PENGUIN BOOKS

A HISTORY OF SCOTLAND

Professor John Duncan Mackie OBE, Hon. LLD, was Professor of Scottish History and Literature at the University of Glasgow from 1930 until 1957. Besides holding office in many historical and antiquarian societies, and serving on a number of boards, he was appointed HM Historiographer in Scotland in 1958. Born in Edinburgh of Scottish parents, he was educated at Middlesbrough High School and received a First in history at Oxford, as well as the Lothian Essay Prize. He was appointed a lecturer at St Andrews at the age of twenty-two and during his occupancy of what Andrew Lang called the 'stool' of Modern History he introduced the subject of Scottish History into the curriculum. He served with the Argyll and Sutherland Highlanders in the First World War, was twice wounded, and was awarded an MC. He returned to St Andrews and in 1926 became Professor of Modern History at the University of London (Bedford College). Among his many publications are *Negotiations Between James VI and I and Ferdinand I of Tuscany* (1927), *Cavalier and Puritan* (1930), *Andrew Lang and the House of Stuart* (1935), *The Earlier Tudors* (1952) and *A History of the Scottish Reformation* (1960). Professor Mackie died in 1978.

Geoffrey Parker obtained his BA, MA and Ph.D. at Cambridge, before teaching at St Andrews University from 1972 to 1986. He is currently Distinguished Professor of History at the Ohio State University. His publications include *The Dutch Revolt* (Penguin, 1977), *The Thirty Years War* (1984), *The Military Revolution* (1988) and, with Colin Martin, *The Spanish Armada* (Penguin, 1988). Together with Bruce Lenman he surveyed the records and patterns of crime in early modern Scotland between 1977 and 1979, in a project funded by the Social Science Research Council and the British Academy.

Bruce Lenman holds an MA degree from his native Aberdeen, and M.Litt. and Litt.D. degrees from Cambridge. He has taught in the universities of Victoria (British Columbia), Dundee and St Andrews, as well as being Harrison Professor in the College of William and Mary in Virginia. His books include four on Jacobitism and a study of modern British politics. He is currently working on the history of the British Empire before 1800 and is Professor of Modern History at the University of St Andrews, where Professor Mackie began his academic career.

To Professor Fowler —
with appreciation
for training two aspiring
biologists, and with
gratitude for educating
an entire family.

Gary, Hilde
Anne + Ben
Brahm

Irvine, California
August, 2006

J. D. MACKIE

A History of Scotland

SECOND EDITION

Revised and edited by
Bruce Lenman and Geoffrey Parker

PENGUIN BOOKS

PENGUIN BOOKS

Published by the Penguin Group
Penguin Books Ltd, 27 Wrights Lane, London W8 5TZ, England
Penguin Books USA Inc., 375 Hudson Street, New York, New York 10014, USA
Penguin Books Australia Ltd, Ringwood, Victoria, Australia
Penguin Books Canada Ltd, 10 Alcorn Avenue, Toronto, Ontario, Canada M4V 3B2
Penguin Books (NZ) Ltd, 182–190 Wairau Road, Auckland 10, New Zealand

Penguin Books Ltd, Registered Offices: Harmondsworth, Middlesex, England

First published in Pelican Books 1964
Reprinted with revisions 1969
Second edition 1978
Reprinted in Penguin Books 1991
9 10

Copyright © J. D. Mackie, 1964
Copyright © J. D. Mackie, Bruce Lenman
and Geoffrey Parker, 1978
All rights reserved

Printed in England by Clays Ltd, St Ives plc

CONTENTS

LIST OF MAPS

INTRODUCTION TO THE
SECOND EDITION

IN revising a text as durable and as distinguished as this one, it has been our aim to introduce only those changes which were essential to keep the book up to date and serviceable. Although there has been a great deal of minor modification, the bulk of the text is still very much that of Professor Mackie, and his revisers have come to admire greatly the extraordinary concision of his style. Substantial changes were only essential at the end and the beginning of the book. At the beginning the decision has been taken to drop the archaeological section, while preserving the very useful topographical introduction. The case for excising the archaeological section rested mainly on the enormous development in archaeological research in Scotland in recent years. This had produced a mass of new evidence, and a host of new problems, on a scale which ensures that no summary of the state of the science can have a very long lifespan. Nor, indeed, can it at present hope to answer many major questions, for the overall effect of the past generation of research has been to throw up many more problems than solutions. At the other end of the text it was essential to expand Professor Mackie's account of modern Scotland, partly because recent developments have ensured that historians look back on Scotland's twentieth-century history with new perspectives, partly because it seemed essential to provide a narrative of events coming closer to the present day than the unrevised text. On the other hand, the point at which history blends with current affairs is a peculiarly difficult one for the historian, and our solution has been to carry a continuous narrative up to roughly 1970, and to mention some of the major factors affecting developments in

Scotland in the 1970s. It is the hope of the revisers that they have combined piety with discrimination in a way which enhances the great merit of this well-known book.

BRUCE LENMAN
GEOFFREY PARKER

Department of Modern History,
University of St Andrews

ACKNOWLEDGEMENTS

The editors would like to thank Miss Lee M. Smith and Mrs Marjorie Nield for their invaluable assistance in preparing this book for publication.

A NOTE ON SCOTTISH CURRENCY

THE silver penny introduced in Scotland in the reign of David I (1124–53) was on a par with the English penny, but thereafter devaluation of the Scottish currency against the English was steady until, in the reign of James VI, the relationship was stabilized, roughly in 1600, three years before James ascended the English throne. The relationship may be illustrated at various dates in terms of pennies.

1373	4d.	Scots	=	3d.	English
1390	2d.	Scots	=	1d.	English
1451	2d.	Scots	=	1d.	English
1456	3d.	Scots	=	1d.	English
1467	3½d.	Scots	=	1d.	English
1483	3½d.	Scots	=	1d.	English
1560	5d.	Scots	=	1d.	English
1565	6d.	Scots	=	1d.	English
1579	8d.	Scots	=	1d.	English
1597	10d.	Scots	=	1d.	English
1601	12d.	Scots	=	1d.	English

Thereafter the ratio of 12:1 remained stable, so between 1603 and 1707 £12 Scots = £1 English. The merk was not a Scots coin but a unit of value equalling two-thirds of £1 Scots, i.e. 13 shillings and 4 pennies Scots. Scottish currency was supposed to be phased out after the Parliamentary Union of 1707, but the process proved protracted and Scots currency remained the normal unit of account at local level in Scotland for many generations.

CHAPTER I

THE LAND AND ITS PEOPLE

In the history of any country the factor of geography plays
a commanding part. Scotland is part of a group of islands
which lie off the north-west coast of Europe, and for
centuries it was upon the utmost confines of the civilized
world.

In the medieval *mappamundi*, which show the world as a
disc with Jerusalem as its centre and ocean as its rim,
Scotland was shown to be almost diametrically opposite to
'Paradise' – which was suspiciously near to Ceylon.
During the long centuries in which the basin of the Mediterranean was the centre of culture, Scotland was far removed
from the mainstream of civilization. Great formative forces,
– those of the Roman Empire, Christianity, and the
Renaissance, for example – reached her relatively late and
with diminished vigour. Moreover, and this is all-important,
these forces had, in most cases, enriched the life of England
before they reached Scotland and, when the southern
kingdom strove to subjugate her northern neighbour, she
came armed, not only with superior might, but with some
of the imponderable values which go with the development
of civilization.

Yet Scotland did not receive all her immigrants by way
of the land which is now called England. In very early
times she received a population which may have come
originally from the Mediterranean by way of her western
coast, and, throughout the whole of her history, she was
able to maintain a contact with Europe by this route.
From the days of the Neolithic men (and perhaps even
from an earlier day) right up to the time of the Jacobite
adventures, the western approach to Scotland from France
and Spain was always open.

From the north-east too, Scotland was open to access by

bold seafarers and, when the hardy Scandinavians dared to take the 'swan's path' across the open sea, it was to Shetland, Orkney, and Caithness that first they came.

As they pursued their adventures, although they came down the east coast, it was upon the west coast that they made their presence felt most definitely. This was no accident. The east coast of Scotland was less attractive than the west, whose innumerable indentations and many islands provided good opportunity for the sheltering of ships and the concealment of raiders.

So much for the general position of Scotland. It is time to consider the configuration and the nature of the land itself.

The total area of Scotland is approximately 30,000 square miles, whereas that of England and Wales is about 58,000. The 8,000 square miles of Wales are largely mountainous. North of the Trent, especially in the Pennine region and the Lakes, there are many hills; in Yorkshire and Northumberland moors abound. Yet a great part of England is composed of gently undulating, well-watered lowlands which, if their good soil with its heavy woodland was too difficult for the early cultivators, yet were conquered by the plough and turned to rich arable soil.

Of Scotland's 30,000 square miles, more than a tenth lies in scattered islands, many of them abounding in rocks and mosses; on the mainland there are mountains, lochs, and moors, not only in the Highlands, so-called, but also in the south country usually known as the Lowlands. South of the Firths of Clyde and Forth are the Pentland Hills, the Moorfoots and the Lammermuirs; the solid watershed which divides the head waters of the Tweed from the Clyde Valley reaches a height of over 2,700 feet at Broadlaw; whilst further west, amongst the mountains which guard rough Galloway are several great peaks, of which Mount Merrick soars to 2,764 feet.

North of the Firths, the dominating feature is a mountain mass which, though it radiates into many branches, may be regarded as containing two great complexes. One of these, stretching from Ben Lomond to the north-east in a great arc, is known under the vague title of the Grampians: while the other, running to the far north in an irregular fashion by way of Ben Nevis and Ben Attow, may represent the *dorsum Britanniae* of the early writers. This complex is penetrated by the Great Glen whose three lochs, Loch Lochy, Loch Oich, and Loch Ness, are now joined in the Caledonian Canal; and another great gap, roughly at right angles, goes from near Oban through the Pass of Brander to Glen Dochart and Loch Tay.

Upon the development of Scotland the great hills exercised a controlling influence. By their very existence they tended to produce two different kinds of society in the country, one of the hills and the other of the plains; and by impeding communication, they tended to break the population up into self-sufficing units, great or small. North of the Grampians, for instance, was the land of Moray which was at one time well-nigh an independent kingdom; and the inhabitants of the numerous glens, until a fairly recent date, owed their first loyalty to their kith and kin.

These generalizations must be qualified. Even a mountainous country is not impenetrable. Today the 'Grampians' may be crossed by motor cars from Stonehaven by way of the 'Slug', from Fettercairn by Cairn O'Mounth, and from Blairgowrie by Glenshee; all these passes lead to the Dee valley. Further to the west the Pass of Drumochter, through which the railway and the great road now run, provides access to the headwaters of the Spey. The hills which lie between the Great Glen and the western sea are now pierced by good roads through Glenmoriston, Glengarry, and by way of Glen Shiel and, besides these main highways, there are smaller roads. These roads are relatively modern, for the Highlanders of old disliked the broad highway. They had, however, their own paths through the mountains, the multiplicity of which has been shown in a book on *The Drove Roads of Scotland.** Yet, though the rough country did not prevent communication, it rendered communication difficult; to this day some glens on the west coast are approached

*A.R.B. Haldane, *The Drove Roads of Scotland* (Edinburgh, 1952).

more easily by sea than by land – and the Highlander of the west was always a boatman.

Again, while it is true that most of the arable land in Scotland lies to the south of the Grampians, there are some very fertile areas to the north. The climate round the Moray Firth, whether or not it owes something to the Gulf Stream, is remarkably mild, and agriculture flourishes in what was once known as 'The Garden of Scotland'. On the west coast too, in certain areas, palm trees will grow in the open air. It is generally believed that the old stories of incomparable fertility are wishful imaginings, yet it is clear enough that much of the sand dune has been heaped up fairly recently over what may well have been good 'machair' land near the coast, and some scholars hold that the great peat-mosses themselves are not so very ancient.

Yet, when all has been said, Scotland before the 'Agricultural Revolution' and the exploitation of her mineral wealth must have been a poor country, in many places wild and bleak. French sayings and stories attest its evil fame as a barren land; the Arabic geographer Idrisi (who, of course, never came near Scotland) described the country, in the twelfth century, as desolate, without inhabitants, towns, or villages; it is plain from the map which graced the history published in Rome by Bishop Leslie that as late as 1578 the wilder parts of the country were still little known; and even in the eighteenth century visitors from England found much of southern Scotland bleak and bare.

From the mere consideration of geography, it might be possible to guess some of the salient features of Scottish history. So hard a mother sent her sons abroad, and valiant sons they were; a land so divided by natural obstacles was hard to reduce to the obedience of a single king, yet such a land was not easily conquered from without. It is true that from the south, where the principal danger lay, the country was open to invasion, and that the best land was within easy reach of an army which crossed the border. Yet though the Border abbeys were burnt and the Lothians ravaged,

14

there remained to the north an intractable land, held by an intractable people; generals and kings sometimes penetrated into the depths of the Highlands, but they seldom succeeded in obtaining complete control.

The mention of the Border calls attention to a fact which could not be deduced solely from geography. When one considers possible frontier lines, it is clear that three distinct possibilities existed at different periods of history. One, which the Romans seem seriously to have considered, would be roughly the 'Highland Line' as it stretches north-east from Loch Lomond to modern Stonehaven. In military terms, this meant closing off the mouths of the glens giving access from the Highlands to the Lowlands and this seems to have been the purpose of the great legionary fortresses built by the Romans at places like Inchtuthill in Perthshire. Further south, the Forth–Clyde line could hardly ever have formed a stable frontier, despite the fact that the Romans tried to make it so by constructing the Antonine wall: it was too easily circumvented by water and it divided two very similar Lowland areas. The only other viable alternative 'natural' frontier lay along the Eden and the Tees. In the mid-twelfth century David I advanced the Scottish border southwards to this line, dividing the island of Great Britain into two roughly equal parts, and ruling his realm from the strategically central stronghold of Berwick-upon-Tweed. For various reasons this proved short-lived, and the present Anglo-Scottish border was stabilized in all but minor details in the early thirteenth century. It represented a point of equilibrium between Scotland and a stronger southern realm, which was for long periods only intermittently interested in northwards expansion. It runs along the line of the Cheviot hills, through an area peculiarly inhospitable to the movement of large bodies of men and animals (such as an army). The long supply-routes on which invading forces had to depend meant that the Border could be efficiently penetrated only at its eastern and western extremities. The stability of this particular frontier line over a long period of history is quite remarkable.

Once a Scottish state had emerged it was, of course, harder to change the frontier materially without breaking the will of the Scots by outright conquest, and this proved extremely difficult. Inadequate as our documentation of the Roman period in Scotland is, it is clear enough that the infinitely changing pattern of Roman frontier policy stemmed from the basic dilemma which faced all would-be conquerors from the south: given the inherent infertility of so much of Scotland, it was extremely difficult to raise revenues in the country which came near to compensating for the formidable cost of conquering and garrisoning it.

The Peoples

Four peoples inhabited the land now called Scotland. The *Picts,* whose name survives in the Pentland Firth and the Pentland Hills, occupied the extreme north and north-east. Their name is first mentioned in two different Latin sources in 297 A.D. It may have been only a nickname given by Roman soldiers to their painted adversaries (like 'Jerries' or 'Wogs'), but it soon came to include all the tribes of the north, who had so long resisted Rome.

The Picts certainly used a form of P-Celtic (the mother of Welsh, Cornish, and Breton), with traces of Gaulish forms. However, it is clear, from the few scraps of evidence which survive, that the Picts also used another language, probably unrelated to any 'Indo-European' tongue and therefore so different from modern European languages as to be incomprehensible to us. In short, the Picts were an amalgam of peoples. The Scots called them 'Cruithni' which is the Q-Celtic (the mother of Gaelic, Irish and Manx) equivalent of 'Pritani' or 'Britons', and there is no doubt that they were the original inhabitants of the land. That they were a separate people appears from their remarkable 'symbol stones' and from their preference for matrilinear descent in the royal house. The Scots, it is true, gave the name 'Cruithni' to some of the inhabitants of Ireland, but though they reckoned all Picts among the Cruithni, all Cruithni

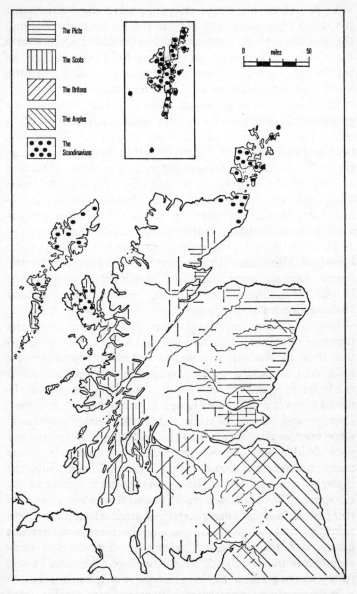

The Picts

The Scots

The Britons

The Angles

The Scandinavians

0   miles   50

1. Scotland: the Land and its People

17

were not Picts. Bede says that they were divided into the Northern Picts, who lived beyond the great mountains, and the Southern Picts. Certainly Columba about 565 found a Pictish king in his fort near Inverness; but later the core of the Pictish monarchy was in Strathmore and Perthshire, and Scone eventually became their ceremonial centre.

If indeed there were two separate kingdoms, the southern prevailed. Brude, son of Bile (672–93) brought all the Picts under his sway, attacked the Scots at Dunadd, and in 685 beat and killed Egfrith, king of Northumbria, at Nechtans-mere (Dunnichen in Angus). By Bede's time the Picts had already occupied Abercorn near Linlithgow; and soon afterwards the strong Angus MacFergus (752–61) established an ascendancy over the Scots. Of the four peoples who coalesced to make Scotland, the Picts were the strongest.

The *Scots* were a Gaelic-speaking people who had established an ascendancy in the north of Ireland, and by the fourth century were assailing the Roman province of Britain. They filtered across to the Southern Hebrides and to the mainland of the country that now bears their name.

Some scholars, arguing from place-names and the presence of round forts, have guessed at an earlier penetration than that which received notice in the chronicles. At all events, about the year 500, a definite settlement was made by Fergus Mor and his two brothers: Fergus established himself in Kintyre; Loarn in the region about Oban (Lorn); and Angus in Isla and Jura. Their 'kingdoms' were very small, but even so the patrimony of Fergus was soon divided between two grandchildren, Comgall, whose name survives in Cowal (near Dunoon) and Gabhran (from whom the Royal house of Scotland descends) in Knapdale. The rock fortress of Dunadd was the capital of this people, but the kings quarrelled among themselves, and possibly would have succumbed to the Picts had they not possessed a rudimentary Christianity and received reinforcements from Ireland. The advent of Columba in 563 (p. 25) had a political as well as a religious significance.

It was perhaps his prestige – he was of high family – and

his personality which strengthened the Scots to resist the Picts, and his statesmanship which united them under the rule of Aidan of the house of Gabhran. Aidan became a powerful king, with a fleet at his disposal, but in 603, having gone south to oppose the advance of the Angles against the Britons, he was beaten at Degsastan (Dawston in Liddesdale?), and thereafter the power of the Scots waned. In 643 one of their kings, Donald Breac, was killed by the Britons at Strathcarron near Larbert. They still tried to struggle south and may have occupied the Campsies, but they succumbed to Angus MacFergus, and for nearly a century may have become something of a client state of the Picts. Armed with the prestige and learning of their Church they may not have 'lost face' as much as has been supposed. At all events, about the year 843, their king, Kenneth MacAlpin, obtained the Pictish throne to which he may have had a claim by female descent. His immediate successors were styled *Reges Pictorum* or *Reges Albaniae*, but they were buried in Iona as Kings of Scots, and the united kingdom took the name of 'Scotia'.

The *Britons* who inhabited the Lowlands were part of that Romano-Celtic world which survived after the province had lost touch with Rome. Some of the tribes had been accepted as *Foederati*; there were Roman names in the pedigrees of their chiefs and some of the people were professedly Christian. The organization of society was aristocratic. There were some hill towns, probably occupied by chiefs, and the typical homestead was a large round farmhouse, which, with its associated buildings, may have been surrounded by a palisade.

In the east lay the Votadini, staunch allies of Rome, whose capital may well have been the great hill town on Traprain Law in Lothian. West of them was the kingdom once ruled by Coel Hen (the original of Old King Cole); from him several princes claimed descent, among them the rulers of Rheged, which may have included Dunragit in Galloway, but at one time extended beyond Carlisle. They too claimed a Roman ancestor: Maximus, who took the troops from

Britain in 383 to support his bid for the imperial title. Further north was the kingdom of Dumbarton or Strathclyde, ruled in St Patrick's day by that Coroticus, or Ceredig, whom the Saint denounced for slave-raiding in Ireland, and the civil wars which vexed the kingdom may have been due in part to the struggle between Christianity and heathendom.

Rhydderch Hael's victory at Arthuret (573) has usually been regarded as a Christian triumph which led to the establishment of St Mungo in the see of Glasgow, but it may have been an incident in a dynastic dispute. Such disputes were frequent and weakened the Britons before the advance of the Germanic invaders.

The Votadini were first to be attacked and a vivid light upon their fortunes was shed by the discovery in 1921 of the famous Traprain treasure. This was a hoard of battered silver, the loot of ecclesiastical and aristocratic houses in the Rhineland; it had been buried only one foot below the last of the occupied surfaces. Traprain must have been occupied, at least temporarily, by sea-raiders, who perhaps in this case were driven out before they could dispose of their spoil.

Later, however, the Britons were subjected to an attack more serious than that of pirates, namely, that of the Angles who had established themselves at Bamburgh about the middle of the sixth century and speedily extended their power. The Welsh poem 'Gododdin' tells of a valiant but vain attack upon Catterick by the Votadini (c. 600?). Yet even in the face of great danger the Britons could not unite, and a concerted attack upon Lindisfarne failed because the assailants quarrelled among themselves.

Before long the Angles took the offensive. By his victory at Degsastan their King Æthelfrith crushed the southern princes and opened a way to the Solway. Under his successors the Angles pushed north along the river valleys; in 750 they broke into Kyle, and in 756, in alliance with the Picts, they subdued the Britons at Dumbarton, though their army suffered loss on the way home.

During the ensuing century the kingdom of Strathclyde

was sorely pressed, though its frontiers may have lain along the Antonine Wall in the north and reached to the Eden valley in the south. In 870 Dumbarton itself was sacked by Danes from Ireland after a long siege and many of its people were enslaved. The shattered kingdom still remained, but possibly it owed its survival to the assaults delivered on its neighbours by the Scandinavians.

It is possible that sea-raiders, perhaps Frisians, made sporadic settlements upon the eastern coast, but the main Germanic attack upon Scotland was made by *Angles* from England. These had made a kingdom named Deira in Yorkshire, and from Deira had come the war-band which seized Bamburgh and expanded into the kingdom of Bernicia. After 600 the two monarchies, in an uneasy alliance, constituted the great kingdom of Northumbria. This was a strong state, able to assail with success the Lowlands, Strathclyde, and Pictland; but it tended to over-expand. It was weakened by quarrels between the rival royal houses, and for that reason its progress to the north was often interrupted.

Æthelfrith, the victor of Degsastan, overran Deira and expelled her king; but in 617 he was overthrown. Edwin of the southern house gained the throne and Æthelfrith's three sons, Oswald, Oswiu, and Eanfrith took refuge with the Picts and Scots. Edwin established an ascendancy far up the east coast of Scotland and it may be from him that Edinburgh takes its name. In 632, however, he was beaten and killed by Penda the Mercian, and two sons of Æthelfrith, Oswald and Oswiu, reigned in succession. They too had trouble with the Mercians (by whom Oswald was killed in 641), but under them the Angle advance was carried to the Firth of Forth, and Dunbar became the stronghold of a Northumbrian alderman.

Oswiu's son, Egfrith, however, advanced too far and was beaten and killed at Nechtansmere in 685. Thereafter the Angles turned their attention to Strathclyde. In 731 an Anglian bishop appeared at Whithorn and before long the conquerors had advanced into Kyle and even to Dumbarton (p. 20). Their progress was facilitated by an alliance with the Picts, perhaps only temporary, and that alliance may have been due, in part, to the fact that Æthelfrith's son, Eanfrith, had married a Pictish bride and, as the Picts counted descent through the mother, had introduced Angle blood into the Pictish royal line.

It is not easy to assess the strength of the Anglian infiltration. Some authorities hold, on philological grounds, that most of the English population must have come in after the Norman Conquest; others point out that while English names are common in the low land, Celtic names abound in the hills. Certain it is that the power of the English began to recoil in the eighth century. Bede noted that the see of Abercorn was no longer in English hands when he wrote, and there is no record of an English Bishop at Whithorn after 805, though the reception there of the Bishop of Lindisfarne with the relics of St Cuthbert (*c.* 880) points to a continuance of the Anglian tradition.

The decline in the power of Northumbria was not all due to Celtic resistance; it was due to internal dissensions which produced anarchy about 800, and to the Scandinavian invasions which cut off the Angles of Northumberland from their kinsmen in the south. The Scoto-Pictish monarchy, however, profited from the English difficulties. Indulf (954–62) captured *Oppidum Eden* (Edinburgh?) and in 1018 (1016?) Malcolm II with the aid of Owen-the-Bald, the last King of Strathclyde, won a victory at Carham which carried his border to the river Tweed.

CHAPTER 2

THE UNION OF THE
FOUR PEOPLES

843 (c.)	Kenneth MacAlpin, King of Scots, gains the throne of Pictland.
1018 (? 1016)	Battle of Carham, Malcolm II gains Lothian. Death of Owen-the-Bald, last King of Strathclyde.
1034	Duncan, grandson of Malcolm II, already ruler in Strathclyde, becomes King of a United Scotland.

THE four peoples united into a single nation. The union took centuries to accomplish, and even today Highlander and Lowlander are alike conscious of separate invididuality. To recount in detail the confused struggles which accompanied the development is here impossible; it is more profitable to regard the main factors which promoted the union. These factors, in their operation, acted one upon another but, by a somewhat artificial analysis, we may distinguish five – a common background, Christianity, the rise of Pictland, the Scandinavian attacks, and the pressure from England.

(i) *Common Background.* Rome may have left some idea of unity, and the Celtic peoples – Pict, Scot, and Briton – had much in common. There are great resemblances between the folklore of the Welsh and that of the Gaels; Pictish art, in its developed form, drew on a stock of forms and symbols which was cosmopolitan, being influenced by both Anglian and Celtic traditions; and primitive Welsh and primitive Gaelic were not entirely dissimilar. What evidence there is shows that the political and social structures of Scots, Picts, and Britons had much in common. All were organized in tribal kingdoms, and the basis of society was a small home-

23

stead, inhabited by a kin group, and surrounded by some land, little of which was tilled, the rest being given to pasture when it was not bare moor. The land of each village was not fixed in amount. In a pastoral society there was no great need to delimit individual holdings. Chiefs may have owned whole villages; certainly they and their kinsmen acquired land, or rights over land, which put them in a privileged position. A good piece of evidence as to the land system of ancient Pictland appears in Gaelic additions (*c.* 1150) to the Book of Deer (Latin, ninth century); these record gifts given to the monastery by a mormaer (Great Steward) who may represent the old provincial sub-king and by a 'toiseach' who may be equated with the later 'thane'.

The Britons of the south may have copied some elements of the Roman system but for them too the tribal kingdom was the basis of society; and if the Angles who settled in Scotland followed the way of Anglo-Saxons elsewhere it must have been very like that of the Celts, though it may have been more 'agricultural' and less 'pastoral'. They too were organized in small kingdoms; they lived in villages of kin groups; and their laws, with their tariffs of blood money, were not very different from those of the Celts. The relations of the two peoples may not have been cordial, especially at first, but the two societies probably co-existed without continual war.

(ii) *Christianity*. To the four peoples the advent of Christianity gave a new cohesion, for the exponents of different types of Christianity all taught the same great truths, brought to savage folk a higher *ethos*, and showed a better way of life. Scotland had her Christianity from two sources. Seeds had been sown during the Roman period and some of the *foederati* may have been officially Christian; it is significant that the first great mission to Scotland of which we know was that of Ninian to the Picts, not to the Britons.*

* 'Ninian' is in fact a later form. The saint's name was Nynia. This means that the evidence of Ninianic dedication, long believed to trace the footsteps of his mission, cannot be so interpreted.

From Bede we learn that Ninian was a Briton, a Bishop regularly instructed at Rome, who built a church at Candida Casa and from there conducted a mission to the Southern Picts. The date usually given is about 400. This is a reasonable surmise, and there is no need to doubt Bede's story, for the Welsh church was organized episcopally and British churchmen had attended some of the great councils. What is doubtful is the extent and the penetration of Ninian's efforts. At all events hagiologists write of little Christian *enclaves* in countries apparently heathen, and St Patrick denounced the 'apostate Picts'.

It was from Ireland that Scotland received a second infusion of the new faith. This was brought in 563 by Columba, a churchman of princely descent and the founder of two religious houses, but one whose high spirit, or excessive zeal, had led to civil war and a bloody battle at Cooldrevny near Sligo. Either condemned, or imposing penance on himself, he exiled himself with twelve companions and established a house on the Island of Hy, whose name survives in its adjectival form Iona (Insula). Armed with prestige, great gifts, unshrinking faith, and high oratory, Columba not only reawakened the dormant Christianity of the Scots but penetrated into Pictland (incidentally worsting a monster in Loch Ness), probably on diplomatic rather than missionary business. Before his death in 597 he had made Iona the centre of a rapidly increasing church which was not episcopal in organization.

Iona was ruled by a succession of abbots, and its units were monastic villages each governed by an abbot, who looked to the Abbot of Iona as his head. Christian communities appeared at or near the small centres of population on the mainland, though a quest for solitude sent anchorites through the Western Islands to Shetland, probably even to Iceland. Before long 'Columban' Christianity spread, with the returning sons of Æthelfrith (p. 21), into Northumbria; there it came into contact with the Roman form of religion which had been brought from the south by Edwin of the Deiran house.

In the sphere of influence of Oswiu the issues between the churches were debated by the Synod of Whitby (663 or 664). Doctrine was not in dispute and little seems to have been said about organization: the differences were about the shape of the tonsure and the method of computing the date of Easter. Yet behind these formal points lay a real conflict. The Roman Church reverenced the authoritative St Peter, the Celtic Church the sensitive St John. The Romans thought it absurd that a few remote schismatics should rend the seamless garment of the universal church, but the Celts could not concede that their saints of old had lived and died in error. Authority won, and the Columbans quietly withdrew. Their withdrawal was a testimony of their faith; for their patroness St Hilda was for resistance, and they were popular – Bede himself paid a glowing tribute to their apostolic virtues. Authority followed up its victory: in 710 Nechtan, King of the Picts, accepted the new way. The Columbans withdrew across the mountains and before long Iona itself received the new teaching.

'The Celtic Church gave love, the Roman Church gave law': the epigram is as true as most epigrams, though doubtless both churches gave both. Authority was necessary to wean turbulent folk from their tribal quarrels; yet the Columban Church stood for a passionate religion which did not all die.

The Scottish Church did not conform entirely to the Roman way. Some of its clergy married, though the appearance of celibate Culdees, who lived in communities, may represent not only the strict tradition of the old anchorites but also a repercussion of the Cluniac reforms. Abbacies might be held by secular men who married, like Crinan, Abbot of Dunkeld, who wedded a daughter of Malcolm II and became the father of Shakespeare's Duncan. After Iona had been repeatedly sacked by the Norsemen, first Dunkeld and later St Andrews became the religious capital. There are a few sporadic references to bishops in the scanty annals. Bishop Cellach of St Andrews appeared on the Mote Hill of Scone with Constantine III

(906). He seems to have been regarded as Bishop of all Scotland (Bishop of Alban).

The giving of liberty to the church by King Giric (878–89) has been regarded as involving the recall of the Columban clergy. Certainly there was an *Ecclesia Scoticana* which went its own way. When the saintly Margaret came north after the Norman Conquest of England, she found irregularities in the Scottish practice, including the saying of Mass 'in some barbarous rite'. She approved the Culdees but she did not, or could not, introduce diocesan episcopacy, and one of her sons became Abbot of Dunkeld.

(iii) *The Rise of Pictland*. Every nascent monarchy must have a solid core, and a factor in the unification of Scotland was the rise of Pictland to a position of predominance. Pictland was fortunate in her geography. She was far removed from the south, and her east coast proved far less attractive to Scandinavians than the indented and island-studded west. Her territory was divided by the Grampians, but there was good fertile land both north and south of the great hills. Again the preference of the Picts for matrilinear descent enabled them to reinforce the royal stem by strong blood from without. The conquering Brude, son of Bile, had a British father; Talorcan (653–7) was the son of the Angle Eanfrith; Kenneth MacAlpin seems to have had some claim, by the female descent, to the Pictish throne; and Duncan's easy accession to Strathclyde after 1018 may have been due to some family connection.

Not only princely blood did Pictland borrow from without. Whether in the days of King Giric or later, the Pictish monarchy made terms with the Scottish Church. And the Pictish Church was very much the same as the Columban Church though with a much stronger development of episcopacy.

The evidence of the later sculptured stones shows that the Picts had a civilization whose aristocrats, women as well as men, rode forth to hunt and to hawk. Scotland might seem to predominate because its king mounted the Pictish throne,

and because of its close connection with Irish learning which
produced the chroniclers; but the idea that Pictland was
submerged by a Scottish conquest is incorrect.

(iv) *Scandinavian Attacks*. Scotland, like most countries of
Western Europe, felt the impact of the extraordinary out-
pouring of men from the Scandinavian countries from the
eighth century on. The Scandinavian attacks, which
wrought much destruction and brought great areas beneath
an alien sway, are yet rightly included among the factors
which unified Scotland. The provinces occupied by the
invaders had always been peripheral to the centre of Pictish
power. That power was compelled to concentrate its forces –
the union of Scotland and Pictland in 843 was made under
Norse pressure; the success of the invaders in England
delayed for almost a century and a half the advance of the
English power against the North; finally, in Scotland as in
every other land the Norse people adapted their own institutions to local conditions and contributed to the population
a strain of competent and adventurous blood. The 'Black
Gentiles' mentioned by the chroniclers have been generally
understood to be Danes, and the 'White Gentiles' Norwegians. Danes from Ireland sacked Dumbarton in 870, and
it was Danes too (perhaps from Northumbria) who ravaged
Pictland in the sixties and seventies and killed King Constantine II in 877. It was, however, with the Norwegians
that Scotland was most concerned.

The Norwegian incursions came in three stages. First,
between 780 and 850 there arrived in Shetland, Orkney,
and Caithness poor peasants who had quitted the barren
soil of western Norway in hope of better land, and they may
have met with little opposition in a sparsely populated
country. Yet along with them, or soon afterwards, came
pirate chiefs who attacked wherever opportunity was found.
Iona was raided repeatedly from 795 on.

Next came the period of the great settlements made by
Norwegian jarls who, after Harold Fair Hair (863–933)
established a strong royal power in Norway, sought dom-

inions overseas. In the Hebrides Ketil Flatnose became king, whose daughter Aud went on to Iceland. Farther south, where at a later date the invaders intermarried with the wild Galloway people to produce a turbulent race of 'Gallgaels', there appeared eventually a strong monarchy based on the Isle of Man. The dynasty founded by Godfrey Crovan in 1075 lasted till 1265.

Meanwhile in Orkney arose a great Norse power. Sigurd the Mighty, who carried his authority into Moray, died soon after his Homeric combat with Maelbrigte Tooth; but 'Peat' Einar, who became Earl between 891 and 894, established a house which lasted till 1231, when a daughter carried the inheritance to the Scottish Earl of Angus. Orkney became a nodal point in the great sea-empire of the Norse, and her earls from their palace at Birsay exercised power not only over Orkney and Shetland, but over Caithness and Sutherland. The Scottish kings were glad to accept their friendship. Malcolm II gave a daughter to Sigurd the Stout (killed at Clontarf by Brian Boru in 1014). The son of this marriage, Thorfinn the Mighty, held Orkney, Shetland, and the Hebrides from the Norse King, Caithness and Sutherland from the King of Scots, and exercised some authority over seven Scottish earldoms. He dealt almost on equal terms with Macbeth, and after his death (c. 1065) his widow (some would have it his daughter) Ingibiorg married Malcolm III (Canmore).

Yet the danger to Scotland was less than might appear. Earls of Orkney and kings of Man were not always in obedience to the Norwegian Crown; moreover, lax marriage customs produced frequent dynastic struggles in both the Kingdom of Norway and the Earldom of Orkney. Finally, the Norse power depended upon ships – services due from Orkney, for instance, were computed in 'ships' and 'oars' – and the ships were small: they could not carry the apparatus for a long campaign – horses or provisions – and they could not sail in winter. It was hard for Norse kings and Orcadian earls to conduct a continuous operation.

(v) *The English Pressure*. During the formative period of the monarchy, as during most periods, the development of Scotland was greatly influenced by her relations with England. When after the Danish conquest Northumbria became a 'no-man's Land' where Angles, Britons, Danes of York, and Danes from Ireland were engaged in constant warfare, Constantine III (900–943) seized the opportunity to press south. Between 913 and 915 he went as far south as Corbridge to help a Northumbrian alderman against the Danes from Dublin. There he had no success, and before long came into contact with the power of Wessex, which advanced through the Danelaw with remarkable speed.

In 921 Edward the Elder (Alfred's son) was at Bakewell in Derbyshire and there, according to the *Anglo-Saxon Chronicle*, the King of Scots 'with all his people', together with the King of the Strathclyde Britons, and all his people, chose Edward for father and for lord. This was no feudal 'commendation'; yet, even if it were no more than the 'coming in' of 'friendlies' to win the good graces of a conqueror, it was of significance. In 927 Athelstan renewed the assertion of West-Saxon power at Eamont, near Penrith, and in effect united Scots, Britons, and the Anglian Lord of Bamburgh against the Danes of York. When, soon afterwards, the Danish monarchy at York collapsed, Constantine found himself confronting an enemy far more dangerous than Danes or Northumbrians. In 934 Athelstan attacked the east coast of Scotland by land and by sea, and according to one account penetrated to Fordun in the Mearns. Thus assailed, Constantine sought the alliance of his old enemies and the result was disastrous. He, along with the Strathclyde men, and Danes from Ireland and Northumbria, suffered at Brunanburgh (perhaps near the Solway) the crushing defeat (937) celebrated in the triumph-song embodied in the *Anglo-Saxon Chronicle*.

Thereafter the Scots sought the friendship of the English. This was easier to obtain because in 940 another Danish king from Ireland established himself at York. In 945 Edmund, after he had devastated Cumbria, 'let it' to Malcolm

I, King of Scots (943–54) on condition that he would be 'his helper both on sea and on land'. Edmund's action was not disinterested; his purpose was to block the road from Ireland into Northumbria, and the Scandinavian place-names, which abound about the Solway and the Lake District, are proof that his precaution was wise.

The English advance, checked by the death of Edmund, and disturbances in Northumbria, was resumed by the powerful Edgar (959–75) and an incident which occurred at Chester in 973 shows how dangerous this was to the Scottish monarchy. The English King, having sailed round the north of Scotland, arranged a water-pageant on the River Dee in which he took the helm of a boat rowed by the King of Scots Kenneth II (971–95), the King of the Cumbrians, and six other kings, Danish and Welsh. The festival was in honour of St John the Baptist, but its significance was unmistakable.

Again the threat to Scotland was removed by the success of the Danes in England. Strong Edgar died, Æthelred was 'Unready', and his employment of Danish mercenaries made him the victim of Danish blackmail and eventually brought him to ruin. The Scots seized the opportunity. Malcolm II, after his victory at Carham, carried his border to the Tweed and virtually annexed Strathclyde, whose king had died, perhaps in battle. The solidity of his realm must not be exaggerated. When Canute came up to Scotland in 1031 he found there (according to the *Anglo-Saxon Chronicle*) two other 'kings' besides Malcolm, and drove them all into temporary submission. None the less, Malcolm II had united under himself a kingdom whose limits, save for the holdings of the Scandinavians in the north and west, were those of modern Scotland.

The Scottish Monarchy of 1034

It is impossible to offer an authoritative assessment of the power of the monarchy of Malcolm II, but a rough estimate of assets and liabilities may be attempted.

The king was head of the state; the carefully preserved genealogies show both the pride in long descent and the respect given to it. About him he must have had some sort of council containing perhaps churchmen, magnates, and a few household officers. As king he had definite rights: he could call out all his men for the defence of Scotland, and some, if not all, for foreign service; he had the right to 'cain' or food-rent and to 'conveth', a night's entertainment, from his land-holders. These rights might be commuted for money, though in Scotland, which had no coinage of her own till the twelfth century, food-rents survived to a very much later date.

The law was his law. We can distinguish the notions of the king's peace, of oath-helping, and the scale of blood-money. The so-called laws of Malcolm MacKenneth are a later invention, with their story that the king reserved to himself only the Mote Hill at Scone and divided the rest of the land among his men; but it is probable enough that the Crown had begun to alienate its rights in revenue, and the execution of its law, to officers who wielded power in the provinces. These were the mormaers or earls, the toiseachs, whom some would equate with the later thanes, and the judges called by some modern writers 'brehons' on an Irish analogy. Beneath the chiefs and the officers were the plain folk occupying perhaps little townships, in some cases, but still tribally organized, and in their economy largely pastoral. In the wilder districts the tribes, or little kin-groups, may have migrated seasonally.

Resting on an unstable basis and limited in its coercive power, the Celtic monarchy could not be secure. The kings, hampered by lack of communications in a difficult country and compelled to use much of their energy in repelling enemies, had little opportunity to build up an administrative system; doubtless they were generally in alliance with the Church but they had not the support of an organized hierarchy. Moreover a curious law of succession delayed the establishment of a single dynasty. In the old Gaelic system the king was theoretically elected from a royal group called the 'derbfine' which included anyone whose great-grand-father had been a king, and in theory there was chosen as successor to the throne a male who by age, strength, and character was most suited to the hour. He was known as 'tanist'. Fresh complications were produced by the Pictish preference for matrilinear descent, and somehow there came into being a system whereby successive kings were chosen alternately from different stems of the royal house, one of which came to draw its power from Atholl and the other from Moray. The alternation was not effected without reciprocal violence, but it persisted. Even when, as in 997, one of the main stems of Kenneth MacAlpin died out, the succession still oscillated between two branches of the remaining stem, and when Kenneth III died in 1005 the crown passed not to his son Boedh, but to his cousin Malcolm II, who was his slayer.

Inevitably the notion of direct hereditary right became familiar, and with it a tendency for a ruling king to keep the succession in his own line by exterminating claimants of the other house. Malcolm II had no son and it became his great objective to secure the throne of Scotland for his grandson Duncan, son of Crinan Abbot of Dunkeld. In pursuance of his plan he killed the grandson of his predecessor (Kenneth III); the murdered man, however, had a daughter or grand-daughter, Gruoch, who had borne a son, Lulach; and she, by a second marriage, became the wife of Macbeth, son of a mormaer of Moray and himself of royal descent (see table on page 37).

Shakespeare's tragedy thus has a historical background, though the dramatist telescoped events. Duncan, who was not a good old king but a headstrong young one, succeeded in 1034, but, having prejudiced his position by a failure against Durham (1039) was killed by his rival in 1040. Macbeth, who with his wife had a good claim by the system of alternate succession, ruled for seventeen years and was apparently able to visit Rome in 1050. He had, however, lost Cumbria to Siward of Northumbria, Duncan's brother-in-law, with whom Malcolm, one of the sons of the murdered king, found refuge. Siward did indeed intervene on Malcolm's behalf with some success in 1054 and may have given him some position in Strathclyde; but it was not till 1057, after Siward's death, that Malcolm slew Macbeth at Lumphanan in Aberdeenshire. Even so Macbeth's stepson Lulach was set upon the royal stone and reigned for four months before he too was killed, in Strathbogie.

So Malcolm Canmore (Bighead) became King of Scots. He came to a troublesome inheritance. The new law of succession was not universally accepted. Lulach's posterity and the House of Moray survived to trouble the House of Canmore for many generations; and even inside the House of Atholl there was trouble, for Malcolm had a brother Donald Bane, who presumably as Tanist claimed the throne when Malcolm died. It was significant, moreover, that it was only with support from England that Malcolm gained the throne. The omens were not favourable. None the less Malcolm Canmore founded a dynasty which was to rule in Scotland for more than two centuries, and to preside over a great development in the Scottish monarchy.

CHAPTER 3

THE HOUSE OF CANMORE

Scottish Kings

1057/8–93	Malcolm III
1093–4	Donald Bane
1094	Duncan II
1094–7	Donald Bane
1097–1106/7	Edgar
1106/7–24	Alexander I
1124–53	David I
1153–65	Malcolm IV
1165–1214	William I
1214–49	Alexander II
1249–85/6	Alexander III
1285/6–90	Margaret

(i) *English Influences in Scotland*

UNDER the sway of the House of Canmore the Celtic monarchy evolved into an organized feudal state and in this development English influences played a great part. The royal house, bound to that of England by many marriage ties, often relied upon English support, provided generally by the Anglo-Norman barons who came to dwell in Scotland, and sometimes by the English Crown itself. Along with English aid came the risk of English domination.

The marriage of Malcolm Canmore with Margaret of the royal house of Wessex gave the Scottish King an interest in the English throne, but William the Conqueror was to prove unshakeable. Indeed, in 1072 he exacted a treaty at Abernethy whereby Malcolm became his man and gave his son Duncan, born of Ingibiorg, as a hostage; and in 1091 William Rufus renewed this arrangement, which might seem to imply the feudal subjection of Scotland. Both kings, however, had given Malcolm land in England and it might be represented that the homage done was in respect of this. At all events Malcolm repeatedly attacked England until in 1093 he was killed at Alnwick.

On his death the Scots, in accordance with old practice, set his brother, Donald Bane, upon the throne. William Rufus supported first Malcolm's son Duncan who, however, was beaten and killed in 1094 at Mondynes (in the Mearns), and later Edgar, the eldest surviving son of Malcolm and Margaret, who gained the throne in 1097. Both Duncan and Edgar paid for the help given by acknowledging the English King as their superior.

The fortunes of the house improved when Henry I married Margaret's daughter Edith (whom he called Maud). David, her younger brother, was educated in England and treated with great favour. In 1113–14 his marriage to Matilda, widow of Simon de Senlis and daughter of Waltheof, brought him the Honour of Huntingdon, with broad lands in the South-Eastern Midlands and even a claim to Northumbria itself.

When in 1107 Edgar died, and Alexander I succeeded as King of Scots, David, apparently with English support, was established in Lothian and Strathclyde; and there as *Comes* he was virtually independent until on Alexander's death in 1124 he became King of Scots. His reign, which lasted till 1153, was one of the most important in Scottish history. Taking advantage of the Civil Wars in England, and supporting first one side and then the other, he succeeded, despite a serious defeat at Northallerton (the Battle of the Standard) in 1138, in carrying his frontier down to the Tees and the Eden; and though he lost Huntingdon he obtained a promise that young Henry of Anjou, if he gained the crown, would give him all Northumbria except Newcastle and Bamburgh.

When, however, the strong Angevin mounted the English throne he forgot his promises. In 1157 he forced Malcolm IV, who had succeeded his grandfather David in 1153, to resign the claim to Northumbria, though he restored to him the Honour of Huntingdon, and gave to his brother William

The House of Canmore

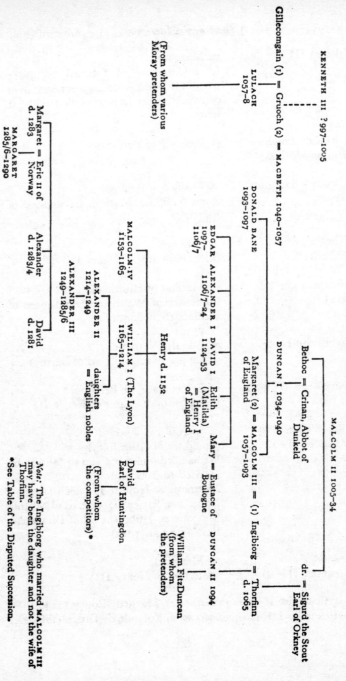

Note: The Ingibiorg who married MALCOLM III may have been the daughter and not the wife of Thorfinn.

*See Table of the Disputed Succession.

Malcolm III
    m. Margaret
    (granddaughter of Edward Ironside;
    sister of Edward Atheling, representative
    of royal Saxon line who died without
    heirs).

Malcolm's daughter
Edith or Matilda
    m. Henry I of England

Malcolm's daughter
Mary
    m. Eustace of Boulogne
    Their daughter Matilda *m.* Stephen of
    England.

Malcolm's son
Alexander I
    m. Sybilla
    (illeg. daughter of Henry I)

Malcolm's son
David I
    m. Matilda of Huntingdon
    (daughter of Waltheof; grand-niece of
    William the Conqueror)

David's son Henry
    m. Ada de Warenne
    (daughter of second Earl of Surrey)

Henry's son William
the Lion
    m. Ermengarde de Beaumont
    (great-granddaughter of Henry I)

William's son
Alexander II
    m. Joan of England
    (daughter of King John)
    William's daughters given to John to be
    married to princes, but
    Margaret *m.* Hubert de Burgh (1221)
    Isabella *m.* Roger Bigod, Earl of Norfolk
    Marjorie *m.* Hubert, Earl of Pembroke,
    Earl Marshal (1235)

Alexander's son
Alexander III
    m. Margaret
    (daughter of Henry III)

Alexander II m. *en secondes noces*, Marie de Coucy (1239).
Alexander III m. *en secondes noces*, Yolande de Dreux (1285).

the barren Liberty of Tynedale. In hope of gaining more, Malcolm in 1159, and his successor William in 1166, accompanied the English King on expeditions to France; but they gained nothing, and in 1173 William joined the conspiracy of Henry's son (the 'Young Henry') who made large promises. His rashness led to his undoing. In 1174 he was captured near Alnwick and forced by the Treaty of Falaise (or Valognes) to become the liegeman to the English King for the whole of his dominions. In 1175 he recovered Tynedale, and in 1186 Huntingdon, which he granted to his brother David; in 1189 by the Treaty of Canterbury he had the Treaty of Falaise cancelled in return for 10,000 marks by Richard I, who wanted money for his crusade. When Richard returned from his captivity, William, who had contributed 2,000 marks to his ransom, stood well with Lion-Heart, at whose second coronation in 1194 he carried one of the swords of state, and he nearly succeeded in recovering Northumberland for the sum of 15,000 marks. The negotiation broke down, and though William renewed his claim on the accession of John, he gained nothing. On the contrary, in 1209 John exacted a treaty whereby the King of Scots gave 15,000 marks for his goodwill and handed over his daughters Margaret and Isabella to be married (according to the Scottish account) to the two Princes of England.

William's son Alexander II joined with the English barons at the time of the Great Charter, and for a time David lost Huntingdon. Friendship was restored in 1221 and Alexander married Joan, sister of Henry III; but partly because his own sisters were cheated of their promised marriages and partly because Henry grew more imperious as he grew older, relations became strained again. Henry opposed, at Rome, the efforts of the Scots King to obtain Papal approval for his unction and coronation, and after 1232 revived the old claim of suzerainty. War was averted, and in 1237 a final settlement of the lands was reached. The King of Scots was granted lands in Northumberland and Cumberland to the value of £200; and these, with the Liberty of Tynedale, were all he had in the North. In the

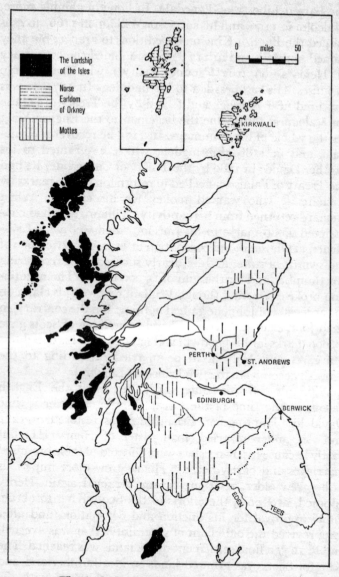

The Lordship of the Isles

Norse Earldom of Orkney

Mottes

KIRKWALL

PERTH
ST. ANDREWS
EDINBURGH
BERWICK
EDEN
TEES

0   miles   50

2. *The Anglo-Norman Penetration, the Frontier and
the Lordship of the Isles*

South his cousin John (son of David) died without heirs in the same year, and the Liberty of Huntingdon was divided between three co-heiresses, whose claims passed to the houses of Balliol, Bruce, and Hastings; any superiority the King of Scots still possessed must have been well-nigh 'naked'.

These lands and rights, and the occasions, perhaps welcome, of visiting England now and again at the English expense, were all the Scots kings had to show for a long connection which had led them sometimes into war, and frequently into doing homage. They denied the assertion, repeated by Henry III in 1251, and by Edward I in 1278, that this homage was for the whole kingdom of Scotland. Yet Henry III, during the minority of Alexander III, who married his daughter, claimed to be 'Principal Counsellor to the Illustrious King of Scotland', and maintained a definite Anglophile party; and Alexander III went south on the summons of Edward. To an age which set great store upon symbols, the frequent sight of a King of Scots on his knees before his brother of England was of high consequence. The English lands of the Scottish kings were a *damnosa haereditas*.

(ii) *Suppression of Revolts*

The English influence which thus threatened the independence of the monarchy was increased by the fact that the incoming Anglo-Normans introduced a new military system. This took two forms: the heavily armed horsemen provided an offensive force which half-naked tribesmen could hardly resist, and the 'mottes' formed strongholds to maintain the ground won.

A motte was simply a wooden tower set on a mound, perhaps crowned with a palisade and surrounded at a short distance by a ditch. The distribution of the mottes marks the progress of Anglo-Norman infiltration (see map p. 40). They are thickest on the ground in the south-west where David, while as yet only *Comes*, introduced English families – Moreville, Soulis, Lindsay, Somerville, and Bruce, for example – many of whom had been his tenants in the Honour of Huntingdon. Significantly they made their appearance in the North where David, after 1130, began to subdue turbulent Moray, and his successors pursued the policy of settling reliable barons at strategic points – at Duffus near Elgin, at Inverurie in the Garioch, at Invernochty near Braemar, and at Lumphanan (between Dee and Don), huge mounds attest the early stages of infeudation. In some cases the mounds were later crowned by stone castles, which came to be the symbols of Anglo-Norman power. Stone castles were more common in Scotland than has been supposed, but they did not appear until the twelfth century and they were mainly royal castles, though some of the greatest, Kildrummy and Bothwell for example, belonged to subjects. Of the 120 or so castles in existence by 1300, a mere thirty were in royal hands – all of them south and east of the Highland Line.

The Crown needed all the help it could get because it was faced with frequent rebellions. Some of these expressed a dislike for the new ways, as, for example, the disorders which followed the death of Malcolm III (1093), the accession of Alexander I (1107) and the return of Malcolm IV from his service at Toulouse with the English King (1160). Others represented a desire for local independence as in risings in Galloway (1160, 1234) and in Moray (1130, 1187). Yet very often the discontented allied themselves to the ambitions of claimants to the throne. These were many. It was only about 1144, when David acknowledged his son as his successor designate, that the hereditary principle was formally asserted; and there seems to have lingered on a feeling in favour of the old tanistry. Descendants of Lulach (p. 34) asserted themselves in 1130, and again about 1150. The MacHeths who troubled William the Lion were probably a base-born progeny of Alexander I. Although William Fitz-Duncan stoutly supported David I, his descendants the MacWilliams rose in 1187, 1212, and 1215, and it was not until a hapless baby girl had her brains dashed out on the market-cross at Forfar in 1230 that the line of Ingibiorg was extinguished.

As the various claimants sometimes cooperated one with

42

another, and sometimes allied with powerful malcontents like the Earls of Galloway, the task of the Crown was far from easy. Yet the kings, patiently advancing their garrisons into hostile territory, ultimately prevailed. Very revealing is a charter of 1267 which shows the King handing his castle on Loch Awe to the MacNaughtans on condition that the MacNaughtans should garrison it and give him a limited but specific hospitality when he demanded it.

(iii) *The End of the Norse Peril*

Not only against internal enemies did the Scottish monarchy prevail. It was able also to deal with the Scandinavians, although not without difficulty.

Between 1098 and 1103 Magnus Bareleg made a serious attempt to make his Western Empire a reality. He compelled the peaceable Edgar to surrender all the Western Islands between which and the mainland a 'helm-carrying ship' could go, and it may well be true that, by having his galley dragged across the isthmus at Tarbert, he claimed Kintyre as well. He established his authority over Orkney, the Hebrides, and Man, and it was a fortunate thing for Scotland that he was killed in an attack on Ireland. But his death did not free Scotland from Norse incursions. Some of the Hebridean chiefs made common cause with the men of Moray, and the Kings of Man were apt to ally themselves with the restless Galwegians. A conspicuous disturber of the peace was Somerled, ancestor of the great Clan Donald; half Gaelic by birth, and married to a daughter of the King of Man, he dominated Argyll and the Southern Hebrides. He assisted one of the Pretenders, Donald MacHeth, in a serious rebellion (1153). He was as much a Gael as a Norseman for he quarrelled with the King of Man, and his buildings at Iona are definitely Irish in character; but he was still a menace, and his death near Renfrew in 1164 was attributed to the special intervention of St Kentigern on behalf of Glasgow, though perhaps the King's officers deserved some of the credit.

In the North, Harold, Matad's son, who had ruled Orkney for very many years, wielded great power. He permitted a great invasion from Orkney against King Sverre of Norway (1192–4), and though he lost a portion of his revenue in consequence, he kept his earldom. When, at the very end of the century, William the Lion, making use of Norse rivals, tried to unseat him, he still managed to maintain himself.

Yet, in the thirteenth century, the Scottish monarchy passed to the offensive. Certainly in 1230–31 an adventurous Norwegian took the Castle at Rothesay; but the building of castles at Dunaverty, Dunstaffnage, Sween, Tirim, and Mingarry bespeaks the Scottish advance to the edge of the mainland. In 1222 Alexander II appeared in force in Argyll, and though he died at Kerrera, off Oban, on a second expedition (1248–9) his coming with many ships told its own tale. Marriage between Harold, King of Man, and Cecilia, daughter of Haakon of Norway, was part of the Scandinavian reply. The marriage was defeated, for bride and bridegroom perished at sea on the way home from Bergen; but when Alexander III, now become a man of twenty-one, after trying in vain to buy the Islands, permitted a brutal raid upon Skye (1262), the valiant Haakon made a final attempt to restore the Norse power. In 1263 he equipped the greatest expedition that had ever left Norway, bade the Orkney Earl provide ships and pilots, and warned the chiefs of the Hebrides, and the King of Man. His total force, if it had ever been assembled in one place, must have numbered 200 ships, and perhaps 15,000 men. For such a venture his organization was inadequate. Only towards the end of August did he muster at Kerrera and some of the Island chiefs would not join him because they were pledged to the King of Scots. He rounded Kintyre, ravaged Bute, and sent up Loch Long forty ships which were dragged across land to Loch Lomond to plunder the surrounding country.

Whilst he was entertained with unreal negotiations, Alexander, who had put his castles into a state of defence,

44

probably brought up a field force; the Norwegians were battered by a tremendous storm in the Firth of Clyde, and when they landed a few hundred men to try to salvage stranded ships, they were easily repulsed. The Battle of Largs (2 October) was not a big affair, but it was decisive. Haakon took his storm-tossed ships back to Kerrera, back to Kirkwall and there he let all but twenty of them go home. He himself died there, in the great hall of what later became the bishop's palace, listening first to readings from the Bible and finally to the sagas of the great Norse Kings – of whom he was the last.

His son Magnus tried in vain for peace, but by 1265 the Scots had taken control of all the Western Islands, including Man; and in 1266, by the Treaty of Perth, Norway ceded to Scotland all her possessions save Orkney and Shetland for a cash payment of 4,000 marks, and a perpetual 'annual' of 100 marks. In 1281 Magnus's son Eric II married Margaret daughter of Alexander III; she died in giving birth to Margaret, the Maid of Norway, and after her death Eric wedded Isabella, sister of Robert Bruce.

Scotland and Norway entered into a friendship which proved lasting. The Treaty of 1266 was honourable. The Norse inhabitants of Northern territory were given the option of staying, or departing with all their goods. Evidence unearthed at Freswick in Caithness seems to show that those who remained kept their own manner of life; to this day inhabitants of Thurso will disclaim any connection with the 'clans', and the huge cathedral of St Magnus at Kirkwall is a splendid monument of Norse architecture. Yet the Norse were absorbed into the realm of Scotland, to which they contributed a virile element of the population, whose virtue continues to this day.

(iv) *The Fabric of the Monarchy*

The political successes of the House of Canmore went hand in hand with the development of a solid feudal monarchy. Feudalism in its developed state specified the obligation between lord and man in the precise terms of a charter conveying the land for which the grantee did homage; but it also involved the taking of an oath of fealty which was an absolute thing, and, since the personal loyalty of man to chief was well understood in Scotland, the new feudalism dovetailed into the old tribal system more easily than has been supposed.

The King. The mainspring of government was the king. According to the new theory he was lord of all the land and was supposed to have granted portions of it in times past to his tenants-in-chief. He was entitled to military service from the lands granted (unless they had been given in free alms) and to very occasional 'aids' (direct taxes); as fountain of feudal justice he exercised power and drew an income from fines and forfeitures. Yet he still kept the old attributes of a Celtic king. He could claim the military service of all his subjects when he took the field. He had a considerable demesne which included new acquisitions made when his enemies were subdued, and also, as it seems, the ancestral lands of his house. From the lands which he did not alienate he drew the old rent, mainly in kind; and the 'thane', though he later developed into a laird, was at first an officer, half royal servant and half landowner, who looked after a portion of the king's land.

From his ancestors the king derived, besides these physical assets, prestige. To this, witness is borne by the prodigious genealogical tree which traced his descent certainly to Kenneth MacAlpin, and almost certainly to Fergus Mor; thereafter it went through thirty-three generations to introduce another Fergus, son of Feredach, to make the Scots senior to the Picts, and through many more to Gaythelus (Gael) who first came from the Mediterranean; and he, as a Greek prince, was evidently superior to Brutus, representative of the defeated Trojans, from whom the English claimed descent. Scriptural dignity was added by marrying Gaythelus to Scota, daughter of Pharaoh, and the line went faithfully back to Noah. It has been said that the first 'international' was a lying match, and that the Scots won easily; but the long pedigree tells not only of ardent pride but of a determination to claim a distinct nationality.

In accordance with the custom of his ancestors a King of Scots was not crowned at the beginning of his reign, but 'set upon the stone' which, though it came to be at Scone, was alleged to have accompanied the Scots in all their mythical journeyings. The stone was sometimes called the 'Fatal Stone' or the 'Stone of Destiny'; a prophecy recorded in Latin by the first formal historian of Scotland foretold that 'wherever the stone should rest a King of Scots would reign', and James VI was crowned King of England on 25 July 1603 in Westminster Abbey, sitting on 'the stone'. One legend, told by an English chronicler, made it 'Jacob's Pillow', another made it 'Columba's Pillow', but the standard Scots tradition brought it with Gaythelus to Spain and thence to Scotland by way of Ireland. Some accounts gave it homes at Iona, Dunstaffnage, and Dunkeld before it came to Scone, and it may well have come into Pictland after Kenneth MacAlpin mounted the Pictish throne.

The old stories generally described it as of marble, and in the shape of a chair, but the stone now in Westminster Abbey is of coarse-grained sandstone fitted at each end with iron staples and rings, arrangements for carrying it, which may have been added by Edward I. The stone may at first have been a fixture – the stone of Dunadd is still *in situ* and it stood for permanence – standing or sitting upon it the new ruler formally assumed the power and the obligations of his predecessor. Latterly it was moveable, as appears from the full account of the coronation of young Alexander III in 1249. The stone was brought into the churchyard, the boy of seven was set upon it and invested with royal robes, then the Lyon King of arms hailed him in Gaelic as Alexander, son of Alexander, son of William, son of Henry, and so up the long pedigree to Gaythelus himself. There is no mention of a crown, and a contemporary Norwegian source, Haakon Haakonson's saga, specifically asserts that the Scots kings were not crowned. One reason for this may have been that

47

the English monarchs did not wish their northern neighbour to hold a sacrosanct office. They prevented the Pope from acceding to Alexander II's request that he should be crowned by a representative of Rome, and it was not until 1329, when Scotland had already asserted her independence, that Pope John XXII formally authorized the unction and coronation of a Scottish king.

On some seals the earlier Kings of Scots are shown crowned; probably they did wear crowns on high days of justice and deliberation as did the Kings of England. The other side of the seal shows the king in another capacity mounted and armed – very justly, for he lived a life of activity. Even when he had no military business on hand, he perambulated his realms, living off his food rents. Stirling was one chosen residence of Alexander III, but he also had castles, manors, and halls in nearly every county of the Lowlands. The list of twenty-three Scottish castles demanded by Edward I (1299) includes a dozen in the north-east.

The Magnates. David I (1124–53) began the practice of establishing Anglo-Norman families in Scotland. Of the early charters none survives save the famous Annandale charter, which gave 200,000 acres to the Bruces; but other grants appear from later 'confirmations'.

Before David's reign was ended, knight-service was well known in the south of Scotland and was being introduced into the north when, after 1130, the king was establishing reliable men in lands taken from the men of Moray. Malcolm IV used the same means to bridle Galloway and William the Lion extended the system. Yet in William's day the total knight-service as evidenced by the Charters was only some sixty-four knights, and five or six sergeants. Doubtless the knights had followers, but even so the king cannot have relied on them alone, and the frequent reservation in the charters of the old 'common service' – *servitium Scotticanum* – shows that the earlier military practices survived.

By the time of Alexander III infeudation and sub-infeudation were well known throughout Scotland. To what extent the old earldoms were brought into the system is not quite clear; certainly some of the earldoms went by marriage to Anglo-Normans. Balliol married the heiress of Galloway, Bruce the heiress of Carrick; Comyn and Umphraville allied themselves with the old lines of Buchan and Angus while the Stewarts acquired by marriage an alleged descent from Banquo. None the less many of the old earldoms remained with the old families: Lennox, Atholl, Strathearn, Fife, Mar, Ross, and Caithness were still predominantly Celtic; Dunbar (March) was part Saxon and part Celtic; Sutherland, though Anglo-Norman in origin, lived in a Norse and Celtic atmosphere.

The magnate came to find that his position was enhanced when he became a tenant-in-chief and exercised a portion of the royal authority, but he kept the prestige of his fore-bears; the old tribal and provincial loyalties survived the assumption of the new feudal dignity.

The Royal Officers. To aid the King in the work of government there appeared a number of officers who, though they might be reckoned household officers in origin, became officers of state. Such officers were known in West European states at least since the days of Charlemagne, but their introduction into Scotland can be noted only by their appearance in the surviving charters. David I had a Chamberlain when he ruled only in the south, and it was to him probably that the introduction of several officers on the English model was due. The officers most about the King in the early charters are the *Constable*, the King's chief military officer – the *Marshal* appeared later – and the *Chamberlain*, who looked after all the King's revenues. The name 'Exchequer' (Scaccarium) was introduced from England, but in Scotland there was no Treasurer until the reign of James I.

The *Chamberlain* was both collector and disburser. He collected the royal rents, developed a special relation with the burghs (the main source of actual cash), and received feudal casualties and fines imposed by the King's officers. Very infrequently he might receive the proceeds of a special taxation to which church, barons, and, according to one account, burghs, contributed during the reign of William I.

The church assessed itself; the barons may at first have paid according to their baronies, though it is probable that in Alexander III's time there was a 'general extent' (assessment) in 'pound-lands; the burghs dealt directly with the Chamberlain. The Chamberlain's disbursement provided for all kinds of public expenditure: the maintenance of the royal household, the payment of fees to officers, the costs of administration, and the expenses of war not covered by the military obligations of tenants. Much of the royal income was collected and spent locally, by sheriffs, bailiffs of the royal lands, and burgh officials, and audit was necessary. Whether this was held annually is uncertain, but for the year 1264 there is evidence of the sitting of a very dignified court. The audited accounts were probably engrossed on the 'Chamberlain Roll' of which, despite the depredations of Edward I, a few examples survive.

The *Chancellor*, who also makes an early appearance, was the most exalted of the officers. He looked after the royal records, kept the Great Seal, and was a sort of Secretary of State for all departments. He was a cleric and had a clerical staff of 'chaplains'; in 1159 appears his special clerk, the ancestor of the Clerk Register. He did not, like the English Chancellor, come to exercise jurisdiction in equity.

The *Justiciar* was the principal law officer of the crown. He was not a 'household' officer. At first he remained much about the king, though he was sent to preside over the 'perambulations' whereby it was necessary to delimit estates, but gradually he came to supervise the working of the royal law throughout Scotland. Much civil justice was done in Church Courts; in Galloway and in Orkney (which was still Norse) the old customary laws remained; yet there was a body of recognized law, known as the *Lex Terrae* and this was supplemented by the '*Assisae*' of successive kings, which introduced new legislation. Admittedly the Crown gave much of its traditional power to feudal tenants, but it still kept the *placita regia* (originally murder, robbery, rape, and arson), and an ultimate responsibility to punish crime and to maintain order.

Along with the new laws came new practice. The 'Jury of Inquest' may go back to David I, and Scotland soon developed procedures parallel to the English *Mort d' Ancestor* (Inquisitio Post Mortem) and *Novel Disseisin*. From the collections known as *Regiam Majestatem* (Alexander II) and *Quoniam Attachiamenta* (1286–1386), which came to be known as the 'Auld Lawis', it is plain that there was much borrowing from England. Yet the borrowing was not slavish; whereas English lawyers sought a procedure to meet every conceivable case, the Scots lawyers relied rather on first principles.

In the days when good government was much the same as good justice, the office of Justiciar was very important, though it never attained the dimensions of the English office. Sometimes it was held by several persons at the same time, and the 'eyres' were irregularly conducted. Still the Justiciar exercised supervision over local officers and had a responsibility in criminal jurisdictions which survives today in the office of Lord Justice-General, now held along with that of Lord President of the Court of Session.

Another office which gained prominence was that of the *Steward*, whose responsibility for the royal household kept him constantly about the king, and from about 1136, when David I gave the office to Walter Fitz-Alan to hold in heredity, the family of Stewart gained in importance. The sixth High Steward married Marjorie, daughter of Robert Bruce, and became the ancestor of the Royal house. Other offices too tended to become hereditary – that of Constable, for example, which is still held by the House of Errol (Hay).

The Royal Council. The Royal Council included members of the Royal family, ecclesiastics, magnates, and officers; it advised the king and authenticated charters. On occasions of importance it might be expanded into a Great Council, at which in theory all tenants-in-chief might attend, and the body thus enlarged might (very occasionally) grant an 'aid'.

Another function of the King's Council was the doing of justice, and the highest justice was done in 'parliament'. The name 'parliament' is given to an important meeting for deliberation in 1173, some seventy years before it occurs in the English annals; but in those days parliament was not 'representative' either in Scotland or in England. In both countries, however, it could be welded into a meeting of the Great Council, and, since England was accustomed to the idea of 'representation' in local government, the English parliament was the sooner able to claim that it spoke for the whole people. None the less, a Scottish parliament certainly functioned in the reign of Alexander III. This may have been primarily a high court, meeting regularly thrice a year, but there existed along with it a parliament or General Council which legislated and advised the king as from the whole community.

Sheriffdoms and Burghs. Much local government was done by the feudal magnates, whom the king had invested with part of his royal power, but much also was done by royal officers appointed *ad hoc*. These were the sheriffs, who dealt with administration, finance, and military affairs, and who held courts at which all tenants-in-chief were liable to appear in person or by proxy. As the central authority gained in might so did the sheriffdoms multiply. Their development was neither regular nor continuous, but some thirty sheriffdoms were in being before 1296.

Closely allied with the sheriffdom was the royal burgh. The early burgh was often little more than a stronghold. Its situation was dictated by geographical factors – a hill, a ford, an estuary, or a road junction – and often, no doubt, there was already a settlement before the stronghold was built. In any case it soon became a place of trade and its original inhabitants – soldiers of the garrisons and their families – were reinforced by incomers, among them Englishmen and Flemings. Yet always it was a place of defence; the earliest burgh was the '*caput*' of the sheriffdom, the headquarters of an omnicompetent officer who came to exercise the authority of local officers who had preceded him. His usefulness must not be exaggerated. The burghs gradually escaped from his sway by gaining, under royal charter, trading privileges, immunity from royal officials, and eventually the right, or liability, of dealing with the royal exchequer. Again, though the sheriff called out the shire-levies, the magnates still led their own retinues, and his authority over the magnates, many of whom came to have burghs of their own, depended on his actual strength. He tended to become a local magnate himself, and in some cases his office eventually became hereditary. Yet, when every qualification has been made, the spread of the sheriff-doms represents the extension of the royal authority. By the day of Alexander III Scotland had a stable government of the ordinary feudal kind.

(v) *The Church*

To represent the development of the Scottish church as either an effect or a cause of the growth of the royal power would be erroneous; yet the royal power was enhanced by its close connection with an institution which organized, as well as spread, religion, and which conveyed social as well as spiritual benefits.

During the period of the Canmore dynasty, a system of diocesan episcopacy was introduced. Whilst he was only ruler of Strathclyde (1107–24), David I founded (*c.* 1115) and richly endowed the see of Glasgow which, perhaps because it represented old Strathclyde, was at times inclined to behave as if St Andrews enjoyed a primacy rather than a superiority. Before David's death in 1153 bishoprics had been created, or restored, in Galloway, Moray, Dunkeld, Ross, Caithness, Aberdeen, Dunblane, and Brechin. The see of Argyll appeared about 1200, but the bishopric of the Isles, to which it had sometimes been united, remained in dispute between York and Trondhjem for many years. The see of Galloway, too, remained a suffragan of York, and though its bishops were sometimes recognized by Popes as

53

Scottish, it was not until about 1359 that York lost effective control. Orkney, naturally, was dependent upon Trondhjem until the islands passed to Scotland in 1472. Still, one way or the other, all the bishoprics which existed at the Reformation were now in being, and into them Scottish influences steadily permeated. There was no archbishop; but in 1225 a Bull of Honorius III authorized the holding of provincial councils, without the presence of an archbishop, under a 'Conservator of the Privileges of the Scottish church'.

Among the reasons for this unusual situation was the claim of England to a supremacy over the Scottish church. This the Scottish kings stoutly resisted, playing off the jealousies of York and Canterbury, and making capital out of Henry II's dealing with Becket; and though bishops like John of Glasgow, and even King William the Lion himself, incurred papal admonition and censure, Scottish persistence prevailed. Either Clement III in 1188 or, more probably, Celestine III in 1192 – the intial 'C' of the Papal Bull is ambiguous – recognized that the *Ecclesia Scotticana* owed obedience to the Pope alone.

The sees were not all equally endowed; in some of them, as in remote Caithness, ecclesiastical revenue was hard to collect. The development of parishes was slow and sporadic. Yet the introduction of a diocesan system not only brought Scottish Christianity into line with the general development of north-western Europe, but exercised upon Scottish society a stabilizing influence which accorded with the centralizing efforts of the Crown. As the War of Independence was to show, the alliance between the Crown and the bishop was an established thing.

Along with the new bishoprics of the secular church appeared the new religious orders. Of these it was the Augustinian canons who first commended themselves to the early kings; but the Benedictines at Dunfermline were already in the field and other orders soon established houses – Cistercians at Melrose, the Tironenses at Selkirk (later Kelso) and Arbroath, Premonstratensians at Dryburgh, Valliscaulians at Beauly and Pluscarden, for example, and there was a Cluniac House at Paisley. The military orders first of the Temple and then of St John gained a foothold too.

The main purpose of a religious house was to sing Masses for the souls of the founders, benefactors, and their families, and to cultivate a holy life among its members; but the religious and their lay-brethren made important contributions to the cultural and economic life of Scotland. They were great builders, and introduced new techniques from Norman England or direct from France. Among the majestic monuments of the age – some of them now sadly impaired by the ravages of time and misfortune – are the cathedrals of St Andrews and Glasgow, the priory of Inchcolm, the abbey of Arbroath, and parts of the great Border abbeys (which were to suffer so much from English invasion). The monks were good agriculturalists too, and good sheep farmers; they became wool-merchants, miners of coal and producers of salt.

There was, however, a debit side to the account. In the first place, the national church recognized by the Pope became subject to papal taxation: a demand was made as early as 1239 and repeated in 1267–8. The king and clergy resisted in the name of precedent, but any success they gained was nominal and after 1274, when Gregory X decided to levy one tenth of ecclesiastical incomes for six years in order to promote a crusade, the danger of the situation became apparent. In 1275, a collector, Baiamundus de Vitia, insisted on assessing clerical incomes on a new basis, and 'Bagimont's Roll' as it came to be called, though it was adjusted from time to time, remained the basis of ecclesiastical taxation for centuries. Scotland lost bullion which could be ill spared by a country without store of precious metals. This was bad, and even worse was the fact that the papacy, regarding Britain as a whole, looked with an approving and hopeful eye upon the proposed crusade of Edward I, and allowed the collection of the Scottish tenths to pass into English hands, to be applied before long to English uses. In fact, one of the readjustments of the Roll

(1291) was made by Edward's servant, John de Halton, who became Bishop of Carlisle in 1292.

While the increase of clerical prosperity thus brought with it a threat from without to the national independence, it brought also a grave danger from within. The church came to own too great a proportion of the good land of the country and to control too great a proportion of the national wealth. It is not certain that James I (1406–37) described his saintly ancestor, David I, as 'ane soir sanct for the Crown', but he may well have done so. And it was not only the Crown which was impoverished by the riches of the church. As early as the reign of David I it became the practice to grant to religious houses the tithes and patronages of the parish churches. This meant that the revenue of the parish was enjoyed by the great house which appointed a 'vicar', very ill paid, to do the parochial work; and he, poor man, struggling to make ends meet, tended to relapse into the ordinary life of the community and to press unduly hard any economic rights still remaining to him (see p. 141).

As the sees also gained control over parishes, the condition of the Scottish church became unsatisfactory. William the Lion's foundation of Arbroath soon controlled thirty-three or thirty-four parishes; on the eve of the Reformation only five of forty-five parishes in Galloway were not 'appropriated', and throughout Scotland the same phenomenon was seen. For the moment, however, the evil consequences did not appear. Faith was strong and the money acquired by sees and religious houses was by no means wasted. To it we owe the beautiful buildings which, defiant alike of English destruction and reforming zeal, still witness to the achievement of generations who saw in beauty one form of holiness. Endowed with abbeys and priories, whose spiritual mothers were, usually, upon the continent, Scotland was brought into touch with a culture which did not necessarily enter by way of England.

Whilst these momentous changes were taking place, how fared the plain folk of Scotland? In areas which felt the impact of the Anglo-Norman penetration, there were certainly great changes, but the advent of a rather small, alien aristocracy did not involve wholesale enslavement or expropriation. Doubtless the newcomers at first held with a heavy hand the land that they had gained. It seems certain that the numerous mottes could have been constructed only with the aid of enforced labour, and some of the mottes were enormous. The Doune of Invernochty in Strathdon is 250 feet long and 120 feet broad at its summit; it was about sixty feet high, and enclosed by a ditch twenty feet deep; and when, about the mid-thirteenth century, the stone castle of Kildrummy arose to succeed it as the chief strength of the earldom of Mar, local labour was surely used, although the good masonry was executed by skilled craftsmen from without.

Doubtless, too, the new lord brought his own soldiers to garrison his castle, and the little township which appeared about it would be peopled partly with Englishmen or Flemings. Yet before long the burgh would become a place of trade for the whole countryside.

Where, as was often the case, a religious house was the new proprietor, the change, though of a different kind, perhaps was more intensive; and for it we have the evidence of the charters. Improved agriculture was introduced and, although we must not expect to find regular dimensions, we hear of the ploughgate, the husband-land, and the ox-gang – terms which bespeak the eight-ox plough, very likely communal. Occasionally, we even hear of 'acres'.

The tenants for the most part owed predial services (e.g. ploughing, reaping, shearing, and casting peats) but they were not unfree. Admittedly there were some serfs who belonged utterly to their masters, but the fact that they are given individual names, usually Celtic, seems to show that servitude was rather the exception than the rule. Where, as sometimes happened, the monks dug coal, or dried out salt, it may be assumed that their work-people were already thirled (bound) to their employment, as they were to remain for centuries. Yet such bondsmen would be relatively few and it seems certain the condition of the shepherds who attended the great flocks which now appeared must have differed little from that of their ancestors.

Moreover, it must be remembered that the total number of incomers was limited. Much of the land remained with Celtic holders. In the fragmentary royal accounts which survive there are many references to thanages which represent the holdings of the old toiseachs, and from these the king derived a revenue largely in kind. Some of them were on the royal demesne; others no doubt passed to members of the new aristocracy; but they were not military tenures: they were heritable estates which paid rent, and, as the years passed, they developed into regular *feu-ferme* holdings.

As this change took place, the position of the subordinate tenants would not be materially altered. In the old thanages there had been gradations of rank – freemen and carls. Under the new dispensation, especially perhaps when new methods of agriculture were adopted, new names appeared and gradations of society were more firmly marked in accordance with the English manorial system; but only the lowest class, the *nativi*, were bondsmen.

All things considered, it may be concluded that the lot of the ordinary folk in the countryside was less altered by the Anglo-Norman invasion than has been supposed. Life in the countryside was certainly simple. Oatmeal, barley, milk, and cheese were the staple foods. For the poorer classes meat may well have been uncommon, and for rich and poor alike fresh meat was unobtainable during the winter months. Owing to lack of pasture, animals had to be killed at Martinmas and their flesh was preserved in brine, since Scotland did not discover dry salt till the beginning of the seventeenth century. The dead animal was known as a 'mart', and the offal sewn in an animal's stomach, and sometimes buried in the 'girnel' (meal-chest) for better protection from the air, was a very early form of preserved meat. The name 'haggis' came from France at a later date.

In the little urban communities, however, there occurred a great development which is of extreme importance as furthering the growth of the 'Third Estate'. The Burgh, as has been shown, was not a mere continuation of the old township, though sometimes it appeared on the site of an already existing settlement. It was a definite creation – a place of strength; its inhabitants had both liabilities and privileges. Because it provided security it attracted traders, and before long craftsmen. In a good many cases its position came to be recognized by a charter, on the Anglo-Norman model, and from the charters there may be gained a fair picture of burghal life. The inhabitants of the Burgh were Scotsmen and Flemings as well as Englishmen. At first they were, in theory, all freeholders of the king, fulfilling prescribed duties, paying tolls and rents to the king's officers; but before long they became corporations anxious to compound as a whole for their liabilities, and elect their own officers. The basis of life was still largely agricultural; every burgher had his own portion of land, and some rights over the common land, and the subsistence economy, thus provided, was practised also when the burghers came, as many did, to follow crafts. The first tradesmen of whom we hear – weavers and tailors, bakers and fleshers, masons and wrights, for example – produced the very things required by a self-supporting community.

The Burgh, however, could not remain entirely self-supporting. Some things like iron, luxury textiles, and millstones often had to be imported, as well as much wine for the king and the magnates; and, on the other hand, hides, sheepskins, and wool could be exported. The presence of Flemings in the early burghs may be indicative of a trade in wool, which rose to considerable proportions in the southern lands, especially where there were houses of Cistercians – Kelso Abbey alone had 7,000 sheep – and Berwick became the great exporting centre. There the Flemings had their own house, the Red Hall, under whose burning timbers they all died during the brutal sack of the city by Edward I in 1296.

Meanwhile the growing importance of the principal burghs had often been recognized by the grant of a royal charter, which made them collective *seigneuries*. The effect

59

of a charter was to make the burgh more independent of royal officers, and also to endow it with valuable commercial privileges. Its inhabitants were given the monopoly of the sale of almost everything except food and drink within the burgh, and usually in the surrounding countryside as well; and country-folk, who might sell their produce at the burgh fair (usually weekly) were compelled to accept prices fixed by the burgh.

As the economy developed the merchants naturally became more important than the craftsmen. Their guild – and most burghs had a merchant guild – soon secured a monopoly of foreign trade, both in Scotland and overseas; for they commended themselves to the king because they could produce ready money. Gradually they gained an ascendancy, and it was from their ranks that the elected officials of the town came to be drawn.

Common interests produced common action to maintain economic privilege and burghal law. The result of this common action was the 'Court of the Four Burghs', at first Berwick, Edinburgh, Roxburgh, and Stirling. During the English occupation Berwick and Roxburgh were replaced by Lanark and Linlithgow; later other burghs came in and the union gradually expanded until it became known as the 'Convention of Royal Burghs' (only abolished in the 1970s).

It and its constituent members were in one sense champions of monopoly; in another they stood for the interest of the Third Estate in Scottish politics. Yet it must be remembered that the Burghs were very small, and in any estimate of the condition of ordinary folk the countryside must take pride of place. There, as has been seen, the lot of the population did not deteriorate seriously during the rise of the Anglo-Norman monarchy. Materially, indeed, it may have been improved. Psychologically, however, it may have been worse, for some of the alien lords were hard-handed, and in any case the native dignity of the Celt would not accord well with the sense of thraldom to the English.

Yet where, as was not uncommon, the newcomer had fortified his position by marriage into the ancient Celtic lines, this sense of thraldom would be greatly tempered and, in the wild countries and the Highlands where the Anglo-Normans had not penetrated, it would not exist at all. And the Highlands were not so far away. It may be remarked that the meat bones found in the ruins of Kindrochit Castle at Braemar were mainly the bones of red deer. Under the new institutions most of the old Scotland still survived.

Secure against its enemies from without and strong at home, with its established government and established church, the dynasty of Canmore seemed to be firmly installed upon the Scottish throne. Yet in a few years all was gone. Alexander III, hurrying from Edinburgh on an ugly night to his new-made wife, Yolande de Dreux, fell from his horse near Kinghorn and was killed. The two sons of his first wife, Margaret of England, were already dead; by his second wife he had no issue, and his sole heir was his grand-daughter, Margaret the Maid of Norway, a girl of three, born to his late daughter, Margaret, who had married Eric II of Norway. The little queen died in 1290 before ever she saw Scotland. The line of Canmore was ended, and before long the kingdom of Scotland was fighting for its life.

CHAPTER 4

WARS OF INDEPENDENCE
1286–1371

1286–90	Margaret
1290–92	First interregnum
1292–6	John Balliol
1296–1306	Second interregnum
1306–29	Robert I
1329–71	David II

The Reign of Margaret

No doubt it was 'in the logic of history' that England should endeavour to absorb Scotland. None the less, the first English attempt at a wholesale conquest resulted from the coincidence of two dynastic 'accidents'. At a time when the Scottish throne passed to an infant girl in a foreign land, there reigned in England a powerful, ruthless monarch with a genius for definition, and this monarch, the great-uncle of the Scottish Queen, had a son of marriageable age. The nature of Edward I's opportunity was apparent to his own generation, and it was made more obvious by events which occurred in Scotland; among the six guardians chosen (all men of good standing), no place was found for Robert Bruce the elder, who had been recognized as heir in 1238, when Alexander II had lost his first wife without issue, and who was then the senior male descendant of David I. Civil wars broke out in Galloway where the Bruce and Balliol interests were mutually opposed.

Yet at first all promised well because Scotland, Norway, and England favoured a marriage between the Maid of Norway and the first Prince of Wales. In a meeting at Salisbury, commissioners from the three countries agreed that the little Queen should come to England or Scotland unbetrothed and without delay, though stipulations were made to prevent her from passing under the absolute control of Edward. He, however, had already applied to the Pope for a dispensation for the marriage of the young cousins, and, though the Scots were not aware of this, they made no demur when the King's intentions were disclosed. In March 1290 the four surviving guardians and many other magnates wrote to the English King cordially agreeing to the marriage and, in July, the matter was formally concluded by the Treaty of Birgham-on-Tweed. The terms of this treaty seem at first sight to make a frank admission of Scotland's independence, yet there were qualifications. There were caveats as to the 'Right of the King of England in the Marches or elsewhere' and Scotland was to return to the legitimate successor only if Edward and Margaret, or *either of them*, should have no heir; apparently Edward, by the marriage, was to obtain a personal right to the Scottish inheritance, which he might transmit to his heirs by another wife. Whether the Scots envisaged this possibility is not clear, but its importance soon became evident, for the marriage did not take place. In September 1290, the Maid of Norway died in Orkney on her way to Scotland.

The death of the little Queen was a turning point in Anglo-Scottish relations. The projected marriage, though it was only a development of a long-continued tendency made possible by happy chance, has been hailed as a piece of supreme statesmanship on the part of Edward I. It has been argued that, had the match succeeded, England and Scotland would have been happily united, and both countries would have been saved from three centuries of bloody warfare and mutual distrust. The argument fails to take count of Edward's mentality. For him, 'union' meant 'suzerainty' and the methods adopted by Edward I to exploit the opportunity which presented itself were marked by sharp practice, arrogance, and brutality, which had the effect of arousing in Scotland a native patriotism and a hatred of England which made the idea of union intolerable to Scottish hearts.

By sharp practice he gained a recognition of his suzer-

The Disputed Succession

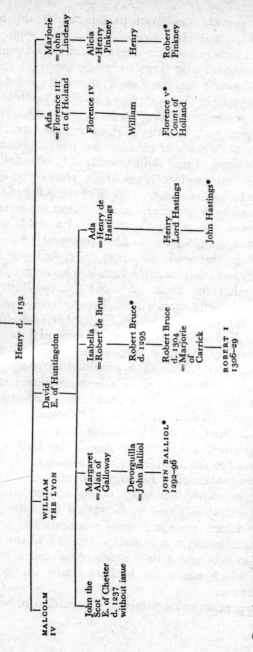

Competitors marked with an asterisk. Kings in capitals.

Note: Florence of Holland based his claim on the allegation that, in the days of William the Lyon, David had renounced, for himself and his heirs, any claim to the crown in exchange for the land of Garioch. His claim was taken seriously by Edward I, Balliol, and Bruce; but the actual instrument of resignation could not be produced, and in the end Florence abandoned his claim (according to one account upon payment made by Balliol).

Scottish Historical Review, XXXVI, p. 111.

ainty; he used his suzerainty to behave as if he might do as he pleased in Scotland; with those who resisted him he held no terms and, regarding them as traitors, he massacred garrisons and executed prisoners. He convinced himself that he was justly entitled to do so but thereby convinced the Scots that from him they had nothing to hope, and that their only chance of salvation lay in independence. He found his first opportunity in the disputed succession.

The Question of the Succession

To modern eyes, it would seem clear that the best claim was that of John Balliol as representing the senior surviving stem of the House of Canmore, but to the men of 1290 the matter was not so clear. To some it did not follow that the sacrosanct dignity of the crown should descend by the rules which governed the inheritance of land – and even as regards land there was doubt as to the respective rights of heirs, male and female. The land of David of Huntingdon had been divided among co-heiresses. Moreover, there still remained in Scotland an attachment to the old idea of 'tanistry' (see pp. 37, 42). In fact, no fewer than thirteen candidates presented themselves. (See Table p. 64).

Some of these may have advanced their claims for reasons of prestige, or on the 'off-chance' that the realm might be divided; six of them relied on illegitimate descent from the royal house. Comyn claimed upon an uncertain descent from Donald Bane (brother of Malcolm Canmore), and Eric of Norway upon the right of his dead daughter. The remaining five could prove descent from Earl Henry, son of David I; all five claimed through female heirs and, if the daughters of Henry were disregarded, there still remained representatives of the three female lines issuing from David, Earl of Huntingdon. Hastings, grandson of the youngest daughter, claimed that the realm should be divided; Robert Bruce the elder based his claim on the fact that he was the son of the second daughter Isabella and that he had already been recognized as heir; Balliol, grandson of the oldest daughter, argued that seniority should outweigh proximity and that the recognition of Bruce in 1238 was nullified by his own birth to Devorguilla, the foundress of Balliol College, Oxford, in 1250.

There was room for dubiety and, to avert a civil war, influential Scotsmen invited Edward to resolve the difficulty. The bishop of St Andrews suggested Balliol. The 'seven earls of Scotland' put in a plea for Bruce.

Recourse to a neighbouring monarch of recognized wisdom was no admission of his suzerainty: in 1263 Louis IX (St Louis) had been asked to settle the differences between Henry III and his barons. Edward, however, was quick to take the chance provided. He set about collecting evidence; ignoring the Treaty of Canterbury (p. 37), but accepting some doubtful evidence, he was confirmed in his view that he was suzerain of Scotland. When he met the claimants at Norham on 10 May 1291, he demanded that they must acknowledge his superiority, and gave them three weeks to make up their minds. At the same time he summoned his northern tenants to join him in arms, including the principal competitors themselves. Reluctant to defy the arbitrator and apprehensive about their English lands, the competitors could not long resist. Edward crossed the Tweed to Upsetlington, exacted from nine of the principal claimants a sworn recognition of his superiority, and took seisin of Scotland and its castles on the ground that he must have these things in hand to give to the successful competitor.

Ignoring a protest made by the 'bone gent' of Scotland (persons of substance) that no reply could be given to Edward's unprecedented claim until Scotland had a King who would answer for himself,* Edward proceeded to act, not as an arbitrator, but as a judge. The procedure he adopted followed strictly legal form, and on 17 November 1292 at Berwick the cause was settled in favour of Balliol. There is no proof that Balliol owed his victory to Edward's favour, or to the fact that he was a known weakling. The Scots called him 'Toom Tabard' (empty coat) after his débâcle,

*The protest was omitted from the official English record.

3. The Wars of Independence

but he seems to have been an ordinary man put into an impossible position by his arrogant overlord.

Reign of John Balliol

Edward demanded from him a humiliating dependence which he himself utterly refused to Philip of France, who was his own overlord for his Gascon possessions. His conduct may have been due to ill-health, domestic difficulty, and a haughty mind; but it may also be interpreted as a deliberate attempt to drive Balliol to his destruction. The vassal king was roughly told that the Treaty of Birgham was a dead letter; appeals from matters on which Balliol was quite entitled to deal were transferred to England; he himself was summoned south on trifling matters. When, in 1294, he was brought to London and told to supply men and money for the King's French War, he found that his subjects would suffer no more. They formed a council of four bishops, four earls, and four barons to whose policy they agreed, and in October 1295, Scotland concluded with France the first formal treaty of the 'Auld Alliance'.

The importance of the treaty has been exaggerated. Scotland and France had already drawn together to resist Plantagenet power. William the Lion (to his great cost) had made common cause with Louis VII (1173); Alexander II had married Marie de Coucy (1239), and Alexander III, Yolande de Dreux (1285). The friendship was not new and the terms of the treaty were unequal, revealing French doubt as to the permanence of Balliol's rule; it was not cited in the numerous renewals afterwards made, which conformed to the Treaty of Corbeuil between Robert I and Charles IV (1326); and it did not at the time aid Scotland.

Balliol renounced his homage to England in April 1296, but Edward had already sacked Berwick with the utmost brutality at the end of March. Next month Surrey beat the Scottish nobles at Dunbar and before long the great castles were in the hands of the English. In July, Balliol yielded at Stracathro in Angus, and surrendered himself and his kingdom into the hands of the conqueror. He and his son Edward were taken by sea to England and a few years later were allowed to retire to France.

Edward marched north as far as Elgin, and on his homeward way collected the Stone of Destiny from Scone, some of the Scottish Records, some plate and jewels, and St Margaret's portion of the True Cross. He collected also oaths of fealty, afterwards entered in the famous Ragman Rolls, from about 2,000 subscribers. His action showed that he would no longer be content with a vassal king. He regarded Scotland as his own and, halting at Berwick on his way south, he held a parliament wherein he arranged a government for Scotland similar to that given to conquered Wales.

The First Interregnum: William Wallace

John de Warenne, Earl of Surrey, was made Governor – of high blood and good capacity, he was ageing and rather indolent; Hugh de Cressingham, a worldly churchman, became Treasurer; Walter of Agmondesham, Chancellor; and William Ormesby, Justiciar. The new government was unpopular from the start. Cressingham was accused of avarice; Ormesby, established at Scone, fined and outlawed those who refused to take the oath, while his clerks took fees from those who did. The escheators were English and, though some of the sheriffs were Scots, all were appointed by the English.

Soon the whole country was participating in a revolt in which the small landowners took a great part. Andrew de Moray was conspicuous in the north; William Wallace, son of a Renfrewshire knight, in the south. In the summer of 1297 some nobles, among them Bruce, the Steward, and Sir William Douglas joined a confederacy, apparently organized by Bishop Wishart of Glasgow, but this fell to pieces, and made an ignominious capitulation at Irvine in July.

The popular movement, however, made rapid headway. Wallace moved north and joined hands with Andrew de

69

Moray who had reduced many castles in his own area, and when an English army under Surrey advanced from Berwick, it found a Scottish army awaiting them at Stirling. The Scottish leaders had chosen their position well, and showed great tactical skill: they allowed their enemy to begin, but not to complete, a slow advance over the wooden bridge across the Forth, caught them in disorder, and routed them utterly. Cressingham was killed, Surrey fled, and, in October, Moray and Wallace wrote triumphantly from Haddington to Lübeck and Hamburg announcing the liberation of their country and hoping that trade would be resumed.

Moray, perhaps wounded at Stirling, must have died soon afterwards, for when the Scots army returned from a raid into England, Wallace alone was its commander as 'Guardian of the Kingdom of Scotland and Leader of its Armies in the name of John, by the Grace of God, Illustrious King of Scotland'. He was probably knighted about this time, but his success was short-lived. The nobility, for the most part, stood aloof and he had little cavalry to encounter the army which Edward brought north in 1298.

When the armies met at Falkirk on 22 July, the English cavalry were at first repulsed by the steady Scottish spears arranged in four solid rings (schiltrons) and lost heavily in horses – the heavy war horse was the 'tank' of medieval warfare and had the tank's inconvenience in that it needed much fuel; but when Edward brought up his archery, the schiltrons, unable to reply, melted away. Wallace escaped from the rout which followed, but his prestige was gone with his army and, after a while, he went off to seek aid in France.

Yet his example was not lost. Edward could occupy only the south-east of Scotland effectively, and Scotland continued to resist under leaders of her own choice. At first Bruce (grandson of the 'Competitor') and Comyn were leaders; but they were rivals too, and a meeting in Selkirk Forest ended in a scuffle wherein Bruce was nearly killed (August 1299). Bishop Lamberton of St Andrews was added as a 'guardian'; but Bruce left his office in disgust and, in

1300, a parliament at Rutherglen appointed Ingram d'Umfraville in his stead.

Apart from the defection of Bruce, who submitted to Edward in 1302, perhaps because he had heard that France was supporting Balliol, the party of resistance was not solid. Yet it had for a while the help of Pope Boniface VIII who claimed that Scotland, converted by the relics of St Andrew, belonged to the Holy See,* and of the French King who arranged truces from October 1300 to May 1301, and from January to November in 1302. In 1303, the Comyn party won a smart victory at Roslin, but thereafter their power collapsed: the French King, beaten by the Flemings at Courtrai in 1302, came to terms with the English; the Pope retired from his position in the two Bulls of August 1302.† Alone the Scots could not maintain the unequal conflict. Comyn surrendered in February 1304, and Stirling Castle, the last stronghold, fell in July. In August 1305, Wallace, taken near Glasgow, was hurried to trial in Westminster Hall and executed with all the horrors of a traitor's death. Some of his bravest supporters followed him to the scaffold.

Wallace was the leader of a *résistance*. He and his men had ravaged England and taken English lives; but a traitor he was not. He had never given his fealty to the usurper. Edward mangled his body and impaled his head on London Bridge; but he became the national hero of Scotland and his spirit lives still.

Robert Bruce

Under the direction of Edward, a commission of ten Scots and twenty Englishmen issued in September 1305 'Ordinances for the Establishment of the Land of Scotland'. These were, in themselves, practical and wise; but they were to be imposed from without and, before they came into operation, the Scottish scene was dramatically changed. On 10 February 1306, John Comyn was slain by Robert

*The Bull, *Scimus Fili* (July 1299).
†*Gravi Mentes Turbatione* and *Inter Assiduas Curas* (August 1302).

71

Bruce in the precincts of the Minorite house at Dumfries. Bruce's supporters suggested that Comyn was about to betray a scheme for a joint attack upon the English, but possibly the incident is best understood as a sequel to the struggle in Selkirk Forest (1299), with the difference that this time Bruce struck first. By his deed, Bruce laid himself open to charges of murder, sacrilege, and, possibly, of treason; and desperation, as well as ambition, would lead him to try to avoid his perils by taking the Crown of Scotland.

Determined to be made a King in the ancient Scottish manner he hurried to Scone and had himself set in the royal seat on 25 March. In the meagre attendance his own kinsfolk were conspicuous. Yet the gold circlet was set upon his head by Isabella, Countess of Buchan, representing her brother, the Earl of Fife, who was in the hands of the English, and the Bishops of St Andrews, Glasgow, and Moray, with the Abbot of Scone, ranged themselves on the side of the new monarch. Such was the ominous beginning of the reign in which Scotland was to win her independence.

All the odds were against the new King. He had aroused the fierce hostility of the powerful Comyns; he had not the sympathy of Scotland, for, though his complaisance to Edward has been exaggerated, he had, at one time, served the English King; before long he was excommunicated; above all, he had awakened the contemptuous hate of Edward, who swore his famous oath upon the swans that he would never rest till Scotland was conquered and gave brutal orders for the slaughter of all who supported 'King Hob' in arms. The evil omens were fulfilled in the first actions of the conflict. The Earl of Pembroke, attacking him improperly upon a Sunday, scattered Bruce's small army at Methven Park near Perth (June 1306) and hanged without trial the lay prisoners taken. Bruce was driven into the Highlands. His wife and daughter, sent north perhaps in the hope of reaching Norway, were captured near St Duthac's shrine (near Tain) and imprisoned. Kildrummy Castle, the strong seat of his sister, the Dowager Countess of Mar, was taken, and his brother Nigel executed out of hand. The young Countess of Buchan was set in a cage at Berwick and, though she was released to a less rigorous confinement after four years, there is no record that she was ever set free.

The new King, struggling to the west, was all but cut off at Dalry near Tyndrum by the chief of the MacDougalls, whose descendants long possessed the Brooch of Lorn, said to have been torn from his shoulder in this action. With difficulty crossing Loch Lomond, he reached the western sea. His movements during the winter of 1306–7 are not really known, but the spring of 1307 found him in Arran. Whether he witnessed in a cave there – or indeed anywhere else – the resolution of the spider is uncertain, but he found determination to try again. And again everything went wrong. A landing in Galloway at Loch Ryan resulted in the death of his brothers, Alexander and Thomas; he himself landed in ancestral Carrick only to discover that the signal bonfire at Turnberry had been lit in error, or by an enemy, and that his people were not ready. English forces from various quarters pinioned him in Glen Trool; yet he broke away from them after a smart action and, on 10 May, beat Pembroke handsomely at Loudoun Hill near Ayr. Two months later came a greater deliverance. Edward I, still striving to advance against him, died at Burgh-upon-the-Sands in Cumberland, and his son Edward II advanced into Nithsdale only to turn back again. The 'Hammer of the Scots' had struck his last blow.

The tide, which had begun to turn, flowed with increasing momentum. Before the year was done, Bruce carried his arms into the territories of his enemies. Finding supporters in Mar and Ross, he attacked John Comyn, Earl of Buchan, and though he himself was very ill, beat him near Inverurie; the 'harrying' of Buchan which followed became a by-word. Having overrun the north, he turned to the west and, in 1308, made himself master of the MacDougall stronghold of Dunstaffnage.

Meanwhile, his fiery brother Edward, along with Sir James Douglas, whose father had well defended Berwick in

1296, took control of the south-west and, in an incursion of the Tweed valley, captured young Randolph who had been taken prisoner at Methven, and who was later to be reckoned, along with his two captors, a famous paladin of Bruce. The surge of victory swept on. The English, it is true, at times invaded, notably in 1310 and 1312; but Bruce repeatedly raided the north of England, and in 1313 seized the Isle of Man. One by one, the English strongholds fell: Forfar, Brechin, Dundee, Perth, Dumfries, and Caerlaverock. Linlithgow was taken by the ruse of a plain countryman in 1313; early in 1314 Roxburgh was captured by Douglas, and Edinburgh by Randolph, in astonishing escalades. Stirling was invested by Edward Bruce and agreed to capitulate if it were not relieved by midsummer 1314.

How is this surprising run of success to be explained? There were several causes. Edward II, inheriting his father's difficulties, but not his ability, was at odds with his nobles; the French King secretly recognized Bruce in 1309; the Scottish clergy in 1310 gave their support to the excommunicate monarch in a provincial council at Dundee. Moreover, Bruce had developed skilful ways of waging war. As early as the day of Loudoun Hill, he had denied ground to hostile cavalry by digging trenches to prolong his short battle line; he avoided pitched battle; he destroyed the castles which he captured, and moved swiftly while his enemy, relying on heavy horses, were sometimes unable to stir until the fields could supply fodder.

It must be remembered too that Bruce had all along stout supporters: some were his kinsmen and friends; others were attracted to him by their antipathy to his enemies. The hostility of MacDougall, for instance, was offset by the friendship of Angus Og, representative of a junior line of Somerled, who was to become, thanks to Bruce's victory, the ancestor of the famous Clan Donald. With him stood the Celtic Earls of Lennox and Atholl, and members of other families which were to become great in Scotland – a Fraser, a Fleming, a Boyd, a Campbell, not to mention a Douglas. What is most important of all is that the people came to trust him. Scotland had not forgotten the days of Alexander III, and English brutality had served to harden the spirit of nationality which still survived beneath the heel of the oppressor. When Bruce proved himself a true champion, he found men to follow him.

Bannockburn. Edward Bruce's rash arrangement about Stirling brought about the pitched battle which the King had so far deliberately avoided: if he were not to lose prestige by permitting the relief of Stirling Castle, fight he must. In the early summer of 1314 Edward II came up with an army which, if far short of the traditional 100,000 men, impressed the English chroniclers as being extremely large. It was evidently far bigger than any force which Bruce could collect, and far stronger in heavy cavalry.

On the 23 June, the English host found their enemy well posted behind the little stream of the Bannock which, cutting through an escarpment in a surprising gorge, entered the River Forth through a plain of marsh and pools a few miles south of Stirling. On the Scots' side of the stream the land, through which the main road passed, rose gently to the 'New Park' and a woodland, whose trees would conceal the movement of the Scottish troops and hinder the use of cavalry against their right flank. The famous 'pits', though they were said to be concealed, were probably designed to defend the places where the deep gorge did not afford protection.

The English, who had marched all the way from Linlithgow, crossed the burn at once. The van, under Gloucester, pushed along the main road, while a party of cavalry endeavoured to effect a technical relief by riding along the edge of the dry ground of the Scottish left. Both attacks failed. When Gloucester tried to enter the New Park, he found the road barred, and one of his knights, de Bohun, charging furiously upon Bruce, who rode a light palfrey, was killed by a blow of the King's battle-axe; Clifford's cavalry was repulsed by Randolph's infantry alone. The English retired and, although during the night some of its

75

elements may have worked their way across the stream, it can hardly be believed that the whole English army, which contained good soldiers, would have bogged itself down in the marshy plain beyond the point where the Bannock enters the Forth.

The action of the following day is not entirely clear, but it seems certain that the English cavalry, jammed on too short a front, was less effective than usual and failed to protect, if it did not mask, the archers, who were dispersed by Bruce's cavalry. The three divisions of Scottish spearmen, ultimately joined by the fourth in reserve, fell upon the opposing host before its attack could gather momentum, and their victory was complete.

Edward, personally a good man-at-arms, reached Stirling Castle along with other fugitives, but the governor warned him that he must capitulate next day and, though hotly pursued, he escaped to Dunbar. He was fortunate. Many of his men were killed on the field; others, as they struggled south to the Border. Many were taken prisoner, some of whom were used to redeem captives – among them the Queen, her daughter, and Bishop Wishart of Glasgow – while the ransom of others and the booty taken flooded Scotland with unfamiliar wealth.

The Triumph of Bruce. The Battle of Bannockburn, though decisive, did not end the war; but thereafter Edward, whose unpopularity grew with his defeat, was fighting a losing battle. The conflict was not all one sided. A Scottish expedition to Ireland under Edward Bruce ended disastrously when its leader was killed at Dundalk (1318); and in 1322, Edward came up, plundered the Abbeys of Holyrood and Melrose and burnt Dryburgh. On the other hand, the Scots captured Berwick (1318), raided the north of England almost at will, and won substantial victories at Mytton (1319) and Byland (1322).

English attempts to use the authority of the Pope were vain. Bruce refused to receive letters not directed to him as King of Scots and, when the legates renewed the excommunication, the Scots nobles replied with the letter to Pope John XXII of April, 1320, whose sonorous Latin bespeaks the vital support of the clergy, and the hand of Bruce's chancellor Bernard de Linton, Abbot of Arbroath. The conclusion of this 'Declaration of Arbroath' rings down the centuries:

> For as long as one hundred of us shall remain alive we shall never in any wise consent to submit to the rule of the English, for it is not for glory we fight, for riches, or for honours, but for freedom alone, which no good man loses but with his life.

In 1323 Edward made a truce for thirteen years, and Randolph, who visited Avignon, softened the heart of the Pope, though it was not until 1328 that his master was fully absolved. By that time Scotland had formally gained her independence.

In 1327, young warlike Edward III celebrated his accession by going to encounter a raid led by Randolph and Douglas. He was nearly captured in his bed and accomplished nothing. Next year, in March, there was concluded in Edinburgh a treaty which, since it was confirmed by the English King at Northampton in the following May has generally been known as the Treaty of Northampton. By this, Bruce was recognized as King of an independent realm, and his son was betrothed to Edward's little sister Joan. The Scots agreed to pay £20,000 and the English to aid in the reconciliation of Bruce with the Pope. There was no mention of the return of the Stone of Destiny, or of the restitution of their lands in Scotland to those who had supported England. It seems likely that Edward's mother hoped, when she brought her daughter to Berwick to be married, to bring also the famous stone and use it to exact concessions for 'the Disinherited', but if there were such a project nothing came of it.

Bruce was now ailing, but he was fully reconciled to the Church before he died; and because he had not been able to fulfil his vow to undertake a crusade, he asked James Douglas to take his heart to the Holy Land in token of his good intention. He died on 7 June 1329, and six days later the Pope issued a bull permitting the unction and coronation of a King of Scots by the Bishop of St Andrews. His great work was done.

The Achievement of Bruce. Bruce was more than an animated battle-axe. While he won the independence of his country, and gained the support of France in a treaty (Corbeuil 1326) far more equitable than Balliol's treaty, he did much to organize and increase the internal strength of his realm. He saw to it that there should be no disputed succession after his death. An Act of 1315 brought in Edward Bruce, failing himself and his heirs-male; in 1318, after Edward's death in Ireland, he brought in, after himself and his heirs-male, Robert (later Robert II), only son of his daughter Marjorie and of Walter, the High Steward. On the birth of his son David in 1324, he had no need for a new statute, but in 1326, clergy, nobles, and people took oaths of fealty to David, and after him, to Bruce's grandson Robert. This was at Cambuskenneth, and the parliament which met there witnessed a great innovation, namely the presence of representatives of certain burghs. It has been argued that they were rather 'at' than 'in' parliament, and that only because the King wanted money. Even so, their appearance is significant, for the tax voted contained new features. Instead of being given a fixed sum, the King now received one tenth of all rents and profits of land, allowance being made for the ravages of war; and the same system was adopted in 1328 when another levy was made 'to pay for the peace'. Doubtless, on both occasions, the clergy made their own contribution; the nobles paid according to the Auld Extent; the burghs dealt directly with the Crown. With regard to the burghs, however, a new practice appeared at this time. Aberdeen, in 1319, and Edinburgh, in 1329, got '*feu-ferme* charters' whereby they paid a fixed annual sum in lieu of the old dues and customs, which permitted the interference of royal officers.

In dealing with the barons, a significant change was

made. For the first time there appeared grants *in liberam baroniam*, for which sixty charters are extant. It is true that the King made grants, in some cases of castles or burghs (in two cases, even of sheriffdoms), to his great servants, and that we hear, for the first time, of grants of 'regality' whereby the King conveyed to trusted adherents most of the rights of the Crown over a given area. Yet the general effect was to regularize the service due to the King and to consolidate the power of the barons. The realm which Bruce left behind him was an ordered, well-established kingdom. Unfortunately, he left it to a minor.

The Reign of David II: 1329–71

The reign of David II is included here under the title of 'The Wars of Independence' because in it David nearly lost all that his father had gained.

The Minority. David was aged five when he ascended the throne. He and his little Queen were crowned with full honours in 1331, but things went ill for him. Valiant Douglas, his face unscarred after so many battles, was killed in Spain (1330) trying to bring his master's heart to greater glory. In 1332, Randolph, Earl of Moray, the last of the great paladins, died at Musselburgh preparing, as it seems, to meet a new thrust from the south. Edward III, who had just sworn to preserve peace, kept his eyes closed when Edward Balliol (son of King John) and the 'Disinherited' sailed from the Humber with eighty-eight ships. The invaders surprised the defence; they landed at Kinghorn, marched through Fife, and in August destroyed at Dupplin a Scots army under the newly chosen guardian, the Earl of Mar, who was killed on the field.

Balliol was crowned at Scone, but before long he was hunted out from Annan 'one leg booted and the other naked'. He won Edward's full support by promising Berwick, and in an attempt to relieve Berwick, Archibald Douglas was beaten and killed at Halidon Hill in July, 1333.

Berwick fell. Next year Balliol not only did homage to Edward III, but gave the land of several of the southern counties to the English Crown. The Scots, in despair, accepted the aid of Philip VI; they sent their little King with his Queen and his two sisters to France where he was maintained in decent state in Château Gaillard (1334–41).

In his absence, a series of regents maintained the struggle as best they might. In 1336, the English King came up in person as far as Lochindorb in Moray and ravaged the north-east, but in 1338 Black Agnes, Countess of March, a true daughter of Randolph, held Dunbar Castle triumphantly for five months. Happier for Scotland than this picturesque episode was the fact that, in this year, Edward III, in pursuit of his claim to the French throne, took his army into Flanders and, with it, his interest. The Hundred Years' War between England and France had begun.

David in Scotland: 1341–6. A gay young prince, who had already accompanied the French King to the field, David probably hoped to emulate his martial father when he returned to Scotland. Scotland, however, impoverished by war and disorder, needed peace and good government, and David gave neither. He idled away his time though the truces were ill kept; and in 1346, at the appeal of Philip VI who was anxious to shake off Edward's grip upon Calais, he rashly invaded England and at Neville's Cross, near Bishop Auckland, he threw away his army by bad leadership (17 October). The Scots suffered heavy casualties, and he himself, wounded by two arrows but still able to knock two teeth from the jaw of his captor, was taken prisoner and, after a convalescence at Bamburgh, lodged in the Tower.

David in England: 1346–57. David's captivity in England was not always stringent. Edward III was his brother-in-law. David had no children and was jealous of his heir designate, Robert the Steward. As early as 1350 he began to listen to proposals that he should do homage to Edward while he lived, and arrange that, if he died childless, the Scottish

Crown should pass to Edward or one of his sons. The Scots, he hoped, would accept his arrangements in exchange for being freed from the payment of an enormous ransom.

The Scots would not agree, though various negotiations followed. When Edward was in France in 1355, they won an action at Nesbit near Berwick and captured the town, but not the castle. Edward was prompt to reply. Early in 1356 he appeared with an army, ravaged Edinburgh and Haddington in the 'Burnt Candlemas', dismissed the puppet King Balliol with a pension, and took Scotland under his direct control. Yet in the following year David was released at last, possibly because Edward's interest, after his son's victory at Poitiers, where the French King was taken prisoner, concentrated itself more than ever upon France. On 3 October 1357, a treaty made at Berwick liberated David in exchange for a ransom of 100,000 marks payable in ten years.

End of the Reign: 1357–71. The returned King found Scotland in a sad state. The country had been wasted, not only by constant warfare, but by the Black Death whose appearance in Scotland had produced a theological, as well as a physical, difficulty, since its visitation of England had been regarded as a just punishment for sin. Evidence of the poverty of the country appears from the taxations which the Estates were persuaded to grant to pay off the ransom which the King probably never intended to repay.

In 1357, a council at Scone ordered a levy which involved, besides new taxes, a complete reassessment of lands and movables. The first instalment was punctually paid. The second was got in rather late and no more could be raised. Nothing could be got from France, and it was alleged that the King wasted much of what had been collected. In 1363, he went to London, and in the course of the visit agreed that if he died childless, his crown should pass heritably to Edward, though an English King was to be formally crowned when he became King of Scotland, the Stone of Destiny being brought back for the ceremony.

The Scottish Estates in 1364 rejected the arrangement, and determined to pay off the ransom. This was increased in 1365 to 100,000 pounds. But the instalments were now fixed at 4,000 pounds and the truce extended to twenty-five years. In 1366 a new assessment was made from which it appeared that the true value of the lands, both lay and clerical, was only respectively a half and two thirds of the ancient assessment.

The Scots got rather better terms in 1369 when England was again involved in France. The arrangement of 1365 was cancelled. The 44,000 marks already paid was deducted from the 100,000 originally due, and the balance of 56,000 marks was to be paid at the rate of 4,000 marks for fourteen years, during which the truce was to endure.

When Edward III died in 1377, 24,000 marks were still owing and this was never paid. Scotland, however, had paid 76,000 marks for the ransom of the King whose capture was due to his own folly, and who was prepared, at least on paper, to sell the independence of his country in exchange for his own release. His last years were unhappy: he had lost his popularity, and showed himself arrogant and self-willed. On the death of his English Queen in 1362, he married Margaret Drummond, widow of Sir John Logie, who was regarded by his nobles as in every way unworthy. He had not quite completed his forty-seventh year when he died in Edinburgh Castle in February 1371.

Summary of the Reign. The long reign of forty-one years was inglorious. In some ways it was picturesque. In this high age of chivalry, great valour went hand in hand with sheer brutality. The ravagings of Scotland were punctuated by knightly tournaments, and feats of arms by the execution of prisoners. Yet there may be detected evidence of healthy growth. As in other countries, when the king was absent for long periods, practical men found new ways of carrying on the government. Nor did David II prove devoid of administrative ability when he returned.

Reference has been made to the experiments in taxation,

and connected with these is a development of great importance: namely, the entry of the royal burghs into national politics. There is good reason to suppose that they were in parliament in 1340 and 1341. The records are not complete; but they were certainly present in the General Council of 1357 and in the Parliament of 1366, both of which were concerned with taxation. Thereafter, though they may not have attended regularly, their place in parliament was assured.

Moreover, the very end of the reign saw the beginning of what was to be a notable feature of the Scottish Constitution, namely the devolution of the authority of parliament, as regards both general business and justice, to small committees or commissions vested with the full power of the present assembly. In 1367 and 1369, commissions were entrusted to finish the work which parliament had begun. In 1370, authority was delegated to two bodies which were directed to report. What may be called the 'business committee' was the parent of the later Lords of the Articles; the judicial committee was the parent of the later Court of Session. The judicial function of parliament was extremely important – as late as 1399 the reason for holding an annual parliament was that the King's subjects might be 'servit' of the law.

Parliament had always been a law court: the *auditores* who first appear in 1341 are identical with the 'triers' and 'terminours' of England and the *maîtres de requêtes* of France. Already by 1370, it was recognized that the civil jurisdiction of parliament was of two kinds – appeals and original business – and, before long, two distinct committees emerged. Appeals were regarded as proper to parliament itself, and the committee 'for Dooms' was expected to finish its work while parliament was sitting. The Committee for Causes and Complaints was simply a central court for dealing with original business, which could sit after parliament rose; and its jurisdiction was afterwards extended into regular 'sessions', quite apart from the parliament itself. These examples of the anonymous development of the constitution are important in themselves – perhaps more important as evidence that Scotland, even under a King who ascended the throne as a minor, was an independent kingdom still. She was fortunate, no doubt, that England was involved in the Hundred Years' War; but her war of independence was won. John Barbour's *Bruce* (*c.* 1375), 'instinct with pride but devoid of savagery', is the birth-song of a nation.

Condition of the People. The condition of the people of Scotland during her struggle for independence was perhaps less unhappy than might be supposed. Certainly there was tumult and bloodshed, and the wastage of war is revealed in the fall of incomes from land already recorded. This, of course, affected the wealthier classes, but they had some compensations from the loot of Bannockburn and the spoliation of the northern counties.

Good stone castles were built: Edward I sent up the great architect of his Welsh castles, James of St George, to work in Scotland. In 1304 he ordered his sheriffs to send up all available masons to assist Master Walter of Hereford who was working there. English improvements may be seen at Kildrummy and Linlithgow for example, and it is clear that some of Edward's adherents in the north of Scotland were able to erect strong and good houses for themselves.

The castles which were destroyed by Bruce in accordance with his policy may not all have been of stone, though it is significant that the great tower of Bothwell Castle was deliberately destroyed by its owner after its recapture in 1337. In any case, during the fourteenth century, the Scottish nobles were able to erect strong castles.

Some of these were simply massive towers, but others adopted the gatehouse tower, which had been a feature of the Edwardian building, and some have seen in this a presage of an alteration in the nature of feudal service, which became more marked as the century developed. The lord tended to take from his tenants money instead of personal service, and, with that, to hire retainers whose fidelity was less certain. He wanted to keep egress and entry under the control of his own household, and possibly too he was thinking of forays as well as of defence.

This departure from strict feudal practice did not alter the position of tenants in theory, but in fact it loosened the strict bonds between lord and master. An English chronicler laments that, even when the Scottish magnates were with Edward, some of their followers and an immense number of Scots ('the community of the land') went to Wallace; and both in the south of Scotland and in Moray it seems that small land-holders joined in the insurrection. As for the lower classes of agricultural workers, they must have lost their security when lands were 'wasted', and there must have been real hardship. There was also danger when many men were called up for service in 'the common army of the realm', the force which won Bannockburn.

Certainly, the wastage was great, and notably reduced the king's revenue from his lands, but that agriculture and pasturage by no means failed is to be seen from the facts that the new system of taxation introduced in 1357 was based on a revaluation of agricultural yield, and that, in spite of everything, great sums were raised by taxation.

While the countryside struggled on there was a marked improvement in the burghs. Reference has already been made to their appearances in parliament, and these were due to their ability to provide the king with money. Berwick, it is true, once described as a 'Second Alexandria', was lost to the English, and so was Roxburgh; but Edinburgh developed a great port at Leith, and Aberdeen and Dundee also prospered. Inverness built her ships; Haddington, Dunbar, and North Berwick benefited from the absence of competition from the south.

As they prospered, the burghs shook off the direct control of the financial officers of the Crown. Even before the War of Independence they had begun to lease the burghal revenues from the Chamberlain, paying him a fixed annual sum in compensation. This sum might be raised from time to time and, perhaps for that reason, Aberdeen led the way in obtaining a feu-charter by which she paid a fixed rent in perpetuity. Other towns followed suit, and the burgh-mails became a fixed asset to the revenues of the Crown. It was not a great asset, especially after Berwick was lost. Indeed in the reign of James III it was worth only some £645 in all.

Another, and somewhat more remunerative, source of revenue obtainable from the burghs was the customs. These were collected by royal officers, 'Custumars', in every burgh whose merchants enjoyed the monopoly of foreign trade. Each such burgh had its own 'cocket' or seal, and no cargo might be exported unless it was vouched by sealed authority as having paid its proper due. At first only exports were taxed and among the exports only wool fleeces and hides.

As the rate of custom was trebled and finally quadrupled in the effort to pay for David's ransom, the increase of revenue noted during the century cannot represent a corresponding increase of trade; on the other hand more wool was probably used for clothing, and some favoured religious houses were excused payment. Computation seems to show that the number of sheep in Scotland in 1378-9 was about a million and a half, very much what it had been in 1327. Still, considering the troubles of the time, these figures show that the towns throve fairly well.

But throughout the country, life was still very primitive. Houses in the towns were usually of wood, and in the country they were often mere hovels. The Lowlanders suffered the ravages of Richard II's army in 1385 with an insouciance which the French observers found remarkable. When the invaders departed, they cheerfully drove back to their blackened homes the cattle they had hidden in the hills: 'Suppose the English turn us out, a few beams and branches will rebuild our houses in three days.'

The Abbeys of Melrose and Dryburgh, burnt by Richard II on his expedition in 1385, were less easily repaired; but repaired they were. The fourteenth century was not a great time for ecclesiastical building, but the buildings were not neglected. The general conclusion is that though Scotland suffered much in a period of political depression, the wounds were not mortal.

CHAPTER 5

THE CROWN AND THE BARONS
1371–1488

1371–90	Robert II
1390–1406	Robert III
1406–37	James I
1406–20	*Robert, Duke of Albany: Regent*
1420–24	*Murdoch, Duke of Albany: Regent*
1437–60	James II
1460–88	James III

FOR more than a century the *Leitmotiv* in Scottish history, as in the history of all western European countries at this time, was the struggle between the Crown and the Baronage which the Monarchy, as it developed, had endowed with much of its own power.

In Scotland the struggle was prolonged and bitter. The country was difficult; England was ready to exploit the over-mighty subject; the 'Auld Alliance' with France, though it brought benefits, drew the energies of the kings away from their business of establishing a strong state. These fundamental difficulties were increased by a series of dynastic accidents. Robert II came to the throne by female descent; he was ageing, almost fifty-five; he had been married twice and there was some doubt as to the validity of his first marriage, though it was made in good faith; by his first marriage he had nine children, by his second four, and he left illegitimate children besides. Robert III was fifty-three when he was crowned, and he had been damaged by the kick of a horse in his youth; he left, besides his surviving son, four daughters. James I succeeded as a boy of eleven; at the very time of his accession, he was kidnapped at sea by the English (apparently in the time of truce) and returned to Scotland only in 1424. He was murdered in 1437. James II became King of Scots at the age of six. He was killed by the bursting of a gun at Roxburgh before he became thirty. James III was crowned at the age of nine; he was murdered before he became thirty-seven after he had been thrown from his horse at the battle known as Sauchieburn.

While the power of the Crown suffered from these misfortunes and recurrent minorities, the baronage was strong. In the north-west and in the Islands, four successive heads of the great Clan Donald, who had assumed the title of Lord of the Isles about 1354, exercised an authority almost independent of that of the King. In the south, the Black Douglases, strong in the prestige of the good Lord James, had actually made a tentative bid for the Crown in 1371. They increased both in power and in reputation by taking a leading part against the English: the second Earl won at Otterburn where he was killed; the fourth Earl, the valiant but unlucky 'Tyne-man' ('Losing man') fought without success at Homildon (1402) and at Shrewsbury (1403) when he was helping Hotspur (see Shakespeare's *Henry IV*); and it was a brother of the eighth Earl who, during the minority of James II, won a resounding victory on the River Sark in 1448.

Both these great houses were connected with the Crown by marriage, and along with their restlessness must be reckoned that of the numerous progeny of Robert II, who had all been provided with lands or benefices. One of the sons of his first marriage, Robert, Duke of Albany, exercised great power under the feeble Robert III and acted as Regent during the captivity of James I. He showed no great desire to rescue the little King from his thraldom and, when he died, left his son to succeed him as Regent. Another son of Robert II was Alexander, the Wolf of Badenoch, who burnt Elgin Cathedral in 1390 and whose son, also Alexander, abducted the widowed Countess of Mar and assumed the Earldom. Of the sons of the second marriage, one, David, was Earl of Strathearn, and the other, Walter, was Earl of Atholl.

When it is added that the minorities gave opportunities for aggrandizement to royal officers, the magnitude of the Crown's task becomes very obvious.

Yet, slowly, the Crown asserted itself. It had certain assets and certain advantages. It had prestige. Robert II was still, according to the romantic reckoning, the ninety-ninth King of Scots from the mythical Fergus; he had been a good fighter in his youth and his descendants, who carried the blood of the Bruce, were some of them good fighters too. Again, he represented the opposition to the English whose tyrannies were not forgotten. It is noticeable that Blind Harry's *Wallace* (1470–80) is imbued with an anglophobia absent from Barbour's *Bruce*, which was written a hundred years earlier. And the administrative machinery, though it was misused and impoverished during minorities, continued to function.

The aid from France during this period was less than that given to France, but still it was something. Much greater was the help given by France indirectly in that she drew upon herself the ambitions of the martial English. Yet the most important advantage Scotland possessed during this time was the continued weakness of England. The old age of Edward III, the youth of Richard II, the accession of Henry IV (only a crowned 'Lord Appellant'), the failure in France after the appearance of Joan of Arc and the inter-necine struggle of the Roses – all these things weakened English power. To them were added economic troubles (exemplified in the Peasants' Revolt (1381), and the very sharp decline in the yield of the wool subsidy) and the vague religious discontents evident in the growth of Lollardy and in schemes for confiscation of the Church wealth.

The Relations of Scotland and England

In these circumstances the English Kings were unable to exploit the difficulties of Scotland. The claim to suzerainty was virtually left in abeyance. It was indeed asserted by Henry IV in 1400, when he wished to proclaim himself in the true succession of English Kings, but he took the matter no further; and when in 1406 his people kidnapped James I, the English King and his successors were content with the practical, rather than the theoretical, advantages of the situation. Henry V took the King of Scots to France with him, and executed for treason Scotsmen captured fighting for France on the ground that they were in arms against their own king; and, when at last James was released, the English demanded a ransom of 60,000 marks in respect of his 'costage' in England for about eighteen years (though the highest sum they expended in any one year was about £700 and that, mostly, in fees to his keepers), but the amount was reduced by 10,000 marks in respect of the dowry of Joan Beaufort who was given in marriage to the King of Scots. James was treated as an ally.

The claim of suzerainty was renewed in 1462 and in 1482 because it was, on each occasion, a convenient cover for English support of Scottish malcontents, but no serious attempt was made to enforce it, although, in 1482, an English army arrived in Edinburgh and might have deposed James III.

There was little direct fighting. In 1385, Richard II came up with an army and burnt Melrose, Edinburgh, Perth, and Dundee as a reprisal for the arrival of French troops in Scotland. The victory of Otterburn (1388) was won by the Douglases. The Regent Albany recovered Jedburgh and Fast Castle, but his 'Foul Raid' (1416) failed. Penrith and Alnwick were burnt by the Scots and Dumfries by the English, but much of the fighting was done by the Douglases and the Percies rather than by royal forces. James I seems to have meditated an offensive against Roxburgh (held by an English garrison) in 1436, but that came to nothing. During the minority which followed his murder, it was the Douglases who bore the brunt of the fighting though after their forfeiture they fled to England and made an unsuccessful attempt to return in 1458. Roxburgh was taken only in 1460 with the loss of the life of James II who, 'mair curieous nor becam him or the majestie of ane king', was killed by the bursting of one of his own guns.

In the following year Berwick was gained for Scotland, but not by arms; it was surrendered by Margaret of

Anjou, hard-pressed by the Yorkists. Scotland, however, was unable to exploit the opportunity offered by the Wars of the Roses because Bishop Kennedy supported Lancaster while the Queen Mother, Mary of Gelders, supported York. Edward IV, the victor in the war, was for some time insecure at home and apprehensive of Louis XI, and for a while he was most accommodating towards Scotland. He made a truce to last for fourteen years, betrothed his daughter Cecilia to the son of the King of Scots, and began to pay the dowry in advance. But after he had settled with France at Picquigny (1475) his policy changed abruptly: he rejected in 1477 proposals for further marriage alliances and demanded back the money already paid in respect of Cecilia's betrothal. When the truce ran out in 1478 hostilities began both on land and sea.

In 1480 the fifth Earl of Angus ('Bell-the-Cat') burnt Bamburgh; in 1481 an English fleet swept the Firth of Forth. In 1482, an English army under Richard of Gloucester, later King Richard III, crossed the Border and, since the Scots host broke up after hanging James III's favourite at Lauder, occupied Edinburgh. The invasion was made theoretically to depose James and set his brother Albany as an English vassal upon the throne – but no effort was made to do this. The main outcome of the expedition was that the English recovered Berwick. Richard III at first gave some support to his old ally Albany but, after his protégé had failed at Lochmaben (1484), he proposed a marriage between his kinswoman, Anne de la Pole (daughter of the Duke and Duchess of Suffolk), and the son of the King of Scots.

Some Scottish captains in French pay accompanied Henry of Richmond to Bosworth (1485), where he defeated and killed Richard III, but the suggestion that Henry was in close touch with Scotland before his accession cannot be upheld. What is true is that in 1487, after he had ascended the throne, Henry VII talked of a triple marriage whereby his mother-in-law, Elizabeth Woodville, should wed the widowed King of Scots and two of her daughters should be united to James's sons. It was a Tudor-like proposal, for Henry would have been delighted to have his mother-in-law at a great distance but, like so many other marriage projects, the scheme came to nothing. James was killed by rebels, professedly led by his eldest son, at 'Sauchieburn' in 1488, and the theory that Henry thereafter supported the party of the dead monarch will not stand examination.

The salient feature of Anglo-Scottish relations, then, during this period was that England did not attempt to assert her suzerainty. But, although at times the countries were officially friendly (e.g. during a dozen years after James I brought home his English bride, and for some time after James II had married the kinswoman of Burgundy, England's traditional ally), England repeatedly tried to weaken the Scottish King by assisting his rebellious subjects. In 1411 she promoted the attempt of Donald, second Lord of the Isles, to realize his claim to the Earldom of Ross. Likewise in 1462 Edward IV made with John, fourth Lord of the Isles, a treaty (called whimsically by Andrew Lang 'Westminster-Ardtornish') for the partition of Scotland between the Lord, one of his kinsmen, and the exiled Douglas. The treaty was not, and probably was not meant to be, executed, but in 1479 Edward was negotiating with the Lords of the Isles again.

Relations of Scotland with France

To Scotland's relations with England, her relations with France form the counterpart. The 'Auld Alliance' was renewed in 1371, 1390–91, 1407–8, 1423, 1428, 1448, 1484, and 1491–2. Its terms were almost unaltered on each renewal. Technically they were defensive but, as has been shown, the French in 1484–5 pushed Scotland into an unnecessary war.

The relations between the two countries were, in the main, intimate and cordial. Scottish churchmen sought higher education in France; Scotland followed France in the 'Great Schism'; and it was to France that the aged

Robert III endeavoured to send his son to safety in 1406. When, after James was captured at sea, the Alliance was renewed, France significantly insisted that Atholl (see p. 89), as well as Albany, should speak for Scotland: she was uncertain of the future of her old ally. When, however, under the pressure of Henry V's attack, the Dauphin sought the aid of Scotland, he met with a generous response. In 1419 the Spanish fleet brought to La Rochelle 6,000 soldiers under John, Earl of Buchan (one of Albany's sons), Archibald Douglas, Earl of Wigtown, and Sir John Stewart of Darnley, ancestor of the Stuarts d'Aubigny in France and of some later Earls of Lennox in Scotland. At first the newcomers made themselves unpopular by their hearty eating and drinking but, in 1421, they beat and killed Henry V's brother, Clarence, at Baugé. In 1423, however, they suffered a heavy defeat at Cravant, and a fresh army which appeared under the fourth Earl of Douglas himself was almost exterminated at Verneuil where the hard-fighting 'Tyneman' was killed.

Honours had been bestowed upon their leaders; Buchan had been made Constable of France; to Douglas was given the Duchy of Touraine, and to Darnley, the Seigneurie of Aubigny in Berry; and, when the Alliance was renewed in 1428, still greater promises were made. The Dauphin was betrothed to Margaret, daughter of James I, who was promised the county of Saintonge and the Seigneurie of Rochefort on condition that, when the English were expelled, he should exchange these territories for either the Duchy of Berry or the County of Evreux. James, for his part, promised to send his daughter to France within a few months, and to come in person with 6,000 men. In the event Margaret did not go to her unsatisfactory husband till 1436 and, meanwhile, Scottish aid was not required. Darnley was beaten and killed at Rouvrai ('the Battle of the Herrings' 1428), but the Scots took part in the defence of Orléans, whose Bishop was a Scotsman, Carmichael, and they had their part in the victories of Joan of Arc – to whom they at least remained constant. With these victories, France's despair vanished, and Scotland never obtained Saintonge, though she continued to put forth her claims till 1517.*

The prestige of Scottish soldiers remained high. It was from their ranks that Charles VII formed his *corps d'élite*, the *Garde Ecossaise*, and when in 1445 he established a regular army by the creation of fifteen companies of men-at-arms, the *Gens d'Ordonnance*, the Scottish company took pride of place. In these two corps, generations of young Scotsmen were to find honourable careers in arms.

In the *Cent Nouvelles Nouvelles* (the first book of 'novels' to be written in French), the Scots soldier appears occasionally as a picaresque hero and James II, with his fiery face, finds place among the *Seigneurs du Temps Jadis* of François Villon. Later, when Louis XI wished to retain a hold on Scottish policy, he sent to the court of James III a famous Scottish scholar of the Sorbonne, John Ireland. Ireland's mission is a reminder that if France got military aid from Scotland at this time, Scotland received gifts of culture and civilization from France. It was from France that she drew her models when, Oxford being infected with heresy and even a King's son unsafe upon the sea, she thought of universities of her own. St Andrews, founded in 1412 by Bishop Wardlaw, adopted the traditional curriculum of Paris and took its constitution from the smaller French universities of the Loire, where the Bishop still kept his authority as Chancellor. Glasgow, established in 1451 by Bishop Turnbull, a St Andrews graduate, followed mainly a St Andrews pattern. Aberdeen, the creation of good Bishop Elphinstone (1495) showed some signs of Renaissance influence, but its first Principal, Hector Boece, who was an acquaintance of Erasmus and wrote excellent Latin, was a scholar from Paris, and Scottish learning, in the main, adhered to the old French discipline with its love of logic.

Scots literature was slow in beginning and followed much the tradition of Chaucer; but towards the end of the century, French influences revealed themselves markedly in the

*When James III renewed the claim, Louis XI characteristically offered instead the Duchy of Brittany which was not in his hands.

work of writers who made much use of French forms and French vocabulary, and whose 'approach' resembled that of Villon.

In architecture French influences were manifest in the flamboyant style preferred in Scotland to the English perpendicular, and in the long gallery. In the College of St Salvator in St Andrews, in the Abbey of Melrose, and in the later parts of Bothwell Castle, may be seen conspicuous examples of good French work. The mace of St Salvator's College – a beautiful thing – was made in Paris and that of Glasgow, a little later in date, is almost certainly French too. If the 'Auld Alliance' led the Scots into some political misadventures, it served also to plant some lilies in the 'cauld kail-yard'.

The King and his Barons

Against the background of contending English and French interests was waged a long struggle between the Crown and the Baronage in the course of which, though two kings were slain by their subjects, the Crown slowly increased its power. The contest is studded with picturesque and brutal incidents, romantically reported in Sir Walter Scott's *Tales of a Grandfather* which can here be mentioned only in passing.

The dramatic Battle of the Clans (1396), fought on the North Inch of Perth, when thirty champions from each side (probably Cameron and Chattan) were all but exterminated in the royal presence, symbolizes well the period of the first two Stewarts when the King appears almost a spectator in the action of the times. Equally illuminating is the death of the King's son, Rothesay, at Falkland in 1402 at the hands of his uncle Albany. The version given in *The Fair Maid of Perth* cannot be taken literally but the essence of the incident is that nephew and uncle were rivals for a power which the King could not exercise. The Battle of Harlaw, 1411, which occurred during the regency of Albany, is an essay on the same theme. Albany fortified himself by an understanding with the Douglases and used his position to promote the interests of his own house. His attempt to secure the earldom of Ross for his son John led to a great invasion by Donald, Lord of the Isles, who had a better claim. This was halted before it reached Aberdeen by a force under the self-constituted Earl of Mar in a battle, misrepresented as a struggle between Highland and Lowland. This contest was long remembered from its savagery as 'The Reid Harlaw'.

James I returned from his captivity, from which the regent had made small effort to deliver him, and at once attacked the House of Albany and executed Murdoch along with some of his kinsmen. He imposed taxes, not really heavy, but unpopular; he was slow to repay money he borrowed from religious houses and burghs; he quarrelled with Rome. Determined to be master of his realm, he conducted an assault upon several nobles such as the Lord of the Isles and many of his Stewart relatives with a vigour which seems sometimes to have lacked justice. His dramatic murder in the Black Friars' Convent at Perth was the result of a conspiracy by some of his victimized relatives.

There is a moral to be drawn from the fact that the hideous execution of the conspirators excited little pity: Scotland had reverenced her king, and his son was crowned without any opposition. He was a child of six; his mother lost prestige by an unequal marriage; the great houses whose support had ensured the continuance of the dynasty stood aloof while the possession of the royal person was contested between two nobles of inferior rank, Crichton and Livingstone. Yet it is significant that the contestants had both been royal officers under James I, and that, when a rival to their power appeared in the person of the young sixth Earl of Douglas, they united to secure his judicial murder in Edinburgh Castle in November 1440 ('the Black Dinner'):

> Edinburgh Castle, towne and toure,
> God grant thou sink for sinne!
> And that even for the black dinoir
> Earl Douglas got therein.

97

The crime went unpunished partly because the great-uncle, who succeeded as seventh Earl – 'James the Gross' – was elderly. His successor, the eighth Earl, however, was bold and vigorous; he regained the lands of Galloway (which had been forfeited after the 'Black Dinner') by a marriage with his cousin, and allied with Livingstone against Crichton. The allies enjoyed the help of the third Earl of Crawford; but the ensuing Civil War was not unequal, for Crichton enlisted the support of Kennedy, the powerful Bishop of St Andrews, and, when in 1445 Crawford was killed in a fracas outside Arbroath, men saw in his death the fulfilment of a curse pronounced by the Bishop exactly a year before upon the ravager of his lands.*

Thereafter the Douglases were busy upon the Borders and, meanwhile, James was growing up. He was called 'Fiery Face' from a birthmark, and he was also fiery of heart. By his marriage in 1449 with Mary of Gelders, a kinswoman of Burgundy, he acquired some of the guns for which the Low Countries were famous – 'Mons Meg' among them perhaps – and no doubt this artillery played its part in his successful wars.† He swooped down upon the Livingstones at once, executed two of their leaders and forfeited others. Having discovered that the eighth Earl of Douglas had made a 'band' with the fourth Earl of Crawford ('the Tiger Earl') and the Earl of Ross (fourth Lord of the Isles), he summoned Douglas to Stirling where, on his refusal to denounce the band, the Earl

*The fracas resulted from a quarrel between Lindsays and Ogilvies for the remunerative office of 'Justiciar', lay protector of the rich Abbey of Arbroath. The Ogilvies were helped by Sir Alexander Seton of Gordon, who was on his way to take up an inheritance in Aberdeenshire, in virtue of which he was to become the first Earl of Huntly and ancestor of the great House of Gordon. He had stayed in their house, and the rule of hospitality demanded that he must fight for them till his last meal with them was digested.

†An act of 1456 authorized the King to request certain great barons each to provide a 'cairt of war', carrying two double-barrelled guns, and to train gunners. James got artillery (1449) with his bride Mary of Gelders, whose dower house, Ravenscraig, was the first castle in Scotland with a gun platform.

was slain, James himself striking the first blow (February 1452).

Immediately the ninth Earl, James, brother of the murdered man, rode in force to Stirling with the King's safe-conduct dragged at a horse's tail. Soon afterwards he offered his allegiance to England. His allies, the Lindsays, rose too – yet the King had the victory. In the north the new Earl of Huntly, as King's Lieutenant, rallied the gentry beneath the royal banner and beat the Tiger Earl at Brechin. In the south, James, having condemned his opponents in parliament, entered the Douglas territory with fire and sword and forced the earl into submission. Ashamed, no doubt, of the perfidious murder he had committed, the King was indulgent to his beaten enemy; but the quarrel had gone too deep for reconciliation and, in 1455, Douglas was in arms again. All went ill with him: the Tiger Earl was dead; he was abandoned by his allies, among them his kinsman the first Lord Hamilton; and the Earl of Angus, head of the Red Douglases 'who rose upon the ruins of the Black', supported the King. When Douglas gave battle at Arkinholm near Langholm he was utterly defeated; two of his brothers were slain and he, with a remaining brother, crossed the Border and became an English pensioner. His ill-starred attempts at Lochmaben in 1458 and 1484 have already been mentioned.

The great House of Black Douglas was fallen and its fall was a turning point in the fortunes of the Scottish Crown. The victor ruled, and ruled well. Even though after his premature death at Roxburgh (1460) his successor was a boy of nine, the minority was, for some years, little troubled by disorders.

After the death of Bishop Kennedy in 1465, however, faction raised its head. The family of Boyd with its allies took control of the royal person and gathered offices and wealth; in 1467, Thomas, the son of Lord Boyd, was created Earl of Arran and married the King's sister, Mary. Next year he went to Norway to complete the arrangements for the King's marriage to Margaret, daughter of

Christian I. This match, for which France had acted as intermediary, was to prove a most happy thing for Scotland: the lady was charming and good; her father, unable to pay much of the promised dowry, pledged the sovereignty and his royal estates in Orkney and Shetland which, in consequence, soon passed to the Scottish Crown.

The Princess came to Scotland in 1469 but, before she arrived, the power of the Boyds had utterly collapsed; Arran, on his return, was saved only by the courage of his wife, Mary Stewart, who came out to his ship to warn him and fled with him to the Low Countries.*

The King, now eighteen years of age, began to rule himself and, for a time, prospered well. He acquired the lands of the Earl of Orkney by exchange and, as the dowry remained unpaid, annexed the Earldom of Orkney and the Lordship of Shetland to the Scottish Crown in 1472. In the same year, St Andrews was made an Archbishopric; this was not due to royal action (p. 111), but the dignity of the realm was increased. In 1476, James was able to deprive the fourth Lord of the Isles of the Earldom of Ross.

When all thus promised well, trouble arose in 1479 from a quarrel between the King and his two brothers, Alexander, Duke of Albany, and John, Earl of Mar. The King's reasons are obscure, hidden deep in his suspicious nature, but his action alarmed his barons: if princes of the royal house could be summarily imprisoned (and perhaps killed: Mar died soon afterwards), what security had others? There was already serious discontent occasioned by bad harvests and currency debasement, and there was criticism of James's ineffectual control of law and order. The barons blamed 'certain low-born councillors' for all these grievances, a charge which has been embellished by later writers (the 'Bell-the-cat' episode and so on). However, it seems clear that the persons denounced were neither low-born nor formal 'councillors'.

*Mary returned to Scotland in 1471 and, in 1474 by papal dispensation, married the first Lord Hamilton, thus giving to the House of Hamilton a contingent interest in the Scottish Crown. Arran remained in the service of Burgundy.

Scheves was a distinguished academic who became Archbishop of St Andrews; Torphichen was head of the Knights
Hospitaller in Scotland; Cochrane and Preston were
obscure and unimportant officials who were hanged by a
group of barons in 1482 not because they were 'wicked
favourites' but because, it seems, they tried to save the King
from being seized by his Stewart relatives as he attempted
to oppose his brother Albany's invasion. James was taken
by his relatives to Edinburgh under guard, but in 1483 he
recovered his powers and Albany again fled.

Untaught by experience, James alienated his nobles by
forfeiting his brother's supporters and by annexing the
revenues of Coldingham Priory to the Chapel Royal which
he meant to develop as a music-school. The Homes, who
had come to regard Coldingham as their perquisite, rose in
revolt and gathered a strong party, which acquired fresh
strength by securing the person of the heir-apparent. The
King, supported by the northern lords, by the burghs and
by his small fleet, should have had power enough to resist
them; but when, after an abortive attempt at compromise,
he met his enemies in a battle near Stirling, miscalled
Sauchieburn, he failed utterly. He led badly; his horse ran
away with him and threw him; and he was murdered by
the hand of an unknown cleric at Beaton's Mill, not far from
Bannockburn, on 11 June 1488. He had not yet reached his
thirty-seventh year.

His death would seem to symbolize the victory of the
barons over the Crown, but it is not so. His conquerors
deemed it right to send an *apologia* to European princes; his
heir succeeded without difficulty to a crown whose dignity
was not impaired, and to a governmental machinery better
than Scotland had ever known.

Constitutional Development

It is time to glance at the constitutional development which
had gone on behind the surge and thunder of a violent age.
Even under the weak Roberts, parliaments had met and,

though the demand for annual parliaments in 1399 was justified on the ground that the King's subjects should be 'servit of the law', some attempts had been made to ensure that the royal action itself should be within the limits of the law. Albany's appointments as Lieutenant in 1404, and as Governor in 1406, were made by general councils. Moreover, during his governorship of fourteen years, no fewer than twelve general councils were held and his successor, Murdoch, held general councils too.

This continuity of constitutional tradition is important; for, although James I on his return in 1424 certainly introduced ideas brought from England, he endeavoured to weld these into existing Scottish practice. His attempts at innovation were not, for the most part, immediately successful, but his reign is a landmark in the constitutional history of Scotland.

His dealings with parliament demand special consideration. During the thirteen years of his active reign, he summoned no fewer than ten parliaments and three general councils. In so doing, he had no intention of sharing his authority with his subjects: his object was to ensure that his subjects should be obedient and should enjoy good laws justly administered. To these ends he endeavoured to make parliament more efficient.

The Scottish parliament was an assembly of tenants-in-chief, and tenurial it would have remained, even if James's designs for its improvement had been accomplished. In 1426 he passed an act bidding all tenants-in-chief attend in person. It is hard to say whether his object was to counteract cliques, or to stop the use of proxies, or to collect fines from absentees; but the act proved unworkable, and in 1428 the King introduced a change designed to make the Scottish parliament approximate to that of England. The magnates, lay and clerical, were to receive special precepts, but the small barons and freeholders were excused from attendance provided that there were sent, from each sheriffdom, two or more wise men chosen at the head court, (except that

Kinross and Clackmannan were to send only one apiece). As these 'commissars' were ordered to choose a 'common speaker', it seems clear that a bicameral parliament was intended.

Yet, even thus altered, the Scottish parliament would have differed greatly from that of England. The act was only permissive. It did not take away the right or the liability of all tenants-in-chief to attend; the 'commissars' were to be chosen in the sheriff-courts where only tenants-in-chief were present. Nothing was said as to the relation of the shire representatives (and their Speaker) to the burghs, who came as collective tenants-in-chief; finally, there was no mention of any hereditary right of the magnates to receive a special summons. In short, neither 'lords' nor 'commons' resembled the English model in certain most essential matters.

The creation of hereditary lordships of parliament, begun under James II, did something to establish a real peerage, but the 'small barons' did not avail themselves of the machinery offered: lairds, as well as lords, continued to attend as individuals throughout the fifteenth century and appear together on the 'sederunts' as *domini*. Acts of 1458 and 1504, establishing property qualifications below which attendance at parliament would be excused, show that the Crown accepted the situation. The lairds, however, did not surrender their right; and, though during the sixteenth century few attended, they came in full force to the Reformation parliament of 1560. It was not till 1587, and then with considerable modifications, that the system envisaged by James I came into force (p. 180).

None the less the King's use of parliament was remarkable. He passed many laws for the good of his people; lepers, beggars, archery, industry, agriculture, weights, measures, coinage, inns, and ferrymen, not to mention wolves and football, were all brought under the royal eye.

No less remarkable is the provision for the maintenance of order and for the giving of good justice. An Act of 1426 for the revision of the old 'Bukes of Law' – *Regiam Majestatem* and *Quoniam Attachiamenta* – was inoperative, but arrangements were made to ensure that the legislation of each parliament should be sufficiently promulgated. Royal officers throughout the land and lords of regalities were sternly commanded to do this duty; parties coming to court were forbidden to ride with large retinues; an attempt was made to improve the method of appeals, and an Act of 1425, far before its time, ordained that a presiding judge must get a 'lele and wyss advocate' to maintain the cause of 'ony pure creature' unable to provide learned counsel for himself.

Not only by its legislation did the King use parliament to promote justice. He used also the judicial powers which it possessed in its own right. He employed it to condemn his enemies in the familiar way, but, as regards its 'civil jurisdiction', he made a bold innovation. Realizing that the judicial committees, which parliament had, since the fourteenth century, appointed to try civil cases, could not possibly get their work done during the brief session, he tried to extend their civil jurisdiction into the periods when parliament was not sitting.

An Act of 1426 provided that the Chancellor, and certain discreet persons chosen by the King from the three Estates, should sit three times a year, in autumn, spring, and summer, to determine original business (as opposed to appeals). This was a notable step in the development of the institution later to be known as the 'Court of Session' or (officially) as the 'College of Justice'. The experiment did not work very well because no provision was made for the payment of judges beyond the hope that they might reimburse themselves from the penalites which they imposed, and because the men on whom the King could rely were constantly being required for other duties. In 1439 the number of 'sittings', now called 'sessions' was reduced to two yearly and, though on several occasions attempts were made to return to the three sessions, no permanent success was achieved until, in the reign of James V, provision was made for the payment of salaries to professional judges.

How was the King thus able to use parliament so freely

for his own ends? Here again he made use of an old expedient. In the fourteenth century parliament had, at times appointed, besides committees for justice, what we may call a 'business committee' which might function after parliament had gone. In James's first parliament certain persons were chosen to consider certain '*articuli*' (agenda) after the others had gone home. From 1426 on, he seems to have used the committee when parliament was actually sitting, and so developed the famous 'Lords of the Articles' who were later to gain an evil name by virtually monopolizing the power of parliament. Perhaps they have been too much condemned; most of them were Privy Councillors and the committee served to correlate the work of parliament with the conduct of government when parliament was not sitting. (Compare the position of the Privy Councillors in the Elizabethan House of Commons.)

James's efforts at governmental reform were not confined to parliament. He did not, as has been alleged, introduce the English 'Order of Chancery' – it was not fully followed in England – whereby all grants had to pass successively through three seals, Signet, Privy Seal, and Great Seal; but, certainly in his day, Privy Seal and Great Seal were in the hands of officers and, by the time of James III, the Signet, associated with the office of secretary, was very important.

As regards finance too, he inaugurated reforms, though not in one fell swoop. During his reign, the Chamberlain ceased to be the great financial officer, and his place was gradually taken by the Comptroller who dealt with regular income, and the Treasurer who handled extraordinary income and expenditure. In the reign of James III, for which we have some fairly complete records, the 'property', handled by the Comptroller, consisted of rents from the royal lands, 'mails' (compositions) paid by the burghs, and customs, mostly upon exports; much of the income received was spent locally, and the royal chest received little actual coin. For this the King depended upon the 'casualty' administered by the Treasurer. His accounts show income derived from feudal dues, from the profits of justice, and compositions for breaches of the law. The Treasurer also handled the receipts of any tax which was imposed. He paid the royal expenses of many various kinds and his accounts are a document of great importance for social history. The royal revenue from all sources was pitifully small; in the reign of James III, it was only £16,380 Scots or about £5,500 English.

The reforms inaugurated by James I affected the whole constitutional development of Scotland. It remains to add something about the work of his successors. James II was much occupied with his wars; but his reign was marked by some important social legislation. An Act of 1450 guaranteed the position of a tenant whose land passed to another lord, and another of 1458 recommended that the King himself and his lords should give their lands in feu instead of in military tenure. No doubt the King, with the example of the French *taille* (1439) before him, had it in mind to reduce the armed strength of great nobles and provide a small regular army for himself; little came of his purpose but the Act paved the way for the substitution of a perpetual fixed tenure in place of the customary leases whose brevity and uncertainty discouraged farmers from making great efforts at 'improvement'.

In the reign of James III, definite advances were made. In 1466, for the first time, began a true record of the sittings of Parliament, now to be kept in a book. The development of the Signet, already noted, marks the rise of the office of secretary, which was closely connected with the Council, and of the Council an increasing use was made. After 1478 the 'Session' became a function of Council rather than of Parliament, and its jurisdiction was greatly increased: not only were laws passed in 1471 and 1478 to facilitate appeals, but its original business was swelled enormously by its handling cases of *spuilzie* (appropriating goods belonging to another) brought by parties who would not trust local courts.

A notable feature of the reign was the growing importance of the burghs; they came to parliament in increased numbers – twenty-three attended in 1471; their commissioners took their place among the Lords of the Articles; they contributed to national taxation one fifth of the total sum granted by Parliament, and they allocated individual contributions among themselves in their own meeting, later known as the 'Convention of Royal Burghs'. No doubt because they could contribute substantial sums, the ecclesiastical burghs, St Andrews and Brechin, appear amongst the Royal Burghs proper; next century, Glasgow, Arbroath, and Dunfermline followed suit.

The constitutional advance of the burghs reflected the increase of their economic importance. When figures are available, in the reign of James III, the customs brought in five times as much as the burgh-fermes, though the total sum was only about £3,300. Since the time of James I duties had been laid on the export of other things besides wool, wool-fells, and leather; but fish of different kinds (salmon, herring, and cod), a little rough cloth, and other things brought in altogether only about a fifth of the total; and the dues received from imports were very small indeed.

Overseas trade, largely carried on with the Netherlands, whence simple consumer goods were imported, engaged the attention of parliament to a considerable degree under the first three Jameses, but it was hampered by the debasement of the Scots currency.

This legislation in itself attests the growing alliance between the crown and the merchants; and that in turn found concrete expression as to the government of the burghs in two Acts in 1469 and 1474. The burghs, as they shook themselves clear of crown control, had developed only very slowly a system of self-government. As yet there was seldom a provost, sometimes called an alderman, and though various Acts of Parliament mention a council it does not appear how this council was constituted. The burghs were really ruled by the bailies who could, upon occasion, summon all the 'good men' of the burgh by whom they were theoretically elected; and they represented, in effect, a few wealthy families, by this time belonging to the merchant guild. An Act of James I (1425) recognized the existence of the 'crafts' by authorizing each craft to elect a deacon as its head, but an Act of three years later emphasized that the deacon must confine himself to supervising the work of his fellow craftsmen. No doubt the crafts resented their exclusion from government, for the 'great trouble and contention' which attended the annual election of officers was advanced as the cause for the Act of 1469 which regulated the matter. This Act provided that the new town council was to be elected by the old one; that the two town councils together should choose the officers with the assistance of one representative from each craft. In 1474 a supplementary Act laid down that four members of the old council should serve on the new. A subsequent Act of 1504 provided that the officers must be changed annually; but it provided also that none save a merchant could hold office, and the effect was that the offices rotated among the members of a small clique, often of blood-relations, which was inclined to disregard any interference from without. The crafts began to take advantage of the doubtful recognition accorded to them by obtaining from the burghs 'Seals of Cause' which established them as definite corporations, and it must be noted that while they resented the dominance of the merchant guild, they were themselves close corporations. The apprentice, when his 'seven long years' were up, could not become a master of the craft and an employer of others unless he was the son or son-in-law of a craftsman, or could pay a prohibitive entry fee. There arose between the crafts and the unskilled labourers a class of skilled workmen who were unprivileged, and, though the burghs in outward semblance flourished, there were bred within them the germs of discontent.

The 'New Feudalism'

Meanwhile in the countryside another aristocratic oligarchy was rising to new heights. The change in the character of feudalism already presaged (see pp. 84–5) had rapidly developed. The nexus of land was by no means broken; but land-service had largely given place to personal service. Some of the old restraints were gone; the new relationship of lord and man fitted in too readily with the old Celtic system; and the great chiefs, depending on their own kinsmen, on hired retainers, on 'bonds of manrent' from inferior chiefs, were possessed of a power over which they had an almost arbitrary authority.

The 'Wolf of Badenoch', son of Robert II, had his great fortresses at Ruthven, Loch-an-Eilean, and Lochindorb. But when he issued forth to burn Elgin Cathedral he was reinforced by 'wild wikkid Hielandmen'; and one of his sons who raided Angus, mustered in his host, besides his illegitimate sons and men of his Earldom of Buchan, the representatives of at least one 'clan'. The character of the clan was changing. Philologically the word should mean children; legally it was used in the fourteenth century to describe groups of kinsmen occupying land to which they might even lack a true title; but in the Highlands it came to mean the adherents of a definite chief. The Lords of the Isles were heads of the great Clan Donald, but Clan Donald mustered in its ranks many who did not bear the name of Macdonald. The clan, in fact, became somewhat synthetic, though many of its members might adopt the patronymic of their lord. Outside the Highlands the same kind of thing occurred; the new chief was head of a family or of a 'name': the Earl of Huntly was head of the Gordons, but by no means all of the 150 houses which claimed the name of Gordon were sprung from the loins of his ancestor. Mention has been made of the rivalries of Lindsays and Ogilvies in Angus. On the Borders the 'names' of Armstrongs, Elliots, Johnstones, and Maxwells were of political importance in the west; Scotts and Kerrs and Humes were further to the east, while in the south-west the domination of the Kennedys was proverbial. The power of Douglas is writ large upon the history of the period.

It is to the existence of these half-tribal, half-feudal lords that most of the disorders of the time were due. They pursued their private vendettas; they seized the royal revenues during minorities; they defied authority and when, as sometimes happened, they made secret 'bands' among themselves, the power of the Crown was in jeopardy.

In such circumstances there was little chance of progress for the 'poor folk that laboured the land', though the king sometimes tried to protect them. Agriculture, even in the Lowlands, was backward. The old heavy plough, perhaps drawn by a mixed team of oxen and horses, was still in use, requiring three men to operate it; and, in the uplands, society was still to some extent nomadic, as the cattle and sheep were driven to higher pastures during the summer. Remedy could come only with suppression of lawlessness and to that end the energies of the 'good' kings turned themselves. The methods they employed may seem to us unscrupulous, but they do seem to have considered the welfare of their subjects and only by their victory could order have been achieved. That is the justification of the New Monarchy.

The Church

To the emergence of the New Monarchy, there contributed an element which enhanced the Royal power, namely its alliance with the Church.

During the great schism (1378–1417) the Papacy had been in a poor way, but when the breach was closed, it pursued a centralizing policy with great vigour. The Popes had, from of old, the right to confirm the appointment of bishops; now they claimed to 'provide' not only bishops (who paid fees on a fixed tariff) to sees, but clergy to other benefices. James I resisted stoutly. He passed laws against the seeking of benefices overseas, and the sending of good money from a land which was short of bullion. He did not hesitate to condemn for treason an apostolic delegate who disobeyed him; but he met with opposition from some of his clergy, and, in the end, was forced to ask for a legate to settle his difficulties. Aeneas Sylvius, later Pope Pius II, was sent; but the King was murdered soon after his arrival and, during the ensuing minority, when the royal power rested much upon the support of Bishop Kennedy, anti-papal legislation ceased.

When James II came to full age, he formally denied the right of the Pope to enjoy the patronage of livings which belonged to a see during a vacancy; but the papacy persisted in its claims, and, during the reign of James III, asserted its right to 'provide' to some great religious houses also. It was by taking the side of Rome in this matter and becoming a papal nominee to the Abbey of Arbroath that Patrick Graham gained his elevation to be Archbishop of St Andrews; but the contest continued until it was settled by a compromise similar to that made by some other European monarchs.

By an 'indult' of 1487 Sixtus IV agreed to let the Crown have the patronage of vacant sees for eight months at most, and to look favourably upon royal nominees; the Crown, for its part, abandoning the legislation of James I, offered no further opposition to 'papal provision' and the payment of regular fees. The effect was to establish a 'sound business arrangement' between Crown and papacy whereby the King obtained bishops whom he could use in the service of the state. The creation of the Archbishop, though by no means of the King's doing, accorded well with the royal effort at centralization.

Freed from trouble with the Church, allied with the growing third estate, steadily improving the machinery of government, the Crown was gradually asserting itself against the baronage. James IV succeeded without any difficulty and, in his first Parliament, the magnates thought it right to record and to send round Europe an explanation of the Field of Stirling (Sauchieburn, p. 110) whereat the father of our Sovereign Lord 'happinnit to be slane'.

CHAPTER 6

THE RENAISSANCE AND THE
NEW MONARCHY

| 1488–1513 | James IV |
| 1513–42 | James V |

IN Scotland there was no large leisured class to devote
itself to the pursuit of the arts, though there was real
interest in the practical art of architecture: the climate did
not lend itself to moonlight discussions on philosophy. Some
learning there was, but it adhered in the main to the old
disciplines. It was not only, however, in art and thought and
learning that the critical creative spirit of the Renaissance
revealed itself. It was in essence a rebellion of the facts against
the theories, and in the field of the state it found expression
in the 'New Monarchy'.

The old 'universalism' of the Middle Ages had seen the
world as a unity ruled, under God, by Pope and Emperor;
the prince of the new age, armed with the force of a national
state, made 'self-sufficiency' his goal. Amoral in outlook, he
made the business of being a ruler an end in itself. He was
head of the state and mainspring of its government; his rule
rested upon authority rather than on consent. He relied
more upon a small council of 'new men' rather than upon
large assemblies of nobles. He used his clergy rather as a
civil service. In place of the old feudal host, he developed a
standing army equipped with cannon and, perhaps, a fleet
too. Because he needed ready money he developed a pro-
tectionist, or even a bullionist economy. Once firmly
enthroned, he might patronize the arts, but he was essentially a practical man and the main thing about the 'New
Monarchy' was that its machinery worked.

Measured by these standards, how does the New Monarchy in Scotland present itself? It had not the administra-

tive machinery or the wealth of England or France but, as in other lands, the monarchy of the fifteenth century contained, behind the façade of old tradition. elements of the new age. These had shown themselves, as has been noted, in the reign of James III (see pp. 106–8). The reliance on 'small men', the development of governmental machinery, the understanding with the Church, the alliance between Crown and third estate, the royal interest in trade and currency, in ships and artillery, the preoccupation of the king in music and building – all these things suggest the 'New Monarchy'. The one thing lacking was the element of force in the royal personality. James III, in the words of his warlike son, was *rex togatus* – 'a king in civvies' as we might say.

It was this son, James IV, who gave to the Scottish realm the effective power which made it a 'New Monarchy'; his reign was the expression of his own personality and its achievements were largely due to his own vigour and his own ability. His colourful personality appears in the stories of native chroniclers and in the reports of foreign observers like Pedro de Ayala, the Spaniard, and John Young, the Somerset Herald; but the best picture of all is that which is given in the *Accounts of the Lord High Treasurer of Scotland*, which reveal every aspect of the royal life, and present the portrait of a true renaissance king.

James was interested in everything; in ships, in guns, in tournaments, in clothes, in music; in surgery too – he bled a patient, he extracted a tooth, he seems to have set a broken leg – even in alchemy, for he financed the adventurer John Damian in his efforts to find the *quinta essencia* which would produce gold. There may be no truth in the story that he isolated a dumb woman with her children in order to see what language the bairns would speak ('some say they spoke good Hebrew'); but he certainly knew something of languages, including Gaelic, though he was not the polyglot marvel described by Ayala.

Yet what shines most clearly through the document is the King's love of good government and of his people. To the sick and the poor, whom he met upon his restless ridings, the

King's face gave grace in a practical way. A single extract reveals the intimate detail of the evidence. Somerset Herald made one qualification to his admiration for the gallant figure of the King – his beard was 'somthynge long'. Its length, perhaps, attracted unfavourable notice from the Countess of Surrey and her daughter, Lady Grey, who accompanied Princess Margaret to her marriage with James in 1503. In the accounts for August of this year appears the entry: 'Item, the ix day of August, eftir the marriage, for xv elne claith of gold to the Countess of Surry of England, quhen scho and hir dochtir Lady Gray clippit the King is berd, ilk elne xxj li., summa cccxxx Li.'

Domestic Policy

For James IV, as for most other Scottish Kings, domestic policy had a twofold aspect, the suppression of actual disorder and the improvement of governmental machinery. In facing the first of these tasks he was so far fortunate in that the nobles of the more settled parts of the realm had no mind to pursue a civil war which had already resulted in the death of a king. The first parliament of the new monarch, which was well attended, not only made an apologia for the unhappy accident, but also ordained that the heirs of all who died on either side at Sauchieburn should inherit without dispute.

With the outlying areas, James inevitably had troubles, and with these he dealt most resolutely. Against the Borders he took advantage of the peace with England (p. 123) to cooperate with Lord Dacre, Warden of the West March in England, in the famous raid of Eskdale (1504) which made short work of captured 'reivers' (robbers, generally mounted); and, in 1510, he himself used at Jedburgh a summary jurisdiction whose memory survives in the phrase 'Jeddart Justice'.

More prolonged was his struggle in the Highlands and Islands. There, disorder was rampant when he ascended the throne. John, the fourth Lord of the Isles, was peacefully inclined and, perhaps for that reason, his illegitimate son Angus, who had married a daughter of Argyll, rose against him, defeated him at the Bloody Bay (1480) at Tobermory and kept the Highlands in a turmoil till he was killed in 1490. Thereafter, John's kinsman, Alexander of Lochalsh, continued the rebellion and laid claim to the earldom of Ross. James met the challenge with vigour: between 1493 and 1499 he visited the Isles six times and exercised the power of his personality. The Gaels always loved a man, and this king who could speak some Gaelic was a splendid, gallant figure. He had some success, as the presence of Highlanders in his army at Flodden shows; but, like all who have dealt with tribal society, he was confronted with the problem of whether to use the clan or to suppress it. His first instinct was to use the chiefs. True, in 1493, he forfeited John of the Isles who surrendered in the next year, perhaps not unwillingly, and became a monk at Paisley; but, at the same time, he granted charters and, in 1496, made each chief responsible for the execution of summons against his own people.

This attempt to treat Highland chiefs as Lowland barons had little success and in 1498 the king revoked all the charters recently given and, when in 1501 young Donald Dubh (son of Angus of the Isles) was rescued by the Glencoe men, he pursued this new Lord of the Isles with unrelenting vigour until, in 1506, he took him in Stornoway Castle where he had sought refuge with the Macleods. Yet he endeavoured to secure by administration the advantages made by force. In 1503 he put the Highlands under three justiciars to sit at Dingwell, Perth, and Ayr (the port for the Western Isles). This device failing, in 1509 he made Huntly heritable sheriff in the north, and gave Argyll the same position in the south-west. In effect, he used the Gordons and the Campbells as government policemen.

Side by side with these strong measures to establish good order went a development of governmental machinery. In this, too, James was favoured by circumstance. William Elphinstone, Bishop of Aberdeen (1488/9–1514), the wisest of his father's councillors, survived his master's fall and doubtless was largely responsible for the maintenance of the constitutional tradition in the early parliaments of the new reign. The 'Articles' and the judicial committees were regularly appointed. Genuine efforts were made to make the King's 'Secret Council' (Privy Council) efficient, representative, and responsible (1490). Attempts were made to control royal grants by the machinery of the Seals, and to supervise the inbringing of the royal revenue. The legislation of subsequent parliaments was marked by wisdom and practicability. Some of this was devoted to the promotion of trade and the regulation of currency; but, in an adolescent society where good government was identified with good justice, much of it was concerned with the business of making the judicial system effective. Acts were passed to ensure that the Justice-Ayres should be regularly held and that sheriffs should do their duty without extortion. At the same time, feudal magnates were ordered to administer their own justice properly, and another attempt to improve local justice took the form of an Act of 1496, which ordered every substantial landowner to send his eldest son to school and university.

One of the objects of these measures was that poor people should not be compelled to seek 'our soverane lordis principale auditoris for ilk small injure'; but in spite of the King's efforts, there was increasing recourse to the central court and the principal feature of James's reign was the resolute attempt to make the working of this court effective. As already shown, the jurisdiction of the parliamentary auditors for original business (Causes and Complaints) was being welded into the jurisdiction of the 'council', which was in being when 'parliament' was not sitting; and, although the judicial business of the council was not separated from its ordinary political work, the council, when it sat to do justice, was increasingly afforced by other lords described as 'lords of session', and the name 'Lords of Council and Session' came into use.

While the court was becoming more professional, various

experiments were tried to improve its actual working. It was at one time decided that the civil court should perambulate along with the criminal justice-ayres; again attempts were made to arrange a 'table' (i.e. a schedule of cases) so that suitors would know when their business would come up. These experiments had but a limited success and, in 1503, in a desperate attempt to clear off arrears, the King held a long 'Session General' at Edinburgh where he 'gretlye lauborit in his propir persone', which marks a point in the development of a permanent court to sit in Edinburgh, now becoming definitely the capital.

Next year saw an experiment which has been misunderstood as an attempt to erect a new court called the 'Daily Council'; in fact what the King did was, as a temporary expedient, to make the central court sit in two divisions (both exercising the same jurisdiction): the Lords of Session sitting in Edinburgh, while the King's Council perambulated with the King. By 1511 Edinburgh was regarded as the normal place of Session, but ordinances for its conduct made for that year show clearly that even then attempts were still made to sway the courts of justice by the exercise of violence.

The real obstacles to the King's well-intentioned effort were two: there were not enough good judges, though an increasing number of laymen were taking to the law; and there was no money to pay a professional bench. The councillors on whom the King relied were apt to be called away for services other than judicial. It is significant that, as evidenced by an act of the first parliament, and by James's own conduct, the best guarantee of justice was felt to be that the King should do it himself.

While the King lived, his realm flourished. John Young, Somerset Herald, who left a full account of the progress of Princess Margaret to the north in 1503, was evidently surprised to find so much civilization in a country which he probably expected to find barbarous.

From internal evidence too it is clear that not only economically, but in culture generally, there was a great expansion. In 1495 thanks to Bishop Elphinstone, and with the support of the King, was founded a third University (King's College, Aberdeen) in which some signs of the new spirit were seen. The first Principal, Hector Boece, who had been a friend of Erasmus when he was in Paris, wrote excellent Latin; there was some teaching in medicine, and a recognition that the neophytes must be taught Latin. Yet Boece, though he tried to use original authorities, was a somewhat credulous historian; and the main purpose of the new foundation was to strengthen the hands of the Church.

In 1512–13 St Leonard's College in St Andrews was founded by the King's son, Alexander (Archbishop of St Andrews, killed at Flodden, who had as a boy been for a short time with Erasmus in Italy), and by Prior Hepburn. Its purpose too was to provide recruits to the Church. Its discipline was strict and monastic, and its teaching followed the standard monastic pattern.

In 1505 a College of surgeons was founded which became 'Royal' next year, and 1507 saw the introduction of printing into Scotland. The King gave a patent to Walter Chapman and Andrew Myllar, burgesses of Edinburgh to 'bring hame ane prent' for the purpose of printing the Books of Laws, Acts of Parliament, Chronicles, and Mass Books after 'our Scottish use', together with legends of Scottish Saints to be collected by Elphinstone. Chapman was a successful merchant in Edinburgh; Myllar was a bookseller, who had already been engaged in printing at Rouen. In 1508 the partners began work in a house in the 'Southgaitt', and their first productions, which survive only in fragmentary form, included tales from the medieval romances, two works of edification, *Orpheus and Eurydice* by Henryson, and a couple of poems by Dunbar. The real promoter of the project, however, was Elphinstone, who wanted to preserve the old Scottish Liturgy against the encroachment of the 'Sarum Use' which was largely accepted in England, and generally to emphasize the individuality of the Scottish Church. The *chef d'œuvre* of the press was the *Aberdeen Breviary* which appeared, along with the accompanying *Legends of the*

Saints, in two volumes 1509, 1510). Of 1,554 pages in all, in clear type, black and red, this was a noteworthy publication; but for some years there is no evidence of any other printing in Scotland, except for the few sporadic traces of the works of John Story and Thomas Davidson.

John Major's *History of Great Britain* (1521) and Boece's *History of Scotland* (1526), both in Latin, were printed in Paris and some of the works of David Lindsay, the Lyon King, were first printed in England in the thirties. No major work appeared in Scotland until about 1536 when Thomas Davidson printed Bellenden's translation of Boece's *History* into Scots. Davidson, who also printed *The Acts of the Parliaments of James V,* was made the King's printer in 1541.

Some have attributed the gap in Scottish printing to the destruction of the period in which Edinburgh was twice burnt, but another explanation may lie in the fact that the Church found the art of printing to be a double-edged weapon (see pp. 149–50). It is among the ironies of history that two projects designed for the defence of orthodoxy, the introduction of printing and the foundation of St Leonard's College, were destined to become weapons in the hands of the Reformers.

Although the Scottish printers produced little it was not for want of material, for this was a golden age in Scottish poetry. Robert Henryson, who survived into the reign of James IV, was something more than an admirable Chaucerian. He had Chaucer's art and, if he lacked Chaucer's breadth, he was not without humour, and to the wide tolerance of his master he added a reflective humanity. To the *Tale of Cressida,* for example, he adds a poignant scene where the prince fails to recognize the unfaithful sweetheart of other days among the lepers to whom he gave alms. His use of Aesop's Fables is remarkable and his moral pieces bespeak personal experience. His successor, William Dunbar, a court poet of James IV, lacked this deep personal sincerity and he too owed much to 'reverend Chaucere Rose of Rethoris All', but he owed also much to France and more still to his own genius. He is a great poet in his own right revealing an impressive mastery both of language and of rhyme in a surprising variety of topics. At one time he sneers at conventional religion, at another, as in the triumphant *Surrexit Dominus de Sepulchro*, he exalts in it. Along with an abounding, and at times coarse, joy in life, there is a sense of unhappiness and uncertainty, as in *All Erdly Joy Returnis in Pane*. The refrain of the 'Lament for the Makaris' – *Timor mortis conturbat me* – was always in the mind of this churchman.

We know little of some of the poets (or 'Makaris') whose passing he mourned, though their very number suggests the presence in Scotland of a creative spirit, and of Dunbar we know less than we should like. Behind much of his work there is a sense of frustration. He enjoyed the royal favour to a large extent for he was given quite a handsome pension; but he never obtained the benefice for which he hoped. There is some evidence that he may have belonged at one time to the Queen's party rather than the King's, but probably he failed to get ecclesiastical promotion because the King could not openly countenance one who mocked at the Church.

Gavin Douglas, his successor on the roll of Scottish 'Makaris', was at the outset of his career far more fortunate, for as a son of the fifth Earl of Angus he was early given good benefices. Having already produced two allegories, *The Palyce of Honour* and *King Hart*, and a translation of Ovid which has not survived, he established his fame for ever by completing, just two months before the fatal day of Flodden, a translation of the *Aeneid*. This is remarkable because it rendered the sublimity of Virgil into good Scots with a truly Scottish atmosphere, and even more because he furnished each book with an original prologue which, though it generally dealt with the subject matter which followed, sometimes expressed his own feelings on other matters – the strength of love, for instance, divine chivalry, the severity of winter, and the beauty of nature. Some critics hold that these prologues reveal a sympathy with men and beasts and nature unknown to Dunbar. His mid-career was marked by high promotion. He became Bishop of Dunkeld and, for a short time, Chancellor of Scotland; but his position rested upon the power of the Douglases and, during a temporary eclipse of that family, he fled to England where, a proscribed rebel and traitor, he died of plague in 1522.

James and the Church

James IV, despite sundry amorous adventures, was strictly orthodox: he wore an iron belt in expiation of his part in his father's death; he was liberal in alms; he showed devotion to shrines; and, though he accepted the working arrangement with the Papacy about promotions, most of his nominees were honourable men. He favoured the Observantines (then the best of the religious orders) and made some effort to transfer religious foundations from sparsely populated areas to places where their example and service would be more effective. He was not unworthy of the Cap of Maintenance and the Sword of Honour sent to him by the Pope in 1507. He genuinely believed in the grand crusade which other princes promoted by lip service for their own ends.

Military Power

With all his conventional piety, with all his energetic labours to give his people good government, James was of martial mind and showed himself a true prince of the Renaissance in developing the military power of his country. Acts of parliament bade his subjects practise archery instead of golf and football, and ordered the regular holding of 'wapynschawingis' to ensure that every man possessed weapons according to his degree. The Treasurer's Accounts show that the King paid much attention to guns and gunnery and, by 1508, he was casting good cannon of his own in Edinburgh Castle.

Equally marked was his interest in the Navy. He had inherited one famous captain, Sir Andrew Wood, and, during his day, the family of the Bartons at Leith provided him with other good seamen. In 1493 he ordered all burghs to provide a boat of twenty tons, and to conscript strong, able men for the crews. Before long he was building ships in new naval dockyards at Newhaven and Pool of Airth; the *James* and the *Margaret* were both of respectable size, and the great *Michael*, completed in 1511, was a wonder of the age. Before his reign was done he had ten big and sixteen small vessels.

In 1502 he was able to lend 2,000 men to Denmark, and in 1508 let France know that he could supply 4,000 men. With a force of all arms he reduced the Highlands and Islands. Yet it was long before he engaged in serious war.

Foreign Policy

James was fortunate in that his neighbours had no desire to embarrass themselves in Scotland. Henry VII was mainly concerned to secure himself on his new throne, and the eyes of France were turned upon Italy. There were, it is true, a few 'sputters of war'. Between 1488 and 1491, England made an unsuccessful attempt to prevent the absorption of Brittany into the French monarchy and, in 1492, endeavoured to restore her prestige by an invasion of France; this the French King easily bought off by renewing, in the Treaty of Étaples, the pension paid to Edward IV.

In all this, James was little concerned. In 1491–2 he renewed the Auld Alliance in the traditional way, but he was not required to take any action upon it. Later his offer of 4,000 men to Louis XII may have aroused English suspicion, and this may have been increased when in 1508 the Scots King received a visit from Bernard Stuart, Sieur d'Aubigny, '*grand chevalier sans reproche*', who had won fame in the Italian wars. Stuart, however, died soon after his arrival. If he had a mission, nothing came of it, and his visit is mainly remembered for the two poems it evoked from Dunbar. Henry VII's apprehensions appeared in his arrest of the Earl of Arran (head of the Hamiltons) and his brother as they passed through England; but the prisoners were soon released and the English King, who made some effort to redress a Border grievance, continued his policy of maintaining peace with Scotland.

This policy is a feature of Henry VII's reign. There was some bickering between the countries. The Scottish Captain, Sir Andrew Wood, had two small naval victories in 1489 and Henry engaged in some dealings with Scottish malcontents, but these cannot be fairly represented as support to the partisans of the murdered James III. As early as 1493, the English King made overtures for a marriage alliance, and next year arranged a seven years truce. This truce James broke when, in 1495–7, he received the pretender Perkin Warbeck as Duke of York, married him to a noble Scottish lady and invaded England on his behalf. Yet Henry, though he retaliated in force, still strove for amity, and in his effort he was aided by his new ally Spain, whose able ambassador, Pedro de Ayala, came up to Scotland in 1496 and again in 1497. On the occasion of his second visit James, who had dismissed Perkin honourably enough, readily came to terms with England at Ayton in September 1497. There, a truce was concluded to last for seven years; this soon developed into a better understanding, and Henry achieved his end when in January 1502 a treaty was made whereby the Scottish King was pledged to the elder daughter of the English King.

The marriage treaty was flanked by a treaty 'for perpetual peace' between the two kingdoms – the first 'peace', as opposed to a 'truce', since that of 1328 – and by an instrument to ensure that 'incidents' on the Borders or at sea should not become *casus belli*. In 1503, the little princess, not yet fourteen, came to Scotland conducted by the Earl and Countess of Surrey and, on 8 August, in the Abbey Church of Holyrood the Thistle was wedded to the Rose. Margaret brought with her a dowry of £10,000 sterling and perhaps a predisposition to dislike her new estate. She gave James six children, of whom only one survived; and James, though not always faithful, was good husband enough to be very apprehensive whenever a birth was impending. There is some evidence that the Queen came to have a party of her own at court. Nevertheless she stood for an alliance with England which remained unbroken as long as her father lived, and the good understanding between the two countries was the background to a period of gaiety at court and prosperity in the land.

With the accession of Henry VIII, the atmosphere abruptly changed. The new King was bellicose and, though he renewed his father's treaties with Scotland and with France – in both cases under papal sanction – he subjected Scotland to a series of pinpricks for which he refused to give the satisfaction due under the treaty and, led by arrogance and by the cunning of Ferdinand of Spain, embarked on the policy which was bound to end in war with France.

France, anxious to keep England out of the Italian wars, had no desire to create a *casus belli* in Scotland, and James, anxious to promote Christian unity in a crusade, tried to reconcile France with her enemies by sending Bishop Andrew Forman on a mission to Italy (1511). His efforts were traversed by the English Cardinal Bainbridge and, in November 1511, Henry joined the Pope, Ferdinand, and Venice in a Holy League against France.

His action placed James in a dilemma from which there was no escape: his obligations under the Auld Alliance of 1491–2 and the Anglo-Scottish peace of 1502, renewed in 1509, were mutually incompatible except when England and France were at peace. In December 1511, James wrote to the Pope endeavouring to denounce the treaty with England on the ground that English aggression made peace more disastrous than war; his letter produced no result. Yet it was only after April 1512, when her ambassador, de Rieux, was rebuffed in London, that France recognized the inevitable, and accordingly tried to use the Auld Alliance as an instrument of war, arguing that James's peace with England had already been broken by English aggression. James renewed the treaty in a slighty altered form in July, but he took no action till 1513, and even then tried to keep both treaties by aiding France 'as an ally only' and sending his fleet to France.

All this time Henry, who meant to shine on the battle-fields of Europe, had been definitely preparing for war against his brother-in-law. In December 1511, he recalled artillery which he had lent to the Netherlands 'on account of my expedition against Scotland'; in 1512 he maintained in the north a skeleton army under the earl marshal, Surrey, who organized levies, studied routes, and arranged posts; and when, in the high summer of 1513, he crossed the sea, he left England well prepared against any attack from the north. James, in a last effort for peace, sent the Lyon King to tell his brother-in-law that unless Henry withdrew from France, he himself must invade England. Henry rejected the envoy with contempt on 12 August; on the thirteenth James was put under papal censure at Rome, where Henry's open breach with his treaty with France had not been noticed.

It was only on 24 July that James summoned the shire levies and, though he brought good artillery with him when he crossed the Border on 22 August, his force, part feudal, part tribal, was far inferior in organization to the army which confronted it. Surrey had begun to mobilize in London as early as 21 July; his artillery had reached Durham before he himself arrived at Pontefract; he was reinforced at Newcastle by his son, the lord-admiral, with a thousand men from the fleet, and his arrangements for organizing the north had been so good that he 'took his field' north of Newcastle on 5 September.

James meanwhile, having reduced Norham and some smaller places, had occupied a fortified camp on Flodden Edge overlooking the river Till; and Surrey, having failed to taunt his opponent into descending to give battle, marched north-west and halted under the cover of Bar Moor. On 9 September the Scots, outflanked and perhaps fearing that Surrey would cut off their supply route, gave battle. The result was a resounding victory for the English. James himself was slain and with him nine earls, thirteen barons, an archbishop, and many more. The English claimed that 10,000 Scots were killed as opposed to a few hundred English. The payroll shows that Surrey lost two fifths of his own picked retinue and, either because his army had been hardly handled or because he knew that Henry would be jealous of a triumph gained by anyone else, he made no effort to follow up his victory.

James's body was found on the field and, though the pious Catherine of Aragon wondered what should be done with the dead excommunicate, it was taken to London and Henry (who perhaps envisaged himself as chief mourner in appropriate magnificence) designed a splendid funeral. This did not take place. The royal corpse lay in its lead at Sheen until the house was despoiled after the Reformation, and eventually the embalmed head was hacked off by Queen Elizabeth's master-glazier who used it as a sort of *pot-pourri* until he tired of it.

All praise must be given to the English who fought a hard action after a long march in bad weather, but James does not deserve the blame which tradition has accorded to him. Not he, but Henry, was responsible for the war, and one reason why he was ill prepared was that he strove to keep the peace till the very last. His conduct of the campaign was not faulty. He could neither have besieged Berwick, nor have marched south with Berwick unmasked at his flank. His defeat in battle was primarily due to the fact that his ill-organized force, numerically not much greater than that of his enemy, was not adequate for its task.

The 'Lilt of dule and wae' was heard all over Scotland, but Scotland remained proud of a gallant King. One of her historians, after mentioning the persistent rumour that the King had survived the battle, concludes simply:

'How ever the matter be, hitherto we want, quhen we want him, a stout, just and devote king', who won great honour both in peace and war when other princes of his day contracted 'ignominie and schame'.

The Reign of James V

Disastrous as it was, the defeat at Flodden did not affect the development of Scotland as much as has been supposed. The death of her King removed the mainspring of her state, yet her spirit was unbroken and the machinery of government remained. The town council of Edinburgh, whose provost was among the slain, at once ordered that women must not wail in the streets but betake them to the churches, and that all must help to build the city wall; the lords, assembling promptly in a general council, ordered the collection of all available war material, and arranged for the coronation of the new king. They arranged too to renew the treaty with France. But their preparations for defence proved to be unnecessary because Henry, realizing that he had been made a cat's-paw by Spain, forestalled his crafty father-in-law by making, in 1514, a peace with France in which Scotland was included.

Freed from outside interference, the nobles reorganized the government in the regular Scottish way. English Margaret was made 'tutrix' of her son, but an invitation to act as Governor was sent to John, Duke of Albany, the heir to the Crown if the little king and his infant brother should die. Albany was the son of that Duke who had fled to France in 1484, and who had married into the great house of de la Tour d'Auvergne; he himself wedded a lady of the same house, spoke French, and was rather a Frenchman than a Scotsman. He arrived in Scotland in 15k5, was made Governor in July of that year, and held office till November 1524; but during that period he paid two visits to France – in 1517–20 and in 1522–3.

To his credit it must be said that he made no effort to supplant his young cousin, that he tried to preserve order, and that when he was abroad the family feuds broke into open violence. In 1520, for example, there was a bloody fight in the High Street of Edinburgh ('Cleanse the Causeway;) in which the Douglases beat the Hamiltons and their ally, James Beaton, Archbishop of St Andrews. Nevertheless Albany stood definitely for France. Soon after his arrival he expelled Margaret, who had lost prestige by her marriage with Archibald, sixth Earl of Angus; the child of this marriage (another Margaret) was born at Harbottle Castle. In after tears, it was important that Lord Darnley, son of this Margaret and the fourth Earl of Lennox, could boast a descent from Henry VII unvitiated by alien birth; but the immediate consequence was that the Douglases became the core of an Anglophile party in Scotland. Albany went on to execute Lord Home and his brother for alleged treason, but the quarrel between French and English interest in Scotland was, for the moment, obscured because events on the Continent made France very anxious to secure the alliance of England.

Accordingly when Albany went to France, he was not very cordially received, and was prevented from returning to Scotland. The terms which accompanied a renewal of the Auld Alliance in 1517 were rather disparaging: by the Treaty of Rouen, James was promised a daughter of France only if there were one to spare after two Hapsburg princes had made choice. It was only when, after the sham splendours of the Field of Cloth of Gold (1520) Henry definitely declared against France, that the Duke was sent back to raise trouble for England on her northern frontier.

His efforts were not successful – Flodden was too recent – and, on Albany's final departure in May 1524, the English interest took control of Scotland. In July 1524, Margaret, with the aid of English money, erected (that is installed) as king her son who was little more than twelve years of age. The ruin of Francis I at Pavia, 1525, set the seal on the Anglophile supremacy in Scotland. This came to be exercised, not by Margaret who, in 1526, divorced Angus and married Henry Stuart (afterwards Lord Methven), but by the Douglases. They defeated two attempts to rescue the King made by the Earl of Lennox at 'Turn Again' near Abbotsford, and at Linlithgow where Lennox was killed; they used their power for the profit of themselves and their friends, and kept the King in a thraldom which he hated until he escaped – not in the romantic circumstances often related – in 1528.

Though he was only sixteen years of age, James was already a personality. The infant boy who, when he could hardly speak, rode on the back of the Lyon King (Sir David Lindsay) demanding a tune upon the lute, grew into a passionate boy, fond of arms, who 'gloomed' at courtiers whom he did not like, and actually wounded one of them. Now, vested in the full dignity of a king, he could give rein to his passions.

Among these was an enduring hate of the Douglases which was not decreased when, having forfeited them in parliament, he besieged them in their stronghold of Tantallon and lost his guns for his pains. Later, in 1537, on a flimsy accusation of conspiracy, he executed the Master of Forbes, brother-in-law of Angus, and burnt his sister Lady Glamis on the Castle Hill of Edinburgh on a charge of witchcraft. Not against the Douglases only did he show his power. In 1529 and 1530 he led expeditions to the Borders where he executed reivers whose fates are immortalized, not with historical accuracy, in the Border Ballads; and even dared to imprison, if only temporarily, the chiefs of some great names – Bothwell, Home, Maxwell, and Johnston, for example. He acted with vigour too against the Highlands and Islands where, though Donald Dubh was still in prison, other claimants to the Lordship of the Isles appeared from among the Macdonalds – Donald of Lochalsh, who died in 1519, later Alexander of Isla and, in 1539, Donald Gorm of Sleat, whose rebellion collapsed suddenly when his own rashness brought about his death at Eilean Donan (on the mainland opposite to Skye).

James, aware that the opposition offered to the Macdonalds by Campbells and Macleans was largely self-interested, refused his countenance to Argyll and tried to win Clan Donald to himself. His personality brought him some little success and, in 1540, he circumnavigated Scotland with a large fleet from the Firth of Forth to Dumbarton, exacting submissions and making arrests. Yet the Isles were not daunted. When, soon after James's own death, Donald Dubh escaped again in 1543, he at once commanded a large following, allied himself with the English, and took to Ireland a force whose power astonished the hard-headed English officials there. He died before he accomplished anything, but the moral was plain to the Scottish government. Argyll might be inconvenient, but Donald Dubh was dangerous; the policy of using Macdonalds instead of Campbells had not been a success.

In these displays of force, the King exhibited one of the characteristics of a Renaissance prince, but he lacked the attribute of practical wisdom: in attacking Borderers, Highlanders, and Douglases, he was alienating some of his best fighting men; and, indeed, much of the finance demanded by his expeditions was found from taxation of the Church with which, for other reasons, he was allied. Yet, though the King proceeded with violence, his reign was marked by healthy development in civil affairs. After he assumed power his parliaments met frequently, functioned regularly, and devoted much attention to the general welfare of the realm. Laws were passed to ensure that the realm was armed, especially with firearms. An act of annexation saw to the preservation of the crown-lands, and arrangements were made for the inbringing of the royal revenue. Efforts were made to regulate the currency, to promote trade, to protect trees and orchards, to preserve fish. Emphasis was laid on the maintenance of good order and local officers were again called upon to administer justice fairly.

Yet local justice did not suffice. Not only did parliament itself hear cases, but there was still frequent recourse to the 'Council and Session' and, during the reign of James, the organization of this court underwent a development which led future ages to suppose that in 1532 the King had created, on the model of the 'Parlement de Paris', an entirely new tribunal called 'The College of Justice'. This he did not do. What he did was to give a new name to the old jurisdiction of the Session and to make that jurisdiction more effective by equipping it with professional judges, properly paid.

The credit for the reform belongs largely to Gavin Dunbar (Archbishop of Glasgow 1525–47) who, as soon as he became Chancellor, endeavoured to exclude from judicial business councillors who were not of 'the Session'. In 1532, a definite establishment was proposed whereby the King was to erect 'a college of cunning and wise men', seven clerical and seven lay, under a president, to sit in regular sessions and administer justice without interference from the other councillors, except on rare occasions. These judges were to have regular salaries. This establishment had become possible because Albany, who served Scotland well after his departure, had succeeded in getting Pope Clement VII to authorize a huge annual tax upon the clergy on the pretext that the King meant to establish a College of Judges. The clergy made a compromise whereby they should provide a large sun down, and £1,400 Scots annually to pay the clerical judges. The Crown was slow in producing the salaries of the lay judges: it was only in 1535 that the Court was recognized by a Papal Bull which used the title 'College of Justice', and only in 1541 that a Scottish parliament ratified the action of pope and king, calling the Court the College of Justice, and its members 'senators'. Thus the tradition that James V created an entirely new court by a single Act of 1532 is erroneous. The realities of the situation appear in the usages of the present day; formally judges of the Supreme Court are called 'Senators of the College of Justice', but in common parlance they are always known as Lords of Session.

Besides the establishment of strong rule, and improved machinery of justice, the reign exhibits other features of the Renaissance. The King went about incognito among his people – 'the gaberlunzie King' – gay, popular, and licentious; he patronized at least one poet, Sir David Lindsay, and, though outwardly orthodox, permitted broad sarcasm at the expense of the Church. He was interested in building; Sir James Hamilton of Finnart, if not a desirable character, was a good architect and notable Renaissance features appear in the royal houses of Holyrood, Stirling, Linlithgow, and Falkland. On the gateway of Linlithgow are portrayed the three orders of which James was so proud – Garter, the Golden Fleece, and St Michael – and, from a picture in the National Portrait Gallery, it may be deduced that the monarch intended an order of St Andrew for Scotland.* The King of Scots should be a king like any other king.

How can we account for the successes of a monarch whose reign began so inauspiciously and ended before he attained the age of thirty-one? We may grant him ability and personal charm, but we must also recognize that he was fortunate in his circumstances. At home he could command the unhesitating support of the Church. The Reformation was upon its way and the clergy, fearful lest James should follow the example of his uncle Henry, could refuse him nothing. They paid two fifths of all direct taxation – after 1544 a half; they submitted to special exactions authorized by the Pope, who also allowed the king to establish five of his natural sons, all minors, in some of the richest benefices in Scotland. Towards the end of his reign, James found his stoutest supporter in David Beaton (Cardinal, December 1538 and Archbishop of St Andrews, September 1539). Moreover, as the tide of the Reformation advanced, many nobles rallied to his side from attachment to the old faith or suspicion of the new.

In his foreign affairs, too, James was fortunate. England and France came together for a while, because France needed English help after Pavia, and Henry needed French support for his repudiation of Catherine of Aragon; in the face of this Anglo-French *entente*, the Emperor Charles V was inclined to seek a counterpoise in Scotland. James found himself 'the most eligible *parti* in Europe'. The vague promise of a French bride, under the Treaty of Rouen, still held. In 1531, Albany came near to obtaining the rich Catherine de Medici for his master, but Francis secured her for his second son (afterwards Henry II) and it was partly as a *solatium* that Clement VII, close kinsman of the heiress, granted the 'great tax', for the College of Justice. There was

*The order of the Thistle was created only in the reign of James VII.

talk of Mary of England; talk also of a series of ladies of the Habsburg house. Courted on every side, James was well able to hold his own with England and when, in 1533–4, first a peace and then a truce was concluded, the Scots managed to get some small territorial advantages about Berwick.

Free to choose a bride where he would, James decided for France. In vain Henry advocated, with scriptural texts and more material arguments, the advantages of a breach with Rome. In March 1536 James betrothed himself to Francis's kinswoman, Marie de Bourbon, and set forth with a gallant train in September. Arrived in France, he found that he preferred the lady so ambiguously promised long ago: Madeleine, third daughter of the French King (who, though he had misgivings on account of the girl's health, yielded to the desires of the young couple). On 1 January 1537, they were married with great pomp at Nôtre Dame. The father's fears were justified. Madeleine survived her arrival in Scotland for only a few weeks, but she was well liked and loved, and, on her death in July 1537, public mourning was worn in Scotland for the first time.

Next year James wedded, as his second wife, the widowed Duchess of Longueville, Mary of Guise, who was conducted to Scotland by Beaton and by him married to the King at St Andrews (June 1538). Making this match, James made his final choice between England and France, between Rome and the new religion. Henry VIII was furious – Mary had been on his own 'little list' – but he swallowed his wrath, for there was talk of a great Catholic crusade against him, and tried to persuade his nephew to follow him into the profitable suppression of religious houses. As Charles and Francis drew more closely together, Henry's advances became more urgent and James, when Beaton was absent in France, promised to meet his uncle at York in September 1541.

Crossing the Trent for the first time in his life, Henry arrived at York to find that James, persuaded by clerical advice, and afraid of being kidnapped, failed to appear.

Henry was enraged and, when the fear of the great crusade died away, he let loose his indignation. In August, 1542, his troops crossed the Border without declaration of war; they were beaten at Hadden Rig near Berwick and their commander, Sir Robert Bowes, was among the six hundred prisoners taken. The scene of the combat was marked by the dead, but Henry insisted that the Scots were the aggressors. He sent forth a fresh expedition accompanying it with a renewal of the claim to suzerainty but, beyond burning Roxburgh and Kelso, his troops accomplished nothing.

If his invasion was a fiasco, the Scottish counter-attack was a disaster: led by the favourite, Oliver Sinclair, it was dismally routed at Solway Moss. The Protestant earls, Cassillis and Glencairn, and many others, were taken prisoner, and James, lying ill at Falkland, died there on 14 December 1542.

He died in despair. His two infant sons were already dead, and the news that a daughter had been born to him at Linlithgow brought him no comfort. 'It came with a lass [Marjorie Bruce] and it will pass with a lass', he said, uttering a prophecy well remembered though it was utterly false. Everything had gone ill with him. It may be that his frame was weakened by his reckless courses; it seems certain that his brilliant personality was brittle. His vendetta against the Douglases, his execution of his favourite, Hamilton of Finnart, his failure to appear at York, his disregard of the precepts and even of the reputation of the Church he defended, all bespeak an instability. Gifted in many ways, he lacked the persistence and the calculation of a true Renaissance King. Exalted when the winds of European diplomacy bore him on a prosperous course, he was ill-fitted to battle against the storms, and his premature death presented Henry VIII with an opportunity which he had long sought in vain.

The realm of Scotland passed to a baby girl whose nearest male kinsman (great-uncle) was the King of England himself, blessed (at last) with a son of suitable age for marriage with the young Queen.

History had repeated itself exactly. On the death of Alexander III the nearest male kinsman (great-uncle) of the infant Margaret, the Maid of Norway, had been Edward I, King of England, who had a marriageable son named Edward, and who knew well how to exploit a situation. Now the year 1286 was come again.

CHAPTER 7

THE REFORMATION

1543–60 Regency of Mary of Guise

THE Reformation was both an extension of the Renaissance and a reaction from it. On the one hand the spirit of criticism bore hard upon an institution whose practice differed so far from its theory; no longer could spiritual satisfaction be obtained from the assurance that outward adherence to the precepts of the Church guaranteed salvation to the soul. On the other hand, the questing spirit recoiled from the bold rationalism of some Italians and a few Germans; it sought security in a return to the practices of God's people of long ago, to the principles of the living Jesus, and of the true Church which he left behind him. It found the truth that it sought in the Bible. The Reformation therefore had two aspects, a negative or critical side, and a positive side, in every country which it touched.

It took varying forms in varying lands and in none of them was it confined to the simple issue of religion; everywhere its operation was conditioned by questions of politics and economics. Yet, while due account of these elements is taken, emphasis must be laid on the fact, too much forgotten nowadays, that religion was the *Leitmotiv*; men do not give their bodies to be burnt save for a thing of the first importance.

To understand the Reformation in Scotland, we must understand the political and the economic factors with which the great religious issue was interwoven; in reality the threads are so closely entwined that they cannot be disentangled, but we may for convenience give separate consideration to each element.

The political background was the rivalry of French and English interests in Scotland and the struggle between the Crown and the Baronage. These time-honoured conflicts took a religious complexion. France stood for the old religion, while England was at least definitely anti-papal; among the Anglophiles were some Protestant enthusiasts, as well as some nobles, like Angus, whose motives were political.

James, as has been seen, had chosen the side of France, and his death following upon the rout at Solway Moss seemed to presage the complete domination of Scottish politics by Henry VIII. He had as possible instruments the prisoners of Solway Moss; his close relationship to the little Queen was a ground for interference; and by proposing a marriage between Mary and his own son he could give to his interference the appearance of benevolence. At first it seemed that he must get his way. A *coup* attempted by Cardinal Beaton and the French Queen Mother failed; the Anglophile Arran was chosen Governor and, in March 1543, Parliament authorized the reading of the Scriptures in the vulgar tongue. Beaton was imprisoned and, by the Treaties of Greenwich of August 1543, the little Queen of Scots was betrothed to the Prince of Wales.

Henry, however, over-played his hand, behaving as if he was already suzerain of Scotland, and the Scottish reaction was prompt. Beaton had already worked himself free and, in December, a new Scottish Parliament denounced the Greenwich Treaties.

Henry's reply was formally to loose his troops upon Scotland with instructions to kill, burn, and spoil, and to hearken to a plot for the murder or kidnapping of Beaton in which a Scot named Wishart was an intermediary. The invasions of 1544 and 1545 wasted southern Scotland, inflicting irreparable damage upon the Scottish abbeys, and the advent of a French force (1545) did little to stay them; but their general effect was to alienate the hearts of many

Scotsmen including that of Angus who, returning to his allegiance, beat and killed Sir Ralph Evers at Ancrum Moor in February 1545. The murder in May 1546 of Cardinal Beaton, slain in his own castle at St Andrews by sixteen resolute men who broke in to avenge the burning of George Wishart (pp. 147–8), shocked Scottish sentiment; and before long the Anglophile party was reduced to the 'Castilians' who maintained themselves stoutly in the castle of St Andrews. Their military strength was little increased by the reception of a few Protestant refugees, among them John Knox who came in with some small boys he was tutoring about Easter 1547, but by that time the situation had changed. Henry VIII had died in January and his successor was a weakly child; the sea was no longer controlled by the English. In July 1547, the Castle of St Andrews was reduced by the gunners of a French fleet; the prisoners were taken to France and some of them, including John Knox, were sent to the galleys.

England endeavoured to restore the situation. The military clique which dominated the Privy Council on the death of Henry VIII was Protestant and, in September, Protector Somerset came up with a strong army and routed the Scots at Pinkie near Musselburgh. He followed his victory by establishing garrisons at Broughty Ferry Castle, Inchkeith, and Haddington; and, though in June 1548 a strong French army arrived under D'Essé, whose army next year was well reinforced by his successor de Termes, the English posts held firm. One result of the invasion was that a Scots Parliament betrothed the little Queen to the Dauphin in July 1548, and next month she was safely conveyed from Dumbarton to France. There she was educated along with the children of the French King who called her his '*Reinette*'.

The climax came when the English forces were defeated in France: Boulogne, taken by Henry VIII, was lost; and, by the treaty which bears the name of that town, the English agreed to withdraw the army from Scotland (1550). The policy of Henry VIII had failed completely. If the English heir-apparent had been happily married to a Scottish

Queen it might have been well for both countries, but the overweeningness of the Tudor ruined all. Scotland might have come to England as a bride, but as a bondwoman she would never come. English aggression drove Scotland into the arms of France.

During the next decade, France made her grip secure. She met with no opposition from the government of Edward VI which hoped for French aid to prevent the accession of 'Spanish Mary', and, later, little from Mary herself who was preoccupied with the religious issue in her own realm. Arran, given the Duchy of Châtelherault, was in 1554 deposed from the Regency in favour of Mary of Guise, on the ground, somewhat proleptic, that the Queen was now twelve years old. Frenchmen were put in charge of finance and of the Great Seal, and the French Ambassador, D'Oysel, appeared sometimes in the Scots Privy Council. In 1556 the Queen Mother attempted, but in vain, to establish a small regular army on the French model; and the hold of France appeared to be complete when, on 24 April 1558, the Queen of Scots was married to the Dauphin.

Both before and after the marriage, Mary, her bride-groom, and his father executed public deeds to preserve intact the ancient liberties of Scotland; yet the Queen signed secretly three documents which would have the effect of conveying the realm to the King of France if she should die without heirs. Mary was now fifteen and may have known what she was doing; but whether she could have defied the coercion of France and her Guise relatives may well be doubted. At all events, by the year 1558 Scotland was in danger of being absorbed by France.

That danger was one of the causes which led to the Protestant revolution. The manifesto of 1559 wherein the 'Lords of the Congregation' justified their rising to the princes of Christendom said almost nothing of religion, but emphasized the intention of France to make Scotland a French province.

The Economic Background

While the fortunes of the old church in Scotland improved or declined with changes in the political balance, its position deteriorated all the while under the influence of economic pressure. The church had too great a share of the national wealth. On the eve of the Reformation its revenue amounted at least to £300,000 a year whereas the Crown's patrimony brought in only about £17,500. Its total income was far less than that of the church, while the increasing expense of government and the fall in the value of money combined to make the royal income quite inadequate for its obligations. The enemies of the church suggested spoliation, and even the Pope agreed that the clergy might supply the royal necessities. In all other countries, after all, orthodox rulers taxed the clergy heavily.

It was not the crown alone which suffered from the depreciation of the currency. The nobles and the landed class generally still lived very largely upon rents which had been fixed by old custom; most of their tenants held by short leases; these to some degree were preserved by the old Scottish 'kindliness', but landlords were now inclined to raise rents when they could. Many benefices were already in the hands of lay 'commendators' and, in some cases, had come to be regarded as family perquisites. The lay lords' desires were realized the more easily because the churchmen, harassed by rising expenses and incessant taxation, began to dilapidate the ancestral wealth of their benefices. The difficulty that the Pope's consent must be obtained for the alienation of church land was easily overcome. Beaton, like Wolsey in England, had himself made *legatus a latere* with full powers; and the stipulation that the income of the church must not be diminished was easily met because many of the leases were held on old customary rents far lower than the real value of the land. Cardinal Beaton, and other prelates empowered by him, might proceed thus: when a lease fell in it was feued, that is, granted by a perpetual charter for a stipulated rent to the highest bidder or to some friend; the rent asked was a little, but only a little, higher than the old lease-rent; and the new feuar, secured for all time in a property at a rent far less than its true value, made a handsome payment in cash to the grantor. By this process the prelates acquired the large sums required for taxation and also the wealth which made them envied by the laity. Beaton gave to one of his illegitimate daughters a marriage portion as large as that given by the greatest Earl in Scotland to his daughter.

This steady enrichment of the higher clergy produced hardship and resentment. Amongst the laity, old 'kindly' tenants were expropriated in favour of new men, and the new men, having their feus at a price, tended to press their sub-tenants hard. The lower clergy had to contribute to the taxation exacted from the prelates and, by this time, many of the teinds were appropriated to sees or religious houses while the parochial work was done by poorly paid curates; even the reforming Councils of 1549 and 1559 suggested twenty marks a year with manse and garden as a sufficient salary for a curate. The luckless curates tended to collect the 'small teinds', if they had any, with rigour, to contract irregular marriages, to take money for performing some of the offices of the Church – the mortuary dues were particularly hated – and, in return for a fee, to pronounce excommunication for trifling matters. In the burghs as well as upon the land, there was discontent. Economic privilege was in the hands of merchants and 'incorporated' craftsmen. The guilds were usually under the protection of some saint in whose honour they endowed an altar in the parish kirk; to the unprivileged journeymen and the badly paid labourer it must have seemed that the church was riveting its fetters upon them.

Pillaged by the crown, envied by the nobles, distrusted by the poor, the church was very open to the attacks of those who hoped to cure their economic grievances by embracing the cause of the Reformation. The prelude to the year of crisis 1559 was the 'Beggars' Summons', posted on the friars' houses on 1 January 1559, calling upon the occupiers to come out and betake themselves to honest work leaving their riches to widows, orphans, the sick, and the poor.

The Religious Issue: Criticism of the Church

Practical politicians and calculating economists do not identify themselves with causes of uncertain value. The cause of reform was in itself strong: the state of the Scottish Church at this time made many men doubt whether the service it rendered was commensurate with the great privileges it enjoyed. Certainly there was much to criticize. There is no need to rely upon the accusations of its confessed opponents: the evidence supplied from its own records and from the dispassionate national archives is sufficient. The communications between Scottish Churchmen and the Father of Christendom, as they have survived in the *Scottish Supplications* still extant in Rome, hardly ever touched on spiritual affairs; nearly all are concerned with the enjoyment of benefices.

The compromise arranged between king and pope in 1487 sometimes led, as has been shown, to unworthy promotions to the highest offices, but among the prelates there were also righteous men like Abbot Mylne of Cambuskenneth, and Robert Reid, Abbot of Kinloss (1526–41), later Bishop of Orkney; and that the higher clergy as a whole were aware of the evils in the Church appears from the statutes of the last three Provincial Councils held in 1549, 1552, and 1559. Attempts at reform were made. Among the things condemned were clerical 'concubinage', the granting of feus with the expropriation of old tenants, non-residence, pluralities, the dilapidation of hospitals, and the lack of good preaching. Against these ills, remedies were provided. The Council of 1549 ordered the principal religious houses to send a specified number of students (often only one) to the Universities, and endeavoured to assign definite benefices to 'preachers'. The Council of 1552 produced, under the name of Archbishop Hamilton, a fine catechism in good Scots, possibly composed by John

Wynram, sub-prior of St Andrews, which reveals an acquaintance with the works of Continental 'reformers' inside the Catholic church. Yet the statute which authorized the use of his catechism emphasized that it should be lent only sparingly to laymen, admitted that many of the clergy were uneducated, and insisted that those who read it to their people must rehearse lest they 'stammer and stumble' in public. The Council of 1559 tried to bring religious truth nearer to the common folk by the issue of a little pamphlet to be read and shown to Christian people when they communicated – 'The Twapenny Faith'.

Yet the fact that the last of the Councils was still denouncing the abuses condemned in 1549 seems to show that the efforts of reform had been ineffective. This assumption can be supported from the writings of men who remained inside the old Church – Archibald Hay, Principal of St Mary's College at St Andrews, who addressed a *Panegyricus* to his kinsman, Cardinal Beaton; Ninian Wingate, the schoolmaster of Linlithgow, who debated with John Knox; the unknown author of *The Complaynte of Scotland* (1548); and Sir David Lindsay, the Lyon King of Arms. The letter of Cardinal Sermoneta to the Pope of 1556 may be cited too, with its tale of clerical abuses in Scotland.

The official records of legitimations provides a counterpart to the conciliar denunciations of irregular marriage. The heads of the church were themselves sinners. Cardinal Beaton had at least eight children, Archbishop Hamilton had several and other great bishops were not free from blame. It is not surprising that laxity was common among the lower clergy, or that laymen should wonder why, whilst concubinage was unchecked, the regular marriage of a priest should render him liable to death.

The expense required for the maintenance of irregular families was added to papal fees, and royal taxation; and the cost of maintaining an estate comparable to that of a nobleman so depleted the resources of the clergy that little was left for spiritual uses. Decent stipends were not paid to curates; little was done for education and the number of students at the Universities did not sensibly increase; there was still good building, but some of the work was scamped and doubts have been thrown upon the attention paid to works of charity. Above all, too much revenue was being withdrawn from the one thousand or so parishes of Scotland to maintain a limited number of ecclesiastical institutions (such as the abbey of Arbroath or the great cathedrals of St Andrews and Dunkeld) and the households of the great prelates.

Faith lives and old tradition endures; it is reasonable to suppose that up and down the land, in some parishes and religious houses, there were still pious men who did their duty. Yet the conclusion cannot be avoided that, taken as a whole, the Church of Scotland was in an ill condition to withstand the criticism so freely directed upon it.

The Positive Side

Criticism is easy; construction is hard; but construction was not lacking. In various ways good men tried to gain the spiritual satisfaction which they failed to find by merely obeying outwardly the established ordinances. Some, despite their doubts, remained in the Church; others were for long unaware that they were moving out of the Church; others again resolutely sought to recreate a Church which would conform, as they thought, to the true rule of Christ and his Apostles.

The forces which gave to the religious *malaise* of Scotland the final impetus to reform came to her from without; all were connected, but we may distinguish three: Lollardy from England, Lutheranism from Germany and the Low Countries, and a more radical 'reform' from south Germany and Switzerland.

John Wycliffe, who was not condemned as a heretic till after he was dead, left behind him the consequences of his doctrine that 'dominion is founded upon grace' – the beliefs that a bad man could not be a true pope; that the doctrine of transubstantiation, as usually taught, was false;

that every good man might be a priest. His institution of the 'poor preachers' may not long have survived but he left also a positive legacy, especially in his translation of the Vulgate into English. Brought probably by fugitive English clergy, his doctrine spread into Scotland. In 1407 James Resby, an Englishman, was burnt at Perth; in 1422 there was an anonymous victim at Glasgow. The combating of heresy was made one of the essential functions of the new University of St Andrews. Contact had been established, probably in the days of Richard II's Queen Anne, between the Lollards and the Hussites of Bohemia. In 1410 four violently anti-clerical letters by a Scotsman were published at Prague and, in 1433, Paul Craw, a Bohemian, professedly a doctor, was burnt at St Andrews.

Doctrines which seemed to threaten the whole fabric of society naturally roused the hostility of the state. James I legislated against heretics and Lollards as early as 1425, and the acts in defence of 'Halikirk' passed by his three successors may indicate uneasiness; but the Scottish Lollards seem to have been quiet, and little is heard of them until 1494. In that year Archbishop Blackadder of Glasgow delated some thirty heretics to James IV who let the matter go with a jest. It is significant, however, that the heresies for which these Ayrshire folk were attacked were precisely those of the English Lollards, that the accused were representatives of good families and that an Ayrshire man, Murdoch Nisbet, translated into beautiful Scots one of the recensions (Purvey's) of Wycliffe's Bible. Plainly the tradition had survived, and there was in Scotland a fruitful soil to receive the seeds of the 'German Reformation' when they were carried across the North Sea.

In 1525 Parliament found it necessary to forbid the importation of Lutheran books. This was repeated in 1535 and meanwhile, in 1528, the Lutheran Reformation in Scotland found its protomartyr in Patrick Hamilton who was burnt at St Andrews in front of St Salvator's College. Of royal descent, made titular Abbot of Fearn in youth, he had studied at Paris, Louvain, St Andrews, and Marburg.

Returned to Scotland he spread abroad his gospel with the use of *Patrick's Places*, a simple catechism founded on the doctrine of justification by faith. His execution, carried out with great cruelty, aroused new sympathy for his cause; one of Archbishop James Beaton's familiars told him that if he was to burn any more he should burn them in deep cellars 'for the reek of Maister Patrik Hammyltoun has infected as many as it blew upon'. After Hamilton's death, St Leonard's College at St Andrews became a centre of unrest. Some critics merely attacked the coves of the clergy; others went further.

During the next few years several distinguished scholars fled abroad, of whom some obtained Chairs in Universities and strengthened the connection between Scotland and the Lutheranism of Germany and Scandinavia. Among these was John Gau (Gow) who went to Malmö and there translated into Scots a treatise of Christian Pedersen as *The Richt Vay to the Kingdom of Heuine*. The doctrine set forth therein is purely Lutheran. Like Luther, Gow inclined to accept all of the old teaching which did not seem contrary to the word of God as he knew it. His book begins with analyses of the Ten Commandments and of the Creed, and ends with an exposition of the Lord's Prayer and of the Ave Maria. Except that it includes Luther's introduction to the Epistle to the Romans and some notes on the nature of Faith, and that it omits the articles of 'the Holy Catholic Church' and 'the Communion of Saints', the work approximates so closely to *Archbishop Hamilton's Catechism* that it prompts the question as to whether a *via media* might have been found between the tolerant men on both sides; but, as with the attempts at reconciliation at Regensburg in Germany and Poissy in France, a settlement was impossible.

Of the followers of Patrick Hamilton who remained in Scotland some recanted, some were burned. The total number of victims was not large, for James V was free-minded and nobles and gentry protected preachers.

After the King's quarrel with Henry VIII made the heretics appear as a political danger, and especially after

146

1538 when Beaton attained to full power, burnings became more common and there is a story that at the very end of his reign James meant to attack some of his greatest nobles including Arran, Cassillis, Glencairn, and the Earl Marischal. In fact Protestant nobles were prominent in the Scots army at Solway Moss, where many were captured (p. 134). In England they were given pensions and as 'assured Scots' were soon sent back to promote the English marriage and the cause of Protestantism.

For the moment it seemed that Protestantism would triumph when the vernacular Bible was permitted and the preachers, Williams and Rough, had great success; but Beaton recovered power (p. 137); burnings began again: and, before long, Protestantism was directed into a new course by the reception of the more radical doctrine which had appeared in South Germany and Switzerland. According to this, the old dispensation of the Roman Church was to be abandoned, and a new Church, founded upon the Scriptures, particularly on the New Testament, was to be established.

The principal agent in introducing this new conception into Scotland was George Wishart who had studied at Cambridge and in Germany; and who translated into Scots the 'First Helvetic Confession' 1536 (under the title of *The Confession of the Fayth of the Sweserlands*). One glance at this document reveals its novelty. Instead of beginning with expositions of the Ten Commandments and the Creed, it starts off with first principles. It sets forth the sources of truth – the Holy Scriptures and the Fathers – and rejects human tradition. Succeeding paragraphs deal with God, man, original sin, free will, and lead up to Christ as Redeemer. Emphasis is laid on preaching and on faith. The only head of the church is Christ, whose officers are the ministers. There are but two sacraments, baptism and Holy Communion. The penultimate paragraph on magistrates and governors contains a definition which moulded the course of the Reformation. The duty of the civil authority is to defend true religion and perform justly the ordinary work of government; so doing, it could command the obedience of its subjects.

Here was the rub. What was the true religion and who was to decide whether the magistrate defended it or not? The authors of the Confession assumed that they themselves were the true interpreters of the Divine Will; hence their doctrine was bound to end in revolution.

Efforts have been made to show that Wishart carried his doctrine into practice; that he was an agitator and may well have been an intermediary in the murder plot against Beaton. It has been answered that his character, on the evidence we have, suggests an evangelist rather than a politician, and that he was condemned for heresy only. The question cannot be resolved. Certain it is that his execution was the signal for the Cardinal's murder, and that, thereafter, Scottish Protestantism became more combative.

While the 'Castilians' still held out, there appeared among them one whose name, more than any other, is associated with the story of the Scottish Reformation. John Knox, born near Haddington about 1514, may have been educated as a priest, though he did not take a degree. He was well versed in Latin, as appears from his English prose, and was fluent in French, but he knew little Greek. At one time he acted as a notary. Later, study of Jerome and Augustine convinced him that much of the old learning was sophistry and, when in 1545 he appeared upon the great stage, he carried a two-handed sword in attendance on his teacher Wishart. The story of his capture when the Castle of St Andrews fell has already been told (p. 138).

By English influence he was liberated from the galleys and in the England of Edward VI he found refuge and advancement. In 1551 he was made one of the six Royal Chaplains and took part in the preparation of the Second Prayer Book of Edward VI. After the accession of Mary, he went to Dieppe, to Frankfurt, and to Switzerland; and though he returned to Scotland with impunity in the autumn of 1555, he was summoned to Geneva next year to be minister of the English congregation there.

During his exile he issued some pithy tracts, in one of which he well-nigh advocated tyrannicide. Among them was the famous *First Blast of the Trumpet against the Monstrous Regiment of Women*, aimed against Mary Tudor and Mary of Guise, which was to lead him into difficulties when Elizabeth ascended the throne.

He did not return to Scotland till 1559 and by that time Scotland was ready for him. Remarkably enough, during the decade of French domination in Scotland, Protestantism had grown apace. France, always opposed to the Habsburgs, had been inclined to support English Protestants against 'Spanish Mary' and was not inclined to awaken odium by burnings in Scotland. Again, the head of the Scottish Church was now Archbishop Hamilton, half-brother of Châtelherault, whom Mary of Guise had displaced. The forces of Catholicism were divided and, at one time, Mary of Guise cultivated the Protestants. In these circumstances, the critics of the old Church became more numerous and more vocal. Not only did inflammable material come in from abroad, but Scotland itself produced books and ballads which evidently circulated widely. Such works had been denounced by Act of Council as early as 1543; the Provincial Council of 1549 ordered them to be burnt and, in February 1552, an Act of Parliament formally condemned printers of 'Ballattis, sangis, blasphematiounis, rymes', whether written in 'Latine' or in 'Inglis'. Special interest attaches to the order of the Privy Council of April 1547 for the arrest of 'John Scott, Printar'; for Scott was probably the printer who produced in 1548 *The Complaynt of Scotland*, a conservative work (important as giving the names of popular Scots songs), and he undoubtedly printed *Archbishop Hamilton's Catechism* of 1552 at St Andrews. Evidently 'printars' were a suspect race. Doubtless it was the vernacular poems which were most dreaded, and an examination of the texts collected in *The Gude and Godlie Ballatis**

---

*Scottish Text Society (1897). The earliest surviving copy was printed about 1578, but from other evidence it is clear that some of the songs were current in the forties.

shows the reason why. Among the compositions are metrical versions of the Catechism and of the Psalms (some of them translations from the German); but others are paraphrases of popular songs, which are freely used to proclaim the new Evangel, and to denounce its alleged opponents. Among these may be noted some well-known ditties whose titles at least (here given in English) are known to us from other sources, for instance: *Hey now the day dawns, Down by yon river I ran, The hunt's up,* and *Ah, my love leave me not.*

In all these instances the argument of the song departs oddly from the text of the title.

> Johne cum kis me now
> Johne, cum kis me now
> Johne, cum kis me by and by
> And mak no mair adow.

goes on surprisingly

> The Lord, Thy God, I am
> That Johne dois the call,
> Johne representit man
> Be grace celestiall.

and continues the theme through many verses.

Again, some well-known refrain might be added to stanzas utterly unconnected with it. Thus the cheerful:

> Hay trix, trim go trix, under the greenwood tree

is appended to each stanza of a poem which begins, 'The Paip, that pagane, full of pride' and goes on to denounce all ranks of Churchmen in terms most uncompromising.

When songs like these were being sung up and down the land it is no wonder that Knox was able to preach with impunity during his mission of the winter of 1555–6; sporadic congregations were springing up here and there, and before long efforts were made at organization.

In 1556 the 'Gentlemen of Mearns' (Lairds of Kincardineshire) bound themselves together in a verbal compact and, in December 1557, there was signed by some great nobles and others the first formal 'Covenant', binding the

Congregation of Christ' to resist the 'Congregation of Satan'. So came into being the instrument which, renewed four times, served to unite the Protestants during the crisis of 1559–60 and, expanded and altered, was to play a great part in the history of the Scottish Kirk till 1689 and even later. It did not always operate for good. Critics have said that it derived, not only from the old Hebrew Covenants but also from the old Scots 'bond of manrent'; but, although at times used as an instrument of oppression, the Covenant was by and large, as Burns claimed, an assertion of religious freedom.

Certainly it was militant: on St Giles's Day, probably both in 1557 and 1558, the Catholic procession in Edinburgh was assaulted by the mob. Plainly the 'Reformers' were preparing for action. And the Queen Mother, for her part, was now ready to meet the challenge. Her daughter was married to the Dauphin in April 1558. The two great Roman Catholic powers, France and Spain, had begun the conferences which led to the peace of Cateau-Cambrésis. She had already burnt Walter Myln; and, in the spring of 1559, she threw down the gauntlet by summoning four of the leading preachers to appear at Stirling, promising to postpone the trial and outlawing them for non-appearance on 10 May.

The Crisis 1559–60

The hour had come and, with the hour, the man. The Protestants had already begun to assemble at Perth, and, early in May, they were heartened by the appearance in their midst of the resolute John Knox. He certainly was one of the preachers whose sermons against idolatry produced despoiling of the religious houses in Perth on 11 May. This provoked the Queen Mother into an immediate attempt at retaliation. Failing in this in the face of strong opposition she tried in vain to temporize. Believing that she felt that no faith need be kept with heretics, the Protestants purged St Andrews on 11 June and on the 29th the Congregation entered Edinburgh while Mary retired to Dunbar. They were speedily expelled as their unpaid troops dwindled, but they re-entered the capital and, in a meeting in the Tolbooth on 21 October, 'deposed' Mary from the Regency. This time, however, the Queen Mother was ready for them.

The death of Henry II in July had made her daughter Queen of France and made her kinsmen, the Guises, the directors of French policy. French troops, bringing their families with them, fortified the town of Leith with the latest apparatus of war, issued forth and drove the Congregation back to Stirling where, on Christmas Day, D'Oysel swooped down on them and cut their forces in two. The westerners retired to the west; the others, headed by the Lord James, Argyll, and Kirkcaldy of Grange, fought a hard rearguard action along the south coast of Fife for three weeks. From a desperate situation they were saved by the appearance of an English fleet which, though England was not at war with France, cut D'Oysel's communications with his base of supplies at Leith and compelled him to retreat under miserable conditions.

Scottish emissaries at once went to meet the English at Holy Island; but Knox proved to be so awkward a negotiator that his place was taken by William Maitland of Lethington, whose subtlety gained for him the sobriquet of 'Michael Wylie' (Machiavelli), and an arrangement was soon made. The Treaty of Berwick (27 February 1560) was represented as merely a contract between Châtelherault (long ago recognized by Parliament as Governor in Mary's absence) and Norfolk, Earl Marshal of England, for the express purpose of expelling the French, and as such it was effective.

An Anglo-Scottish army beleaguered Leith; the Queen Mother took refuge in Edinburgh Castle (not for the only time regarded as neutral). After her death there on 10 June, Leith capitulated and on 6 July the Treaty of Leith or Edinburgh was signed which ended the French domination of Scotland.

Ostensibly this was a treaty between England and France,

but its importance lay in an appended section concerning Scotland. Mary and Francis were recognized as Sovereigns of Scotland, but they were thereafter to abstain from using the arms and the title of England; French troops were to withdraw from Scotland; the Scots might summon a parliament of the usual kind and that parliament should present a list of twenty-four names of whom it should choose five, and the Queen seven, to form a provisional government. It was provided, however, that Parliament should make no decisions about religion but only formulate proposals to be submitted to Mary and Francis.

The effect was to leave power in the hands of the Protestants. Parliament met on 1 August. In its composition, although the lairds appeared in abnormally large numbers, it was quite legal, for the lairds had never lost their right to attend; when, however, it legislated about religion its action was outside the treaty. 'That we litill regarded, or yit do regarde' wrote Knox: revolutions are a law unto themselves.

A Confession of Faith was passed in the face of feeble opposition on 17 August; a week later three Acts destroyed the authority of the Pope in Scotland. All Acts not in conformity with the Confession were annulled, the Sacraments were reduced to two, and the celebration of Mass was made punishable by a series of penalties culminating with death for the third offence. The contrast between this settlement and that of Elizabeth in 1559 is illuminating. The English Act of Supremacy endowed the Crown with the privileges taken from the Pope; the English Act of Uniformity made obligatory the use of one form of public worship. The Scots Acts merely destroyed the papal authority and condemned the use of only one particular rite.

In fact, the new Kirk came to use the *Book of Common Order*, which embodied the form used by the English congregation at Geneva, though the two services were not identical; as it came to include a number of metrical psalms, it was sometimes called the *Psalm Book* as well as the *Geneva Book*.

The Scottish settlement assigned to the Kirk, which accepted the Confession of Faith, a sovereign authority, while the authority of the State was limited. No doubt the consequences of the assumption were not obvious to men who believed that a 'Godly Prince' must needs arise from the ashes of the old error; but implicit in it was the doctrine of the 'Twa Kingdomes' enunciated (but not invented) by Andrew Melville.

This Confession of Faith followed the Swiss Confession in proceeding upon first principles, but it applied the principles with more precision. Rejecting the claim of Rome, it defined the visible Kirk as that distinguished by the true preaching of the Word of God, the right administration of the Sacraments, and ecclesiastical discipline rightly administered. It asserted that truth and righteousness could be established from the Bible, but it gave to the Spirit of God the sole right of interpretation; by implication, the ministers would be the most likely interpreters, and they themselves were confident that their Confession could not be impugned from the Scriptures.

The *Book of Discipline*, prepared less rapidly than has been supposed, and perhaps not entirely completed, was an astounding document aimed at organizing, not only the Kirk, but the whole nation in accordance with the Will of God.

It proceeded on the assumption that the whole spiritual revenue of the secular clergy of the old Church would be available and it envisaged the establishment of ministers throughout Scotland, a national system of education, and some arrangement for poor-relief. The minister, who was the centre of the fabric, could be appointed only after a process of election, examination, and admission, and it was the congregation who elected. An instructed congregation was, therefore, a necessity, and there was outlined a scheme of education as complete as anything ever devised in Scotland: provision was made for primary, secondary, and university education; the importance of vocational training was recognized; the student's career was checked by examination and inspection; the curricula were so arranged that the study of theology should be its very apex.

Foreseeing that time must elapse before a sufficient number of good ministers could be trained, the authors provided for the appointment of 'readers' who might do some parochial work under supervision, and for 'superintendents' who, besides preaching in a 'chief' town, would oversee the surrounding districts. As the superintendents were to be better paid than ministers, and as the district assigned to them represented a sensible readjustment of the old dioceses, it has been thought that Knox favoured Episcopacy. But Knox, by nature a master if ever a man was, never became a bishop; he may have thought that the superintendent would be a convenient officer from an administrative point of view, but further he did not go. It is perhaps more useful to see these superintendents as performing the functions of a pre-Reformation archdeacon. In fact, only five superintendents were ever appointed; some of the bishops became Protestant; others, undistinguished for spiritual service, survived to do administrative work, especially that connected with Church livings. The organization of the new Kirk proceeded only slowly. The hopes of the ministers with regard to Church property were dismissed as 'devout imaginations' and an Act of the Council of 1562 ordained that two thirds of the old wealth was to remain with the existing incumbents – by no means all spiritual men – and the remaining third divided between the Crown and the ministers. Thus the magnificent scheme of education went by the board; the clergy were ill paid; as late as 1567, there were only 257 ministers for 1,080 churches with some 600 readers and 'exhorters'.

The institutions of the new church took shape only in a haphazard way. Kirk Sessions existed in some parishes even before the Reformation (in St Andrews from 1559) but in more remote areas they only appeared in the seventeenth century. The General Assembly, though it appeared in 1560, was at first a predominantly lay body, and for some time met twice a year; only in 1563 did a Moderator make a somewhat hesitant appearance. The Synod, or provincial assembly, was introduced in 1562; but the Presbytery came into being only in about 1580, and then partly in imitation of English practice and not in all areas.

Because of the severity and narrowness which emerged from the Reformation, the Scottish Church has often been compared unfavourably with that of England. In the minds of some critics the Book of Discipline is connected with the Stool of Repentance, though 'Discipline' in that context meant the outward order of the Church as distinct from 'Doctrine'; and in fact public repentance was not unknown in the Elizabethan Church.

A general explanation of the divergence between the two Churches is that Scotland accepted Calvinism whole-heartedly, while England did not. (This explanation is not entirely true. The doctrine of the Lambeth Articles of 1595 is uncompromisingly determinist, with their assertion that God predestined some to salvation and others to damnation; the Calvinistic 'Discipline', however, did not commend itself.) It was only in the reign of James I of England that Armin-ianism began to take control, and even so, the Puritans, for the most part, adhered to the Calvinistic doctrine. After the defeat of the King in the Civil War, the official religion of England was, for a short time, Presbyterian, and it was from England that Scotland was later to receive 'The West-minster Standards' (see p. 212); and indeed some of the austerity most denounced in Presbyterianism stems rather from English Puritanism than from Scotland.

It may well be true that Scotland as a whole accepted the logical system of Calvin, whereas England found a means of tempering its austerities; but the fundamental cause of the differences which emerged between the two Churches lay, not in doctrine, but in discipline, and that in turn was informed by the circumstances of their origins.

In England the Crown arrogated to itself all the power of which the Pope was deprived. The monarch was head of the Church, and the government of the Church was authori-tarian. As head of the Church, the English monarch could persecute religious dissidents on the ground that they were enemies of the state, and in times of crisis under Elizabeth, and in the days of Laud, the English government used its power with a heavy hand. In normal times, however, the Church, conscious of its strength, could afford to shut its eye to minor aberrations and interfered little with the private peccadilloes of law-abiding citizens.

The Scottish Church, on the other hand, was born in revolution against an absentee Queen who was a Papist. It received as a rule only a half-hearted support from the Crown, and for long lived in dread of Papist invasion from without and the apostasy of Protestant rulers within. It could not rely on the state to suppress its opponents – as regards executions, its record was far better than that of England. Always it must stand upon its own defence, and, not unnaturally, it developed the Calvinistic doctrine that civil government, though regarded as a necessity, was to be recognized only when it was conducted according to the Word of God. Two great consequences ensued. In the first place the Church inevitably came to advance the doctrine of the 'Twa Kingdoms', claiming in fact a right to interfere in civil affairs. Again, because their authority rested upon moral conviction and not upon physical force, the ministers must display in their own lives, and must demand from their people, an exact obedience to the 'Word of God' as they understood it, and so tried to regulate not only the public affairs of the state but the private lives of individuals. To them the slightest yielding might open a breach to the storm which beat against the wall. Moreover, they felt it incumbent upon them to see that their people were instructed; confident in the truth of their faith, they felt that every member of the Church had the right to know the foundations upon which it stood, and the Scottish people, as a whole, was better educated than most populations.

It has been thought that this constant discipline established in the minds of the Scottish people the idea of a God arbitrary and severe, and made them God-fearing rather than God-loving; and it may be that a consciousness of being elect bred a spiritual arrogance. On the other hand it did inculcate high moral standards, and a desire for education, since every individual was reponsible for himself. It fostered a spirit of independence which at first sight seems odd in those who believed in predestination, and a consciousness of being right with God led sometimes to a lack of manners towards fellow men.

The revolution of 1559–60 fell far short of its hopes. Yet it was an event of the first significance. It overthrew the Roman Church and, though it did not realize its ideals, it set forth the pattern of a nation organized for the worship of God according to a system which made personal righteousness the duty of every individual.

Not all men became truly religious. For some, religion was a supersitition to be disregarded or scorned; for others it was a way to be followed when piety became fashionable; for others it became an insurance against eternal punishment; and for others a cloak to conceal an evil life. Yet in the main the Scottish people became not only God-fearing but God-trusting. The measure of their trust appears in their general adherence to Covenants which expressed the belief that the whole nation was specially at one with Jehovah.

Those who denounce the narrowness and the disregard of beauty of the early reformers should remember that the Kirk they produced trained up a people strong in faith, patient of discipline, ready to venture, and even to die, for their beliefs. If the loftiness of the idea led sometimes to disillusionment and sometimes to hypocrisy, it led also to achievement.

The picture of religious life in Scotland here presented is not complete. Outside the bounds of the national Church, Roman Catholic communities still existed, especially in the north-east and the Highlands, and among the Protestants were those who looked back with regret to the organization and the ritual of the Old Church.

CHAPTER 8

THE COUNTER-REFORMATION
AND THE CLAIM
TO THE ENGLISH CROWN

1561–7	Mary Queen of Scots (in Scotland)
1568–87	Mary Queen of Scots (in England)
1567–87	James VI (with Regents)

WHEN, by the settlement of 1560, a state professing the Protestant faith owed allegiance to an absentee Queen who was a convinced Roman Catholic, Scotland inevitably was cast for an important part in the politics of north-western Europe. The Counter-Reformation was already upon its way. The Roman Catholic Church, soon to be reorganized by the Council of Trent, reinforced by the Jesuits and backed by the crusading King of Spain, was setting itself to recover its lost dominions, and Protestantism must stand to its defence.

The contest, however, was not the simple Armageddon seen by many of the protagonists on both sides. The forces of Catholicism were divided by the imperialism of Spain, which alienated the French and some of the Italian princes and, at times, even alarmed the Pope. The Protestants, for their part, were not united. There were differences between Lutherans and Calvinists, between Anglicans and Presbyterians. They, too, were not actuated purely by religious enthusiasms; the Protestant zeal of England, for example, was bound up with an assertion of English nationality. Out of this turmoil there arose a doctrine formulated in France, but known elsewhere, that the prince should be a *politique*, putting the welfare of his state before the claims of contending faiths.

To tell here the whole story of the complicated drama is impossible. It suffices to show that, for a moment, Scotland was the hinge upon which world-politics turned. Her Queen was not only a convinced Catholic, not only connected by the closest ties with France and with the great house of Lorraine, but she also had a claim to the Crown of England. Roman Catholics had never recognized the marriage of Henry VIII to Anne Boleyn and, for many of them, Mary was more than true heiress to the English Crown – she was actually Queen of England.

Before long the great action was transferred to Scottish soil. On 5 December 1560, Mary's weakly young husband died. The young Queen Dowager soon found her position in France uncomfortable and, since her Scottish subjects expected her in her native land, Mary sailed from Calais for Scotland in 1561.

She arrived safely at Leith but, even before she came, the difficulties which must encompass her had become obvious. She had refused to ratify the Treaty of Leith (on the ground that its terms were so worded that she must abandon the claim to England forever) and, for that reason, Elizabeth had declined to give her a safe conduct across the North Sea. In these circumstances her dilemma is writ plain: was she at once to lay claim to the English throne and let herself become the spearhead of a grand Catholic Crusade organized by the Guises? Or was she, by playing the *politique*, to continue the understanding with England achieved by the Congregation and, by abandoning her immediate claim to the English throne, gain recognition as the accepted successor of Elizabeth, should that Queen die before her and without heir?

The decision was not easy. On the one hand there was no guarantee that Spain, which had looked on unheeding whilst Elizabeth established Protestantism in Scotland, would support a crusade to enthrone a French princess; on the other, Elizabeth, who was only nine years older than Mary, might well outlive her and might well marry.

Not unnaturally, she took a middle way and, until the year 1565, her conduct was marked by political wisdom, in accordance with the advice of her half-brother, the Lord

James, and subtle Lethington. She had wisely refused to accept the invitation of the Earl of Huntly to land in the north-east and make herself a Catholic Queen of Scots with the aid of the Clan Gordon. Instead, she at once issued a proclamation forbidding her lieges to attempt anything against the form of religion which she found 'public and universally standing' on her arrival, or in any way to molest any of the company whom she had brought from France. She made no effort to suppress the infant Kirk though she did not encourage it (see p. 155) and, in 1562, she overthrew the Roman Catholic House of Gordon which, to be sure, had shown itself overweening.

Yet, at the same time, she promoted the interests of her own religion by insisting first on having her private Mass, and later that the Mass should accompany her on her progresses; and she let her own inclination be plainly seen in establishing herself in the hearts of her subjects by 'some inchantment whareby men ar betwitched', as reported in the pages of John Knox. To this period belong the famous 'interviews'. From the naïve accounts of these, which Knox gives in his own history, some things are plain. The interviews, conducted in French (the only language in which both Knox and Mary were fluent), were always of the Queen's seeking; he refused her invitations to admonish her privately; the Queen was more than his equal in tact and sometimes even in logic. It was only when he had justified his preaching on the subject of her marriage that she wept, and only when he had taken upon himself to summon the lieges to resist the spread of the Mass that he was brought before her in the presence of the Council. His patrons, with whom the Queen was at that time allied, were able to rescue him from real danger on this occasion, but they seem to have felt that he was an embarrassment. He fell out with Lord James (now Earl of Moray) with whom he did not communicate for a long time; and, though his personal influence remained great, he played little part in public affairs.

In these the Queen persevered upon the middle way, still

hopeful of gaining recognition as Elizabeth's heir in return for abandoning her present claim. But, at the same time, she kept other irons in the fire. In the diplomacy of the times, an unmarried queen was an asset of the first importance, and there was talk of Mary's marriage with some great Catholic prince (Archduke Charles son of the Emperor Ferdinand I, Charles IX of France, the young Duke of Guise, or Don Carlos son of Philip II), or with some Protestant suitor (Arran, Eric XIV of Sweden, or Leicester).

Mary, affecting to regard Elizabeth as a friend and seeking a personal interview, tried to arrange a match which would have the approval of the English Queen; but it became apparent that Elizabeth would oppose any but a disparaging match – the offer of Leicester was an insult – and, in the end, the young Queen settled the matter for herself by choosing her cousin, Henry Stewart, Lord Darnley, who came up to Scotland in February 1565, ostensibly against the wishes of Elizabeth. Darnley, son of the fourth Earl of Lennox, who had taken the English side, and his wife Margaret (née Douglas), had a claim to the English throne unvitiated by alien birth (p. 128). His suit was approved by Catholics, both abroad and in England. He was tall and personable. He and Mary fell in love and, in July 1565, they were married according to the Roman rite without awaiting the necessary dispensation from Rome.

Before long, however, Darnley was being denounced as arrogant, incompetent, and faithless and, though it is not fair to accept all the contumely hurled upon him when he lost the royal favour, he seems to have been something of a 'young fool'. The marriage was a turning-point in Mary's career. Having made her choice she cast away prudence, spurned the representations of the General Assembly, and hunted the leaders of the Protestant nobles, who had attempted a *coup*, into England, riding herself with the foremost in this 'Chase About Raid'. Before long she was in touch with the Pope, Spain, and Shane O'Neil and, early in 1566, the English were sure that she had signed the famous League to suppress heresy. A 'formal' League may not have existed, but the fears of the Protestants were not vain, and they suspected that the Pope had a secret agent in David Riccio.

Of Riccio little is known save that he was a Piedmontese who came to Scotland in 1561 as a musician, commended himself to the Queen and was advanced till he became a secretary in the small household which Mary maintained as Queen Dowager of France. By 1566 it seemed that 'Seigneur Davie' was supplanting Darnley, not only in the Queen's counsels but in her company. The jealous Darnley conspired with Morton, Ruthven, and others to bring back the leaders of the 'Chase About Raid' (Moray among them); Lethington approved; the English government was cognisant; and on 9 March 1566, Riccio was murdered at the door of the Queen's apartment in Holyroodhouse by assassins who had gained access by the husband's private stair. Next day Moray and his friends arrived in Edinburgh and were received by the Queen.

She, however, soon detached Darnley from his allies, summoned her supporters and exiled all who had taken part in the slaying of Riccio. Her son, the future James VI, was born in Edinburgh in June. She did not forgive Darnley and when, in December, the infant, handsomely treated by his godmother, Elizabeth, was baptized at Stirling, his father was virtually ignored.

Meanwhile the Queen had fallen under the influence of James Hepburn, fourth Earl of Bothwell, a reckless man who, having served Mary of Guise well, had been exiled for turbulence in 1562 and had returned unbidden in 1565 to be given command of the royal forces in the 'Chase About Raid'. The Queen's councillors accepted the fact of his dominance over their mistress and framed with him a plan for the removal of Darnley, from whom the Queen would not be divorced lest her son should be prejudiced. The doomed man was conveyed by his wife from Glasgow, where he had lain sick, to the house of Kirk O'Field on the old Flodden wall in Edinburgh. Early in the morning of 10 February 1567, the house was blown up and the body of

Darnley, who had been strangled, was found in a nearby garden. Public opinion at once cast Bothwell for the part of 'first murderer' and did not spare the name of Mary.

Undismayed, the bold Earl had himself acquitted in a farcical trial, and obtained from some of the nobles a recommendation that he should marry the Queen, 'abducted' her near Cramond and took her to Dunbar. He was soon divorced from his wife, Huntly's sister, and on 15 May, having been created Duke of Orkney, he was married to the new-made widow in the Chapel at Holyroodhouse, by Protestant rites.*

Scotland was shocked, not so much by the murder as by the marriage. Shocked too were Mary's friends abroad who, trying to convince themselves that the plot had been aimed at the Queen herself, urged her to take a strong hand against the conspirators. She, however, though her union with Bothwell was far from happy, would not desert him and, when the lords rose against him, rode by night in male attire to join him at Dunbar. Thither he summoned his friends, but, when the hosts met at Carberry Hill near Musselburgh, his army melted away. Mary fell into the hands of the lords, who promised her good treatment, but who could not protect her, if indeed they tried, from the threats of the Edinburgh mob crying 'burn the whore' – death by burning was the fate of a wife convicted of murdering her husband.

A few days later, on 17 June, Mary was imprisoned in the island castle of Loch Leven by the lords who, alleging that

*There is an immense literature as to the complicity of Mary in the murder of Darnley. Against her may be urged her conduct, both before and after the deed, and the evidence of the 'Casket Letters' found with a follower of Bothwell, who had removed the Casket from Edinburgh Castle. If one of these letters is genuine, Mary can hardly be acquitted. The originals have disappeared and there is some doubt as to the circumstances of their production. In any event, it seems probable that Mary had been led to suppose that Darnley's removal would be 'approved' by parliament; that the murder had been arranged in a way to suggest Mary's complicity – it would have been easier to have got rid of a sick man by poison – and that some of Mary's accusers were as deeply involved as she herself may have been.

she still adhered to Bothwell from whose oppressions they had risen to save her, compelled her to abdicate on 24 July and to appoint her half-brother Moray as Regent. James was crowned at Stirling on 29 July; and when Moray, who had been in France for four months, returned in August, he accepted the situation and on the twenty-second was proclaimed Regent.

The Regencies: 1567–78

James, Earl of Moray (Mary's half-brother)	August 1567–January 1570
Matthew, fourth Earl of Lennox (Darnley's father)	January 1570–September 1571
John, sixth Earl of Mar (Keeper of Stirling Castle)	September 1571–October 1572
James, fourth Earl of Morton (among the slayers of Riccio)	November 1572–March 1578

After the formal abdication of Mary, Scotland was governed for over a decade by four successive Regents. All were supported by England and under their rule the party of Mary was crushed and the Protestant cause was maintained in Scotland. Yet the task was not easy. Mary, whose apologists argued that her misfortunes were due to her steadfast adherence to Rome, had many friends; while England, after Elizabeth's excommunication allied with France (Treaty of Blois 1572), was at times hesitant in support of her Scottish allies. Some support, however, England did send. France was unable to intervene; and the result was the destruction of the Queen's men in a barbarous civil war.

During the regency of Moray, Bothwell, after a brief career of piracy in northern seas was hunted into Norway; there he was arrested by the King of Denmark and placed in a captivity which ended only with his death in 1578. Mary, having made a romantic escape from Loch Leven on 2 May 1568, rode south to Hamilton. There her Hamilton relatives rallied an army, but in moving north to link up with the bulk of her supporters, Mary was beaten at Langside, near Glasgow, on 13 May, lost courage at last, and fled into England.

Her arrival embarrassed Elizabeth who, none the less, exploited the situation. Making no scruple to judge a sister Queen, but professing impartiality, she compelled Mary's enemies to produce their evidence, including the Casket Letters; and then, refusing to condemn either side, she kept the illustrious refugee in a detention which was to last more than eighteen years. She was, in truth, afraid of Mary, whose position as legitimate Roman Catholic Queen of England became more dangerous after her own excommunication in 1570, and in 1572-3 she proposed in great secrecy to send her cousin back to Scotland to be judicially murdered. The base plan miscarried, and Mary's captivity was, in the main, honourable enough; but Elizabeth would not let her go.

Meanwhile, in Scotland, the struggle continued. In January 1570 Moray was murdered in a Linlithgow street by Hamilton of Bothwellhaugh; a few months later the palace, castle, and town of Hamilton were destroyed by an English army. In April 1571 the Castle of Dumbarton was captured by a bold escalade and Archbishop Hamilton, who was among the prisoners, was hanged at Stirling for complicity in the murder of Darnley; in the following September, Darnley's father, the Regent Lennox, was murdered at Stirling in the course of a sudden raid by Mary's men.

The next Regent, Mar, died 'because he loved good peace and could not have it'. It was his successor, the cold-blooded Morton, who ended the business. In February 1573 the Hamiltons and the Gordons were driven to make their peace in the 'Pacification of Perth' and, in May, Edinburgh Castle, defended to the last by Kirkcaldy of Grange, fell before English artillery, brought up by Sir William Drury. Morton insisted on hanging Grange; Lethington had died just before the capitulation and as John Knox, having vainly warned his former ally Grange not to prolong the defence, had ended his days in Edinburgh in the preceding November, the stage was cleared of most of the protagonists in the great drama.

Morton remained – ruthless, greedy of a life which hardly

seems to justify his complete confidence in the hour of death, but extremely competent. He it was who, while very mindful of his own interest, re-established order in Scotland and confirmed a religious settlement whose foundation had been laid during the regency of Mar.

In September 1571 the Council had appointed ministers to be Archbishops of St Andrews and Glasgow without consulting the Kirk and next year a General Assembly reluctantly accepted a concordat made at Leith whereby Episcopacy was re-introduced. The bishops, it is true, were to have only the power of superintendents and their examination and admission was to rest with local committees to which the name of 'chapters' was given. Their nomination, however, rested with the Crown which adopted the English system of *congé d'élire*. The new bishops were nicknamed 'tulchans', from the stuffed calf-skin which was put beside a cow to induce her to give milk, and they made very little contribution to the spiritual life of Scotland.

Against this Tulchan Episcopacy the stalwarts of the Kirk rallied under Andrew Melville, a scholar of European reputation, who had returned from Geneva in 1574 to become Principal of Glasgow University. Thence he was later transferred to St Mary's College (as it is now called) in his *Alma Mater* of St Andrews. Under his leadership, and after consultation with English sympathizers, was produced the *Second Book of Discipline* (1581) which was accepted by the General Assembly.

Asserting that the Kirk derived its power directly from God, the Book erected a spiritual authority outside that of the state and, founding upon Scripture, alleged that the names 'bishop', 'pastor', and 'minister' had the same significance: ministers were set above doctors (teachers), elders and deacons, but they were equal among themselves. Assemblies in 1580 and 1581 categorically condemned the whole estate of bishops 'as they are now in Scotland'. Thus arose within the ranks of the Scottish Protestants a deep cleavage which persisted even in the face of the threat from the Counter-Reformation. The Crown favoured the authori-

tarian bishops; the Presbyterians held that the re-appear-
ance of bishops might presage a return to Rome and, in any
case, represented an absolutism. Their political doctrine
resembled that of Hildebrand, but in the world of affairs
theory often avails less than practice; the Melvillians found
little support in exalted quarters (principally because the
nobles and lairds resolutely opposed all demands for the
return of clerical property), whereas the Episcopalians commended themselves to the King at home and to the Roman
Catholics abroad.

The King and his Mother 1578–87

While the great controversy in the Kirk was developing, a
new figure appeared upon the Scottish stage. James VI, not
yet twelve years of age, began his active reign when, early
in 1578, Morton was coerced into resignation by a group of
hostile nobles. He recovered his power for a short time in
1579, but in 1581 he fell to his destruction.

The King had come under the influence of a fascinating
cousin, Esmé Stuart, Seigneur D'Aubigny, who arrived from
France with the benediction of the Guises in September
1579. Speedily endowed with the Earldom of Lennox and
the Abbey of Arbroath, the newcomer formed an alliance
with audacious James Stewart, son of Lord Ochiltree and
brother-in-law of John Knox, who had served as a soldier
in Sweden. The pair of them brought Morton to his
death in June 1581: he was condemned for being art and
part in the murder of Darnley and beheaded by the 'Mai-
den', a sort of guillotine which he himself had introduced
into Scotland. Stewart was made Earl of Arran.

The situation which had developed in Scotland was now
attracting universal attention: both Spain and France were
wondering whether to deal with the infant King or the
captive Queen. Mary was in no mind to be ousted from the
position of Catholic champion and she succeeded for a time
in preventing Henry III from accrediting an ambassador to
her son. In 1579 she tried to get into direct touch with

James, but her secretary was not received because his letters were directed '*au Prince d'Écosse*'. The irate Queen, fearing that France was deserting her, promised in 1580 to put herself, her son, and her realm under the protection of the King of Spain. Meanwhile her friends in France promoted a scheme of 'Association' whereby the mother should still be Queen while the son actually ruled.

This plan, which might be represented as beneficial to England as well as to France, was at first favoured by D'Aubigny; but it had little substance and, by 1582 the Frenchman was involved in one of the grand schemes of Catholic invasion which filled the years until the Armada sailed. These schemes had little reality. Philip was expected to supply the money and the forces; but he had no belief in the far-flung combinations devised by priests. Moreover he did not intend that Spain should conquer England for a French Princess. Persuaded that he himself had a claim to the English throne, he regarded the fate of Mary with indifference and, though he kept in touch with James, he had no intention of erecting him as King of a United Britain. His purpose, however, was kept very secret, and the Scottish Protestants, imagining that the Roman Catholic forces were uniting, lived in constant dread.

James, for his part, enacted the part of 'Mr Facing-Both-Ways'. Ostensibly he remained the Protestant ally of England; but he was determined to be included in any great action by the Catholics and kept in touch with their eternal conspiracies.

The domestic history of Scotland reflects these uncertainties. When the growing influence of Lennox awakened suspicion, James sought to disarm it by himself signing, and having his favourites sign, the 'Negative Confession' – or 'King's Covenant' – an abjuration of Popery, in the winter of 1580–81. When the execution of Morton and the rumours of Catholic plots increased Protestant alarm, a group of nobles seized the King in the 'Raid of Ruthven' (August 1582) and ejected Lennox. Early in 1583, as the result of machinations of two French ambassadors, the 'Raiders' were overthrown, and much power was exercised by the unscrupulous Arran. By 1584, James was in touch with Guise and with Pope Gregory XIII, to whom he held out hopes of his conversion. Arran, however, though he abhorred the claims of the ministers, was a Protestant, and his attack on the Kirk took the form of a royal assertion of the royal supremacy: an attempt by the Ruthven raiders was crushed and William Ruthven, Earl of Gowrie, was executed; the leading ministers were menaced and ejected; even Andrew Melville fled. In May 1584, Parliament passed the so-called 'Black Acts' which asserted that the King was head of the Kirk, that no Assembly should meet without his leave; that Bishops should be appointed by the Crown; that ministers were not to preach politics.

Arran's innovations commended him to the Elizabethan government with whom in July 1585 he laid the foundation of a Protestant league between England and Scotland to counteract the League between Philip II and the Guises. Yet already the ground was slipping beneath his feet. The English realized that his brutality made him unpopular in Scotland; they were aware of James's *démarches* to Rome, and felt that the ministers and the Ruthven raiders were the safest representatives of the Anglophile party in Scotland. Elizabeth's ministers therefore dealt with the Scottish malcontents and they skilfully engineered Arran's downfall. He was blamed, quite unfairly, for the death of Sir Francis Russell, son of the Earl of Bedford, in a Border fracas, and the king felt obliged to imprison him. Then in October 1585 the Ruthven raiders were allowed to cross the Border from their exile in England and, with surprising ease, they regained control of James's person. Arran fled.

The action of England was dictated by the belief that an attack by Spain must soon come. Despite the expulsion of the Spanish ambassador, Mendoza, in 1584, Roman Catholic conspirators were active still and, in 1585, Parliament ratified an 'Association' made by the Protestants whereby the Queen was empowered by special commission to exclude from the succession any person taking part in a plot or invasion, and every person in whose interest a plot against the Queen was made. The act was plainly aimed against Mary, and it was followed by a close *rapprochement* between Elizabeth and James.

In 1586 a formal league for mutual defence was made, and Elizabeth promised to pay James a pension of £4,000 a year. The king was not content, for he had been led to expect £5,000 a year and some recognition of his place in the succession – his father's English lands, perhaps, or an English dukedom; but for years the 'gratuity', though it was not paid regularly or in full, was a welcome addition to his revenue. Yet he was not so subservient as has been supposed.

Secure of James and aware of Spanish preparations, England made short work of Mary, Queen of Scots. In August she was arrested; her papers were seized and in October she was condemned by a commission under the Act of 1585. Elizabeth, though pressed by both Houses of Parliament, hesitated long to sign the warrant for execution, and tried to avoid the responsibility. Yet on 1 February 1587 sign she did and, on 8 February, Mary was beheaded at Fotheringhay.

Froude regarded the death of Mary as the victory of truth over falsehood, and has shown her death-scene as the exist of a great actress dishonest to the last. For Mary this must be said: a sovereign, she had come to England voluntarily to seek asylum and she had been kept in long captivity; certainly she knew of the plot to set her free and she may have known, or guessed, that there was a design against Elizabeth's life. Yet the court which tried her had no competence; the evidence against her, alleged decipherments of ciphered letters written by her secretaries from dictated notes, would hardly be admitted in a modern court of law. Moreover, though she had threatened to disinherit her son in favour of Spain, she had not done so.

That son has been much denounced as one who said that 'he would not be so fond as to prefer his mother to the title'. Yet it must be pointed out that James had been taught to regard his mother as a murderess of his father; that he did endeavour to preserve her life only to be told that a threat of the strong hand was the certain way to provoke Elizabeth to sign the fatal warrant; that rascals like the Master of Gray, James's agent in England, concurred with Walsingham in the determination that Mary must die. Moreover his whole political position must be considered. He had been set upon his mother's throne (as Elizabeth was always telling him) and maintained upon it, with the potent help of England; he had been reared a Protestant, and it was as a Protestant king that he reigned; some of his great nobles were Catholic, but many of the lairds and most of the burghs were staunchly Protestant; and in much of the countryside as well as in the towns the ministers had great power. If he took up arms for Mary he might not enjoy much support in his own country, and the events of the last two decades had made it clear that, despite some conspiracies fomented from abroad, the majority of the English Catholics were Englishmen first of all. To challenge England in battle might well be to throw away at once the foundations of his own power in order to engage in an enterprise which promised little hope of success and threatened the gravest danger. In the event of war with England, he would almost certainly be crushed before the Roman Catholic powers abroad could come to his aid; and if they did come and prevailed, there was no probability that they would set him upon the English throne, and no guarantee that they would maintain him upon the throne of Scotland even if he apostasized from his own religion. Finally, though this may have weighed with him less than his own interest, he had an obligation to the country over which he ruled. His was a hard choice, and he must not be too hastily condemned for choosing as he did.

And what of Elizabeth? Had she had no cognizance, when she was a prisoner in the Tower, of Wyatt's conspiracy against her own half-sister? Was her reluctance to sign the warrant due to womanly pity? She had profited from Mary's downfall to buy cheaply the famous Medici pearls from one who had no right to sell them. She had plotted to have her cousin sent to Scotland to be killed there; and, according to her trusted servants, she had blamed Sir Amyas Paulet, Mary's gaoler, because he did not compass his prisoner's death in some quiet way. The truth seems to be that a long-standing jealousy was stimulated to fear for her own life, by the constant plots against her. She was willing, perhaps even anxious, that Mary should die; but she wanted to thrust the responsibility upon the shoulders of others. It was a matter of policy. Mary was a Queen in her own right and there was already too much talk of regicide. All the monarchs of Europe might turn against the slayer of a fellow sovereign.

Whatever foreign potentates might think or do, Elizabeth's action was supported by her own well-instructed subjects. As so often in her career she contrived to make her own wishes seem to express the desire of England. Mary's death was celebrated with public rejoicings, bells, and bonfires. Yet it was in the very next year that the long promised Armada sailed at last. Philip, under the impression that Mary had already declared him her successor, wasted no time on regrets. There was now no fear that he might conquer England for a French princess; he could safely venture, in the cause of the Faith, no doubt, but also in his own interest.

CHAPTER 9

THE UNION OF THE CROWNS
1587-1603

THE year which saw Queen Mary's death saw also the attainment by King James of the age of twenty-one. The tragic Queen was followed by one whom history, not uninfluenced by the pen of Sir Walter Scott, had tended to regard as a King of comedy. Spindle-shanked, goggle-eyed, sloppy-mouthed, James shuffles across the Scottish stage, witty of speech, irresolute in action, influenced by personable young men, flinching at the sight of a drawn sword. But Scott's portrait in *The Fortunes of Nigel* was founded upon a contemporary satire, and it shows the King when he was getting old; the real James was much less amiable and much more competent than has been supposed. After all, his achievement speaks for him. He did prevail against the nobles and against the Kirk in his own country. He did unite the Crowns of Scotland and England and so doing he put a term to the secular quarrel which could hardly have been ended in any other way. Since England was so much stronger than Scotland, Scotland would not accept the rule of an English King who might try to enslave her; England, conscious of her strength, had no fear, though naturally she had some reluctance, in recognizing the accession of an alien King who had a title to the Crown according to the accepted rules of descent.

To gain the Crown of England was the supreme desire of James, and from the moment that he himself could influence the policy of Scotland, all his efforts were directed to this single end. But his accession to the English Crown was not a matter of course. The Scots were aliens in England, and unpopular aliens at that. Moreover, the English Parliament had affirmed that the Crown could regulate the succession by will, and the will of Henry VIII, founded on statute, had set aside the rights of his elder sister Margaret, from whom James descended, in favour of his younger sister Mary from whom had sprung (in both cases by female descent) scions of two noble English houses. Even if Henry's will were set aside there was in Arabella Stuart (1575–1615), daughter of Darnley's brother Charles, a representative of Margaret Tudor whose descent was not marred by alien birth. Again, it was possible that James's claim was barred by the English Act of 1585 under which his mother had been executed, as a person who would have benefited if the murder plot had succeeded. Finally there was a feeling among some English politicians that if James succeeded to the throne he would take vengeance upon those who had slain his mother.

Apart from these dynastic uncertainties there were other reasons which might make a union of the Crowns difficult. The governmental machinery of Scotland was not so different from that of England as has sometimes been asserted, but it was less developed and far less well organized; the Scottish Kirk was not the same as the Church of England; Scotland was poor, her economy was weak, and England despised her indigent neighbour; and behind all loomed the great question of whether Elizabeth's successor would be a Protestant or a Roman Catholic.

Enthusiastic Romanists remembered that Henry VIII had been a schismatic rather than a heretic; that Elizabeth's settlement, except for the Royal Supremacy, departed so little from the old practice that it was accepted by ninety per cent of the English clergy who had been Catholic under Mary; that Elizabeth, though by her birth she must play the Protestant, was no lover of Puritans. To them it seemed that a nation which changed its allegiance so easily had little religious conviction wherewith to oppose the *Semper Eadem*. Amongst the priests, and particularly the Jesuits, and in political circles where the voices of Catholic exiles from England could be heard, there was great hope, formulated in Clement VIII's breve of 1600, that when God 'should remove that woman whom His inscrutable Will had permitted to reign so long' her successor on the English throne would be a good Catholic and a son of the true Church.

Truly the path of the Scottish King to the English throne was beset with difficulties, and to the overcoming of these difficulties the King could not devote the whole of his attention and energy. He had to deal with the troubles of his own country, a turbulent nobility, a discontented Church and an inadequate revenue.

It cannot be assumed that in solving his everyday problems James consciously had the English Crown always in view; none the less it is true that the solutions which he found were such as to make possible the realization of his great ambition. Admittedly he was fortunate, but plainly he had abilities. He lacked courage and his physique was indifferent; yet as a French observer noted, he was extremely anxious to be thought hardy; and though he was somewhat feeble of foot he rode very well. If he was personally timorous, he was sometimes sudden and resolute in action. Occasionally he went with his armies to the field. When he wanted a wife he sailed over rough seas to bring her home, scorning the example of his great-uncle Henry VIII of England with his 'mail-order' bride Anne of Cleves. His policy was tortuous, but he lived in a tortuous age; his opponents and some of his supporters too were dishonest; he was dishonest himself but possibly less dishonest than has been supposed. Some of his tergiversations represent a definite development in his own character. In his youth he was brought up by men who inculcated the belief that his mother was the murderess of his father, and that, given the chance, she would overthrow not only his own sovereignity, but also the Protestant Kirk which he had been told was the only true church. After his mother's death he came to believe that she had been sinned against rather than sinning. In 1590 he quite possibly believed, as he told the General Assembly, that the Anglican Liturgy was 'an evill said masse in English' and that there was no warrant for the observance of 'Pasche and Yuile', but he certainly held

176

other views on these matters before the decade ended. His main fault was an overweening conceit, a belief in the inspired wisdom which was proper to Solomon. Convinced that he could produce from inner resources solutions to the great problems of the day, he felt himself entitled to use every means to make essential right prevail.

Foreign Policy

In the field of foreign policy his method and spirit reveal themselves with peculiar clarity. All along he posed as the Protestant ally of Elizabeth. In 1589 he sailed to Oslo and married a Protestant bride, Anne of Denmark. Next year, reviving a project which he had announced in 1585–6, he sent envoys to the German princes in the hope of creating a general league for the defence of Protestantism. (The projected league was perhaps rather anti-Spanish than anti-Catholic and before it is dismissed as fantastic, critics should remember the 'great design' ascribed by Sully to Henry IV.) That he was sincere in his endeavour to keep the goodwill of England is probable. As he said in his pithy way, he could expect no favour from Spain save that which Ulysses had from Polyphemus: namely that he would devour him the last of all his fellows.

At the time of the Armada he crushed an incipient revolt by Maxwell in the south-west; next year, advised from England of the dealings of Huntly and Errol with Parma, he brought the northern earls to submission at the Bridge of Dee. After the discovery (in the sleeve of a sailor's shirt) of the 'Spanish Blanks' – incriminating pledges given by Huntly, Errol, and Angus to Spain – he found strength to suppress the insurgents in spite of their victory at Glenlivet in 1594 and threw down the houses of Huntly and Errol at Strathbogie and Slains.

Yet all the time he discreetly held out a hand to the Catholics. Many of his nobles, including some whom he personally liked, were Catholics, and he allowed the rebels of 1594 to reconcile themselves by very doubtful submissions to the Kirk. Among the officers on whom he relied after the death of Chancellor Maitland (Lord Thirlestane) in 1595, were Crypto-Catholics. His own Queen, Anne, was converted to Rome in 1600, though she afterwards returned to Protestantism. Throughout his reign he declined to prosecute Roman Catholics on the ground of religion alone while at the same time he resisted the importunities of the Presbyterians. In so doing he was not necessarily insincere. He believed that he could find a middle way. To him it seemed that the anti-monarchic doctrines of Protestant extremists were very like those of the more violent Catholics. He was aware that there were grave differences between the Jesuits and other priests and he came to realize that some Catholic powers – Venice, Florence, and even the Pope himself – were alarmed by the ambitions of Spain. Above all he had before him the example of Henry of Navarre, that champion of the Huguenots, who 'received instruction' in 1593 and thereafter reigned as a Roman Catholic, guaranteeing to the Protestants toleration and a sure place beneath the aegis of the King of France.

James, it is true was more inclined to give than to receive 'instruction'. He thought that he could provide the necessary formula to embrace all sound forms of Christianity. He would accord the Pope a place of honour though he would not grant him a supremacy over Kings. As he said himself, he could not communicate officially with Rome because he could not give the Pope the titles he demanded, but he was quite prepared to bargain unofficially through the agency of others. Admittedly his hope of a *rapprochement* was not all due to a belief in Christian unity; it was due to a desire to exclude any Catholic competitor from the succession to the English throne. For all that, his dealings with Rome, though certainly they led some devout enthusiasts to expect more than James could grant, did not proceed from a fundamental dishonesty.

These dealings can here be summarized only, although from 1595 a definite policy emerges. The King's objectives were to ensure that moderate Catholics stood aloof from the Spanish claim, to prevent his own formal exclusion and possible excommunication by the Pope, and if possible to get money on the ground that he must hire a guard if he was to protect his Roman Catholic subjects. From France he probably hoped to get some recognition of his title and the reconstitution of the old Scots Guard and the Scots Company of men-at-arms.

James's method was to send first an agent with a verbal message and, if his overture had any success, to follow up with formal instructions. Venice met caution with caution; Tuscany went so far as to discuss a marriage between one of her princesses and James's son; but the Pope, while expressing gratification at James's friendliness, would make no promise until James himself returned to the Catholic Church. It is commonly said that James deliberately deceived the Pope, for his wife Anne, who became a Catholic herself in 1600, alleged that her husband knew of her correspondence and hinted that he might follow her example. It is likely enough that James knew of Anne's dealings and thought them useful as a precaution against excommunication; but it is also likely that Anne, under the influence of the Jesuit who converted her, and of her Catholic entourage, carried matters further than her husband knew. There is no proof that the King really addressed the Pope as *Beatissime Pater*; he made no promise that his son should be educated as a Catholic; he asserted that he himself remained in the religion in which he was born; and in fact he informed the English Government of the 'Instructions' brought from Rome by Sir James Lindsay in 1602. He did try to extend toleration to his Catholic subjects, and he probably thought that when he became King of England he could repeal the Recusancy Laws.

After the death of Philip II he negotiated with Spain and with the Archduke Albert in the Netherlands; there was actually an ambassador from the Archduke at his court on the very eve of his accession to the English throne. The net effect of his policy was certainly to immobilize Roman Catholic opposition to his beloved 'Title'. At the same time he forbore to quarrel with England. At one time he ran a dangerous course by dealing with Essex, who hoped for his support in the *émeute* of 1601, but on the fall of the Earl, his ambassadors, Mar and Kinloss, got in touch with the powerful Secretary, Sir Robert Cecil, and thereafter his road was clear.

Domestic Policy

As for James's domestic policy, it too was coloured by his determination to secure the English throne. One of his first acts in 1587 was to try and reconcile old feuds by holding a whimsical 'love-feast'; and throughout his reign he made personal efforts to quench the mutual hates of his nobles and consolidate all the forces of Scotland against the great day.

To the 'constitutional' development of his country he made some contribution. In 1587 the smaller tenants-in-chief were again encouraged to attend Parliament (partly to help James secure a grant of 40,000 marks) but the Act of that year did not really bring into operation James I's Act of 1428 (see p. 103). The forty-shilling qualification was certainly introduced, but there was no suggestion now of any second chamber; and the King, who plainly regarded Parliament as a means of getting money, showed himself as the reign proceeded more and more inclined to use instead of Parliament the 'Convention', which was in theory the old General Council (which could vote money), but in fact sometimes was like an expanded Privy Council. When Parliament did meet, control could be exercised through the business committee known as the Lords of the Articles, whose place when Parliament met was not unlike that of the Privy Councillors in the Elizabethan Parliaments.

Money remained the difficulty. Parliamentary grants, when given, were contributed according to antiquated assessments and yielded little, and efforts to effect economies and increase the ordinary revenue had only a limited success. In 1596 James appointed a special Exchequer Commission known to history as the 'Octavians', but their efforts at reform excited an unpopularity which helped to produce the riot of 17 December (see p. 182), and led to their resignation. Subsequent attempts by other commissions produced little result and optimistic nobles who undertook the office of Treasurer usually found themselves charged with debts incurred on behalf of the King, which were irrecoverable, though it is possible that some of them gained indirectly.

In a word, James's ideas embodied the Tudor notion of the overriding authority of the Crown and the Tudor preference for conciliar action. What was lacking to him was the force and the financial strength of the Tudors.

The Kirk

Naturally James's dealings with the Kirk reflected the foreign policy which has already been described, but they too were directed to the achievement of the English Crown. Just as, under the threat of the Armada, Elizabeth forbore to attack the Puritans by statute, so James, while the Catholic menace persisted, showed himself accommodating to the Kirk. In 1592 was passed what Calderwood called 'the Golden Act' which in the main affirmed the Second Book of Discipline. Authority was given for an annual meeting of the General Assembly, providing that should the King, or his Commissioner, be present he should appoint, during the sitting of the Assembly, time and place for the next meeting (but providing also that, if neither King nor Commissioner attended, the Assembly itself should make the arrangements for the following year); the functions of provincial assemblies (Synods), Presbyteries, and Kirk-sessions were recognized; Episcopacy was ignored.

Thereafter the wind changed. James was irritated by the Kirk's assertion of the doctrine of the 'twa kingdoms' and by the vehemence of Andrew Melville who on one occasion called him 'God's "sillie" (weak) vassal' and generally showed no regard for the inherent dignity of a King. The extremists however carried their claims so far as to assert that they could not answer in a lay court for things spoken in the pulpit, and thereby gave James his chance. In 1596 David Black, minister of St Andrews, attacked Queen Elizabeth in the pulpit and as Elizabeth, now persecuting her own Puritans, felt that she could dispense with the support of the Scottish Kirk, James could deliver his counter-attack without fear of English intervention. His determination to hold ministers responsible for their utterances in the pulpit produced a discontent which culminated in an important riot in Edinburgh on 17 December (fomented, it is true, by those courtiers who hated the Octavians). The King's reply was to remove the law-courts to Linlithgow, making it plain that he no longer regarded Edinburgh as his capital. Beneath this threat the burgesses submitted and the King re-entered Edinburgh as a conqueror on 1 January 1597.

He used his advantage to make a frontal assault on the Kirk, attacking both the General Assembly which was the main expression of its political power, and the doctrine of ministerial parity which had been used to claim for every minister the right to speak as he would in the pulpit by virtue of being an instrument of the divine truth. Ignoring the Act of 1592, which seemed to recognize the right of the Kirk to hold a General Assembly every year, he arrogated to himself, by degrees, a complete power of appointing time and place for meetings. Aware that the ministers had some support from the Edinburgh mob and that the country ministers of the north resented the pretensions of Edinburgh, he summoned meetings to Perth and Dundee in 1597, to Dundee in 1598, to Montrose in 1600, to Burntisland in 1601, and to Holyroodhouse in 1602. It had now become the practice that 'the king appointed the Assemblies when and where he pleased, by proclamations at the mercat croces'.

Meanwhile he had taken control of the business transacted in Assemblies. Taking advantage of the reaction to the riot of December, 1596, he induced a special meeting which he convened early in 1597 to abandon the claim of complete liberty of speech; and in a regular Assembly held in May and attended by the 'Northerners' in force, he induced the Kirk, under pretext of the necessity of planting churches throughout the land, to appoint a Standing Commission. It is unfair to say that at first the members were mere puppets, though Andrew Melville was excluded and of the others some were beguiled by James's charms. Yet before long the Commission acted as 'the King's led horse', in the words of Calderwood, and became the means whereby the King could assert that the innovations he made were approved of by the Kirk. These innovations were significant.

For some time there had been a demand, not among the clerics only, that the clerical estate in Parliament should recover its medieval strength, and in December 1597, on a petition of the Commission of Assembly, Parliament enacted that such ministers as the King should promote to the dignity of prelate should have a seat in Parliament. Next year an Assembly at Dundee, from which Andrew Melville was excluded on the ground that he was not 'a pastor' but a 'doctor', listened to a speech from the King who explained that he did not wish 'to bring in Papistical or Anglican bishops, but only to have the best and wisest of the ministers appointed by the General Assembly to have place in Council and Parliament'. After debate a small majority voted that fifty-one ministers – the number of bishops, abbots, and priors in the medieval Parliament was reckoned at fifty-one – should have seats in Parliament and that the election of these should belong partly to His Majesty and partly to the Church.

But the clergy never entirely trusted the King. Their confidence was shaken both by his unscrupulous methods and by the absolutist aspirations revealed by the discovery in 1599 of a copy of the *Basilicon Doron*, written by the King as an instruction to his son Henry and printed only in seven copies. In this James, claiming that 'the office of a King is a mixed office betwixt the civil and ecclesiastical estate', adopted a very high doctrine which would allow him to claim a 'supremacy'; and though the Assembly of Montrose in 1600 tried to limit the position of the new bishops by a series of '*caveats*', their resistance was too late and ineffective.

The only ministers to be 'promovit' to prelacies were three who were appointed to vacant bishoprics with reduced revenues, but before the King went over the Border in 1603 he had taken the decisive step of making the Kirk of Scotland conform more closely to the pattern of England.

The Gowrie Conspiracy

Yet, though he thus prevailed against the Kirk, James VI's years in his native kingdom were not free from anxieties. To the year 1600 belongs the famous Gowrie Conspiracy, whose mystery is even today unsolved. John Ruthven, third Earl of Gowrie, a young man of about twenty-two, having returned from Italy and having been well received in England, came to Scotland and made himself conspicuous by opposing the King's demand for money in the Convention of 1600. What is certain is that on 5 August the King rode suddenly to Perth along with the Earl's brother, the Master of Gowrie (a boy of nineteen), followed by a small attendance, and that in Gowrie House a fracas occurred in which both the young noblemen were killed. James asserted that there had been a plot to assassinate him and ordered public rejoicings for his escape. Some of the ministers refused without further knowledge to accept the royal version of the affair, and the King's enemies roundly asserted that he had arranged the brutal murder of possible opponents of whom he was jealous, perhaps on account of the Queen. That the handsome young brothers meant to slay the King is extremely improbable; but that the son of a 'Ruthven Raider' (and grandson of one of Riccio's murderers) planned to kidnap the King, whose doubtful relations with the Papists excited suspicion, is not impossible. It is, in fact, extremely hard to see why the King, if he meditated murder, came into his enemies' stronghold with a slender attendance, or why the Gowries, attempting a *coup d'état*, should not have provided themselves with a sufficient force.

His good name tarnished (perhaps unjustly) by this episode, his relations with his wife (who was friendly with the Ruthvens) uncertain, his Treasury well-nigh empty, and his attempts to arm Scotland unsuccessful, James had cause for anxieties. Yet in his dealings with England as they are shown in the State Papers, the King himself showed little apprehension. He was unmoved by stories of Spanish invasion; he tried to reduce the Borders to obedience, riding himself to do the business; he offered his wild Highlanders to assist Elizabeth's Deputy in Ireland; and he affected to treat the Queen of England as a fellow Sovereign. No doubt his confidence was due to his knowledge that Cecil was on his side, and indeed it is clear from the evidence that the able Secretary, secure in his secret understanding with the strong Protestant candidate for Elizabeth's throne, promoted James's interest in a way which contrasts strangely with the suspicious attitude he had adopted when he knew or suspected that the Scottish King was in relation with Essex.

'Incidents' on the Borders and at sea which had hitherto provoked violent repercussions were now smoothly adjusted. The King informed 'his dearest sister in England' of the fact that he had received communications from the Pope by the hands of Sir James Lindsay, and on one occasion the English Councillors, guided by Cecil, listened to the reading of a letter from James with bared heads. Before Elizabeth breathed her last, on the night of 24 March 1603, all was made ready for the accession of the Scottish King.

There is no evidence that, at the very end, the dying Queen recognized James as her successor, and the famous ride of Robin Carey who rode from London to Edinburgh in three days to be the first to salute his new Sovereign has a romantic rather than a political significance. The Privy Councillors, amongst whom Cecil's influence was paramount, had James proclaimed in the City of London without delay, and it is possible enough that, before the gallant but ambitious horseman presented himself at Holyroodhouse, James had already been informed by Cecil that the Queen was at the point of death and that his own accession was assured.

CHAPTER 10

THE CROWN AND THE KIRK
1603-25

Think not of me as of ane King going frae ane part to another, but of ane King lawfully callit going frae ane part of the isle to ane other that sae your comfort be the greater.

(Speech of James in St Giles, 3 April 1603)

I am the Husband and the whole Isle is my lawfull Wife; I am the Head; and it is my Body; I am the Shepherd and it is my flocke; I hope therefore no man will be so unreasonable as to think that I that am a Christian King under the Gospel should be a polygamist and husband to two wives; that I being the Head should have a divided and monstrous Body.

(Speech of James to his first Parliament, March 1604)

THE accession of James VI to the English throne increased his power, but it also confirmed him in his exalted concept of the sovereign power of a king. He arrived in England convinced that he could effect a complete union of the two kingdoms by force of personality alone. To be sure, he was well received by the people as he rode south, though he aroused some suspicion by having a cut-purse hanged without trial, and by creating a large number of knights; but his popularity declined with the advent in London of numerous Scots ('needy'– as they appeared to the English), and by his smug speech to his first Parliament which contained clear hints that he regarded his powers as absolute.

Nevertheless, in deference to his wishes, Parliament appointed forty-four commissioners to meet thirty-one Scots to discuss union. There were able men on both sides, Francis Bacon and Thomas Hamilton ('Tam o' the Cowgate', later Lord Haddington and Earl of Melrose) among them, but little resulted. James led the way by adopting by proclamation in October 1604 the title of 'King of Great Britain, France and Ireland'. He also thought up a happy motto, *Henricus rosas regna Jacobus*, while the first simple 'Union Jack' bore his name. But his example availed little: the only real achievement was the abrogation of the Border Laws and, in 1607, the English Commons broke off the union talks with rude emphasis. The only other significant advance in this field was gained by legal decision and not by statute: namely the recognition that subjects born after James's accession to the English crown had a common nationality. The crucial case concerned a piece of land which was bought in the name of Robert Colville, infant grandson of Lord Colville of Culross. His title was challenged, and Colville's guardians brought an action both in the King's Bench and Chancery divisions of the English High Court. In both cases, the defendants argued that the Colville was an 'alien' and therefore not competent to bring a prosecution, but the matter was taken to the Exchequer Chamber where all the judges sitting together declared that the infant's claim should be heard.*

In Scotland the same meagre results were obtained in a more regular way. Parliament, though not anxious for a complete union, was prepared to agree to the royal plan, but in view of the English attitude, it could do no more than repeal the Border Laws, and give common citizenship to subjects born after the Union.

Scotland under an Absentee King

To the same Parliament was read a commission appointing the Duke of Lennox to represent the King in Scotland. This was significant. James in his farewell speech at St Giles, which moved his audience to tears, had promised to revisit his native land every three years; but now it was plain, as indeed it was natural, that he would devote most of his

---

*The case is known in England as Calvin's Case; the English know that the Scots are Calvinists and sometimes assume that they cannot spell their own names.

attention to the greater and wealthier kingdom. Only in 1617 did he find time to obey 'the salmon lyke instinct' to see 'the place of his birth and breeding' and he stayed for only twelve weeks.

Yet he did not neglect Scotland. From the *Register of the Privy Council*, and the correspondence of the time, it is clear that he was keenly interested in her affairs, and there was justice in his claim that 'this I must say for Scotland, and may truly vaunt it; here I sit and govern it with my pen; I write and it is done'. How was this achieved? There is little doubt that, in distant London, the King was safe from kidnapping nobles and hectoring ministers, but that is not the sole explanation. During his absence his interests were maintained by able ministers, among them the redoubtable 'Tam' (Lord President), George Home, Earl of Dunbar, (Treasurer), the seventh Earl of Mar (who became Treasurer on Dunbar's death in 1616) and Gideon Murray (Treasurer Depute). Between them these men made the central power effective. 'Tam' saw to the machinery of government and the others at least scrutinized the royal pension-list and kept a watchful eye upon revenue and expenditure. The control over the Kirk was placed in the hands of the bishops, especially of John Spottiswoode (Archbishop of Glasgow, 1610, of St Andrews, 1615–39).

Suppression of Disorder

An essential part of the government's duty was to bring into order the 'peccant' parts of the realm – the Borders, the Highlands, and Islands. This was done ruthlessly and sometimes by means more than doubtful. The Borders were daunted by a small, but permanent, police force under Sir William Cranston, whose efforts were furthered by a *deportatio juvenum* which sent wild Armstrongs and others to serve in the Continental wars; and, in 1612, some influential lairds pledged themselves to deliver up every criminal found on their lands. Violent measures were taken against the Macgregors who, on the eve of James's departure for

England, had slipped down the western side of Loch Lomond and carried out a bloody and lucrative raid in Glen Fruin – 'the slaughter of the Lennox'. Argyll was given the task of inflicting punishment and, when the Macgregor chief crossed the Border under safe-conduct to state his case to James, he was arrested under the pretext that the safe-conduct was not valid in England and hanged in Edinburgh. In 1610 a commission of 'fire and sword' was issued against the whole clan and, in 1617, Parliament confirmed a Privy Council ordinance of 1603 and abolished the very name of Macgregor.

Against the southern Hebrides the Crown prevailed, partly because the Macdonalds of Isla were divided amongst themselves. The doubtful expedient of employing Argyll as Justiciary and Lieutenant had some success but, in 1608, a more drastic step was taken. A powerful army appeared in Mull under Andrew Stewart, Lord Ochiltree, who enjoyed the cooperation of Andrew Knox, Bishop of the Isles. The chiefs were invited to a conference in the Castle of Aros, lured aboard ship to hear a sermon, kidnapped, and confined to various prisons. Under this compulsion they accepted next year from the Bishop 'the Band and Statutes of Icolmkill (Iona)', which, though largely concerned with the establishment of the church and the improvement of morality, made each chief responsible for the conduct of his clan. The improvement which followed was steady, but it was slow. Clandonald remained recalcitrant and, in 1614, its leader, Angus Og, gained the Crown lands of Isla by trapping Bishop Knox himself. Only with the aid of the Campbells, with whose help Angus Og was treacherously taken and hanged, did the Crown manage to assert itself. The plantation of Ulster (1608–10), though mainly directed against the Irish, had the effect of depriving the Islesmen of support from Ireland, where the house of Isla had long been established.

Fresh attempts to colonize the Isle of Lewis, however, failed and in 1610 the surviving 'gentlemen adventurers' sold their claim to Mackenzie of Kintail who assumed authority, though the long-resisting Macleods remained, and still remain, the predominant element in the population.

In Orkney Patrick (son of an illegitimate son of James V and builder of a beautiful palace) carried feudal tyranny to such a height that the name of Earl Patrick became a byword for oppression. In 1609 he was arrested, but his natural son, Robert, raised the standard of revolt. In 1612 the lands of Orkney were permanently annexed to the Crown, but it was only in 1615, after a further attempt at rebellion, that the matter ended with the execution of son and father in Edinburgh.

As Argyll had been overmuch used in the south, so the Earl of Caithness had to be given extensive powers to preserve order in the north. None the less, the royal policy, despite its use of doubtful expedients, had given Scotland an order better than that which it had hitherto enjoyed. Royal power was thus considerably enhanced.

Constitutional Development

The growth of the royal power went hand in hand with some development in constitutional machinery. The Privy Council, whose numbers were gradually reduced till it was composed mainly of royal officials, gained in authority, and was linked more closely with Parliament through a manipulation of the committee known as the Lords of the Articles, upon which many of its members appeared. By James's reign, this parliamentary committee was normally composed of eight members from each estate plus certain royal officials, whose number was limited to eight in 1617. Taking advantage of some uncertainty whether a committee chosen in the first session of a parliament could automatically act in subsequent sessions, the King in 1606 sent in a list of his own nominees which was accepted, and this procedure may have been followed in 1607 and 1609, though theoretically the election was made by the whole Estates.

In 1612, however, the King, reverting to former practices

with a difference, ordained that the prelates should choose eight representatives from the nobles, the nobles eight from the clergy, and the prelates and nobles jointly eight from the smaller barons and eight from the burghs. Possibly it was not all the prelates and all the noblemen, but only the sixteen already elected who were to choose the barons and the burgesses; certainly this was the procedure used in 1621 and on subsequent occasions. As the prelates were virtually the King's nominees, the obvious result of this system was to produce a committee amenable to the royal wishes. In 1621 'Tam', now Earl of Melrose, could report that the names of all the Lords of the Articles chosen, save one, had been on a private list prepared beforehand.

Thus, even without the nominated royal officials, the committee was in the pocket of the government. It had become the practice that after the election of the 'Articles' the Estates did not meet, even as separate bodies, until the committee reported. Then, assembling together, they saw all the conclusions of the committee turned into statute on a single day by the application of the sceptre in the hands of the King's representative. The royal control over Parliament would seem to have become complete. The machine, however, did not always act with precision. There was a feeling that certain great nobles had a prescriptive right to be elected to the Articles and sometimes the nobles openly resented governmental interference. Sometimes the King did not get his legislation without opposition, but get it through he did, though finance remained a difficulty.

Over local government, too, the King stretched forth his hand. He took some control over the election of burgh officials, and, though his attempt, begun in 1610, to establish Justices of the Peace on the English model had only a limited success, yet it accomplished something.

The Kirk

The reorganization of the Scottish Church was perhaps the central feature of James's policy. Secure upon his southern throne, and becoming, under the influence of the Anglicans, ever more 'high' in his outlook, he set himself to complete the work which he had begun before 1603. That work was both destructive and constructive.

His first business was to overthrow the General Assembly. Disregarding the intention and the text of the Act of 1592, he avoided the holding of Assemblies in 1603 and 1604 and, when a meeting was arranged for 1605, the Privy Council outlawed in advance any persons who should dare to attend. None the less a few ministers constituted themselves an Assembly and named time and place for the next meeting. Those who stood to their protest (thirteen in number) were prosecuted by the King's advocate, found guilty, and confined till their sentence was known. James, despite the advice of his officers, insisted that their offence was high treason and six were brought for trial. In spite of the use of undue influence, only nine out of the fifteen jurymen concurred in finding the accused guilty, but the six were exiled and never saw Scotland again. By means more discreditable still, James rid himself of the doughtiest of his opponents. In 1606 he summoned eight leading ministers to England for a discussion and only six of these were allowed to go home. James Melville was permitted to live in the north of England, but his Uncle Andrew, who had added to his misconduct a rude Latin epigram upon the formal ritual of the English Church, was imprisoned in the Tower where he remained for more than three years. He was released in 1611 through the good offices of the Duc de Bouillon, but to Scotland he never returned. He became a Professor in the University of Sedan and died there in 1622.

Meanwhile the King was hurrying on with the constructive part of his programme. In 1606 an Act of Parliament restored 'the Estate of the Bishops', amongst other things undoing in part the Act of 1587 which had annexed to the Crown the temporalities of all prelacies. Later in the year, a ministerial convention at Linlithgow agreed that, mainly in order to counteract the machinations of the Papists, each Presbytery should have a constant Moderator – a permanent

Chairman. In April 1607 the astonished clergy found that the convention was reckoned a General Assembly, and that it had voted for constant Moderators for provincial synods as well as for presbyteries. Thus was the authority of the bishop over the clergy of his diocese firmly established. An Act of 1609 restored to the prelates the jurisdictions they had lost at the time of the Reformation. In 1610 each archbishop was given a Court of High Commission.* In the same year, not without undue influence, a General Assembly accepted all the innovations and in 1612 these were confirmed by Parliament.

Meanwhile the King had sent Spottiswoode and two of his brethren to receive the Spiritual Touch from three English bishops – not from Canterbury or York lest the independence of the Scottish Church was hazarded. The 'synthetic' bishop was complete.

Had James stopped here his policy might have been counted a success. The extremists were outraged, but many of the moderate Presbyterians were prepared to receive bishops though they did not welcome them. The local Church courts and the ordinary services were little altered; Popery was condemned and, in 1615, the Jesuit John Ogilvie executed. It is the case that some ministers, later to be champions of the Kirk, accepted episcopal ordination, among them Baillie and Dickson. But being doctrinaire, and moving to the practice though not to the theology of the Arminians, James could not call a halt, and he went on to prejudice the victory he had won in two ways: he used the bishops in political affairs and he began to interfere with the ordinary ceremonies of the Church. When, after a long interval, a General Assembly was held at Aberdeen in 1616, there were projects for a new Confession of Faith, a new Catechism, and a new Liturgy, and the design might have been completed had not James announced that he intended to introduce ceremonies uncongenial to most Scotsmen, and, to some, savouring of Popery. These were

*In 1615 the Courts were united under the Archbishop of St Andrews.

five in number – kneeling at Communion, which might involve the doctrine of the Real Presence; private Communion in case of necessity, which might give opportunity for a secret *viaticum*; private baptism; observance of the great feasts, which contradicted the belief that every Sabbath Day should be as holy as man could make it; and episcopal confirmation, which magnified the bishops.

Spottiswoode warned the King that the time was not yet ripe, but in 1617 James came north in person to enforce his policy. Holyrood Chapel was prepared to receive an organ and choristers, and there was a proposal to introduce statues of patriarchs and Apostles, though this was dropped. When the King arrived in May, bringing Laud and others with him, he introduced the English service into the Royal Chapel; but his attempt to give the bishops an increased power was defeated by Parliament, and a clerical convention at St Andrews held that the innovations could be accepted only by a General Assembly. An Assembly held at St Andrews after the King's departure made concessions accompanied by *caveats* which roused the King's fury; but next year an Assembly at Perth, not without some coercion, accepted the King's proposals. Finally, in 1621, the 'Five Articles of Perth'* were ratified by Parliament. The chance of a united Episcopal Kirk in Scotland was lost.

The consequences of James's persistence did not immediately appear, for Spottiswoode was a Scotsman and, in some ways, moderate; and James had not lost all his native common sense. 'Laud,' he said, 'knows not the stomach of these people.'

A Colonial Venture

The peaceful years, which concluded James's reign, witnessed Scotland's first attempt to establish a colony in North America, where England and France had already estab-

*The Five Articles were not rigorously enforced, but they had been made law and the day was to come when Laud's influence was to prevail.

195

lished themselves. This was made by Sir William Alexander, poet and courtier – a sort of Scottish Raleigh, later Secretary of State and Earl of Stirling, and an unsuccessful experimenter with the currency who died bankrupt in 1640.

After a project advanced by English 'Undertakers' for Newfoundland had failed, Alexander obtained in 1621 a Charter for Nova Scotia in America which embraced, besides the Nova Scotia we know, New Brunswick and all the land between New Brunswick and the St Lawrence. The English New Plymouth Company offered no objection because the country concerned was unattractive in itself, and because the Scots would provide a barrier against the French. Yet the great design had little success, though in 1624 James offered the title of baronet to reputable persons who would give practical assistance.

The outbreak of war with France gave the venture the support of English ships and in 1629 a little colony was founded at Port Royal, originally a French post, much later known as Annapolis, and another small settlement was started on Cape Breton by Lord Ochiltree. Just at this time, however, England made peace with France and, when a final settlement was reached at St Germain-en-Laye in 1632, Charles I surrendered all the Scottish settlements, partly because he wanted a lever to extract the balance of his wife Henrietta's dowry.

Not unnaturally, Scots have held that they were betrayed in the interests of English policy, but in fact the prospects had never been good. Country and climate were hard; Scots labourers and craftsmen were not inclined to emigrate; the thirty-five gentlemen who became baronets took seisin on the Castle Hill of Edinburgh, and did not personally visit their new domains; the 'younger sons' and lairds whom James hoped to attract preferred a career of arms with the French, with the Dutch, with the Danes, or with the Swedes, to the adventure of opening up a wild land in distant America.

Though the colonial enterprise failed, Scotland's economy seems to have thriven. A book of customs of 1612, though it deals with rates and not with actual transactions, shows that a varied trade was contemplated; much of this, under the superintendence of the Convention of Royal Burghs, was conducted through the Staple at Veere in the Netherlands, but there was active business with France, Ireland, and Scandinavia. A list of the year 1614 shows that the bulk of the exports were raw materials, corn, skins and hides, wood, lead, ore and coal, as well as much fish, particularly herring and salmon. There were some manufactured articles – cloth of various kinds, hose, linen, yarn, salt, and leather goods. Many of the imports were luxuries, but others were of practical use – timber, metals, and metal-work. Some were obviously for military purposes. The total value of Scots exports in 1614 was reckoned at £736,986 Scots.* That business was prosperous appears from the fact that the merchants, sometimes little to their profit, were able to lend substantial sums to the government – in 1598 the Crown admitted a debt of £160,552 Scots to Thomas Foulis and Robert Joussie.

With increasing prosperity came a development of the liberal arts. Literature made some progress under a King who admired good letters. His own poetry is undistinguished, though no doubt it adhered to the rules which he had published in 1584; but his prose could be both witty and pithy. His use of the Scots idiom diminished as the years passed and what is true of him is true of other men of letters: Alexander Scott, and Alexander Montgomery, who flourished in the early days of his reign, wrote in Scots, but Drummond of Hawthornden (d. 1649) and Sir William Alexander wrote in English. A comparison between the language of Robert Lindsay of Pitscottie (the sixteenth-century historian) and that of Archbishop Spottiswoode (1565–1639) for example, is revealing. As for painting, it is now certain that the first James Scougall was working before 1612, and George Jameson, usually reckoned the

*The total value of Scotland's exports around 1614 was therefore only £61,415 Sterling compared to a value of £2,487,435 Sterling for England's total exports at the same time.

first of Scottish portrait painters, was busy too. Architecture flourished. In the early days of the century the first Marquis of Huntly restored Huntly Castle in a beautiful fashion whose oriel windows recall those at Blois; while in the north-east, castles like Craigievar, completed in 1626, carried the Scottish vernacular 'towerhouse' tradition to its apogee.

James died on 27 March 1625. During his long reign Scotland, it has been said, made a greater advance from barbarism to civilization than in any whole century of its previous history. Spottiswoode's panegyric may be to some extent discounted, but the estimate of Arthur Wilson is worth regarding: 'He had pure notions in conception but could bring few of them into action . . . yet peace was maintained by him . . . Peace begot Plenty and Plenty begot Ease and Wantonness.' Wilson's judgement is not unlike that pronounced by Clarendon upon the state of England on the eve of the Great Rebellion. Neither historian saw the whole truth for, in both countries, beneath the surface of prosperity lurked a discontent due not to plenty alone, but to long-standing religious grievances, which meant more to the people of the early seventeenth century than is readily understood by a 'secular' age.

The apparent ease with which James accomplished his ecclesiastical programme has misled some modern observers as it misled the King himself. Behind the acquiescence was a steadily growing resistance. The *History* of David Calderwood* bristles with stories of deprivations, confinements, banishments, and protestations; and though his work represents the attitude of some resolute ministers, the conclusion that the opposition was purely clerical cannot be maintained.

In the Lothians and Fife, particularly, recalcitrant ministers had the support of their congregation. Even from Edinburgh burgesses streamed forth to attend country churches where the new regulations were less strictly en-

*David Calderwood (1575–1650): author of *The History of the Church of Scotland*, not published till 1678, and of controversial tracts.

forced, and the opposition grew steadily more general as the consequences of James's policy revealed themselves.

The bishops showed themselves to be agents for royal absolutism. As early as 1615 it was noted that in Glasgow the Bishop 'had the chief management of the University in his hand', and in 1621 Principal Robert Boyd, French-trained, moderate, and scholarly, was expelled because he would not accept the Five Articles. Next year he was expelled also from Edinburgh which had sought his services. Plainly the Crown meant in the future to control the opinions of churchmen.

Yet it was not only churchmen who felt alarmed. The High Commission Court wielded an increasing jurisdiction which affected the lives of ordinary folk; and, by the ingenious use of the 'Lords of the Articles', the bishops played the decisive part in rendering Parliament submissive. Some figures are significant. In the General Assembly which passed the Five Articles of Perth, the Crown obtained a convincing majority – eighty-six against forty-nine – the bishops, of course, voted *en bloc* for the King and so did almost all the lay-elders; but when the matter came before the Parliament in 1621, although the bishops and most of the great nobles voted with the Crown, fourteen lords and lairds ventured to oppose; the shires were evenly divided and, amongst the burghs, there was a small majority against the measure. The King himself, though characteristically he was prepared to argue and hesitated to proceed to extremities, supported his policy by all the means in his power. He ordered that great feasts of the Church should be observed and encouraged the use of sports on Sunday. When he came north in 1617 he counselled the members of the High Commission to deprive recalcitrant ministers, not only of their livings, but of their offices. 'We took this order with the Puritans in England,' he reassured them.

James spoke truly, but he misjudged the situation. In England too his policy had had the semblance of success. After the Hampton Court Conference, some ministers had been deprived, but many others, thanks to the policy of Archbishop Bancroft, had conformed, though in their hearts they had remained Puritan. Puritanism had taken what may be called an inward turn. Released from the urgent necessity of resisting a probable Roman Catholic invasion, it found an outlet in the insistence on a higher morality; 'Salvation Yeo' of *Westward Ho!* gave place to 'Zeal-of-the-Land Busie' of Jonson's *Bartholomew Fayre*. That active elder is no doubt a caricature, but many honest men, bred on the Bible and Foxe's *Book of Martyrs*, looked askance at the government's attacks upon the Sabbath, and at the evil example of the Court. The proceedings of the High Commission Court went hand in hand with the insistence on ritualism in the Church. There was a feeling that all this savoured of a return to Popery, and this was heightened by James's foreign policy, well-intentioned in its pacifism.

In Scotland too the fear of Popery was never absent. In a word, James was driving into the same camp the religious malcontents of both his kingdoms and, in the reign of his son, the fruits of his action were to appear.

To the understanding between Scottish Presbyterians and English Puritans the King unwittingly made a contribution by his patronage of the 'Authorized Version' of 1611. Before he left Scotland some of the more scholarly clergy had already been conscious of defects in the Scottish Bible (a recension of the Geneva Bible) approved by Parliament in 1579. He himself, in the General Assembly at Burntisland in 1601, approved the idea of a new version, himself giving, extempore, examples of mistranslations in the existing text. It was remitted to certain ministers to prepare new versions of doubtful passages, but before long the Assembly lost its power (p. 193) and nothing came of the project. But the good qualities of the 1611 version commended it to Scotland, and it had an impact, not only upon the religious life of Scotland, but also upon her literature. It accelerated the movement (p. 197) from the Scots tongue to the English.

CHAPTER II

THE PRESBYTERIAN
REVOLUTION:CHARLES I
1625–49

The National Covenant, 1638

THE uncertain basis of the peace which James had given to Scotland became evident on the accession of Charles. The father had divided his opponents by making innovations gradually: the son united them all against the Crown. Charles, born in 1600, had left his native land as an infant; until his brother Henry died in 1612 he had been little regarded, and he may have developed that inferiority complex which asserts without being able to achieve. When he mounted the throne he had personal dignity, but he knew little of the art of government and still less of Scotland. For Scottish affairs he had, at first, little time. He was at once embroiled in inherited difficulties in England, which ended with his complete breach with Parliament in 1628–9 and his determination to rule without Parliament in the future.

This early encounter with the constitutional spirit of England confirmed him in the idea, inculcated by his father and soon exemplified by Richelieu in France, that monarchy should be absolute. In this opinion he was strengthened by the support of William Laud (Bishop of London, 1628, Archbishop of Canterbury, 1633) and other Arminian divines who, liking the trappings of Rome but refusing papal supremacy, magnified the King as Head of the Church. Everything combined to make Charles believe that opposition to his absolutism was not only folly but sin.

To him, therefore, the ecclesiastical situation in Scotland was a challenge, and he accepted it at once. Archbishop

Spottiswoode was given precedence over all other subjects, made President of the Exchequer and, along with four other prelates, appointed to the Privy Council from which, in 1626, every one of the Lords of Session was excluded. Plainly the Bishops were to take a still greater part in the government of Scotland.

While the prelates were thus exalted the nobles were to be depressed. An Act of Privy Council of October 1625 recalled to the Crown all property alienated since the accession of Mary in 1542. It is true that similar Acts of Revocation had been passed at the beginning of a reign or at the end of a minority, but Charles had never reigned as a minor. Moreover, this Act affected most of the wealth which had passed from the Old Church since the Reformation, including the thirty-five religious houses which had been 'erected' into temporal lordships, and the teinds (tithes) of other lands which had long been acquired by persons little interested in the welfare of parishes. For Charles, it must be said that he wanted to bring the teinds into relation with the properties from which they were derived and provide decent livings for the clergy; and the Act was not rigorously interpreted, for a commission which sat between 1627 and 1629 arranged a compromise whereby holders of lands and teinds might secure themselves by payment of stipulated sums. Even so, however, there was hardly a landed family of standing which was not threatened; the nobles were forced to pay money outside regular taxation, and their hearts were turned from the King who, sure that he had acted justly, and relying on the Church, made no effort of conciliation.

When he came to Scotland to be crowned in 1633, though he distributed some honours, he did little to increase his popularity. He brought Laud up with him, introduced a service in the English manner into the Royal Chapel and the Kirk of St Giles, and established an episcopal see in Edinburgh. He refused to look at a petition of the ministers and, after his return to England, directed that the English service should be used at Holyrood and St Andrews and gave stringent instructions regarding clerical apparel – 'rags of Popery'.

To the Scottish Parliament which met during his stay, Charles showed himself uncompromising. Well-organized preparations had ensured 'Lords of the Articles' who produced, and a house which accepted, 168 Acts on a single day, including taxation, the Act of Revocation, and confirmation of the ecclesiastical innovations of James. When these were put to the meeting the King, who was present, openly noted down the names of dissentients. He refused to receive a Supplication in which some nobles expressed their grievances and later insisted on prosecuting one of them, Lord Balmerino, for treason. The Crown got a verdict by only eight votes against seven and admitted the condemned man to mercy; but the trial, which lasted for more than a year, aroused immense hostility.

Charles went on unheeding. In 1634 he gave a new Court of High Commission extended powers; in 1635 he made Spottiswoode Chancellor. In the same year, without reference to General Assembly or Parliament, he authorized a *Book of Canons* which gave the King the title of Head of the Church, ordained an unpopular ritual, and commanded the exclusive use of a new Liturgy which had not yet been published. This new Service Book when it appeared was found to be more 'Papistical' than the English Prayer Book. It has wrongly been called 'Laud's Liturgy', for Laud would have preferred the introduction of the English Prayer Book; indeed, the Scottish bishops played a central role in drafting the new liturgy. Nevertheless, the attempt to use it in St Giles Kirk produced the riot with which the name of Jenny Geddes is associated.

Under the leadership of Alexander Henderson, minister of Leuchars, and with the legal skill of Archibald Johnston of Warriston, there was produced the 'National Covenant' which was to stand for so much in the history of Scotland. In this instrument the 'Negative Confession' (p. 169) was repeated *verbatim* and followed by a citation of Acts of Parliament with which the recent innovations were declared incompatible. Then followed a solemn oath whereby the signatories bound themselves to support the King 'in the defence and preservation of the aforesaid true religion, liberties, and laws of the kingdom'; as also to their own mutual defence 'in the same cause of maintaining true religion and his Majesty's authority'; likewise each one in his own conduct to behave 'as beseemeth Christians who have renewed their Covenant with God'.

'Wednesday 28th Februar' was, according to Warriston 'that glorious mariage day of the Kingdom with God'. On that day the Covenant was signed, by the nobles and gentlemen, in the Kirk of the Greyfriars in Edinburgh; next day ministers and burghs signed four principal copies 'in another building'; only on March 2 and 3 did the general populace sign. Thereafter other copies were sent all round the country and, by 5 April, representatives of all the shires and all the towns save three had given their adherence.

The Conservative 'Aberdeen Doctors', justly famed for piety and learning, steadfastly refused to separate themselves from a large part of Christendom by embracing the Covenant and it is not to be supposed that elsewhere whole communities were committed by the action of their Commissioners. Yet it is clear that the Covenant, appealing to deep-seated religious conviction, to real fear of Popery, and to a national determination not to surrender Scottish institutions into the hands of the English, was very well, and in some areas very enthusiastically, received.

This was a direct challenge to royal power and it could not be met. Charles's ministers in Scotland have been blamed for their incompetence, but it was the King who had divided the Privy Council in the manner already shown. While he failed to give it the means to suppress revolt, at the same time Charles refused all compromise, believing that his very 'Majesty' would quell a storm raised by a malignant few. All 'Supplications' were disregarded and the upshot was that the Supplicants organized a machinery of their own: each of the four orders – nobles, lairds, burg-

hers, and ministers – chose four representatives to sit permanently, and in December 1637 these Tables (as they were
called) drew up a joint Supplication demanding, now, not
only the withdrawal of the Liturgy, but also a removal of
bishops from the Privy Council. The reply of Charles was
refusal, supplemented by a warning that the authors of such
supplications would be punished as traitors; but his formal
proclamation in Stirling, Linlithgow, and Edinburgh was
met publicly and at once by formal Protestations in the
name of the four orders. The Tables, in fact, had constituted
themselves as an Opposition; but they soon realized that
mere opposition was not enough, for the opponents of the
King were not all of one mind. The old 'Melvillian' party
denounced bishops altogether; others would accept a
moderate episcopacy, but not the Five Articles; others,
again, repudiated only the new Liturgy. Some unifying
bond was needed and it was found by recourse to a precedent which had served well in the crises of the Reformation,
namely, a 'Covenant'.

The Covenant was meant to be defensive but, when it
professed to maintain both Charles I and Presbyterianism,
it brought not peace but a sword. 'Now,' said Spottiswoode
(as reported), 'all that we have been doing these thirty years
past is thrown down at once.' He himself fled to England
and most of his brethren fled too.

It was the bishops who were the core of absolutism in
Scotland and, with their fall, Charles was brought to the
brink of civil war. 'Thorough', as Charles's policies were
known, was beginning to wear thin in England too, and
before long all three kingdoms were involved. Yet it was in
Scotland that the struggle began, and the first hostilities
were 'The Bishops' Wars'.

The Bishops' Wars, 1639–40

The 'Covenanters', steadily becoming more exigent, went
on to demand a 'free Assembly' and a 'free Parliament';
and it was plain that, if they could not gain their end under

the existing government, they would erect a government of their own – always under the king – which would give them what they wanted. On that point, Charles had no illusions: as long as the Covenant existed he would have no more power than 'the Duke in Venice'. Yet, true to his nature and believing that his opponents were not united, he tried to temporize. By September he instructed his Commissioner in Scotland, the Marquis of Hamilton, to promise a free Assembly and a free Parliament, while at the same time he invited subscriptions to the King's Covenant, which repeated that of 1581, but condemned the National Covenant and questioned the right of lay elders to attend the General Assembly.

His manoeuvres had little success, and the General Assembly which met in Glasgow Cathedral in November persisted in sitting on (though the Commissioner dissolved it), and abolished episcopacy, condemned the 'Five Articles' and the Liturgy, and asserted the right of lay elders to attend. It deposed, and in some cases excommunicated, the bishops and other clergy who opposed the Covenant, and it secured the support of Argyll, not a good soldier, but almost an independent prince. Ambitious and narrow, Argyll yet adhered to his principles: he said upon the scaffold in May 1661, 'God hath laid engagements upon Scotland. We are tied by Covenants to religion and reformation ... and it passeth the power of all the magistrates under heaven to absolve from the oath of God.'

War was inevitable, but the two campaigns which followed were one-sided affairs. Charles intended to make a tripartite attack in the spring of 1639: on the Border, from the Firth of Forth, and from Ireland. But money was short and recruits were reluctant; with difficulty he mustered 21,000 ill-trained men at Berwick while an attempt by Hamilton in the Firth of Forth accomplished nothing. In Scotland, on the other hand, there was an enthusiasm which sent ladies of quality to carry earth for the fortifications near Edinburgh; Covenanting nobles raised regiments in their own countries and none were busier in bearing the rub-

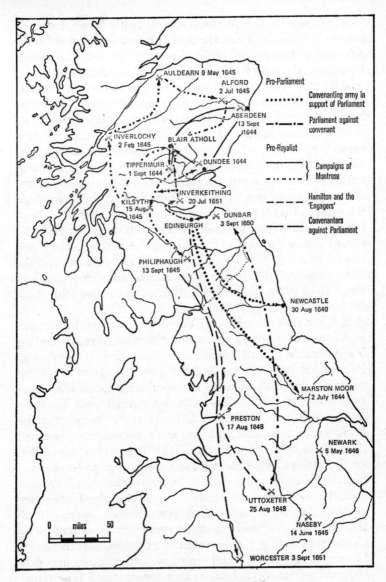

Pro-Parliament

· · · · · Convenanting army in support of Parliament

— · — · Parliament against convenant

Pro-Royalist

———— Campaigns of Montrose

— · · — · · Hamilton and the 'Engagers'

— — — Convenanters against Parliament

AULDEARN 9 May 1645
ALFORD 2 Jul 1645
ABERDEEN 13 Sept 1644
INVERLOCHY 2 Feb 1645
BLAIR ATHOLL
DUNDEE 1644
TIPPERMUIR 1 Sept 1644
INVERKEITHING 20 Jul 1651
KILSYTH 15 Aug 1645
DUNBAR 3 Sept 1650
EDINBURGH
PHILIPHAUGH 13 Sept 1645
NEWCASTLE 30 Aug 1640
MARSTON MOOR 2 July 1644
PRESTON 17 Aug 1648
NEWARK 5 May 1646
UTTOXETER 25 Aug 1648
NASEBY 14 June 1645
WORCESTER 3 Sept 1651

0 — miles — 50

4. Scotland During the Civil Wars

bish for use in the fortification of Leith 'than ladies of honour'. Veterans from the Swedish service hurried home. Alexander Leslie, the defender of Stralsund, was made General; Alexander Hamilton of Redhouse, inventor of a mobile gun, was made General of Artillery; and Robert Munro, the main prototype of 'Dugald Dalgetty', became Major-General, Commander of the Foot. Doubtless national patriotism and local loyalties played their part, and certain areas – episcopal Aberdeen, for example, and most of the Highlands – stood aloof; but that a great wave of religious enthusiasm swept across Scotland is not to be denied. When the armies came face to face at Duns Law, the Covenanters, who did not wish to fight against the King, extracted from him a promise that he would concede all their demands; he would not acknowledge the Glasgow Assembly, but there should be a free Assembly and a free Parliament, and, if the Scots dissolved the Tables, disbanded their army, and restored the castles, he would withdraw his forces (the Pacification of Berwick, 18 June 1639).

Neither side was sincere. The King, after trying to win over some of his opponents, went off south without attending the Assembly or Parliament; and, when the Assembly met in 1639, it not only ratified the proceedings of 1638 but asked the Privy Council to make subscription of the Covenant obligatory. The Privy Council agreed, and Traquair as Commissioner ratified all its Acts; he knew that the King would not yield and that the Covenanters weakened their cause by denying to others the liberty they demanded for themselves. When the Estates met (August to November) fresh difficulties arose. There being no bishops, Traquair himself nominated the nobles to sit on the Committee of the 'Articles'; but, when the Articles approved all the Acts of Assembly and recommended constitutional changes including the permanent exclusion of the clergy, he refused to give the royal assent to their findings and prorogued Parliament without its own consent until June 1640.

Charles, for his part, again prepared to fight; but the English 'Short Parliament' (April–May 1640) granted no supply, and he could muster but a weak and half-hearted army. The Scots, on the other hand, not only equipped a strong army but effected a constitutional revolution of great importance. Disregarding a further prorogation, the Estates met on 2 June and, finding no royal commissioner, elected their own President and asserted themselves a valid Parliament. They abolished the clerical estate; they ratified all the Acts of the late General Assembly, including that of making the Covenant obligatory; passed (in advance of England) a Triennial Act, and voted supplies on an improved assessment.

Two other things they did of the first importance. They dispensed with the 'Articles' and, following a fourteenth-century precedent, entrusted the authority of Parliament to a Committee of the three Estates. The earls and lords, though they attended in strength, were outnumbered in a unicameral assembly, and the Committee chosen could and did make common cause with the Commission of the General Assembly. The Presbyterian Church took a firm hold upon politics and found an influential leader in Argull. In a session which lasted less than a fortnight, the whole face of the constitution was altered.

The clash between the armies was brief and decisive. Leslie crossed the Tweed on 20 August, forced a crossing of the Tyne at Newburn and, about a week later, entered Newcastle, at once taking control of the coal trade and, before long, he occupied the whole of Northumberland and Durham. Charles, unable to resist and coerced into summoning a new parliament in England, was driven to a meeting of Commissioners at Ripon. There a bargain was made whereby the Scots should advance no further and should receive subsistence from the occupied lands at the rate of £850 a day (16 October 1640).

The first consequences of the Scottish success were seen in England. The Long Parliament, which met on 3 November, launched a violent attack upon the King's ministers and, in 1641, swept away the whole apparatus of 'Thorough' in England – 'No feare of raising the Parliament as long as the ladds about Newcastle sitts still', wrote the Scots divine, Robert Baillie. The English Parliament, which had refused to be dissolved without its own consent, ratified the terms of Ripon in 1641, and the triumphant Scots army marched home with £200,000 to its credit.

Charles in Scotland, 1641 – August to November

Meanwhile, Charles had decided to try his fortunes in Scotland, where dissensions had appeared in the ranks of his opponents. The remains of the old episcopal party still survived; many Scots still held that the King after all was the King; some of the nobles were alarmed to find that the power wrested from the Crown was passing to mere lairds and ministers; others, feeling that the recent constitutional changes were outside the terms of the Covenant, had united themselves in the 'Band of Cumbernauld'. In the last-named group was the young Montrose who, in 1639, had been conspicuous in enforcing the Covenant in the north-east, had captured Huntly in a very questionable manner and had been the first man to cross the Tweed. He, however, was imprisoned in Edinburgh Castle because he could not substantiate his accusation that Argyll was seeking the Crown for himself.

Charles had hoped to gain popularity by confirming the Acts of 1639 against episcopacy, but he found that the Scots considered their own ratification sufficient, and they now went on to demand that Officers of State, Privy Councillors, and Lords of Session should be appointed by him with the advice of Parliament. This point he reluctantly surrendered; but while his complaisance did not win him new adherents the efforts of his old friends who plotted to kidnap Argyll, Hamilton, and Hamilton's brother the Earl of Lanark, made things worse. There is no evidence that Charles knew of any such design, but 'The Incident' served to discredit him; and he had made little progress in creating a party when he was recalled to London by the news of the Ulster massacres. He may well have hoped that England, and possibly Scotland too, would unite behind him for rescue and vengeance.

The Solemn League and Covenant, 1643

There had been close links between Ulster and Scotland for centuries. Lowland Protestants had settled in Ulster in some numbers after 1603, but Highland Catholics, especially Macdonalds, had conquered the glens of Antrim several decades before. In 1641 the religious tensions in this complex and unstable society erupted in a great Catholic rising marked by massacres of the Protestants. This Ulster crisis brought things in England to a head: plainly an army was necessary, but Parliament would not, and the King could not, agree to the other party controlling it. The tension between the Crown and the Commons steadily increased. The King's attempt personally to arrest five members failed in January 1642; he left London for York in the following spring, and, after a futile negotiation, raised his standard at Nottingham on 22 August. In October the first battle of the Civil War was fought at Edgehill (drawn) and, before the year was done, King and Parliament had each appealed to the Scots.

The Privy Council would have received only the King's message, but the Standing Committee of the Estates (known as the Conservators of the Peace), hand in hand with the Commission of the General Assembly, insisted that the message of the English Parliament should also be read.

The issue was not long in doubt. A Convention held in July and a General Assembly which met in August accepted the overture of the English Parliament, and the resultant treaty took the form of 'The Solemn League and Covenant'. By its terms, the contracting parties engaged themselves to preserve the reformed religion in England and Ireland 'according to the Word of God and the example of the best reformed Churches'; to try to extirpate Popery and Prelacy, to maintain the rights of Parliament and the

King's personal authority in preservation of the true religion and liberties of the kingdoms, to suppress all opponents of the League, to preserve peace between England and Scotland; and mutually entered into the Covenant, acknowledging their own short-comings and professing their desire to amend their own lives.

The English were 'for a civil league', wrote Baillie; 'we for a religious Covenant'. Yet the treaty is not to be attributed entirely to Scottish coercion. The Westminster Assembly had been brought into being by the vote of both Houses in England and members of that Assembly, as well as members of Parliament, negotiated the Scottish Treaty. Moreover, the object of that Assembly was professedly to produce a unity with other reformed Churches – those of France and Holland, for example – besides that of Scotland, and one of the wisest Scotsmen, Alexander Henderson (see p. 203) had already written: 'We are not to conceive that they will embrace our form. A new form must be set down for us all'. It is fair to remember too that Scotland abandoned her own standards in favour of those of the Westminster Assembly – the Directory of Public Worship (1644–5), the Confession of Faith, the two Catechisms, and the metrical versions of the Psalms (1647). It may be added that the redoubtable 'proofs', which accompanied the larger Catechism, were demanded by the English Commons, and that the six Scottish Commissioners who 'attended' were not members of the Westminster Assembly.

What is true is that the Scottish Commissioners in London failed to realize that, though both Capital and Commons were at this time Presbyterian in sentiment, a great part even of Puritan England was not; and that the overture to Scotland had been dictated partly by the desire of the Commons to gain an ally against sectarianism. On both sides of the Border the example of 'the best reformed Churches' was understood to be that of Scotland; and to tempt Anglicans, English Independents and Irish Papists into the Presbyterian fold was a folly, if not worse. For that folly, however, Scotland was not alone responsible.

In Scotland the Solemn League and Covenant was approved by the General Assembly and ratified by a Convention only very doubtfully authorized by Charles (17 August); in England it was passed by both Houses, after which the Commons and the members of the Westminster Assembly took the oath (25 September), and a few Lords gave their adherence later. Only in the spring of 1644 did the two English Houses establish a Committee of both Kingdoms, but, by that time, the alliance was already in action. In mid-January 1644 Alexander Leslie, now Earl of Leven, crossed the Border with 18,000 foot, 3,000 horse and guns. The first of the 'Articles of War', which set forth his discipline, was that every soldier was to give his oath 'according to the heads sworn by me in the Solemne League and Covenant of the three Kingdomes'; the following regulations enjoined strict morality as well as resolute performance of military duty.

Sweeping the royal forces before him, Leslie advanced to York which was besieged by the Parliamentarians, and played an important part in the victory of Marston Moor over Rupert, who had hurried north to relieve the city (2 July); the victory was mainly due to Cromwell, but the Scots were annoyed that their own services were belittled. Leven returned to the north, occupied Newcastle in October and made his winter quarters there. Thereafter the Scottish share of the war, though it occupied numbers of the King's forces, was not dramatic and was marked by growing antipathy between them and their allies.

Pressed by the English to move south, Leven declined to do so, being conscious of the fact that the Scots were regarded as aliens. He was also apprehensive about Montrose, who was stirring up Royalist opposition to the government of the Covenant in Scotland. In the end Leven did descend as far as Hereford, but he soon went back and he was besieging Newark in Nottinghamshire when, unexpectedly, Charles presented himself at the quarters of the French

Ambassador, Montreuil, who was in the Scottish camp (5 May 1646).

The arrival of the King heightened the misgivings between the allies which had become evident. The truth is that England did not like the Covenant. Parliament, when it abolished episcopacy in 1646, kept the new 'Presbyterian' establishment under its own control and to the Scots this was Erastianism; the Parliamentary Ordinance that every member of the army should take the Covenant was not obeyed. Many of the soldiers, including Cromwell, were Independents and there appeared a widening breach between them and the Presbyterians: the latter were still Royalist and there grew a suspicion that they did not want to beat the King absolutely.

Charles, whose belief that England really wanted a King was not ill-founded, felt that, though the Presbyterians would insist on the Covenant, they would leave him with political power; and that the Independents, though they would curb his authority, would interfere less with his religion. Determined to exploit the situation, he had broken out of Oxford ready to deal with either side, and his arrival in the Scottish camp was almost an afterthought. The Scots had pledged themselves to the Covenant; Charles was equally plain that he would not sign the Covenant; but some arrangement was made. Newark surrendered at the royal command, and the Scots marched north with the king to Newcastle. There, though he refused to take the Covenant, he allowed the moderate Alexander Henderson, at whose door death was already knocking, to try to remove his scruples.

In London there was great anger. Parliament and Army alike were shocked; on 19 May the Commons voted against the continuance of the Scottish Army in England, and offered £400,000 (instead of the £2,000,000 demanded by the Scots) to pay off that army provided it surrendered the King's person before it left England. The Scots accepted, but they were in a quandary. They could not remain in England; nor could they return to Scotland with an intransigent monarch. They therefore tried ineffectively to stipulate for the safety of his person before they marched away, and Charles was taken to Holmby House in Northamptonshire where, on 3 June, he was arrested by Cornet Joyce in the name of the Army. Even so he by no means lost heart. Already he had been receiving reasonable offers from both Presbyterians and Independents, and dissensions had appeared in the ranks of the Army itself. A case for the re-establishment of the royal power above the contending factions was gaining strength. In England the Solemn League and Covenant had failed of its purpose.

Its fortunes in Scotland must now be considered. Here, too, it bred enmity as well as support. Support it certainly had; for, without any great physical force at its disposal, it exercised a stringent coercion over the Scottish people. Failure to take the Covenant was punished with severe penalties; there was a fierce attack upon witches, and a fresh crusade against the 'monuments of idolatry' which survived in some churches. Intolerance, cruelty, and vandalism are not to be defended, yet they must be compared with the other intolerances of that age. It was not only in Scotland that witches were burned. To us it seems a shocking thing that a good and learned man like Professor John Forbes of Aberdeen must be banished for mere inability to take the Covenant; yet Scotland did not descend to the whip, the pillory, and the hangman's knife in the manner of 'Thorough'. Scotland, in the main, accepted this harsh discipline; it was not all terrorism. There was a sense of cooperation in individual dedication. The true Covenanter saw life *sub specie aeternitatis* in a manner not easily understood by a materialistic age.

Montrose's Venture, 1644–5

Although opposition smouldered beneath the surface, its one great expression was founded less upon resentment against 'discipline' than upon the tradition of the Highlands and the genius of one man – James Graham, Marquis of Montrose (1612–50).

Montrose would have no part in the Solemn League. When first he offered his sword to the King at Oxford, he had met with a very cool reception, doubtless in view of his early support for the National Covenant. When, however, the King felt that the Hamiltons were useless to him, he listened to the overtures of the bold, handsome, eloquent young man. In the spring of 1644 Montrose was offered the commission of Viceroy and Captain-General in Scotland. This he declined for fear of arousing jealousy and the commission was given to the King's nephew, Maurice, brother of Rupert of the Rhine. Montrose himself went north with the title only of Lieutenant-General. His hopes of gaining recruits from the Borders and the Lowlands and of obtaining reinforcements from Ireland were disappointed and, after Marston Moor, there was nothing to expect from the north of England. The few friends remaining to him rode for Oxford. He started with them, but doubled back and, disguised as the servant of two officers wearing the uniform of Leven's troopers, entered Scotland and made his way to his own country.

For a time he was safe among his own Grahams, but even they would not rise for a chief who brought nothing with him but an empty title. Suddenly help came to him. One thousand or so wild Irishmen and Islemen landed on the West Coast under the command of the gigantic Alasdair MacDonald, known sometimes by the name of his father, Coll Keitach, which appears in Milton's sonnet as Colkitto. With him came Manus Roe O'Cahan. Both men had bad records in the Ulster massacres. They had courage, however, and their men were skilled in arms, had some discipline, and understood guerilla warfare very well. Round this small core there gathered a little force with which Montrose achieved a series of astounding successes.

Erupting suddenly from Blair, he routed Lord Elcho at Tippermuir on 1 September 1644, and occupied Perth; on the thirteenth he gave the city of Aberdeen to the sack;

then, finding only limited support from the Gordons, who remembered his capture of Huntly in 1639, he vanished into the hills. In December, having crossed passes deemed impassable in mid-winter, he carried fire and sword through the lands of the Campbells. On his retiral it seemed that he must be trapped in the Great Glen, but he surprised his pursuers at Inverlochy (February 1645), and inflicted a bloody defeat upon his enemies whose chief, Argyll, fled in a galley. In April he seized Dundee; then, trying the north again, he beat Covenanting Armies at Auldearn near Nairn in May, and at Alford on the Don in July. Next month, having gathered all his forces, he won a pitched battle at Kilsyth (between Stirling and Glasgow) so completely that the Lowlands lay at his feet. Jubilant, he planned to cross the Border with a great army and redeem the cause which seemed to have been lost at Naseby (see map, p. 207).

His hopes deceived him. He found few recruits, his Highlanders melted away and, on 12 September, he was surprised and routed at Philiphaugh near Selkirk by David Leslie, nephew of Leven. The Covenanting victory was stained by a massacre of some prisoners, like that which followed the Battle of Naseby. Montrose, who escaped, tried in vain to raise the Highlands again, and in July 1646, at the royal command, disbanded his army near Blairgowrie and sailed for Norway. Four of his distinguished followers were executed in St Andrews and in Glasgow after parliamentary proceedings which resembled those taken in England against Strafford and Laud.

Montrose's victories have been discounted on the ground that they were gained against unseasoned troops whose commanders were overruled by ministerial committees; but it is impossible to deny him military ability of a high order and a personality which could win the hearts of the Highlanders. What is to be criticized is the recklessness which attended his conduct. His spirit appears both in his prose and in his poetry. Sovereignty must be absolute:

> As Alexander I will reign
> And I will reign alone
> My thoughts did ever more disdain
> A rival on my throne.

Single-minded in his desire to save the monarchy and convinced that he alone could do it, he did not count the cost. He loosed upon Scotland Irishmen whose hands were red from the Ulster massacres and Highlanders who, in their own feuds, neither gave nor expected quarter. At least ten thousand died as a result of the 1644–5 campaign, alienating Royalists and neutrals alike. Brilliant as was his campaign, it restored to his opponents the moral ascendancy which they had lost by their intolerance, and served to unite all moderate men in a party prepared to support the King upon moderate terms. But events were to show that moderation did not obtain even the limited success which had attended reckless resolution.

The Engagement, 1647–8

The union of the moderates was the more easily achieved because the soldiers of the Solemn League who recrossed the Tweed in February 1647 came home disillusioned. Scotland had helped to beat the king; she had surrendered the old Scottish theological standards for those of Westminster; and England was not performing her part of the bargain. It was obvious that the English army, now gaining an ascendancy in politics, would do nothing for the Covenant, and it seemed a not unworthy thing that the Covenanters should try for at least part of their end by joining those who were prepared to restore the King on condition that he gave Presbyterianism a trial.

In December 1647 King Charles, now a prisoner of the Army in the Isle of Wight, made a secret 'Engagement' with three Scottish Commissioners who promised him the aid of Scottish armies on condition that, once restored, he would establish Presbyterianism for three years, and suppress Sectaries, though the Covenant was not to be made obligatory.

When the Scottish Estates met in 1648 a change of spirit was visible. The General Assembly had lost its influence; the Covenanters were in a minority and there was general support for Hamilton who led the 'Engagers'. Something like an ultimatum was sent to England, demanding the liberation of the King, the fulfilment of the Covenant, and the disbanding of the English army; but, when in July Hamilton crossed the Border, he met with utter disaster. He came too late, for English and Welsh risings were already suppressed; his army was no longer the well-organized force of the 'Bishops' Wars', for it had been raised in the face of a 'protest' from the stalwarts of the Kirk; and Hamilton had little save his courage to recommend him. He advanced down the Western route with incredible slowness and, in mid-August, Cromwell came down on his left flank through Ribblesdale and shattered his army at Preston, Wigan, and Warrington (17–19 August). He himself, with the few troops left to him, surrendered at Uttoxeter in Staffordshire on 25 August. Seven months later he was beheaded outside Westminster Hall, though he was a Scottish officer carrying out a duty with which he had been charged by a Scottish Parliament.

The Death of the King, 30 January 1649

On the news of Hamilton's defeat the opponents of the Engagement at once took control of Scotland. Under Loudoun and Eglinton, 6,000 western Covenanters advanced upon Edinburgh in the 'Whiggamore's Raid'.* They were well received. Argyll and the anti-Engagers or 'Protesters' at once took office and made haste to come to terms with Cromwell, who arrived in Edinburgh early in October, supped with Argyll and Warriston, and agreed with them to oppose all forms of 'Malignancy' (Royalism). This *entente* between a party professing complete acceptance of the Covenant and the soldier who was the embodiment of

---

*Possibly the origin of the word 'Whig'. 'Whiggam' was used in the west country to encourage horses.

'Independence' was dictated by both expediency and logic. Both sides profited immediately, but the gain of the Protesters was short-lived.

They made their policy plain at once: the Estates which met on 4 January repudiated the Engagement, renewed as a body the Solemn League and Covenant, and passed the 'Act of Classes' which distinguished four degrees of wickedness among the enemies of the Covenant and disabled all from holding any office until they had shown true repentance. Yet already they knew that all was not well between them and their new ally. They are found urging the Scottish Commissioners in London to avoid any pretext for war with England and yet to dissociate themselves from any sentence to be pronounced upon the King. For Cromwell had used his settlement with them in a way of which they disapproved. Secure now from Scottish interference, the army in England pressed on its attack upon the 'Man of Blood'. The Scottish protest was vain. The King, sentenced by a court which he did not recognize, was beheaded outside the Palace of Whitehall on 30 January.

He died with the utmost courage, still convinced that he had been right all along. As he looked out into eternity, he warned his hearers that unless they gave what was due 'to God, the King, and the people, they would never be happy ... A subject and a Sovereign are clean different things'.

In his belief that on his death England would be without a sovereign he was wrong: yet he was prescient. England was proclaimed a free Commonwealth, governed by the representatives of the people in Parliament; but, in fact, the matter had 'returned to the sword again', and all Cromwell's endeavour to provide a Constitution availed only to 'put a wig upon the point of a sword'. The new sovereign of England was the matchless army. For the moment the English army had no control over Scotland, and the first thing Scotland did when she knew that her King was dead was to proclaim King Charles II. War between Scotland under Argyll and England under Cromwell was now inevitable.

CHAPTER 12

CROMWELL

'K. Charles behedit at Whytehall gate, in England, by that traiterous parliament and armey (all honest men being formerly remoued,) one Tuesday, the 30 of Januarij, 1649, . . . Prince Charles proclaimed King of Grate Britane, France and Irland, at Edinburghe crosse, by Illa and Snaudon herauldes; the Lord Chanceler, Loudon, black veluet goune, read the proclamatione.'

So the dispassionate words of the Lyon King, Sir James Balfour of Denmilne, record a momentous transaction. Scotland had her King, and with him came new difficulties. On the one hand her hope that she could blame the English army for the execution and continue the Solemn League with England was vain; for now the army ruled all. On the other Charles II would not accept the Covenants; he would agree to maintain Presbyterianism in Scotland, but for England and Ireland he would promise nothing without consent of the parliaments of these countries.

Behind this strictly 'constitutional' attitude he was marking time; he still had adherents in Britain and Ireland, and he hoped that his family connections would bring him help from abroad. When this hope failed he allowed Montrose to make another venture in Scotland, which in public he disowned. The venture failed disastrously: on 27 April 1650 the little expedition was crushed at Carbisdale in Sutherland by a vigorous 'Protester', Colonel Strachan, and a few days later its leader was captured. He was led to Edinburgh with many indignities, brought before parliament, and sentenced to be hanged on a gallows and his body afterwards dismembered.

The sentence was carried out at the Market Cross on 21 May; but the handsome face of the victim, his resolute speech before his judges, and his undaunted courage gave him a place in the hearts of Scotsmen which he still holds, though their minds may not approve his full career. He died to no purpose. Charles had already decided that he must accept the Scottish offers. This he did at Breda on 1 May; and on 23 June, before he landed at Garmouth at the mouth of the Spey, he signed both the Covenants.

At last Scotland had a 'Covenanted' King. Since the King was Charles II the impossible situation had an element of comedy. Yet those who denounce its absurdity should remember that the exile got no help from his illustrious friends abroad, and came to Scotland only because there he could find men to fight and die for him as the figurehead of an unrealizable ideal. The incongruities involved soon revealed themselves. The Covenanting leaders treated the King with outward respect, but they found it necessary to persuade the world – and perhaps themselves – that they were still true to their old cause, and, hearkening to the Commissioners of the General Assembly, they demanded concessions that could only be regarded as indignities by Charles, among them a profession that, though he must honour his father, he was humbled and afflicted in spirit before God for his father's opposition to the work of God, and for his mother's idolatry.

Even so the Scottish Government could not satisfy the zealots, and already danger threatened from the English, who had a fixed principle for dealing with Scottish recalcitrants: namely, invasion. Fairfax refused to take command on the ground that the alliance still existed, but the army had no hesitation. In July Cromwell crossed the Border with 16,000 men, mainly veterans, and a fleet sailed up the east coast in support. Cromwell hoped, indeed, to obtain his end without fighting and his advance was preceded by an appeal to 'all God's elect to unite with their fellow elect in England' and by a letter to the General Assembly containing the sentence 'I beseech you in the bowels of Christ, think it possible you may be mistaken.' When the Scots replied with an appeal to the Covenant, he stated his case with great clarity – it did not induce to the interest of Godliness that 'a King should be taken in by you to be imposed upon us' especially when that King was the very Head of the Malignants for whom a Popish army was now fighting in Ireland.

His appeal had no effect upon the Scots, and soon he found that they were as ready in arms as in argument. They had gathered a host which, though it was weakened by the exclusion of 'Malignants' by the Act of Classes (January, 1649), had some of the virtue of the army which had fought the Bishops' Wars. Leven was made general, but as he was now ageing it was his nephew, David Leslie, who did the business, and he did it well. When Cromwell, who needs must keep contact with his fleet, endeavoured to secure Leith, he was repulsed by a well-disposed defence; and when, having marched round Edinburgh from the south, he attempted Queensferry, he found Leslie strongly posted on Corstorphine Hill and made nothing of it. Deprived of supplies he withdrew to Dunbar in bad shape; and there he was saved by a mistake of his enemies. Confident that the English were retreating to their ships, and suffering from atrocious weather on the high ground, the Scots came down from Doune Hill to find that the Brock Burn and the broken ground which had covered their front now deprived them of all tactical freedom. Cromwell, with a soldier's eye, saw his opportunity. He broke the Scottish right after a stiff action and then rolled up the whole line. Over 3,000 Covenanters were killed and no mercy was shown to the fugitives. The 10,000 or so prisoners taken were treated with callous disregard; some, who were dismissed, were in such a condition that they were unlikely to fight again; of the others few survived to reach 'the Plantations' to which they were exiled.

Cromwell at once occupied Edinburgh, visited Glasgow, and set his grip upon the Lowlands, whilst the Scottish party which had condemned the reception of the King sent to the Committee of Estates a 'Remonstrance' wherein they rejected Charles until he had proved the sincerity of his profession. Yet the clear-sighted Cromwell saw that the business was not yet ended; the Kirk, he thought, had 'done their do', but he believed the King would 'set up on his own score now; wherein he will find many friends'.

His prediction was correct. The defection of the 'Remonstrants' made easier an alliance between the moderate Presbyterians and the Royalists. In November the Committee of Estates passed a Resolution condemning the 'Remonstrance', and most of the ministers became 'Resolutioners'. Charles was crowned at Scone on 1 January 1651, but though it was Argyll who placed the crown upon his head, the power of the Covenanters steadily declined. When the Estates met in May the Act of Classes, already disregarded, was formally rescinded and vigorous measures were taken to provide a new army. Meanwhile the English were pushing on; the differences between 'Remonstrants' and 'Resolutioners' aided them, and may have had their part in the easy capitulation of Edinburgh Castle. With his rear secured, Cromwell in June 1651 advanced against Stirling where again he found Leslie so well posted that he did not try direct attack. Instead he sent a force across the Firth of Forth under Lambert, who won a sharp action at Pitreavie near Inverkeithing, followed up at once himself and pushed on to Perth. Charles and his army, seeing their flank threatened and the road to the south open, set off boldly to England. There they found no recruits, and on 3 September, the anniversary of Dunbar, Cromwell obtained his 'crowning mercy' at Worcester where he annihilated the invaders.

Meanwhile, in Scotland, Monck took Stirling. Soon afterwards he captured the whole acting government of Scotland, the Committee of Estates, at Alyth, and on 1 September sacked Dundee, with the massacre of its citizens. By the spring of 1652 Dunottar Castle alone held out for Charles, but it too fell on 25 February, though the Regalia, saved by the ingenuity of two women,* were buried under the floor of the Kirk of Kinneff where they remained until the King enjoyed his own again. Argyll

* Mrs Granger, wife of the minister of Kinneff and Mrs Ogilvie, wife of the Governor of the Castle.

was compelled to come to terms. The cause of Charles was utterly lost and himself a fugitive.

Attempts at Union

The first inclination of the victors was to treat conquered Scotland as a mere province, but early in 1652 Commissioners appeared at Dalkeith with a 'Declaration' of the English Parliament. By the terms of this the Gospel was to be preached, and liberty of worship assured to the whole people; Scotland and England were to be made into one Commonwealth; the expenses incurred by England were to be met by confiscation of the estates of those who had served in Hamilton's expedition; and the whole nation was to enjoy all the privileges of English subjects. Accordingly, burghs and shires were to elect representatives to give assent to the Union, and a tax was imposed on every county for the payment of the English army. The representatives of shires and burghs found that they must simply accept the idea of Union without discussion; and when, later, Scottish deputies were sent to London to discuss its terms, they found that they were to be offered only thirty seats in the joint Parliament. The ejection of the Rump in April 1653 delayed progress, and though in Barebones's Parliament (which contained only five Scots members out of 140) an Act for Union was read twice, that Parliament was dismissed with its work unfinished. Then Cromwell took office as Lord Protector under the 'Instrument of Government', a document which gave Scotland thirty members out of 460, and an Ordinance of Union was produced by Council in April 1654. According to this, Scotland was to send twenty members from the shires and ten from the burghs; some of the shires were grouped together; and whilst Edinburgh was given two members, the remaining fifty-six burghs were divided into groups of half a dozen or so. In the event, only twenty-one members were chosen, and many of these were government servants. It was only in the Protector's second Parliament (1656–7) at which thirty

225

members sat for Scotland that the Ordinance of Union became an Act. To the Parliament summoned by Oliver's son (1658–9), Scotland also elected thirty members, only eleven of them Scots (including the Marquis of Argyll who was returned unopposed for Aberdeenshire despite general unpopularity and heavy debts); the rest were English and included ten army officers. However, the recall of the Long Parliament in 1659 threw doubt on all the Cromwellian legislation and a new Bill foundered on the vexed question of religious toleration, which the Presbyterians regarded as wicked. No settlement was reached and, though some Scots still hoped that the 'Free Parliament' which Monck promised would be a Union Parliament, that hope was vain.

Throughout the whole negotiation the English attitude had been one of condescension to a conquered people; the Scots counted for little at Westminster and one Englishman remarked that 'Scottish members are like a wooden leg tied to a natural body.' Plainly the Union was not everywhere popular in England, nor was it really popular in Scotland, though the English governed well. The Reverend Robert Blair was not alone in his opinion that 'As for the embodying of Scotland with England it will be as when the poor bird is embodied into the hawk that hath eaten it up.'

The English Administration

The eight Commissioners sent to administer Scotland, and the Council of State which replaced them in 1655, were tolerant as well as firm. They made and kept good order, suppressed the 'moss-troopers', and in 1654 crushed a serious rising headed by Glencairn and by Middleton who had come from Charles with Commissions.* Commander-in-Chief Monck was tireless and efficient, and in July 1654 one of his officers, the capable Morgan, broke Middleton's force so utterly at Dalnaspidal that it never rallied again. For the rest, the military occupation was not oppressive,

* For their later careers see p. 232.

though the Cromwellian soldiers were not all saints; they killed unnecessarily at Dunbar and Dundee, and in Dunfermline they broke the 'Kirk-brod' and stole the accumulated collections. Yet they were well disciplined; and the four great citadels which were erected at Ayr, Inverlochy (Fort William), Leith, and St Johnston (Perth), as well as many other forts served to give employment to areas whose economy had been shaken by the turmoil. It was the Cromwellians who ejected the Dutch from their post at Lerwick* and built a fort there to prevent the abuse of the Scottish fisheries by the Hollanders. It is true that Scotland was heavily taxed to maintain the garrison, and that severe burdens were imposed upon houses which had supported the King; but a great part of the finance required for the army came from England.

The good order established by military force was supplemented by good civil justice. The jurisdictions of Privy Council and Court of Session were replaced by seven Commissioners – four Englishmen and three Scots – who showed themselves more equitable than their predecessors because they were outside the close-knit ties of family and friendship. It is not true that after the Restoration Lord President Gilmour explained their impartiality on the ground that they were 'a' kinless loons', but he does seem to have said 'De'il speed them! they had neither kith nor kin'.

The form of religion which the English practised was very like that of the Scottish Kirk; but they declined to accept that Presbytery was *de jure divino* the one true form, and established their own more tolerant system. This they did more easily because the Scottish Kirk was weakened by the continued struggle between 'Remonstrants' and 'Resolutioners' and because the piety of the Protector was obviously sincere. By the terms of the Humble Petition

*Before the advent of the Dutch, Scalloway was the capital of Shetland, but the Dutch fishing boats congregated in Bressay Sound in such numbers as to stimulate the growth of a trading village at nearby Lerwick on the east coast of the mainland to supply the fresh food, clothes and recreation (which included pony-trekking) of these seasonal visitors.

toleration was not extended to Papists and Prelatists, but even they were left alone if they did not call attention to themselves. Sectaries enjoyed full toleration; and though the Presbyterian Kirk was no longer able to make civil penalties follow upon its censures, Kirk-Sessions, Presbyteries, and Synods functioned as before. In its general policy the Government upheld the Protesters because their opponents, the Resolutioners, seemed to hanker after monarchy, and because the General Assembly, where they predominated, continued to claim independence from the secular state. Colonel Cotterell in July 1653 simply marched the fathers and brethren out of town between files of soldiers. Thereafter there was no Assembly and the Resolutioners met only informally in 'Consultations' of ministers. Both sides sent deputations to the Protector; to both he gave a fair hearing, but reconcile them he could not.

None the less in Scotland religion flourished. As upholders of morality the Puritans were as strict as the Presbyterians, and it has been argued that the ministers, now debarred from politics, gave more time to their parishes and were stirred to emulate the earnest preaching of the Sectaries.

The Universities, still regarded as the nurseries of the Church, fared well financially, though there the Protesters began to predominate. Their small revenues were increased from the patronage of vanished bishops and deans, and they received grants from the Customs. At Glasgow the Protester Patrick Gillespie, who was made Principal, was able to complete the famous College in the High Street, a lovely example of Scottish Baronial (now, alas! vanished) and Principal John Adamson of Edinburgh was on excellent terms with Colonel Fairfax, who interested himself in Scottish antiquities. Economically the Universities were prosperous, though the academic standard seems to have fallen.

Prosperity did revive after 1650, but it was not spread evenly over the country: amongst the burghs, for example, Aberdeen and Glasgow seem to have fared well, whereas Dundee and the Fife ports continued to decline. More generally, the money spent by and for the soldiers encouraged trade. The good order encouraged industry, and some new manufactures were introduced; glass was made at Leith, and tradition says that Cromwell's men introduced the knitting of stockings, and the planting of kail. In the words of Burnet, 'We always reckoned those eight years of usurpation a time of great peace and prosperity.' Yet the prosperity was not founded on an enduring basis. The free trade granted by the Declaration of Union brought Scotland into competition with the far stronger English commerce and the greater English shipping. The evidence of Thomas Tucker, sent up to report on the Revenues and Customs of Scotland in 1656, shows that Scottish shipping was in a very poor way.

In the main Scotland fared well during the Usurpation. A Presbyterian could write: 'There were more souls converted to Christ in that short period of time than in any season since the Reformation.' It is possible that from English Puritanism Scotland borrowed the idea that religion was a thing of gloom; but it is clear that the generality of Scotsmen accepted the occupation, if not with enthusiasm, at least with a fair content and, as has been said, some Scots were loath, on the return of the King, to break the Union made by the Protector.

None the less for most Scotsmen the end of the English domination came as a relief, not only because taxation had been heavy and the 'Usurpation' a disgrace, and not only because the Scots were Royalists at heart. Scotland as a whole was wedded to the discipline and doctrine of the Presbyterians which emphasized the direct responsibility of every individual to his Maker, and the eternal significance of his every act. Zeal was not limited to a few enthusiasts. Moderate men, no doubt, had come to realize that the high ambitions of the Solemn League were unobtainable, but many were still convinced that an oath taken by the whole nation, and by every individual, in the presence of God and to God, was a binding thing which could not be loosed either by Protector or by King.

CHAPTER 13

THE RESTORED MONARCHY

1660–85   Charles II (proclaimed 1649;
               crowned 1651)
1685–89   James VII

WITH the recall of Charles II in 1660 Scotland was little
concerned. The enigmatic, tobacco-chewing Monck gave no
indication of his policy when he marched off south, save
that he told an assembly of burghs and shires in Edinburgh
that he was going to restore the liberties of the three nations,
and that they must maintain order whilst he was away.
Possibly he himself had not yet made up his mind; but he
and his army decided the issue. Under his aegis the excluded members of the Long Parliament were recalled;
they re-affirmed the Solemn League; adopted the findings
of the Westminster Assembly and then at last dissolved
themselves. The 'Convention Parliament' which followed
made offers to Charles, recommending that he should
promise complete oblivion of the past and complete toleration for the future. To these suggestions the King would not
entirely agree but, in the famous 'Declaration of Breda'
(April 1660), he promised that any exceptions to an Act
of Oblivion should be settled by Parliament, and that the
arrears of pay should be given to the army. Most important
of all, he declared a 'liberty to tender consciences' to be
ratified by a future Parliament, so that no man should be
troubled 'for differences of opinion in matters of religion
which do not disturb the peace of the kingdom'.

The enthusiasm which greeted him, when he arrived in
Dover on 29 May, probably took him by surprise, and in
Scotland too his return was hailed with a delirious joy. On
19 June, the day of public thanksgiving at Edinburgh, the
spouts of the Cross ran claret, hundreds of glasses were
emptied in the streets, bells, trumpets, drums and cannon

resounded and fireworks from the Castle Hill showed Cromwell chased by the devil to disappear with his pursuer in a grand explosion.

The whole nation rejoiced at the removal of the English yoke and anticipated relief from heavy taxation. The nobles particularly, and ordinary folk, who could not stomach such a strong dose of 'godly discipline', welcomed the passing of the severe rule of the Saints; the 'Resolutioners' were mis-led, perhaps, by the last Acts of the Long Parliament, and some of them believed that they had a 'Covenanted King'; the Protesters, a small minority, were divided amongst themselves – Gillespie himself was soon to try to make terms with the new government. Any doubts in the minds of the Resolutioners, at least, were allayed by a letter from Charles to the Presbytery of Edinburgh (3 September) wherein he said: 'We do also resolve to protect and preserve the Government of the Church of Scotland, as it is settled by law, without violation.'

The general enthusiasm concealed what Burnet, writing after the event, realized as the essence of the situation: 'They had called home the King without a Treaty.' The fact was that Charles had, or soon came to have, two fixed resolves in his mind – on no account to 'go on his travels again'; and to rule, as far as he could, as an absolute King. He understood that the second of these projects would be hard to realize and he did not disclose it openly; but he set to work without delay. The enthusiasm which greeted his return seems to have convinced him that his father had been right all along, and that his subjects, or most of them, now shared his father's views. These views he endeavoured not only to realize, but to expand.

A comparison shows that his conduct of government followed the same lines in Scotland as it did in England. First, he developed arbitrary government with the help of the bishops; then he buttressed his policy by a profession of toleration which might appease Dissenters but would help Roman Catholics.

He did not come to Scotland himself to assume the

regalia saved from Dunottar;* he ruled by Commissioners and the policies of these Commissioners corresponded to those of Charles's ministers in England. In Scotland the period of Clarendon is represented by the commissionerships of Middleton and Rothes; the period of the Cabal is paralleled by the commissionership of Lauderdale; and Charles's 'absolute' period was marked by the commissionership of James, Duke of York (James VII and II).

The first acts of the King were significant. He appointed the Officers of State and the members of the Privy Council without any regard to Parliament. Glencairn was made Chancellor; Rothes, the drunken but able son of a Covenanting father, became President of the Council; some of the councillors were to sit in London along with English councillors, amongst whom Clarendon was conspicuous. This Scottish Council in London had the ear of the King; and Lauderdale, who had redeemed his attendance as an elder at the Westminster Assembly by nine years' imprisonment in the Tower after his capture at Worcester, selected for himself the post of Secretary of this Council which kept him close to his royal master. No new Parliament was called. Instead the 'Committee of Estates' captured at Alyth in 1651 (see p. 224) was assembled under Glencairn and occupied itself in arresting some Protesters, including the fiery minister, James Guthrie, and in forbidding unwarrantable meetings and conventicles held without the King's authority.

Middleton

When, on 1 January 1661, a well-prepared Scottish Parliament met, there appeared as Commissioner John Middleton, a rough soldier newly made an earl. The Estates proceeded

*These were used on formal occasions, as at the riding of Parliament, to represent the royal presence. After the Union of 1707, they were put into a chest and did not see the light of day till 1818 when the romantic Sir Walter Scott got the chest opened.

to rid Charles of some of his enemies, and to endow him with great power. They had been charged by royal authority with the trial of all persons concerned in the late troubles and, though most of the Protesters were released, four victims were found. Argyll, who had himself crowned Charles, had gone to seek an interview with the King in London; he was arrested in the presence chamber, taken to Edinburgh, condemned for compliance with the Cromwellian government (on the evidence of persons who had served Cromwell far more than he) and executed on 24 May. Courage and religious conviction made his last hours a shining example of Christian fortitude. Four days later there suffered the vociferous James Guthrie and a lieutenant, William Govan, who was believed to have been on the scaffold of Charles I. In 1663 Warriston was captured in France, brought home, broken in mind and spirit, and executed. No other lives were taken, whereas in England there were fourteen executions; but in Scotland there were no regicides and if Englishmen had been executed on the same grounds as those which sufficed in Scotland, the number of victims would have run into hundreds.

Much more important than the vengeance taken on a few offenders was the positive achievement of the Estates. During a session of some six months they passed 393 Acts, the most important of which made the King almost absolute. One Act restored the Lords of the Articles; another declared that the sole power of appointing officers, privy councillors, and lords of session, and of calling parliaments lay with the King; yet another ordered all holders of public office to take an oath of allegiance acknowledging the King as 'only Supreme Governor of this Kingdom, over all persons and in all causes'. The final stroke was the 'Act Rescissory' which annulled all legislation passed since 1633, including that of 1641 passed in the presence of Charles I himself, and the 'Engagement' of 1648. The effect was to make 'the Government of the Church of Scotland as it is settled by law', which Charles had promised to maintain, not Presbyterianism but the episcopal system created by James VI and Charles I. Another act of the same day preserved the powers of Kirk sessions, presbyteries, and synods; and, because the Act Rescissory did not 'cut off' presbytery, there was some hope of a compromise which helped the passage of the act. Charles, however, intended nothing less than a complete episcopacy.

For this the ground was already prepared. James Sharp, minister of Crail, who had gone up to London to represent the interests of the Resolutioners, changed sides without informing his principals, arranged with Clarendon for the restoration of episcopacy and emerged himself in December 1660 as Archbishop of St Andrews and Primate of Scotland. Along with him were consecrated the saintly Robert Leighton and two others. Before long a whole bench came into being, and the Crown had an instrument which could ensure its control of the 'Articles' and could work hand in hand with the Privy Council.

Next year, 1662, the bishops were further advanced. One Act restored to them all their old ecclesiastical powers (though they were warned not to encroach on the prerogatives of the nobles in the governance of the realm – the fatal error committed by the bishops of Charles I). Another ordained that no minister who had not been collated by a bishop should retain his living. To the astonishment of Middleton and Archbishop Burnet of Glasgow, who thought that the strong hand would succeed, at least 270 ministers declined to obey, though the day of grace was prolonged till 1 February 1663.

The King's confidence in Middleton's high-handed policy may have been shaken, and it was lost altogether when Charles saw that a fresh Act, compelling all office holders to declare the two Covenants unlawful and seditious, was part of an attack on his chosen servant, Lauderdale. Lauderdale kept his post; Middleton was recalled.

Rothes, who succeeded him, was very much Lauderdale's man, and the machinery of absolutism was steadily developed. Provision was made for an armed force; James VI's method of electing the 'Articles' was restored; and an Act, 'the Bishop's Dragnet', imposed heavy fines for absenteeism from Church.

Parliament was dismissed and did not reappear till 1669. The work of government was carried on by the Privy Council, and for a short time, by the Court of High Commission which was revived in 1664. The Privy Council continued to rule in a way which provoked great discontent. The parishes of the excluded clergy had been given to 'the King's curates' who, if they were not all as scandalous and ignorant as has been said, failed to satisfy the people, many of whom sought the services of their old ministers. An Act of Council, designed to keep the deprived clergy away from their flocks and in remote places, was so worded that it would have been almost impossible for the old ministers to live anywhere. None the less 'Conventicles' continued. The curates were used as informers and the fines were collected by methods which produced a revolt.

On 15 November 1666 a small party of Galloway men captured at Dumfries Sir James Turner, who commanded the government's very inadequate forces in the area, and with him in their hands (he was not ill-used) advanced upon Edinburgh. They found few recruits. Their numbers never exceeded 3,000 and had been reduced to 900 when they were defeated, after a sharp action, at Rullion Green in the Pentlands. Fifty prisoners were taken and the Council insisted that the quarter granted to them on the field was only a temporary respite. Thirty-three were hanged, two of them after torture; others were shipped to the Barbadoes; suspects were persecuted. The brutality used bespeaks the nervousness of the government, who feared collusion with the Dutch, against whom England was now at war. Their alarm was quite groundless: the rising had no political affiliations. The insurgents were simple men, badly armed, some of whom believed 'the horses and chariots of Israel' would fight upon their side. Charles, worldly-wise and tolerant, is said to have advocated leniency in a letter which Sharp suppressed. This may not be so, but the cruelties produced a strong reaction. Sharp, whose position at about this time was shaken by the fall of Clarendon, lost much of his influence and an indemnity for the Pentland Rising was proclaimed – with a severe 'Bond of Peace' to be imposed upon accessories. Rothes was recalled and Lauderdale ruled in his stead.

Lauderdale

Coarse-fibred, and one to whom (as he said when Middleton tried to ruin him) 'a cartful of oaths' meant little, Lauderdale adopted to religious questions a policy of limited toleration based on indifference. Letters of Indulgence were issued in 1669, 1672, and 1679 in an attempt to distinguish non-conformity from political disaffection – the evicted ministers might return to their charges if they would live peaceably and orderly, and he could not understand why they should not. True, bishops had been introduced and the General Assembly did not meet; but synods, presbyteries, and kirk-sessions functioned much as they had always done. No attempt was made to enforce the Five Articles of Perth. No liturgy was made obligatory; some ministers, like Burnet (later Bishop of Salisbury) at Saltoun, used the English Prayer Book, but others used extemporary prayers. An English non-conformist, who attended the University at Glasgow because he was debarred from Oxford and Cambridge, 'much wondered why there should be any dissenters in Scotland' till he was told of the denunciation of the Covenant and the imposition of a hierarchy. In fact, two thirds of the ministry in all, and most in the east and north of Scotland (except for Fife), accepted what was given them. Yet, as appears from *An Accompt of Scotland's Grievances*, a pamphlet issued against

Lauderdale (1674), many who complied in obedience to the royal will grieved that 'what the most part took to be the labour of their Fathers, and the work of God, were at that time unconcernedlie regarded'. Of the ousted ministers, 150 refused the Indulgence on the ground that a Solemn Covenant with God was broken, that it stood for Erastianism, and presaged a return to Rome.

While 'toleration' thus failed to win over the Presbyterians it alienated some of the Episcopalians. The first Indulgence had been accompanied by the 'Assertory Act' from which it appeared that the royal supremacy enabled the King to establish any religion he pleased, and it was followed by a violent pamphlet from Archbishop Burnet of Glasgow, so violent that the author was removed from his see, to which Leighton, from Dunblane, succeeded.

For several years this charitable churchman, with the support of other liberal-minded men, tried to promote a compromise whereby bishops should cooperate with Presbyters; but he made no progress. He failed to see that real principles lay behind a quarrel which he regarded as 'a drunken scuffle in the dark' and, in 1674, he retired from his see to live an unworldly life till his death in 1684.

The failure of attempts at reconciliation were accompanied by growing severity against the non-conformists. To preach at a field Conventicle was made punishable by death; to accept the ministrations of an ousted minister was to incur severe penalties; absence from Church on three successive Sundays involved a fine. Other disabilities were imposed, and the sums exacted from the non-conformist gentry were enormous. From the shire of Renfrew alone the sum of £36,800 Scots was taken in a few years; and though some heritors managed to compound, others lost their estates. In 1674 heritors and masters were made responsible for their tenants and servants. Next year an Act provided for 'Letters of Intercommuning', in effect a complete boycott against recalcitrants; and, in 1677, an Act of Council ordered heritors and masters to sign bonds for all persons whatever residing in their lands. Many

237

landowners refused to undertake an impossible obligation and, in 1678, the government loosed on the south-west, particularly upon Ayrshire, the Highland Host, a body of 6,000 Highlanders and 3,000 Lowland militia to live in free quarters whilst they exacted the bonds and disarmed the country. Not only was the land looted but, as the result of fines and forfeitures, estates changed hands, and to the fury of the victims, money and lands were often kept by Lauderdale and his friends. The west was simmering to revolt and, in 1679, occurred an event which brought things to a head – the murder of Archbishop Sharp.

This was not premeditated. Sharp had long been hated on many grounds, particularly for his hounding to death of James Mitchell, whom he had induced to confess to an attempt at murder by promising him his life. When, by sheer chance, the Archbishop encountered a few desperate Covenanters, including Balfour of Kinloch, Burlie, and Hackston of Rathillet, who were on the lookout for one of his creatures, his appearance was regarded as a 'Providence' and he was brutally murdered on Magus Muir near St Andrews. Hackston, lest his personal hate should enter into an act of divine vengeance, refused to strike a blow, and stern Covenanters noted that only he was brought to justice for the deed.

The slayers rode to a west already in a ferment. On 29 May a body of Covenanters at Dumfries extinguished the bonfires lit on the anniversary of the King's return, and, on 1 June, an armed Conventicle at Drumclog repulsed with considerable loss an attack led by John Graham of Claverhouse ('Bloody Clavers'). The insurgents, however, were beaten off from Glasgow, and though their numbers swelled to 5,000, they were divided amongst themselves. In spite of the valour of Hackston, they were routed at Bothwell Brig by a royal force under Monmouth, who was Charles II's favourite illegitimate son, sent up hastily to take command. Two ministers who were taken were hanged; some of the other prisoners were executed at Magus Muir and all were treated with barbarity. Four hundred who took a bond not to rise in arms were allowed to go home, but 250 were sent to the Barbadoes in a ship which sank off the Orkneys with 200 of the captives, who were battened below hatches. Monmouth himself, who had advocated clemency, succeeded in getting an Act of Indemnity and the third Indulgence. His success was a proof that Lauderdale was no longer trusted. Bothwell Brig ended his career as Rullion Green did that of Rothes.

The Duke had long been disliked for his arbitrary conduct, his avarice, and his use of power to benefit himself, his kinsmen, and friends. In 1673 he had managed to survive a sharp attack in Parliament made by Hamilton and his party; but rancour still pursued him and, after the rising of 1679, he passed into obscurity. Presbyterian historians on the whole have dealt with him lightly; his Indulgences, after all, had been accepted by the great majority of the ministers and, possibly, his reputation benefited by comparison with that of his successor – James Duke of York.

James, Duke of York

James, Duke of York, usually referred to in Scotland as 'Duke of Albany', was sent north by his skilful brother largely because his unpopular presence in London was an asset to the promoters of the 'Exclusion Bill' designed to bar him from the English throne. Though personally brave, he was cold-blooded and narrow-minded. He took his seat on the Privy Council in December 1679 and appeared as Royal Commissioner only in July 1681. During the interval he paid two visits to Scotland and, no doubt, appraised the situation there. The 'indemnity' granted after Bothwell had not put a stop to the dragooning and the fining. The 'indulged' ministers kept their places but the strict Covenanters, reduced in numbers but not in resolution, continued to resist with increased fervour. Led by the minister Donald Cargill and by Richard Cameron, a St Andrews graduate, they became known as the 'Society

People' or the Cameronians.* Boycotted, hunted, and half-starved, but never betrayed though prices were on the heads of their leaders, they wandered in the hills. On 22 June 1680, a few of them fixed to the Market Cross at Sanquhar a *Declaration* disowning Charles Stuart as King. Next month a small force was surprised at Airds Moss in Kyle and, after a fierce action, Cameron was killed. Hackston, who was taken, was mutilated before he was hanged.

Undismayed, Cargill at the Torwood Conventicle formally excommunicated the King, the Duke of York, and other Royalist leaders; thereafter, his followers cut themselves off from all other Presbyterian ministers, Cargill was captured in May 1681, maintained his principles with constancy, and inevitably was hanged along with four of his people.

When things were in this posture, the Duke appeared as Royal Commissioner and at once held a Parliament in which he showed his quality. To him, the failure of the 'Exclusion Bill' appeared as a clear proof of his indefeasible title to the throne and his first measure was an Act which declared that no difference of religion could divert the right of succession to the Crown by lineal descent. Another Act ordered that every holder of public office should as a 'Test' take an oath whose terms seemed to be self-contradictory, but emphasized the principle of non-resistance. Eight of the Episcopal clergy resigned, so did Sir James Dalrymple, President of Court of Session. The ninth Earl of Argyll, son of the great Marquess, who had said he would take the oath in so far as it was consistent with itself, was condemned for treason, but managed to escape disguised as a page holding the train of his step-daughter, Lady Sophia Lindsay. The 'Test' was presented, not only to every official but to every suspect, and fines were rigorously collected. Conscious of public unrest, the govern-

*The regiment which bears his name has the sobriquet of 'The Covenanters'; till recently they took their rifles to Church and posted sentries outside.

ment proceeded against Scotsmen alleged to be concerned in the Rye House Plot (1683). Several well-known men were tortured, and one (at least) was hanged in 1684.

In that year the Society People provided another excuse for severity. Few now in number, they were wandering about in physical misery and religious exaltation; in November, 1684, they posted on several market-crosses and churches in the south-west the *Apologetical Declaration* wherein they declared that every servant of the government who sought their lives should do so at the risk of his own. Thereafter, the task was easy for the dragoons of Claver-house and for Sir George Mackenzie, the Lord Advocate. The suspect was asked if he would abjure the *Apologetical Declaration*. If he said 'no' he was shot out of hand; if he said 'yes' the criminal court might deal with him. It is fair to say that 'Bluidy Clavers' and 'Bluidy Mackenzie', who kept to the letter of the law, were not the monsters of Covenanting tradition; but the laws were cruel and the men were ruthless.

On 6 February 1685, Charles died. During his reign in England he had never visited Scotland. For his rule there he had precedent from the reigns of his father and grand-father and he was clever enough to avoid the peril of 'Laud's Liturgy'. His two great aims he had realized: he had kept his throne secure and made himself well-nigh absolute. He had also secured the succession of his brother who was openly a Roman Catholic.

James VII

James was proclaimed King of Scots on 10 February 1685. He omitted to take the Coronation Oath to defend the Protestant religion, and the Indemnity which he proclaimed excluded all his Covenanting enemies. When Parliament met in April, a fresh Act once more declared the taking of the Covenants to be treason, and made mere presence at a Conventicle punishable by death. An excise was granted in perpetuity and provision for a national army was promised.

The strength of the Crown was emphasized by the complete failure of an invasion by Argyll which was meant to synchronize with Monmouth's venture in the south-west of England. The expedition was ruined by divided counsels, and Argyll, after a vain attempt to shoot himself, was taken and beheaded. Like his father, he died with great courage but his supporters and sympathizers were hardly handled: 167 Covenanters were imprisoned under dreadful conditions in the vaults of Dunnottar and those who tried to escape were tortured.

This was the year in which Louis XIV, who had already begun to persecute the Protestants, repealed the Edict of Nantes, and the news of his severities produced a rising in Edinburgh against the Catholic priests. Yet James went on unmoved. He appointed converts to Roman Catholicism to the offices of Chancellor and Secretary of State, and recommended the Parliament of 1686 to repeal the penal laws against innocent Roman Catholics. When Parliament demurred, he simply ordered the Council itself to annul the laws. He met with opposition. The Council was purged; some of the bishops were deprived; and he found it necessary to include Protestant Dissenters (with limitations), as well as Catholics, in his generosity. Letters of Indulgence, which he issued in 1687, permitted people of both faiths to serve God after their own way and manner, provided they did not teach disloyalty. The Indulgence did not extend to field Conventicles and it brought no relief to the 'Society People' who would acknowledge 'no King but Christ'. The last of their ministers, James Renwick, was captured and executed in 1688. Yet, besides awakening suspicion, it produced a result which James did not foresee. The 'outed' Presbyterian ministers were enabled to return to their parishes, where the influence they exercised was to play a great part in the Revolution. And, in 1688, the Revolution came.

The birth of a Prince of Wales in June convinced England that James's policy would survive his death, and the arrest of the 'Seven Bishops' stirred into activity resentment already awakened by the promotion of Roman Catholics to power and office. Before long William of Orange received an invitation from English magnates, both Whig and Tory, to which, after some negotiation, he replied that he would come to ensure that all pressing questions of Church and State should be settled by a free Parliament.

To Scotland he sent a special address offering to rescue her from the tyranny of James. But the Episcopalians had no wish for a Dutch Calvinist and when, in October, false news came that William's expedition had been broken up by storm the Scottish bishops declared their loyalty to James VII. Yet when William landed at Tor Bay in November, James's cause in Scotland was already lost. He had violated the fundamental but unspoken compact between the Crown and the nobles which formed the basis of the Restoration settlement in Scotland: he had challenged the right of the aristocracy to control Scottish society at local level. The Privy Council, divided within itself, was powerless against open discontent, for some of the regular troops had been recalled to England, and the levies raised from the country refused to fight. Before James quitted England for ever on 23 December, the Chancellor Perth had been driven from Edinburgh and the Roman Catholic Chapel at Holyrood had been pillaged. The men of the west were rising against their 'curates' and on Christmas Day began a visitation which ejected some 200 households of Episcopalian ministers without bloodshed, but without consideration of the cruel winter weather.

The news of the King's flight brought representatives of all Scottish parties to London, where William, in response to a request from over a hundred nobles and gentlemen, agreed to undertake the administration until a national assembly should decide as to the future government. Accordingly he at once sent out letters summoning the Estates to a meeting on 14 March 1689. Such a meeting could only be a Convention, since there was yet no king; but the elections were now free from official control. Recently imposed disabilities were ignored, and both sides not only strove to secure a majority, but brought in armed men.

Claverhouse, now Viscount Dundee, returned from England with sixty horse while the Whigs introduced zealots from the west. There being no Royal Commissioner it was necessary to choose a President and the 'Williamite' candidate, the Duke of Hamilton, had only a small majority. Both James and William had sent letters. William's letter, urbane and ambiguous, was read at once, but the Jacobite party remained formidable: the Duke of Gordon from Edinburgh Castle could menace the Parliament House; both archbishops and seven bishops had exercised their right to attend, and it was hoped that new adherents would be obtained on the reading of James's letter. This however contained nothing but fulminations. The Royalists were dismayed. Dundee, after a word with Gordon on the Castle Rock, rode off to Stirling where it was proposed to hold a rival convention. When this came to nothing, he went off to the Highlands to emulate the action of another famous Graham.

Left to themselves, the Estates followed in the main the precedent set by England. On 11 April they issued a 'Declaration' consisting of a *Claim of Right* and an offer of the Crown to William and Mary. There were, however, significant differences between these documents and their English counterparts. The Tory element which had been operative in England was absent from the Scottish Estates, and their Claim of Right was radical. In the enumeration of the King's tyrannous acts it was firmly declared that:

Prelacy and the superiority of any office in the Church above Presbyters is, and hath been, a great and insupportable grievance and trouble to this nation . . . and therefore ought to be abolished.

Moreover it roundly asserted that the King had 'forfaulted' his right – no fiction of 'abdication'– and that the throne was thereby vacant. Two days later this enunciation of the 'contract theory' was emphasized in the

244

Articles of Grievances which condemned the whole machinery of the restored monarchy – the Committee of the Articles, the Act of Supremacy (1669), the keeping of a standing army in time of peace, and arbitrary justice. A new Coronation oath was also drawn up.

William, though he did not like to have his hands so much tied, even by implication, accepted the offer brought to him at Whitehall by representatives of the Three Estates and took the Coronation oath in the Scottish fashion, though he balked at the promise 'to be careful to root out all heretics' until he was assured that this could be interpreted in a tolerant way. The Scottish Revolution was achieved; but great difficulties still remained.

It has been contended that the history of the Restored Monarchy in Scotland has been too much written in terms of the religious conflict. It is true that sufficient attention has not been paid to the intellectual and economic developments which took place. Certainly, within the narrow bounds of determinism, minds tended to stagnate, and sound learning suffered from religious polemic. On the other hand persecution drove men to lands abroad where thought was more free. It should not be forgotten that the first secretary of the Royal Society was Sir Robert Moray and that among its early members were the Earl of Tweeddale, who made a great contribution to the art of navigation, and James Gregory, who planned the first observatory built in Britain and had a share in the discovery of differential calculus. It was in 1681 that Sir James Dalrymple, Lord Stair, published *The Institutions of the Law of Scotland* in which the old-established 'practicks' on which the lawyers had so long relied were digested into a treatise based upon principles of Roman Law and Dutch and French commentaries. His book remains a masterpiece. In the same year Sir Thomas Murray of Glendoick, Clerk Register, produced an edition of the Acts of Parliament from 1424 to his own time which was to serve Scots lawyers for many a day. To this period belongs also the foundation of the famous Advocates' Library, now the National Library, and also of the Snell Exhibition, which was to send so many young Scotsmen to Balliol.

The Edinburgh School of Medicine expanded and the Royal College of Physicians came into being. Among the physicians was Archibald Pitcairne, at once a lawyer and a man of letters; he wrote good Latin verse and also some satires upon the Kirk which led to the suspicion that he was an atheist. Owing to the influence of the Court, plays, especially those of Dryden, were produced in Scotland. Sir George Mackenzie of Rosehaugh, known as 'Bluidy Mackenzie' from his persecution of the Covenanters, was also a 'Christian Stoic' whose moral essays, and legal and historical works, were written in good prose.

Portrait painting was represented in the work of two members of the family of Scougall, and architecture by Sir William Bruce, who designed the rebuilding of Holy-roodhouse, which was carried out by Robert Mylne, the King's Master Mason, between 1671 and 1679. The portraits of the Scottish Kings, many legendary, which adorn its walls were all painted in a couple of years by a Dutch artist, Jacob de Wet, after alleged originals.

Along with this intellectual and artistic activity went an important constitutional development. An Act of 1661 extended the parliamentary franchise to include, besides the old-established holders of 'forty shilling lands' of 'auld extent', other tenants (mainly feuars) of the King, who had an annual rent of £1,000 (Scots); and, by a subsequent Act (1681) the property qualification was reduced to £400. In spite of government manipulation there began to emerge (e.g. in 1673, as already noted) a definite opposition supported by the enlarged electorate.

In the realm of economics there was progress. An Act of 1672 gave to burghs of 'barony' and of 'regality' a share in the monopoly of foreign trade hitherto enjoyed by the Royal Burghs; and aristocrats got charters which enabled them to exploit the resources of their lands. A 'Committee of Trade' was set up in 1661. and there was some trade with the English colonies across the Atlantic. Thanks to the goodwill of the 'proprietors', a small Quaker-Scottish colony was established in East New Jersey, and in 1684 a Presbyterian settlement was made at Stuart's Town in South Carolina. There the Scots were welcomed as a buttress against the Spaniards, by whom, in fact, the little colony was destroyed in 1685, when only twenty-five fit men survived to face the raiders from Florida. Yet, despite these stirrings of new life, Edinburgh boasted only 60,000 inhabitants at the end of the period and Glasgow, reckoned much the more beautiful, 30,000.

It is true that many ordinary folk, like Scott's 'Cuddie Headrigg', cared little about 'Covenants' and 'Testimonies'. It is true that the Covenanters were divided amongst themselves, and that the majority stood aloof from the extremists: some of them under persecution would acknowledge 'Nae King but Christ', but others, who accepted the doctrine of *Lex Rex* in theory, did not mean to dispense with the King altogether. It is true also that the Covenanters were no apostles of toleration. Yet, when every limitation is made, Presbyterianism played a great part in the Revolution. The country was interested in religion. According to a statesman of the time 'two thirds of the business of Scotland was related to the business of the Church', and in the constitutional struggle the Covenant became for many a shibboleth corresponding to *Magna Carta* in England.

For the Crown was absolutist. It had the support of Episcopalians, who reverenced the principle of authority, and in resisting despotism the Covenanters were champions of liberty, the more heroic because the struggle in which they engaged was so unequal. Against enormous odds they maintained the truth as they knew it, defying suffering and death, confident that beyond the grim gallows, or the firing party, they would find a welcome in the Everlasting Arms.

It was not from their own efforts that salvation came. The Protestants of Great Britain had long watched with horror the treatment of the Huguenots by Louis XIV, and when

James VII and II openly showed his purpose of making his whole realm Roman Catholic he alienated the hearts of nearly all his subjects. When he laid his hands on the Church of England and arrested the Seven Bishops it was evident that to resist the Crown in the name of conscience was an entirely respectable thing. It might seem that the Covenanters had been right after all.

They did not believe in religious freedom; they had no formulated scheme of constitutional government; yet as has been said 'it was from the impact of Stuart steel upon the Covenanting flint that our modern freedom of thought and belief was born'. Scotland does not err in reverencing the tradition of her martyrs.

CHAPTER 14

THE REVOLUTION SETTLEMENT
AND THE UNION OF
PARLIAMENTS
(1707)

THE Union of the Parliaments, it has often been shown, was
a direct consequence of the Revolution Settlement. The
personal union of the Crowns would suffice only as long as
the Crown itself governed directly in both countries, or at
least in one of them. When the 'Lords of the Articles'
disappeared (pp. 191, 253), and Scotland as well as England
strove to develop responsible government, grave frictions
were liable to develop. It is, however, too simplistic to see
the parliamentary union of 1707 as the inevitable result of
the events of 1689. There were several possible patterns of
development.

In the first place it was uncertain whether the revolution
settlement would survive the attacks of malcontents and of
Jacobites who could count on the help of powerful France.
Again it would have been possible to maintain the purely
personal union if William, while governing 'constitu-
tionally' in England, had been able to continue in Scotland
the system of 'management' by Commissioners used by his
predecessors, and William would have been not ill-pleased
to do so. Finally, experience might have shown that the
differences between the demands of these two parliaments
were so acute as to convince each that it must go its own
way.

The Revolution Settlement

It soon became apparent that William's acceptance of the
Crown did not guarantee the immediate emergence of a
'limited monarchy' in the modern sense. William was

tolerant in religion and broad-minded, but he was also authoritative. His experiences in his native land had implanted in him the *idée fixe* that France must be resisted at all costs and, also, the belief that the resistance could be best maintained by the strong rule of one man. He was delighted to have the full cooperation of Britain in his struggle against Louis XIV, which must needs be intensified since Louis recognized the exiled James VII and II as King of Great Britain. But while he of necessity sought the cooperation of the English Parliament, his main concern with Scotland was to hold the Jacobites at bay. For 'constitutional government' as such he had no particular regard. It was only with reluctance that he acceded to some of the vital principles in the Claim of Right, and some of his implied promises he merely disregarded. The Claim of Right had demanded the frequent calling of Parliament: William recalled the Convention which had invited him as a Parliament in June 1689, and kept it in being in nine successive sessions during the whole of his reign. The Claim had demanded the abrogation of all oaths save the new oath of allegiance but, in 1693, William demanded that all officers, civil, military, and ecclesiastical, should swear to the 'Assurance', recognizing him as King *de jure* as well as *de facto*. When the Scots Parliament tried to put pressure on William by refusing to cooperate in essential administrative procedures, William, on his own authority, both nominated Lords of Session and ordered the Signet to commence business. In 1692 he dismissed an intractable General Assembly without arranging the date of the next meeting. He followed the unpopular Stewart precedent of keeping the Secretary of State for Scotland in London, and in 1691 appointed as a Joint-Secretary Sir John Dalrymple, who had been an apostle of absolutism in the days of James VII. In his firm resistance to 'Popery' and to the might of persecuting France, William commanded the support of a great part of Scotland; but in other matters he made himself unpopular.

The settlement was opposed from various quarters. The Jacobites were still active; the Episcopalians resented the establishment of Presbytery; the Cameronians were outraged by the disregard of the Covenant; and disappointed politicians in the name of Scottish patriotism united themselves loosely in the 'Club'–the 'Country Party'.

None the less, the active opposition to the government was easily overthrown. Some inept conspiracies came to nothing. Dundee, as James VII's Lieutenant-General, gathered some western clans and, on 27 July 1689, routed the Williamites under Major-General Mackay at Killiecrankie; but 'Bonny Dundee' was killed in the action and, when his successor, Colonel Cannon, from Ireland, advanced on Dunkeld, he was repelled by the newly embodied regiment of the Cameronians (21 August) who, mindful of the Highland Host and Killing Times, inflicted such losses upon him that his undisciplined force melted away. Next year Cannon's successor Buchan, also from Ireland, was routed at Cromdale and thereafter there was no serious resistance. Mackay had built Fort William; the Earl of Breadalbane had made some arrangement with the Highland chiefs at Achallader and, in August 1691, the government promised indemnity to all who would take the oath of allegiance before 1 January 1692.

The government, and especially the Joint-Secretary, Dalrymple, realized that shortage of resources ruled out any adequate military action to contain the Highlands, so it was tempted to try to terrorize the bulk of the chiefs by an act of severity. Macdonald of Glencoe, partly through truculence and partly through bad weather, was a few days late in giving his pledge. 'Letters of Fire and Sword' were issued against his small clan which had an ill name for thieving, and was hated by those on whom it preyed; on the night of 13 February, thirty-eight persons, including two women and two children, were treacherously murdered by a party of soldiers, led by Captain Robert

Campbell of Glenlyon, which had been quartered in their midst. It is possible that the exact circumstances of this 'Massacre of Glencoe' have been misrepresented but, on any interpretation, it was a foul and bloody act from which the government of William could not excuse itself.

The Ecclesiastical Settlement

The first session of William's Parliament, in accordance with the Claim of Right, abolished prelacy; but it did not establish Presbyterianism, and it seems plain that the King, who realized the importance of the prelates in Parliament, would gladly have kept the bishops if he could. His hesitation was overcome, perhaps by the counsel of William Carstares, his adviser on Scottish ecclesiastical affairs,* but even more by the negative response of Alexander Rose, Bishop of Edinburgh, to a personal appeal from William late in 1688: 'I will serve you, Sir', Rose answered William, 'as far as law, reason or conscience shall allow.' It was not enough, so the King authorized his commissioner to the second session of Parliament (1690) to approve the establishment of Presbyterianism and to abolish patronage, though the right of 'presentation' was transferred to heritors and elders. The importance of the Presbytery was asserted in the Barrier Act of 1697, when the assembly decreed that all legislation proposed and approved by the assembly must be ratified by a majority of the Presbyteries before it was enacted as law by a later Assembly.

The Act of Supremacy (1669) was abolished; the ministers ousted in 1662 were restored; and a Presbyterian Settlement was authorized, based on the Act of 1592 and silent as to the Covenant and the Divine Right of Presbytery, though the Westminster Confession of Faith was read and formally recorded. Episcopal incumbents and Episcopal professors were expelled and, in 1692, the General Assembly refused

*Carstares had been subjected to the thumb-screw for alleged knowledge of the Rye House Plot (1683).

to readmit even those Episcopalian ministers who would recognize Presbyterian government and accept the Westminster standards. The King was more tolerant than the Kirk: in 1693 and 1695, successive acts granted a form of 'indulgence' to Episcopalians who would acknowledge William, and a hundred Episcopalian ministers took advantage of the opportunity. The non-Jacobites received toleration in 1712, but the true 'non-jurors' were excluded until 1792.

Although, during this period, secular interests were replacing religious enthusiasm the Kirk continued to assert itself in Parliament. Acts were passed against blasphemy and profanity, under one of which an unfortunate young student, Thomas Aikenhead, was condemned in 1696 and, by the insistence or indifference of the ministers, hanged.

A more pleasing result of clerical insistence was an Act of 1696 compelling the heritors of every parish to provide a commodious house for a school and a small salary for a schoolmaster. This legislation was not designed to establish new schools; it was aimed to provide for the masters teaching in the already numerous existing schools. By the early 1690s Scotland appears to have had extraordinarily good provision for schooling, at least in the Lowlands. Out of a total of 179 parishes in the Lothians, Fife, and Angus, at least 137 supported schoolmasters and at least 156 had either latin or 'Scots' schools. The Scottish people during the eighteenth century were far better educated than those of most other lands.

The King and the Parliament

The relations between the King and his Scottish Parliament were by no means always happy. William strove in vain to retain the Committee of the Articles, but the compromise as to their election, which he suggested, was rejected, and Parliament was dismissed without its acts being touched by the sceptre. The second session (1690) was more amicable. The Articles were abolished; Presbyterianism, as already stated, was established; twenty-six members were added to the shire representation (two each to eleven large shires and one each to four smaller shires); in accordance with William's measure of 1689, the franchise in the royal burghs was now exercised by all the burgesses instead of by the town-councils, and the burgesses began to recover their importance in Parliament. In 1690 Parliament cancelled the greater part of the Act of 1672 which had conferred trade privileges upon the non-royal burghs, but it is fair to add that the enjoyment of these privileges, which was accompanied by a liability to pay taxes, was not regarded as an asset by the smaller royal burghs, some of which tried to escape from their status, though Cromarty alone succeeded in its attempt.

Confronted by a Parliament becoming more independent and more representative, William relied upon the expedient of offering posts and gratifications to nobles and burgesses, but his relations with Scotland remained uneasy. Apart from the causes of friction already mentioned, there was a permanent underlying cause of difference in the matter of foreign policy. William from 1689 to 1697 was at war with France, and France was Scotland's old ally. Scottish money was spent, and Scottish lives were lost – the Cameronians, for example, suffered dreadfully at Steenkirk (1692) – in a quarrel which was repugnant to Scottish sentiment and which injured an old-established Scottish trade. The ill-will between the two governments came to a head with the failure of the 'Darien Scheme'.

The 'Darien Scheme'

With the dawning of the secular age, Scotland had become more conscious of the importance of trade. In spite of the Navigation Acts, Scots merchants had conducted a trade with the English 'Plantations' and, by arrangements with the proprietors of the Colonies, small settlements had been made (p. 247) in New Jersey, and a small post, Stuart's

Town, established in South Carolina where it served as an outpost against the Spaniards for two years.

By this time there was great interest in the establishment of companies and an Act of Parliament (1693) authorized the establishment of companies to trade with any country against whom the King was not at war. In pursuance of this Act, the Crown in 1695 authorized the establishment of a 'Company trading to Africa and the Indies', which might establish depots in any uninhabited place, or in places not possessed by any European sovereign. This project represented the Scottish desire for a colony, and for the expansion of trade; but it also received support from London merchants anxious to break the monopoly of the East India Company and, as at first designed, its capital was to consist of £300,000 sterling from Scotland and as much from England.

In the minds of the first promoters the possibilities of Africa played a great part, but under the influence of the experienced William Paterson (the Scottish founder of the Bank of England, 1694) interest turned to the scheme of establishing on the Isthmus of Darien an entrepôt which would command the trade of two great oceans.

The money was readily subscribed, but the merchants of the East India Company, who had great influence in the House of Commons, took alarm. There were threats of impeachment, most of the English directors withdrew, and Scotland put up £400,000 herself, equivalent to almost the entire value of the coinage of Scotland (as revealed by the recoinage of 1707–8). The King, saying that he had been ill-served in Scotland, offered every impediment he could, preventing the borrowing of money in Hamburg, the buying of ships in Holland, and the giving of aid by the English colonists. His hostility was due in part to his knowledge that Darien was claimed by Spain, about whose possessions he was trying to arrange the Partition Treaties with Louis XIV. None the less three Scottish ships and two tenders sailed from Leith in July 1698 and, in October, founded the township of New Edinburgh; but fever, dissension, and English opposition ruined the venture, and the colony was abandoned after great loss of life. A later expedition of 1699 reoccupied the deserted settlement and beat a Spanish force at Toubacanti, but the Spaniards returned in force by sea, as well as by land, and Fort St Andrew capitulated in March 1700.

Scotland had lost 2,000 men and upwards of £200,000. The anger of the nation was intense, and it was not allayed by a letter sent by William to the ninth session of Parliament, which assembled in October 1700. In this he explained that to have accepted the Company's right to Darien would have disturbed the peace of Christendom. However, he promised to support every measure which would promote Scottish trade, and especially repair the losses of the Company. How bitter was the feeling appears from the fact that in 1705 an English Captain, Green, was hanged with two of his men for an alleged act of piracy upon one of the Company's ships – the Company still sent an occasional ship to the East – of which they were almost certainly innocent.

Meanwhile the relations of the two kingdoms were worsened by an affair of great consequence. In 1701 the English Parliament, forseeing that Anne, William's inevitable successor, might leave no heirs when she died, provided that the succession should in that case pass to her nearest Protestant kinswoman, the Electress Sophia of Hanover, and her heirs, stipulating also that the new sovereign must be a communicant of the Church of England. This Act of Settlement was passed without any reference to Scotland. There was no obligation upon Scotland to accept this arrangement and, in view of its terms and of the state of feeling between the two realms, there seemed little likelihood that Scotland would offer her Crown to the person favoured by the English. There was a risk, at least in the eyes of English politicians, that the Old Pretender (son of James VII, who died in 1701) might return and seize the throne of Scotland. William saw the danger, and to him it appeared that the only remedy was a complete union between the two realms. He had indeed suggested this immediately after his accession, but though the Scottish Convention favoured the idea, the English would have nothing of it. In 1700 the House of Lords, at his suggestion, passed a Bill for appointing Commissioners to treat with Scottish Commissioners for 'the weal of both kingdoms' but the English Commons rejected it. By this time there was no guarantee that the Scottish Parliament would favour union.

Yet William, realizing that war with France must soon come, was more urgent than ever and, on 28 February 1702, only a week before his death, he sent a message to the English Parliament recommending a firm and entire union with Scotland. Experience had shown him that the purely personal union of the Crowns would no longer serve.

The Union of Parliaments

The accession of Anne did not seem to augur well for the complete union so desired by her predecessor. The Revolution Settlement was Whig; William's advisers had been Whig; the scheme of Union was Whig. Anne was a Tory, and a devout Churchwoman; moreover she was popular, and free from the tarnish of Glencoe and Darien. The Scottish Tories looked forward to a period when William's policies, if not in part undone, might well be halted and the scheme of Union be relegated to the background. The event belied their hopes. Anne undoubtedly had an affection for the House of Stewart; but as a firm Anglican she could not contemplate with pleasure the claim of her Papist half-brother and, in any case, since he (the Old Pretender) had already been recognized as King by Louis XIV, she could not form an alliance with the Jacobites without uncrowning herself. She must perforce continue William's policies. Within two months of her accession Britain, with her allies, declared war upon France and, meanwhile, the new sovereign had already invited the English Parliament 'to consider of proper methods towards attaining a Union with Scotland'. In May 1702 she gave her assent to an Act of the

English Parliament empowering her to appoint Commissioners and in June recommended Union to the Scottish Parliament which reassembled on the ninth of that month. In that Parliament the opponents of union with England suffered a reverse of their own making. Hamilton, complaining that Parliament had not met, according to an Act of 1696, within twenty days after the King's death, protested that its sitting was illegal and then dramatically walked out with fifty-seven of his supporters.* His action was popular in the streets, but in the House it left control to the Court interest which passed a series of Acts confirming the Revolution Settlement to win Presbyterian support and asked the Queen to appoint Commissioners to negotiate with those of England. In November Commissioners fr m both sides met at Whitehall but, though they agreed on general principles, they differed on economic details and, in February 1703, adjourned without reaching a conclusion.

Whilst they were still sitting, Scotland was electing a new Parliament and, to the disappointment of the Country interest, the Queen's supporters remained in power. The government still retained some means of gratifying nobles and of influencing local elections while Presbyterian ministers swayed their congregations. Lord Queensberry, who appeared again as Commissioner, was moderate in opinion and able in management, and Seafield (who succeeded the zealous Presbyterian Marchmont as Chancellor) concealed beneath a handsome presence and an engaging manner a firm will, and an art of management. Both had served under William, and Seafield under James VII too.

The task of the government was not easy. The Court Party in the House had a majority, but it was opposed both by the 'Country Party', headed by Hamilton, which professed to champion Scottish interests, and the 'Cavaliers' ('Jacobites' or 'Episcopals') who opposed the Revolution Settlement altogether; moreover, it was confronted by the single-minded Fletcher of Saltoun, a true idealist who

*Hamilton was right: the failure to summon Parliament was a device to enable the executive to declare war on France.

advocated an independent Scotland, a Church without dogma and, if a republic was impossible, a monarchy so limited that the sovereign was merely the guardian of the law. Fortunately for the government the opposition groups were mutually opposed; yet they were agreed in antipathy to England and they succeeded in passing two Acts which did not improve the relations between the two realms. The *Act anent Peace and War* ordained that no successor of Queen Anne should declare a war involving Scotland without consulting the Scottish Parliament. The *Act of Security* provided that the Scottish Parliament, twenty days after the death of Anne without issue, should name as her successor a Protestant and a descendant of the House of Stewart, but not the person designated by the English Parliament unless under conditions which guaranteed to Scotland freedom of government, of religion, and of trade. Provision was also made for the re-arming of Scotland. It was made plain that until this Act were passed there would be no supply; and although Queensberry, at the close of the session of 1703, announced that he was empowered to ratify all Acts except the Act of Security, no supply was given.

For the session of 1704 Tweeddale replaced Queensberry as Commissioner, and two somewhat incidental gains were made by the government. Tweeddale's supporters emerged as the 'New Party' or *Squadrone Volante* which, though jealous of Scotland's interest, was yet not opposed to Union. In August, Godolphin, First Lord of the Treasury and Anne's principal English adviser, anxious about affairs abroad, gained the royal assent to the Act of Security (5 August), and obtained a vote of supply. The news of the victory of Blenheim (4 August) made the English government feel that it had surrendered unnecessarily and, in February 1705, the English parliament passed the (miscalled) 'Alien Act' which threatened that, unless Scotland accepted the Hanoverian succession by Christmas Day 1705, Scots would be treated as aliens and Scottish commerce would be severely penalized. Yet, as the Act also empowered the Queen to appoint commissioners to negotiate a union, the door was not closed and, despite the ill-feelings manifest in the case of Captain Green, definite progress was made in the session of 1705. This time there was named as Commissioner the young Duke of Argyll, a soldier rather than a politician, but straightforward and one who commanded the sympathy of Presbyterian Scotland by reason of the deeds and the sufferings of his grandfather and great-grandfather. At his back he had Queensberry as Privy Seal and Seafield as Chancellor. Under their direction, a moderate policy was prepared. It is unlikely that this would have succeeded had not Hamilton betrayed his supporters, presumably for money, by carrying, on a snap vote, in a thin house, the provision that the Commissioners to negotiate the treaty with England be appointed by the Queen. The Commissioners to be appointed to negotiate were not to touch the ecclesiastical settlement. Anne was merely asked to repeal the insulting Alien Act, and the objectionable clauses were in fact repealed before Christmas 1705.

Early in 1706, the Queen appointed thirty-one Commissioners from each country. The English representation was virtually all Whig, but the Scots included some of the critics of Union, including Lockhart of Carnwarth, a professed Jacobite, but overlooking Hamilton. Argyll declined to act.

The Commissioners met in Whitehall on 16 April and, by 16 July, had agreed on the terms of a treaty which were to be kept secret until they were presented, first to the Scottish Parliament, and then to the English. That they achieved in nine weeks so momentous a result was due to the fact that the wise men on both sides dreaded the consequences of failure and that there were the elements of a bargain. England, at war with France, could not afford to have behind her back a hostile Scotland under a Jacobite ruler, and demanded a complete union and acceptance of the Hanoverian succession. The Scots wanted free trade at home and abroad. They would have preferred federation to complete union, but could not insist upon it since the English were adamant, and they themselves knew that the break-down of the treaty might involve them in civil war and French intervention on behalf of a 'Popish King'.

The essential points of the Treaty were these. The two kingdoms were to be united into one in the name of Great Britain, with a common flag, a common great seal, and a common coinage. The monarchy of Great Britain was to descend to the Hanoverian Princess and her heirs. The two countries were to have one and the same Parliament, styled the Parliament of Great Britain; the Scottish representation in this was reckoned according to a ratio, based both on populations (perhaps five to one), and on taxable capacities (about thirty-six to one), and Scotland was to send only sixteen peers to join the 190 English peers and forty-five commoners to join the 513 from England and Wales. Scotland was to retain her own law and her own judicature free from any appeal to any court sitting in Westminster Hall; the Privy Council and the existing Court of Exchequer were to remain until the Parliament of Great Britain should think fit to ordain otherwise. The matter of a right of appeal to the House of Lords was left deliberately ambiguous.

Arrangements were made for an equitable distribution of public burdens with some concessions as to customs in the interest of Scotland; and, in as much as these would include the service for the National Debt (that of England was nearly £18,000,000 and that of Scotland, £160,000), Scotland was to receive a cash payment of £398,085 10s. with a promise of a further payment at the end of seven years to balance the increased revenue to be expected from the Scottish customs and excise. The yields of these 'Equivalents' were to be used to recompense private losses due to the standardization of the coinage; to reimburse investors in the Darien Company, which was to be extinguished; to pay the public debts of the Scottish Crown and to provide, for seven years, £2,000 a year to aid wool-manufacture, fisheries, and other industries. The Scottish nobles were to keep their heritable jurisdictions, and the Scottish burghs their old privileges.

When the draft Treaty was presented to the Scottish Parliament in October 1706, and its terms became public, it was met with a howl of execration throughout the land which was, no doubt, fomented by Jacobites, but which also represented a feeling that Scotland had been sold to the English. In Edinburgh, Glasgow, and Dumfries, there was mob violence and, as the debates in Parliament continued, petitions came in from about a third of the shires, a quarter of the royal burghs, and from some presbyteries and parishes who feared that the Kirk was in danger. None the less, when it came to the point, the Articles were approved one by one and, on 16 January 1707, the entire treaty was passed by 110 votes to 69, there being a majority in each Estate, that of the nobles being the most pronounced.

In the course of the debates, certain necessary amplifications were made. Article XXII had remitted to the Scottish Parliament the duty of deciding as to the manner of elections to the new Parliament, providing that an Act to be made on this subject by the Scottish Parliament should be as valid as if it were part of the treaty itself.* The arrangement made was that the sixteen peers were to be chosen by their fellows in open election and plurality of votes; of the commoners, thirty seats were given to the shires and fifteen to the burghs. In adjusting the excess of the 'constituencies' over the number of members, Cromwellian precedents were available, though they were not exactly followed. Six of the smaller shires were paired to send one member at alternate elections; Edinburgh was given one member and the remaining sixty-five burghs were formed into nine groups of five, and five groups of four.†

*The Scottish peerage then numbered 154 in all – ten Dukes, three Marquesses, seventy-five Earls, seventeen Viscounts, and forty-nine Lords. There were sixty-six burghs.

†These arrangements were far from perfect. The shires of Bute and Caithness had nothing in common except approximate importance; the declining Fife burghs still provided one fifth of the total representation; the arrangement that each burgh of a group should send a delegate to vote at the election meeting led to absurdities as the burghs developed unevenly – Glasgow, which by the end of the century had a population

With regard to religion, a sensible procedure was adopted: the Scottish Parliament passed an Act for Securing the Protestant Religion and Presbyterian Church Government, which was to be regarded as part of the Treaty and a corresponding Act for securing the Church of England to be passed by the English Parliament.

The three Acts were passed by the English Parliament. The royal assent was given. An 'Exemplification' under the Great Seal was read by the Commissioners to the Scottish Parliament and duly recorded. As Chancellor Seafield handed the signed document to the Clerk, he said, with a jest which had surely a tear in it: 'Now there's ane end of ane old song.' Parliament was adjourned on 19 March until 22 April. But it never met again and, on the twenty-eighth it was formally dissolved. On 1 May the new Parliament of Great Britain came into being.

The Act of Union was a remarkable achievement. It made two countries one and yet, by deliberately preserving the Church, the Law, the Judicial System, and some of the characteristics of the smaller kingdom, it ensured that Scotland should preserve the definite nationality which she had won for herself and had preserved so long. It realized some of the desires of both countries. To England it gave security, in face of French hostility, for the Hanoverian succession and for the constitutional settlement of the Revolution; to Scotland it gave a guarantee of her Revolution Settlement in Church and State, and an opportunity for economic development which was sorely needed.

Yet John Richard Green was not entirely right when he said that 'all that passed away was the jealousy which had parted, since the days of Edward I, two peoples whom a common blood and common speech proclaimed to be one.' The jealousy remained and it was heightened by the patronizing attitude of the English who represented that Scotland

of 200,000, had an equal vote with Dumbarton, Renfrew, and Rutherglen, who mustered only 11,000 between them; the exclusion of non-royal burghs deprived a few fairly big towns (Greenock and Paisley, for example) of any representation.

was 'merged' into England, and that on terms of great generosity. And there was some truth in this view. Though in theory after 1 May 1707 there was no English Parliament, but a wholly new 'British' legislature, in practice the English Parliament simply absorbed the Scottish one. Scottish membership was small, particularly in the House of Lords, and the constitutional assumptions on which the legislature operated were entirely English. The financial provisions of the Treaty tell a similar story. 'Equivalents' were the capital value of the Scottish obligations as computed by competent financiers, and by the Treaty part of the capital sum of the Equivalents was to be used – in fact more than half was required – to recoup the shareholders of a Scottish company which had been deliberately ruined in the interests of English commerce. These are the facts. Yet within a few years of the Union, Treasurer Harley told the Scottish members that when England gave them the Equivalent she had bought the right to tax them.

The idea that Scotland was 'sold' is due, partly, to the assertions of Scottish opponents of the Union that it was effected by bribery. Of course, in the eighteenth century it would have been most remarkable if a major transaction of this sort had taken place without money changing hands in considerable quantitites. All public servants at that time, and for long afterwards, expected some rewards from their governments as a matter of course. In this case, of the £20,000 secretly sent from England, far the greater part was already due to Queensberry and other officers in respect of unpaid salaries and allowances, and £1,000 went to Atholl who was, and who remained, a vigorous opponent of the government. Many nobles favoured Union to preserve the trade with England which they had already established (pp. 246–7).

No doubt money and gratifications passed, but the Union was not brought about solely by the bribery of Parliament. That it was unpopular in the country at large cannot be denied; but among those who disliked it there were many who were nevertheless not prepared to embrace

Jacobitism, now the only viable alternative. It was only later that a very significant proportion of the Scottish governing class was willing to contemplate the use of force against the Union. Yet must it be said that this hostility was due, not only to sentimental attachment to the 'old song' or to regret that the Scottish Parliament should have been extinguished just when it was thriving well, but to the attitude of the English themselves in misinterpreting the spirit of the Act of Union and sometimes even ignoring its text.

CHAPTER 15

THE UNION IN OPERATION: THE JACOBITES

ON both sides of the Border the men who had made the Treaty tried to make it work. Evidence of good intent is shown by the creation of a third Secretaryship of State which was given to Queensberry, and by the zeal with which the country rallied behind the government against the invasion from France which was attempted in 1708. None the less, the first years of the Union were marked by friction – a friction so serious that by 1713 Seafield himself felt that the Union had failed – and in England and Scotland alike there was great uncertainty as to what would happen on the death of Anne.

Behind the immediate occasion of friction lay one underlying cause. This was the patronizing attitude of the English – their assumption that England had 'bought' Scotland, and that this was no equal partnership. The Scots were well aware that the Equivalent was no *ex gratia* payment. They knew too that their soldiers contributed in no small measure to the effort of Britain against France, and that, if their gentlemen found employment in the British army, they earned any promotion they got. The Cameronians, for instance, lost very heavily at Blenheim as well as at Steenkirk; it was the Colonel of the Scots Fusiliers who led the assault on the village of Blenheim and gave the signal to open fire by striking the palisade with his sword; he was killed there. One Ayrshire family had five sons serving of whom four were killed; and, among the cavalry, the Scots Greys (Grey Dragoons) won great distinction in all Marlborough's battles. To the Scots it seemed an unworthy thing that, in the question of war or peace with France, Scotland should be little regarded.

Against the background of this political dissatisfaction

emerged a series of grievances, economic, constitutional, and ecclesiastical.

The dominant factors in the economic situation were that, since Scotland was much weaker than England, she inevitably suffered at first from the (now free) competition of England, and that, when fresh taxation was needed to support the war, Parliament considered at first the English interest. The Treaty of Union had provided that malt should not be taxed in Scotland during the war, and that in the imposition of new burdens, regard should be paid to the respective capacities of the countries. Parliament did in fact endeavour to impose a malt duty on Scotland during the war and, in its fiscal legislation, seemed to penalize Scottish linen and Scottish timber, while the appearance of English customs officers added to the general irritation on both sides.

In constitutional affairs too, Scotland felt that she was abused. The Privy Council (whose possible disappearance was indeed envisaged in the Act of Union) was abolished out of hand on 1 May 1708, and the commissions to the new justices of the peace, whose powers were extended, were issued in the name of English councillors, including the Archbishop of Canterbury.

The 'Masters', eldest sons of peers, were debarred from sitting for shires and burghs, and even from voting at elections. The conferring on Hamilton of the title Duke of Brandon in 1711 was made the occasion for a resolution in the Lords that no Scottish peer should become a member of their House by virtue of an English title granted after the Union; yet such peers were forbidden to vote at the election of the sixteen representative peers. A new Treason Act, though it abolished torture, was bitterly resented in Scotland because it introduced the draconian penalties stipulated by English law.

Ecclesiastical grievances were added when, after 1710, Tory influence prevailed in the English government. James Greenshields, an Episcopal clergyman who had arrogantly defied both civil and ecclesiastical authority in Edinburgh, and had been refused redress by the Court of Session, had the decision reversed by the House of Lords. Very many Scotsmen learned with surprise that the House of Lords was not one of the 'Courts sitting in Westminster Hall' precluded from exercising jurisdiction in Scotland by the Act of Union. No doubt the Scottish lawyers must have been aware of this, but in any case the Scots felt that civil jurisdiction, exercised in an affair of the Kirk, was a breach of the Act of Union.

The Toleration Act of 1712, though repugnant to Presbyterians, was good in itself; but tacked on to it was the provision that all clergymen must take an oath of allegiance and abjuration which was in fact difficult for a conscientious Presbyterian to accept. Lay patronage was restored, in open breach of the Act for the Security of the Scottish Church. The general effect of the legislation was to promote the belief that Episcopacy was to be introduced. The Episcopalians showed themselves supremely confident. Meanwhile the extension of the oath to officers of the Crown expelled some Whig officers of the army and, at the same time, grants of money were being made to Highland chiefs of doubtful loyalty who began to re-arm their clans.

The outcome of these accumulated grievances was the introduction of a motion in the House of Lords (1713) to rescind the Act of Union; this was supported by all the Scottish members, Whigs and Tories alike, and it was defeated in the Lords only narrowly and by the votes of proxies. It has been doubted if the Scots meant to force the issue; anyhow the necessity disappeared. On the death of Anne (1 August 1714) the Whigs, amongst whom Argyll was conspicuous, acted with resolution. To the surprise of the Jacobites, George I ascended the throne 'amid acclamation' and with the establishment of a mainly Whig ministry the danger to the 'Revolution Settlement' seemed to fade away. But it did not disappear altogether. Discontent in Scotland was both wide and deep and, in both England and Scotland alike, there was still the instinctive feeling that as long as the 'legitimate' monarch was extant there was no hope of permanent peace. For three decades it seemed possible that the exiled dynasty might return.

The Jacobite Attempts – 1708, 1715, 1719, 1745

The efforts of the Jacobites to reinstate the Stewarts upon the throne have attracted much attention. They have importance as well as romance, but their influence upon the development of Scotland was slight. It may be too much to say that they were foredoomed to failure, but certainly they were founded upon false hopes. While the Jacobites were justified in counting upon discontent in Scotland, they and their agents deceived themselves and deceived others as to the extent to which this discontent would express itself in arms. The growing economic prosperity inclined men, especially the wealthier men, to accept with complacency a rule of which perhaps, in theory, they did not approve.

Again, they overestimated the amount of help which would, or could, be supplied by their allies overseas; a stroke on their behalf was only one of various possibilities open to continental diplomatists and, in any case, uncertain seas and a competent navy were interposed between Scotland and the invader. Finally, there was the matter of religion. James VII and his son, the Chevalier de St Georges (the Old Pretender), were resolute Catholics; and, though the Young Pretender did at one time join the Church of England, his hopes continued to rest upon the Catholic powers. To the majority of Scotsmen 'Popery' was anathema, and in England and Scotland alike its restoration was dreaded as presaging a return to absolutism. It is with regard to these overriding factors that the Jacobite attempts must be considered.

1708. Anxious to avenge Marlborough's victories and aware that Scotland was ill-defended, Louis XIV launched in March 1708 a powerful fleet conveying 6,000 men, and graced by the presence of the Chevalier. This was destined

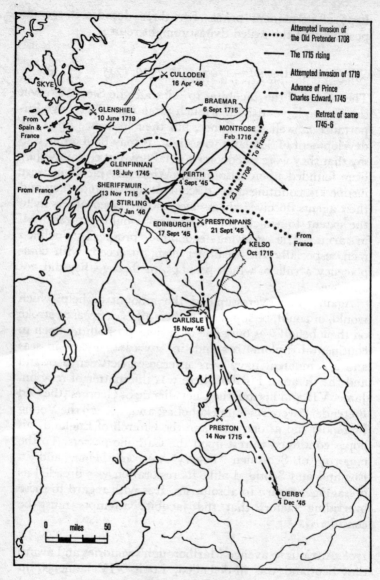

Legend:

•••••• Attempted invasion of the Old Pretender 1708

——— The 1715 rising

– – – Attempted invasion of 1719

–·–·– Advance of Prince Charles Edward, 1745

—— Retreat of same 1745-6

SKYE

CULLODEN
16 Apr '46

BRAEMAR
6 Sept 1715

GLENSHIEL
10 June 1719

From Spain & France

MONTROSE
Feb 1716

To France

GLENFINNAN
18 July 1745

PERTH
4 Sept '45

From France

SHERIFFMUIR
13 Nov 1715

23 Mar 1708

STIRLING
7 Jan '46

EDINBURGH
17 Sept '45

PRESTONPANS
21 Sept '45

KELSO
Oct 1715

From France

CARLISLE
15 Nov '45

PRESTON
14 Nov 1715

DERBY
4 Dec '45

0   miles   50

5. *The Jacobite Rebellions*

for the Firth of Forth, but bad weather, faulty navigation, a marked lack of enthusiasm amongst the French soldiers and sailors, and the arrival of English ships prevented the invaders from making any landing. Yet in England and Scotland alike, it was felt that a very real danger had been averted by fortune alone.

1715. The 'Fifteen' at its outset seemed to have all the elements of success. The Scots were by now tired of the Union. The Jacobites, who felt (quite erroneously) that they had been within an ace of success in England on the death of Anne, were optimistic.

The eleventh Earl of Mar who led the enterprise was more considerable than his sobriquet 'Bobbing John' suggests. True, he had been in touch with the Court of St Germain whilst he had served the English government. He had twice held the post of Secretary under Queen Anne and had made his choice only when repelled by George I. Yet he could represent that he had tried to make the Union a success and found that it would not do; and the speed with which he rallied a party in Scotland shows that he had the sympathy of a large following and a power of organization. At first sight his optimism would seem to have been well founded. Apart from the possibilities inherent in the general discontent, he had positive assets. He could count on the support of the Episcopalian clergy: in the north-east of Scotland they had strong congregations and in many places these congregations included gentry. Moreover in the countryside the influence, and the actual power, of the family was often almost feudal, and loyalty to the chief might be supplemented by actual pressure. When the laird rode, some of his tenants would normally ride too; and the coercive power of a great noble against the reluctant may well be judged from the letter of Mar himself to Black George Forbes, his bailie at Kildrummy. It begins: 'Jocke, ye was in the right not to come with the 100 men ye sent up tonight when I expected four times the number.'; it goes on 'particularly let my own tenants in Kildrummy know that if they come not forth with their best arms, I will send a party immediately to burn what they shall miss taking from them,' and concludes by making his servant personally responsible for seeing that the gentlemen came both well-horsed and well-armed. Similar orders were issued by Lochiel, Glenlyon, and others.

Coercion of this kind might be used against the unruly Highlanders but it was less necessary in more orderly districts, and Mar could not afford to wait. Yet he delayed. Having raised the Royal Standard at Braemar on 6 September with the support of a few Scottish nobles, mainly Lowlanders, he was soon at the head of a force of 12,000 men. By the end of the month he had occupied Inverness and Perth and controlled a long coast-line which invited aid from France. Yet his venture failed utterly.

The towns south of the Tay held fast for the government; Glasgow, for example, was quick to raise a company. The Whig lairds began to form 'Associations'. The Earl of Sutherland raised the extreme north for the Crown. No help came from France, for the Regent Orléans, who governed France after the death of Louis XIV (8 September) sought an English alliance; and Mar himself was not equal to the occasion.

He dallied at Perth, although Argyll, a good soldier, could muster barely 4,000 men at Stirling; and his attempt to turn the position by sending Mackintosh of Borlum across the Firth of Forth was fruitless, for that bold leader joined with the Jacobites of south-west Scotland and northern England only to find that the country would not rise, and to share in the surrender at Preston (12–14 November). When at length he himself advanced on Stirling, he was met at Sheriffmuir near Dunblane by Argyll, who had only half his numbers. Though the Battle of Sheriffmuir (13 November) was only drawn, he threw away his opportunity by returning to Perth. His failing cause was not restored by the arrival of the Chevalier at Peterhead (22 December), for the Prince, though personally brave and courteous, was formal and obviously discouraged. His army melted away as it moved north and he himself, along with Mar, slipped off by sea from Montrose on 4 February 1716, leaving his supporters to shift for themselves.

Although Argyll, who favoured some accommodation, was dismissed, the obvious sympathy throughout Scotland for the prisoners deterred the government from undue severity. Of the leaders taken at Preston, only Derwentwater and Kenmure were executed; the others 'escaped' and, of the Scots condemned to death at Carlisle, none was executed. In 1717 the government passed an Act of Grace and Free Pardon to all except Macgregors (whose name was forbidden and who were deprived of their civil rights until 1774) and, when next year it endeavoured to prosecute for treason those who had fled overseas, juries would not convict.

With regard to the 'forfeited estates' of those condemned, Scottish reluctance to proceed to extremes was obvious. The Court of Session held that creditors must first be satisfied and the factors named to see to this were Jacobites. When the commissioners offered the estates for sale, few bidders appeared, although the York Buildings Company came forward to purchase, and when the accounts were closed in 1725 it was found that, of the £84,000 received, the expenses of realization had amounted to about £83,000. The balance in the hands of the government was £1,107.

1719. The 'Fifteen' had involved the whole of the Jacobite interest in Scotland. In contrast the attempt of 1719 was a mere side-issue of European diplomacy – one of the devices whereby Cardinal Alberoni sought to immobilize the powers which might ally with Austria to frustrate his ambitions in Italy. After a grandiose attempt to unite the Jacobites and the Swedes had failed, he promoted a 'nuisance raid' on the north-west of Scotland by sending from Spain two frigates and a few hundred men under the command of the tenth Earl Marischal (who had been out in the 'Fifteen'). After visiting Lewis the invaders established a base at Eilean Donan on Loch Duich (opposite Skye) in April, but they met with little support and in June they were routed about half way up Glen Shiel. The few chiefs who had come in went their ways, taking what arms they could, and advising the Spaniards to do likewise. They promptly surrendered. As far as Scotland was concerned, the event was of no substance.

The Forty-Five

The 'Forty-Five' has attracted great attention for its romance, and because it seemed to come very near to success. Yet it was not the spontaneous rising of a great part of Scotland. It owed its being to the diplomatic situation in Western Europe and to the personality of one young man.

During the twenty years which separated it from the affair of Glen Shiel things had changed for the Jacobites both in Scotland and abroad. In accordance with an Act of 1725, General Wade had disarmed the Highlands, at least nominally, and during the next eleven years, he had constructed 250 miles of roads. In fulfilling these tasks he had used the aid of friendly Highlanders and, in 1729, six regular companies were formed. These, supplemented by four other companies, were organized into one regiment – the Black Watch (1739–40) – which served with distinction at Fontenoy. Moreover in 1738 Duncan Forbes of Culloden, newly appointed Lord President of the Court of Session, had proposed to raise from less well-affected clans 4,000 or 5,000 men to serve under their chiefs and gentlemen, and his suggestion had been seriously considered.

Meanwhile abroad things had gone badly for 'the King Over the Water'. Expelled from France by the Peace of Utrecht he had sought refuge with the Pope, first at Avignon, later at Rome; his little court was discredited by quarrels and scandals; no prince save the Pope recognized him as king; endless diplomatic intrigues proved futile; George II succeeded easily to the British throne in 1727; France and Britain remained at peace.

A gleam of hope appeared when France and Britain

drifted towards hostility after the war of 'Jenkins' Ear' but, though in 1738 the English Jacobites formed a council and solicited aid from France, their terms were impossibly high. Meanwhile, however, seven distinguished Scottish Jacobites formed an Association which suggested reasonable conditions: they might put 20,000 men in the field if France would send arms, munitions, some money, and a few troops to guard these supplies whilst they mobilized. These *démarches* produced no result; but they became important when, in 1744, Louis XV prepared a coup of his own in revenge for British participation in the battle of Dettingen (1743), fought while Britain and France were not yet at war. He concentrated at Dunkirk a formidable expedition under Marshal Saxe and secretly summoned from Rome Charles, son of the Old Pretender, who speedily arrived in disguise bearing a commission to act as Regent of his Kingdoms in the name of King James.

The Young Chevalier was then twenty-three years of age. At the age of fourteen he had seen war with the Spanish army at Gaeta; fêted in Italy, he had come to believe in his destiny, and deliberately developed his strong physique against the great day. When Saxe's expedition was brought to nought by a violent storm, Charles raged in vain for neither the Scottish Jacobites nor his allies in France would countenance an unsupported rising. Nothing daunted, he pawned his jewels, borrowed money, purchased a few arms, and embarked secretly at Nantes with a few followers.

On 25 July he landed in Moidart. Of the seven men who accompanied him, one was English, three were Irish, and one was a Macdonald from Ulster. His coming was fortunate in that, during 1744, the Scottish government had been in very acute financial embarrassment; and it had 'at its disposal only 3,000 men, mainly raw', under Sir John Cope. Yet in other respects the invasion was most inopportune. The great chiefs were naturally reluctant to risk their people, and their children's heritages, in the cause of a prince, unknown though royal, supported only by a few adventurers who had little to lose besides their heads, and some of whom might even save their heads by pleading commissions in the French army. Macdonald of Clanranald, in whose country he landed, would not come out, nor would Macdonald of Sleat or Macleod of Dunvegan, the heads of the principal clans in the northern Hebrides. Yet the Prince's charm and the adventurous spirit of the Highlands brought initial success. Young Clanranald joined him and the turning point came when Lochiel, chief of the Camerons, was won over in spite of grave misgivings and wise counsels: 'No, I'll share the fate of my Prince, and so shall every man over whom nature or fortune hath given me any power.'

Seven hundred men of a clan renowned for its valour came out at once, and though the Prince had only a thousand followers all told when he raised the Royal Standard at Glenfinnan on 19 August, the snowball soon gathered. Eluding Sir John Cope, who had advanced in the hope of confining the disaffection to the Western Highlands, he occupied Perth, where he proclaimed his father as King. Hastening on, he secured hesitant Edinburgh on 17 September and, four days later, at Prestonpans he routed Cope, who had returned by sea to Dunbar.

During the next few weeks he remained at Edinburgh organizing his forces into what may be described as Clan Regiments. By this time the Macdonalds of Clanranald, Lochgarry, and Glencoe had come in; so had the Stewarts of Appin and the Macphersons, so also the Robertsons and the Atholl men, who formed a complete Brigade, though their chief was with the government. These men all wore the kilt. There were only a few Lowland Regiments, and the four companies of cavalry, consisting of gentlemen and their servants, mustered fewer than five hundred all told. The artillery consisted only of the guns taken at Prestonpans and a few French pieces.

During his stay in Edinburgh, though he kept court at Holyroodhouse, the Prince worked hard among his troops, but though he enchanted the ladies of Edinburgh he found few recruits among the men, and there were desertions from the Highlanders, especially from the Atholl Brigade, whose members could easily reach their own homes. Quite early in the venture, Lord George Murray, Atholl's brother, wrote to Tullibardine (Atholl's son) urging him to destroy the houses and crops of the deserters as an example to others.

No doubt the deserters brought back welcome loot to an impoverished countryside. The harvest had been bad in the Highlands: if the harvest had been good, it might have been very difficult to bring the men out at all. As it was, the Prince's strength was less solid than it appeared. From the lists of prisoners published after the collapse of the Rebellion it seems that among his followers were not only devoted Jacobites and loyal clansmen, but uncertain adventurers, including even a few deserters from the British army. In these lists of prisoners the Macdonalds were much the most numerous (173); and there were sixty-six Camerons; but there were also fifty-one Campbells, whose chief, Argyll, with his clan, was one of the mainstays of the Government.

Charles, always optimistic, may not have realized the instability of his position, but in any case he was right in deciding on an immediate advance in order to forestall the return of the British army from Flanders. He set off south on 31 October. Well advised by Lord George Murray, who had seen much service, he deceived Wade who was in Northumberland, by a feint, crossed the Esk with 5,000 men, captured Carlisle, and marched boldly on. Till he reached Derby on 4 December he was still full of optimism, gaily discussing what clothes he should wear when he entered London; but, by this time, his officers were disillusioned and despondent. Some of the Highlanders had deserted when the Border was crossed; except for a few hundred men from Manchester, he had hardly any recruits; there was no word of a general rising of Jacobites and Roman Catholics or of a French invasion and, on 6 December, the retreat was begun.

Charles was furious, and to this day there are some who assert that he should have gone on since London was in a state of alarm, Wales was stirring, and the victors of Fontenoy would be able to send help. Yet his position was well nigh desperate. Cumberland was at Lichfield with 10,000 men. Wade was on his flank with 8,000 more, and regular troops were returning from the Continent. In Scotland there was counter-revolution as soon as the Prince's forces moved south: the Campbells mustered strongly in the west; Forbes was rousing the Whig clans of the north; some of the towns Charles had occupied, including Edinburgh, were in the hands of the government; and the British navy patrolled the seas. Though he himself sulked and discipline slackened, the retreat was conducted without serious loss save of some guns and, at Clifton, Lord George Murray inflicted a check upon the pursuers. However, the Jacobite garrison at Carlisle surrendered, being mainly Englishmen of the 'Manchester Regiment', and some of them were afterwards executed as traitors.

Yet when the Prince reached Scotland new musters of the Jacobites and the arrival of a few French troops gave him an army of about 8,000. He besieged Stirling Castle and handsomely defeated at Falkirk a relieving force under Hawley (17 January 1746), but there his good fortune left him. His magazine exploded; supplies were short, his army melted away as he retreated north, slowly pursued by Cumberland. He reached Inverness whence he could have escaped into the hills, but, still confident, he insisted on fighting, and at Culloden on 16 April 1746 his valiant men, half-starved and exhausted, were routed with the loss of over 1,000 dead. He escaped from the field, but he made no endeavour to rally his forces sufficiently to make terms, mainly because he no longer possessed the funds to pay any troops. A French attempt to convey a large sum of money to the Prince had been foiled by the Royal Navy just before Culloden. Charles's followers were therefore abandoned to the brutalities of Cumberland and Hawley, while he wandered through the Highlands and Islands until 20 September, when he sailed for France from Moidart where he had at first landed.

His flight was a desperate business. He was an embarrassment to the chiefs into whose land he came; only reluctantly did Flora Macdonald, whose father was with the government forces, convey him to Skye; he was bitten by lice and midges; he suffered from dysentery; he was often hungry. He was saved by the fidelity of the people and by his own courage and endurance: 'Show me a King or Prince in Europe cou'd have borne the like, or the tenth part of it,' wrote Lochgarry.

Arrived in Paris he was the hero of the hour until he was forcibly expelled after the Treaty of Aix-la-Chapelle (1748). From Avignon, whither he had resorted, he disappeared in 1749 and began a course of life which discredited himself and his cause. Probably in 1750, and possibly in 1753, he visited England, but neither there nor abroad did he find support; and when his father died in 1766, the Pope, though he received him in Rome, would not recognize him as King. He died without legitimate issue in 1788 and the stem of the White Rose survived only in his brother Henry, Cardinal of York, who survived till 1807 having been supported in his latter years by a pension offered with great delicacy by George III.

Meanwhile his supporters paid heavily for their loyalty – apart from the ravages by the navy and army which followed Culloden. One hundred and twenty of the prisoners taken were executed: peers like Kilmarnock, Balmerino, Lovat, and Derwentwater by the axe; the rest by the rope. About 1,150 were banished or transported and the fate of almost 700 is unknown. Argyll and Forbes of Culloden, who had done so much to stem the rebellion, found themselves little regarded. The office of Secretary of State was abolished and, thereafter, the Lord Advocate, under the direction of the Secretary of the Northern Department, came to represent the royal power in Scotland. Rigorous laws were passed against Episcopalians. The Disarming Act, as now renewed, banned the kilt and condemned the pipes. An Act of 1747 abolished the 'Heritable Jurisdictions' of landowners, which had been specifically guaranteed by the Act of Union and the compensation paid (almost £600,000 sterling), though perhaps not unfair, was far less than what was demanded.

There were many pardons, free or conditional, but the lands of attainted or 'declared' traitors were forfeited and, with regard to them, the government, prompted by the Lord Advocate, William Grant of Prestongrange, proceeded wisely. Some of the lands were 'annexed' to the Crown and the management of the income (about £5,000 a year) was assigned to trustees who were directed to apply it to the promotion of Protestantism, good order, and education in the Highlands. The trustees did their work well. Order was soon restored. Schools were established. The system of land-tenure was improved, and some afforestation was begun. Handicrafts were introduced.

So completely did the Jacobite cause evaporate that, in 1782, the ban on the kilt was removed and, in 1784, the forfeited lands were restored to their former owners upon payment of moderate sums (which were used in part for the building of the Register House in its commanding position overlooking North Bridge in Edinburgh and, in part, for the construction of the Forth and Clyde Canal). The changed attitude was due, in part, to the feats of the Highland Regiments in the British Army. In 1757, William Pitt adopted the policy commended by Forbes in 1738 and enlisted men even from the disaffected clans. His action did not proceed from generous motives alone. He commended it to Hardwicke on the ground that 'not many of them would return'. It was only in 1766 when the Highland Regiments had distinguished themselves in Germany and in America that he paid tribute to their valour – and to his own wisdom. In all, between 1757 and 1799, about a dozen regiments were raised, whose performances form a bright page in the annals of the British army.

The Forty-Five facilitated further change in the economy of the Highlands. The chiefs, no longer reckoning their wealth in fighting men, began to demand rents from their principal tenants, the 'tacksmen',* whose main obligation

*A 'tack' is a lease.

280

hitherto had been to maintain the military strength of the clan and act as officers. Many tacksmen emigrated; those who remained demanded rent from their sub-tenants and, as the population increased – and it increased until 1831 – the small family holdings became even smaller. The introduction of the potato after 1739 produced a significant increase in the productivity of Scottish agriculture. This was particularly important in the Highlands, but the ordinary crofter could obtain ready money only by going south to work in the harvest or by breeding black cattle which were driven south for sale. Meanwhile the encroaching sheep advanced.

Yet the Forty-Five did not greatly affect the development of Scotland as a whole. The march to Derby was a fine military achievement, but it was achieved against a government and a people unprepared. The Prince did not command the support of all the Highlands and he did not enlist many recruits as he advanced. The attitude of many contemporaries seems to have been that 'something ought to be done about' this Highland raid; and, in fact, the King's servants, once recovered from the initial shock, did pretty well.

The failure of the rising ruined the Scottish supporters of the White Rose and convinced foreign powers that it was not profitable to support a losing cause. As a political issue Jacobitism never recovered. Yet in Scottish sentiment it survived and, under the stimulus of the romantic movement, it produced a literature still well loved – the novels of Sir Walter Scott, for example, and the songs of James Hogg and Lady Nairne. Burns himself wrote verses (not of his best) to the 'Bonnie Lass of Albany' (Charlotte, the illegitimate daughter of Charles and Clementina Walkinshaw). *Tout finit par des chansons*. Yet, rightly, has the tradition endured. The Prince, in the end, proved himself unworthy and ungrateful, and his cause was more than doubtful; but courage and hardihood, loyalty and sacrifice are very precious things.

CHAPTER 16

THE EIGHTEENTH-CENTURY
DEVELOPMENT

THE main reason why the Jacobite risings, except in the Highlands, had little effect on the development of Scotland is that the country was adjusting itself to new situations, and its attention was much directed to the south.

Constitution

The government of the country resembled that of the seventeenth century in that it was still directed from the south; yet there were two differences of importance. Government was now in the hands, not of the commissioner representing an absolutist king, but of a king whose officers changed according to the parliamentary majority. Again, seats in the Parliament, hitherto little sought, had risen in value with the abolition of the Articles, and had become even more valuable when the government depended on a parliamentary majority. Hence there came into being an unofficial 'manager' whose business it was to see that the Scottish representation at Westminster accorded with the policy of the party in power.

To this end the 'manager' employed methods of control already practised in England. He had at his disposal places on the civil list of Scotland, at least one third of the ecclesiastical patronage; he could offer pensions or posts in the customs, excise, and postoffice; he could help to procure commissions in the army; and sometimes, though rarely, offices under the British government. His task was rendered the easier by the nature of the Scottish representative system. Amongst the peers (about 150 in all) who elected sixteen of their own number were many whose wealth did not match their dignity, and who were open to offers for themselves or for their sons. Before the century was very old, the Crown was able to send down before an election of representative peers a list of its own nominees, and this 'King's List' was invariably accepted.

In 1734, for example, when a very powerful group tried to organize opposition, its most successful candidate obtained twenty-five votes, whereas fourteen of those on the King's List got fifty-nine apiece, and the two others sixty and fifty-eight respectively. 'Management' was evidently efficient, and as regards the Lords the government fortress was well nigh impregnable, though the peers were occasionally recalcitrant at by-elections.

Control of the Commons was the easier because the electorates were very small. In the shires, the elector must hold from the King either a 40 shillings land of 'Old Extent' or £400 a year from land. During the eighteenth century the shire electors throughout the country never numbered more than 2,700; the name and quality of each elector was readily ascertained; 'influence' could be used; and, owing to the now obscure qualification of 'Old Extent',* manipulation of votes was possible.

It was well understood that great magnates might control a whole shire, and that everywhere noblemen and lesser magnates had some power. The issue was not always simple. 'Interest' might be used to further the ends of kinship or friendship as well as of politics, and sometimes there might be a conflict of interests within the shire. Where this occurred it might be possible to 'do a deal', but sometimes there was a genuine contest. Yet in every case the Crown was sure to have some means of exerting influence.

In the burghs the franchise was restricted to the members of the town councils. They, too, were open to pressure from

*'Old Extent' was a traditional assessment for taxation long out of use. An Act of 1743 prevented further creation of 'faggot-votes', but the method it prescribed for determining what was a qualification under 'Old Extent' led to fresh difficulties; and the complexities of the Scottish land-laws as to the relative rights of 'superiors, possessors, life-renters, and "wad-setters"' (mortgagees) led to further uncertainties. (See Thomas Thomson's *Memorial on Old Extent*, Stair Society, 1946.)

local magnates, or promises from would-be candidates, but the situation was complicated because the burghs voted in groups of four or five, and each member might be under obligation to a different magnate. Argyll had great power over the four burghs of the Glasgow group, but his 'interest' in Ayrshire was shared by Bute, Eglinton, and Loudon; and where, as in the Dingwall group, rival families disputed, the result was never easy to predict. Moreover, some town councils – Ayr and Dundee, for example – sometimes showed independence; and Lord Queensberry in 1734 was uncertain of the prospects in Dumfries, though he himself had been drinking among the electors. Coercion, influence, and venality were general, but there is no record of the actual purchase of a seat for money. One small Fife burgh, at least, let it be known that it would give its vote to the candidate who promised to do most for the burgh; but, even so, it could offer only one vote in a constituency of five burghs. In Scotland the phrase 'rotten borough' should be used with care.

None the less, generally speaking, 'management' had the means to prevail, and the political history of Scotland during the eighteenth century reflects the influence of 'managers' who were changed from time to time with the rise and fall of parties at Westminster. For long there was no thought of using the Tories, suspected of Jacobitism, and the government had to decide between two parties of Whigs – the 'Old Party' which came to be called 'Argathelian' after its leader Argyll, and the representatives of the old 'Squadrone' who were at one time known as the 'Patriots' since they professed to regard the interest of Scotland as well as the Revolution Settlement and the Hanoverian succession.

Because George I disliked Argyll, his early government relied on the Squadrone whose leader, Roxburghe, was made Secretary of State for Scotland; but Walpole inclined to Argyll and, in 1725, angered by Scottish opposition to the Malt Tax (which involved a brewers' strike in Edinburgh, the burning of an M.P.'s house in Glasgow and the use of troops to disperse the mob), dismissed Roxburghe and Lord President Dundas. No new Secretary was appointed, but management passed to Argyll who, with his brother Islay (third Duke, 1743) and their agents Colonel Campbell of Mamore (fourth Duke, 1761) and Andrew Fletcher, Lord Milton (Justice-Clerk till 1748), established an almost complete control over Scottish affairs. The effort of the 'Patriots' after 1737 to join hands with the 'Leicester House Party' of Frederick, Prince of Wales, and thereby to exploit the rivalry between George II and his son, had little effect: Islay and his brother Argyll, despite distant personal relations, began to build a formidable political machine.

Argyll, however, began to lose favour with Walpole after his action in the Porteous Affair* and made a half-hearted alliance with the Patriots, which defeated the Court in the election of 1741. Yet the Patriots gained little; for, though Carteret, who succeeded Walpole in 1742, revived the office of Secretary in favour of Tweeddale of the Squadrone tradition, he still operated the machine through the Campbells, and Islay, now third Duke of Argyll (1743–61), became 'the uncrowned King of Scotland'. He lost some of his influence because his pleas for clemency after the Forty-Five led to his being accused of Jacobitism; but he and his machine were indispensable. In 1746 the office of Secretary of State was abolished, but the Rebellion had tended to drive all Whigs into the same camp, and the Pelhams, who valued the support of the Scottish bloc in the Commons, carried into Scottish affairs the principle of the 'Broad

---

*In 1736 Porteous, the blustering Captain of the City Guard of Edinburgh, fired upon a crowd at the execution of two popular smugglers; four onlookers were killed and eleven wounded. He was sentenced to death for murder, reprieved by the Queen, and expected a full pardon, but the mob took him out of the Tolbooth and brutally hanged him. Investigation by the Scottish law-officers was met by a conspiracy of silence. In February 1737, the Scots judges were made to stand at the Bar of the House of Lords, and in the House of Commons humiliating penalties on Edinburgh were proposed. All the Scots members protested, including Argyll, whose English peerage had been granted before the Union.

Bottom' and disarmed the opposition by giving it a share in the Crown patronage.

On the death of Argyll and the revival of the Tories, power passed to John Stewart, Marquis of Bute and favourite of the young George III. He operated the patronage through his brother, Stewart Mackenzie, but his régime was marked by no great extension of favour to Scotsmen. After Bute's fall (1763), remote control was exercised from England, often by the Secretary of the Northern Department; but the management of Scottish affairs tended to fall into the hands of the Lord Advocate. Yet four successive Advocates, Grant of Prestongrange, Robert Dundas, Thomas Millar, and James Montgomery, to whom high public office came in the course of professional careers, were distinguished rather by their promotion of good legislation than by their political power.

The country was not altogether supine. In 1761, when public feeling had been aroused by the refusal to allow Scotland a militia like that provided for England in 1757, Edinburgh stoutly rejected Argyll's nominee for one of its parliamentary seats, and next year the 'Poker Club' was founded by a group of the Edinburgh *literati* to stir up the spirit of Scotland. In 1774 again the King's List was resolutely attacked by some of the peers, though the Crown got its own way in the end. And, under Henry Dundas (Lord Advocate 1775–83), the system of management reached its apogee.

Born to the proud tradition of a legal family Dundas was appointed Solicitor-General at the age of twenty-five; in 1774 he was elected for the county of Midlothian and, although thereafter he lived much in London, he endeared himself to his compatriots by speaking good Scots at a time when polite Edinburgh was learning to speak English from teachers from the south (Irish Sheridan amongst them). He was bluff, approachable, and free from venom; free, too, from rigid adherence to party – he held office under administrations of differing political hue. At first a Whig, he served with distinction under Lord North, then under two

Whig governments until, in 1783, he sided with Pitt whom he followed thereafter. He was not a turncoat: in his day parties changed their political complexions. Brougham and Cockburn, Whigs both, regarded him as a great servant of Scotland.

In his early days he promoted an Act which began the redemption of colliers and salters from the servitude to which earlier legislation had condemned them; in 1779 he refused, in the face of popular and clerical pressure, to support a Bill against the removal of Roman Catholic disabilities; it was under his superintendence that, in 1782 and 1784, Acts were passed to relieve the Highlands from the penalties imposed after the Forty-Five. Meanwhile he had taken vigorous measures for the strengthening of the British fleets and, in 1782, joined to his office that of Treasurer of the Navy. Dismissed by the Fox–North Coalition, he joined hands with Pitt, whose scheme of parliamentary reform he supported in 1783. When Pitt became Prime Minister the next year he regained his post as Treasurer of the Navy and then went on to serve in many offices, among them Secretary for War, First Lord of the Admiralty, and President of the Board of Control for India. It cannot be said that he used the machinery of management for his personal advantage; but certainly he used it to gratify his friends and fellow-countrymen in the furtherance of ends which he thought beneficial to Scotland. The evidence shows that he scrutinized the lists with immense care to secure the representation he wanted in both Houses and that, at first, it was North rather than himself who commanded the allegiance of some of the peers, but before long his machinery was in full operation.

Though his rule came to be known as the 'Dundas Despotism', it was not founded entirely upon machination. There was, it is true, some sympathy for the rebellious colonists and, later, with the French Republic; but the most influential part of Scotland approved of what he did. In the 'eighties' there were rumblings of discontent. Led by the able Henry Erskine (brother of the Earl of Buchan), the

Scottish Whigs raised their heads while the Rockingham administration ruled in England. There were proposals of parliamentary reform and, in 1783, Henry Erskine was made Lord Advocate by the Coalition; but before the general election came in 1784, Pitt was in power and Dundas was supporting him. Defeated at the election, the Whigs began a campaign against parliamentary corruption, especially against the enrolment of unqualified voters, and they had some success. William Adam and Henry Erskine prepared a frontal attack and, by 1788, to that end had had prepared a nominal roll of every shire vote in Scotland (there were 2,662 in all) which showed the family, the affiliations, and the financial position of every single man so far as that could be ascertained. Before long, however, political opinion in Scotland was shaken by the outbreak of the French Revolution; Pitt became steadily more Tory and his henchman, Dundas, followed his example.

Economic Growth

During the eighteenth century Scotland experienced an economic development which greatly impressed writers of about 1800, who could compare what they saw about them with what their fathers or grandfathers had told them of the abject poverty into which Scotland had been plunged by the 'seven ill years' of William's reign, by the collapse of the Darien Scheme, and by the failure of the Union to produce any immediate relief.

The rise in prosperity was in part due to new opportunities presented by the Union, and in part also to the ability of the Scots to seize the opportunities. It has been said that, in a reaction against the religious furies of the seventeenth century, Scotland developed a secular spirit, turned to money-making, and according to some, magnified the virtues of thrift, abstinence, and hard work into a kind of piety expressed in the fact that copies of the *Shorter Catechism* issued to children bore the multiplication tables on the back. To state the matter so is to exaggerate. Capitalism existed before Calvinism. Certainly the secular spirit of 'reason' advanced in Scotland as elsewhere, but frequent controversies are proof that there was still an active interest in religion and there is ample evidence that simple piety was maintained in many ordinary households.

What is true is that the regard for truth and honesty inculcated by the discipline of the Kirk was a good foundation for success in business, and that Scottish people, trained to the 'economic' virtues in a long struggle against a hard environment, were quick to exploit the advantage offered by better conditions.

Agriculture. The impetus to improving agriculture came from the nobility and gentry. Gentlemen going to and from Parliament must have noted the prosperous English fields, while farmers, and especially cattle-breeders, assured themselves of bigger and better markets. It was Lady Henrietta Mordaunt (daughter of the Earl of Peterborough), married in 1706 to the son of the Duke of Gordon, who introduced hay-making, foreign grasses, and the English plough into Moray; and, in the more general advances made in the Lothians and the south-west, it was the aristocracy who led the way. The sixth Earl of Haddington was conspicuous for his afforestation and for the sowing of rye-grass and clover; the Earl of Rothes has been credited with the introduction of the turnip about 1716; and the second Earl of Stair not only planted turnips and cabbages in fields, but enclosed lands, drained marshes, put down lime, made roads, and planted woods in Galloway and West Lothian. The Honourable Society of Improvers, founded in 1723, included among its three hundred members dukes and peers, judges, professors, and landlords, all interested in the new agriculture. The Duke of Perth, afterwards ruined by the Forty-Five, was the great 'improver' in Perthshire; and, later in the century, Lord Kames and his son, employing a gigantic water-wheel made at Alloa, turned into fruitful fields hundreds of acres of bogland in Menteith.

Everywhere English methods, drilling, sowing, and the

rotation of crops, came into use; so did the iron plough which could be drawn by two horses, though, in backward parts, the old plough with its big mixed team was still in use towards the end of the century.

A necessary part of 'improvement' was the substitution of compact enclosed fields for the old run-rig system. The enclosures were unpopular as restricting liberty, diminishing free grazing, and presaging unemployment; and in Galloway, where proprietors were enclosing land to breed black cattle, there broke out in 1724 a serious rising of 'Levellers' (destroyers of fences) which had to be suppressed by military intervention. There, somewhat late, Craik of Arbigland led the way in the new agriculture, but it was in the Lothians and afterwards in Aberdeenshire that farming obtained its greatest eminence. At Ormiston John Cockburn was a model 'improver' who provided, in a new village, craftsmen and their families to do the work ancillary to farming. Like many of the early improvers Cockburn went bankrupt. However, at Monymusk, Sir Archibald Grant, between 1716 and 1760, transformed a miserable property into a prosperous estate, granting long leases to his tenants to encourage 'improvement', providing local industries for those displaced by his enclosures and education for the children. John Wesley in 1761 was much impressed by what he saw; but our admiration is tempered by the knowledge that Grant had been expelled from the House of Commons for corruption in 1732, and is said to have acquired considerable 'tochers' (dowries) with three of his four successive wives.

The cultivation of the potato, first grown in fields near Kilsyth in 1739, spread rapidly and greatly improved the diet of the peasantry. As the century progressed labourers were better housed and better paid; in 1765 a ploughman's wage had been increased by at least fifty per cent, and by 1796, it was three or four times what it had been in 1765, though we must remember that inflation had reduced its purchasing power.

The average weight of animals was doubled during the

century; in 1723 30,000 cattle were sold at the great fair at Crieff, mainly to be fattened in England and, by the end of the century, the annual figure of 100,000 was reached. In Berwickshire and the Lothians rich crops of grain were raised. Ayrshire excelled in dairy farming, Galloway in stock-breeding, and the Borders in sheep. All along the eastern side of Scotland new implements and the new husbandry were being introduced by landlords and by tenants. Yet upon this fair picture must be noted some blots. In remote places the untidy, uneconomic farming persisted. The cost of living tended to rise. Not all landlords were considerate. Great sheep farms appeared and with them unemployment, especially in the Highlands, where sheep farmers from the south-west began to come in 1762, for there was no alternative occupation. People moved into towns or across the Atlantic, and it must not be forgotten that there were emigrations from the Lowlands as well as from the Highlands.

The difference between the developed and the under-developed areas became very evident during the long struggle with France from 1793 to 1815 when high prices for foodstuffs at last made improvement a profitable policy. In the developed areas agriculture prospered enormously, but in the north and west only the sheep prospered, though for a short while the kelp industry provided work along the shores where peasants collected and burned seaweed to make kelp (or industrial alkali). However, there was never enough work and, despite a great enlistment in the army, a surplus population was driven into the town or across the seas.

Industry and Commerce. During the eighteenth century Scotland experienced remarkable developments, both in industry and commerce, but in neither case was progress visible immediately after the Union, mainly because a weak Scottish economy was ill-fitted to cope with English competition. The Scottish Parliament in the reigns of William and Anne had made genuine efforts to improve matters, but its efforts were hampered by the privileges of the royal burghs and of the incorporations (craft-guilds) within them. As for the 'unfree burghs of barony'– about one hundred and fifty in number – attempts to secure for them a share (upon payment) in the monopoly of foreign trade had produced little result, though Paisley and Greenock were now far larger than some of the little towns of the east which were still 'royal'. In the more substantial of the baronial burghs, monopolistic incorporations controlled the main industries; in many others, burgh status involved little more than the right to hold a weekly market for local goods and an occasional fair.

There was extensive mining of coal, iron, and lead, but the workers in coal and salt, mainly about the Firth of Forth, were for long hereditary serfs (p. 287). Coarse plaiding was manufactured, but weaving and spinning were for the most part domestic industries carried out by the people of the farms. Of these the healthiest was the linen industry. This was well-nigh a staple, and an attempt by Parliament in 1711 to impose an export duty upon linen, while leaving English wool untaxed, united all the Scottish members into an opposition before which the government bowed. The industry throve. By 1726 one foreign visitor reported that the poor people all span, some of them very well, and that Scots flax was better than Dutch; and Edward Burt from England said that he found good linen everywhere, but chiefly in the Lowlands. In 1727 the industry received a fresh fillip. The Act of Union had provided that the surplus of the Equivalents was to be paid at the rate of £2,000 a year for seven years to encourage coarse wool manufacture and, thereafter, the fisheries and other industries. Nothing had yet been done; but now, in response to an application from the Convention of Royal Burghs, the government established a Board of Trustees which was to provide annually for six years the sum of £6,000 – £2,650 for the linen trade, £2,650 for the fisheries, and £700 for the wool trade.

The fisheries and the wool trade made little of it in the

face of English and Dutch competition, but the linen trade developed enormously. Paisley, using Dutch methods, began the spinning of her famous yarn; other towns, including Glasgow, manufactured for the export trade, which doubled between 1725 and 1738. An Act of 1751 set linen-weaving free from craft restrictions and the bold action in 1746 of the British Linen Company (which became the British Linen Bank in 1763) in advancing cash credits stimulated production all over Scotland.

Before long the industry was being organized by 'manufacturers' who supplied flax to the spinners, bought back the yarn, supplied it to the weavers, and bought back the cloth which they sold. This system lasted long, for it proved very difficult to apply machinery to the spinning of flax. Machines were used before 1800 but they produced only coarse yarn, and it was only after 1825, when Kay discovered a process which made the brittle fibre more tractable, that a great industry sprang up about Dundee and in north-east Scotland generally (see pp. 348–9).

Meanwhile the cotton industry had advanced with enormous strides. In the last quarter of the century the textile 'mill' appeared, largely as the result of the inventions by Arkwright (1769–75) and Crompton (1779). The first cotton mill – a very small affair – appeared at Rothesay in 1778 and the next year a mill was built at Penicuik, but it was mainly in Lanarkshire and Renfrewshire that the development was greatest. Labour was readily available owing to the influx from the Highlands; by 1780 one mill near Glasgow employed 1,300 people and in 1786 David Dale erected at New Lanark the famous mill in which he began those social experiments for the good of the workers which were to become famous under his son-in-law, Robert Owen.

These early experiments in the use of machinery were at first confined to spinning and, even after their introduction, much of the work inside the factories was done by hand till about 1800. The introduction of machinery into weaving was a slow affair. A power-loom, indeed, was used in Glasgow in 1792, but the motive energy was provided by

Newfoundland dogs; it was not till 1807 that the power-loom was used on a large scale at Catrine in Ayrshire and, even so, it was not suitable for the finer cloths. The hand-loom weaver was still essential and, when self-employed, could maintain a sturdy independence; but eventually he fell under the control of the 'manufacturer' who came to pay him a wage, though he worked on his own loom, and one explanation of the slow introduction of machinery may be that, with a plentitude of labour, the wage paid was so small that the employer had no incentive to mechanize.

Steam-power was first used in a cotton factory only in 1792, though in 1765 James Watt had produced his improved steam engine which was employed in coal-mining. Yet, in one way and another, the cotton industry expanded enormously. In 1792, American cotton was first used and, by 1800, the annual output of cotton, mainly from Glasgow and Paisley, was worth £3,000,000 as compared with £1,000,000 for linen. John Galt, writing early in the nineteenth century, called Glasgow 'the city of muslin-makers'. Meanwhile, the wool industry grew with the increase of sheep, especially in the Border country.

In 1759 the beginning of the ironworks at Carron marked the birth of large-scale production in an industry which had been attempted sporadically where timber for smelting could be procured. New methods already employed in England demanded the use of coal, as well as of wood and of water-power, and it was largely English knowledge and English capital which fixed upon Carron as a place which would provide these requisites, though William Cadell of Cockenzie played an important part. At first, only small articles were produced, but the reputation of the company was established when, in 1779, the navy adopted the carronade, a gun quickly reloaded, which did great execution at the Battle of the Saints (1782). Before the century closed, furnaces were opened near Glasgow, in Lanarkshire, and in Ayrshire; there, and in Lothian, coal-pits were opened to provide the necessary fuel. Yet, as late as 1814, the annual output of iron was worth only about £230,000, and coal and iron were considered as only secondary industries compared with the textiles.

Meanwhile, a traditional industry took a new lease of life. The fisheries, in spite of some government help given after 1727, had made little progress, but in 1786, the British Fisheries Society set up three 'stations'– at Ullapool, Tobermory, and Lochbay (Skye) – and next year established Pulteneytown near Wick; the long-continued war with France compelled Britain to look to herself for food supplies and, before long, Scottish fishing was in a thriving way.

Concurrent with this industrial expansion came a notable improvement in communications; a Turnpike Road Act, 1751, followed by half a dozen similar Acts, led to the provision of many Toll Roads; by 1786 the journey from Edinburgh to London by stage-coach could be accomplished in sixty hours. The practice of using small stones to make a surface was in use in Renfrewshire before it was popularized by Macadam early in the new century, and Macadam's roads were scorned for lack of a deep foundation by Thomas Telford (1757–1834), who began his career as an apprentice mason at Langholm and became one of the greatest 'civil' engineers.

Along with the development of roads came an increased use of waterways. As early as 1710 courageous Greenock embarked on a very expensive scheme to enlarge its harbour, which succeeded so well that the debt was cleared off by 1740. The Forth and Clyde Canal, begun in 1768, was not opened to navigation till 1790, but meanwhile James Watt had personally surveyed the construction of seven miles of canal to bring coal into Glasgow from the pits at Old Monkland. In 1759 was passed the first of several Acts for deepening the Clyde so that ocean-going ships might reach Glasgow, and in other Scottish ports, docks were enlarged and improved.

Overseas Trade. The expansion of overseas trade during the eighteenth century was remarkable. Its main feature was the

295

rapid growth of the American trade, and the consequent shifting of commerce from east to west. Glasgow merchants soon began to send out the kind of goods likely to be wanted in a colony – hard-wearing cloths, all kinds of iron implements for farming, for carpentry, and for house-building, glass, and leather goods. At first Glasgow tended to use hired ships, the local ships being small; but by 1735 she had 67 ships, of which a third traded with the Colonies, and by 1776 she had no fewer than 386 vessels. Greenock, too, sent a ship of her own to America in 1719 and soon was actively engaged in the import of sugar and rum. Glasgow, for her part, made herself the emporium of the tobacco trade, buying from the colonies and re-exporting, mainly to France. As early as 1724 she re-exported three quarters of the 4,000,000 lb. which she imported and, in 1771, 43,000,000 lb. of a total import of 46,000,000. Her wealthy merchants were the 'Tobacco Lords' who acquired great fortunes, though they were not quite the red-cloaked purse-proud aristocracy of popular belief. They dealt in other things besides tobacco, such as mahogany, lemons, and limes; of course, they exported too, and many of them were public-spirited citizens. Their downfall came with the outbreak of the American War of Independence. By 1778 the total trade of Scotland was only fifty-eight per cent of what it had been in 1771. Yet, though some great houses were ruined, the country showed a remarkable resilience. In 1783 Glasgow established a Chamber of Commerce, the first ever founded, to study markets and promote sales. The growing trade in textiles did much to redeem the situation; and by 1791 Scottish trade had regained the figures of 1771 with an advantageous difference in that the value of home-produced exports had been almost doubled.

The population of Glasgow, which in 1708 was about 12,500 had risen to 25,000 by the middle of the century and, thereafter, increased so rapidly that by 1831 she mustered 200,000 people. Paisley, which in 1782 had 17,000 inhabitants, boasted more than 31,000 in 1801 and the surrounding parishes (Old Monkland, for example) showed a corresponding increase. It was not only in the west that the urban population increased. Seaports with their hinterlands – Leith, Dundee, and Aberdeen, for example – flourished and so did inland towns too.

Edinburgh, which retained its place as the capital, expanded in the second half of the century from the many-storeyed 'lands' in and about the High Street into the beautiful New Town. In 1772 the North Bridge was constructed and, in 1781, the Old and the New were more firmly linked when the Nor Loch was drained and the Mound erected. In the seventies the Theatre Royal and the Register House were built at the east end of Princes Street and, by 1800, George Street had been completed with St Andrew's Square at the east end and Charlotte Square at the west.

Banking. As a necessary concomitant to this remarkable expansion came a great development in banking. As the Bank of Scotland, founded in 1695, was suspected of Jacobitism, the Royal Bank was established in 1727. About the middle of the century local banks were established in Glasgow and other towns; some of these failed disastrously – the Ayr Bank in 1772 and the Glasgow Arms in 1793 – but others such as the Thistle were united with other houses to form banks which survived until after the Second World War. The most remarkable venture was that of the British Linen Bank already noted. Its boldness was justified by the event and its example was followed. Increasing capital was used to develop home industries, to improve communications, and to promote overseas trade. Altogether the economy of Scotland was in a thriving way. The Industrial Revolution was by no means complete by the end of the eighteenth century, but it was already well advanced.

Ecclesiastical

It is not to be supposed that the increase of Scotland's attention to economics swept away her concern for religion. Domestic piety was still generally maintained, and public interest in ecclesiastical affairs is attested by the vigour of controversies.

The Revolution Settlement had established a Kirk based on the Act of 1592 in structure and on the Westminster Confession in doctrine, but this Kirk did not embrace all Scotsmen. The Roman Catholics, Episcopalians, and some of the Presbyterians did not accept it.

The Roman Catholics decreased in numbers during the century. The Pope appointed a Vicar Apostolic, who was consecrated bishop in 1694, and reorganized his charge into 'districts'. By 1703 he enjoyed the services of thirty-three clergymen, but thereafter the fortunes of his church declined with each failure of the Jacobite Cause. A framework was preserved; in 1731 the country was divided into two vicariates each under a bishop; clergy came quietly in and services, though forbidden by law, were maintained. Yet 'Popery' was still esteemed a real danger; the aftermath of the Forty-Five took its toll; and by 1755 it was reckoned that there were only some 16,500 communicant Roman Catholics in Scotland, distributed over the shires of Banff, Aberdeen, Inverness, and Argyll. The figure (for, especially in the remote Highlands, there is little evidence) is probably too small; but this church, though still it continued, played almost no part in politics.

The Episcopalians underwent the same experience as the Roman Catholics, but in a less extreme form. Taking advantage of the measure of toleration offered by William, a fair number of their clergy subscribed to the oath of allegiance and kept their livings; the bishops remained 'Non-Jurors', but they survived to consecrate pastors to the new 'meeting-houses' which appeared as the parishes were filled by Presbyterians. The Episcopalians prospered under

Anne, but their vigorous adherence to the Fifteen cost them dear; some of their clergy, especially in Aberdeen, were deprived, and an Act of 1719 closed all 'meeting-houses' where prayers were not offered for King George. Yet in 1720 they established a definite constitution when, on the death of the last pre-Revolution prelate, a bishop was appointed 'Primus' without reference to a particular See. This system continues to the present day. Yet there was internal dissent over certain 'usages'; the failure of the Forty-Five brought new restrictions; the number of the clergy and the size of the congregations alike declined though Aberdeenshire remained a stronghold. Yet a church which included in its members many nobles and gentlemen had the power to survive. It organized itself territorially; in 1784 it consecrated a bishop for the revolted American Colonies; and in 1792 the main body of the 'Non-Jurors' made their peace with the Hanoverian régime. Stronger in influence than in numbers, the Episcopal Church was still a force to be considered.

The Cameronians (pp. 239–40), for their part, steadfastly refused to accept an uncovenanted Church, but their numbers were few, and they abstained from political action, though on one occasion their reproaches nearly drove the Assembly into a 'Declaratory Act' as to the independence of the Church. Their three remaining ministers were admitted to the Established Church but the 'Society Folk', as they were called, still held aloof and, having obtained the adherence of two ordained ministers, established themselves in 1743 as the 'Reformed Presbyterian Church' proclaiming itself the only true Kirk of the Covenanters. It continued in a quiet way, unyielding in its principles, aloof from politics to the extent of refusing to vote. Its strength was at first in the west, especially among country people, but it came to establish itself in some towns. In 1876 most of its members joined the Free Church whose origin in the Disruption (see p. 331) seemed to be a vindication of its own position.

The Secession (*1733–40*). The National Church had to reckon not only with these Churches which remained outsïde it, but also with dissensions in its own midst, which before long produced the 'Secession'.

The immediate occasion of the rupture was a contention about 'patronage' which had been re-introduced by the Act of 1712, but its root cause was the coexistence of two conflicting approaches to religion. On the one hand, some churchmen and laymen, alike influenced by the dawn of 'reason', began to doubt whether the Westminster Standards had an eternal validity, and whether the restrictions upon life imposed in the name of piety were really justified. The 'enlightened' views commended themselves to philosophical thinkers, in the universities and elsewhere, and also to easy-going people, often, though not always, of the more prosperous classes, who were happy to think that the severe discipline of the Kirk was part of an old superstition which might well be discarded.

On the other hand there were in the Kirk many who still revered the Covenanting martyrs, and who, while they accepted the Westminster standards, were inclined to emphasize 'Free Grace' as against Law. Logically, therefore, they were liable to be denounced as 'Antinomian'; but, in fact, their view of religion was very austere, insisting upon exact morality, and regarding most forms of pleasure as sin. These devout folk in many parishes formed praying societies,* wherein they supplemented the services of the Church, to which they still adhered, by communal devotions, in some cases heartily approved by the ministers. For the most part they belonged to the humbler classes of society, and were not assertive politically; yet their religious profession induced a feeling of equality, perhaps even a superiority in spiritual things. They despised preaching which seemed to be a 'blash of cauld morality' instead of a soul-warming and sin-denouncing gospel; and their vital

*They are not to be confused with the 'Society Folk' (the Cameronians who stood outside the Kirk). Their position was that of the 'Prayer Circles' of pre-Reformation Germany.

belief led them into a headlong conflict with the supporters of patronage, which was to take a public and, in some sense, a political aspect.

The early years of George I were marked by omens of the coming storm. In 1714 John Simson, Professor of Divinity at Glasgow, was attacked for teaching 'Arminianism' (broadly, freewill, as against 'predestination'), but managed to clear himself. Twelve years later he was accused of favouring 'Arianism' (Unitarianism). After a full examination of this charge he was suspended from teaching in 1729, but he was allowed to keep his Chair; and other professors, both in St Andrews and in Glasgow, who went on to preach what seemed like a new theology were also allowed to keep their Chairs.

Their critics met with far harder measures. Thomas Boston, minister of Ettrick, partly republished an English Puritan book of the seventeenth century, *The Marrow of Modern Divinity*, which emphasized the part played by 'Grace' in conversion. It was violently attacked as antinomian by Principal Hadow of St Mary's College, St Andrews, and the General Assembly of 1720 condemned it. Twelve devout ministers, the 'Marrow Men', were publicly rebuked, admonished, and threatened.

Meanwhile, the General Assembly upheld the action of patrons, who had begun to exercise their powers, and tended to present moderate men in preference to evangelical hot-heads; when grievances about 'intrusions' multiplied, it took to overruling recalcitrant presbyteries by appointing 'riding commissions', and in 1732 the Assembly passed an Act against congregational elections. Ebenezer Erskine, minister of Stirling, himself earlier a victim of 'intrusion', defied the Assembly in a sermon, and next year he and three of his supporters were declared to be no longer ministers of the Church. Nothing daunted, the four 'Secession Fathers' in a meeting at Gairney Bridge in December, 1733, constituted themselves a separate Presbytery. In 1737 they were joined by four others including Ebenezer's brother Ralph, and appointed a teacher to instruct their young men. The Assembly, more tolerant than the Commission, tried in vain to win them back. Only in 1740 did it expel them and in 1744 the 'Dissidents' formed themselves into the 'Associate Synod', quite outside the Established Church.

The new Secession Church grew very quickly for it had the nucleus of congregations in the 'Praying Societies' and, although its founders had been ministers in Perthshire and Fife, the forty congregations which it had established by 1740 were widely scattered. Almost all were in towns, some of them small, though churches were early founded in Edinburgh, Glasgow, Dundee, and Newcastle. Very soon 'congregations' and 'synods' appeared in Ulster and, before long, 'presbyteries' in North America. The members came mainly from the middle class, though one of the original four ministers, Moncrieff of Abernethy, was a laird, but they were fairly prosperous folk, who could build churches and pay ministers.

Although the Seceders gained the sympathy of George Whitefield, who was a Calvinist and who took part in a great 'revival' at Cambuslang (1742), he did not adhere to them, finding their outlook too limited. Yet narrowly exclusive though they were, they soon quarrelled among themselves as to the admissibility of taking the Burgess Oath. This was, in fact, aimed against Jacobitism in 1745, and applicable only to a few cities, but its wording seemed to assert that the only true religion in Scotland was that of the Established Church. The 'Burghers', amongst whom were the Erskines, held that the oath could properly be taken; the 'Anti-Burghers' excommunicated the Erskines and, before long, set up a 'General Associate Synod'. The 'Breach' thus made in 1747 was not healed until 1820 and, even then, not entirely. *

*The position subsequently became almost impossibly complex. In 1799 new dissensions appeared in both communions. The 'New Lichts', in effect, upheld the voluntary principle that there should be no state church; the 'Auld Lichts' believed that there was still a national established Church of which they were true representatives. In 1820 the 'New

In the face of these disputes among their enemies the 'Moderates' took control of the General Assembly, which, however, still contained men of evangelical spirit. They asserted discipline in church government, favoured the new intellectualism in theology, and endeavoured to elevate the social status of the clergy. In 1752 the Assembly censured the presbytery of Dunfermline for refusing to induct a presentee, and deposed one of the offending ministers, Thomas Gillespie of Carnock. Gillespie at once surrendered his charge, but preached in the open air at Dunfermline until his followers built him a 'meeting house'. In 1761 he and two others founded the *Relief Church* which was not opposed to 'establishment', but which, on the basis of a common 'evangelical' principle, ultimately joined with the United Secession Church in 1847.

The spirit of the 'Moderates' is well revealed in the autobiography of Alexander Carlyle, minister of Inveresk, (called 'Jupiter'), who danced, played cards openly, and courted the disapprobation of the Assembly in 1756 by attending with great publicity a performance of the tragedy *Douglas*, written by a fellow minister, John Home of Athelstaneford, who found it wise to resign his charge almost at once.

The real leader of the group, however, was William Robertson who, as a young minister, had led the attack in 1751 and paved the way for the 'restoration of the ancient discipline' by the Act of 1752. Of deserved repute as a historian, he was made Principal of the University of Edinburgh in 1762 and, thereafter, annually attended the Assembly, which he came to dominate. To great ability and personal integrity he added a power of 'management'

Lichts' of both communions joined the United Secession Church which (in 1847) joined with the Relief (above) to form the United Presbyterian Church (U.P.s). Most of the 'Auld Licht' Burghers joined the Established Church in 1839, but the Anti-Burgher Auld Lichts continued in the old way till 1852 when the majority joined the new 'Free Church' of 1843, while the minority went on as the 'Original Secession Church' until 1956, when it joined the Church of Scotland. For further complexities see p. 361 below.

and, though he did not personally administer Crown patronage, his policy commended itself to the Government, which put in moderates where it could. The ministers appointed under his régime were of good address, and in touch with the intellectual development of the time; but, though many of them were diligent pastors, the improved status of the clergy attracted in 'Mr Worldly Wiseman', and even 'Jupiter' Carlyle began to feel that the standard was falling. In 1780 Robertson announced that he must resign the leadership, perhaps because he foresaw that the coming agitation about 'Popery' would compel him either to abandon his principle of toleration, or to defy the majority of the Assembly. His successor, however, Professor George Hill of St Andrews continued his policy, and, in alliance with Dundas, maintained his authority for some thirty years, though his own teaching in St Andrews seemed to lack inward conviction. It is of significance that, in 1796, the General Assembly refused to countenance support for foreign missions, though this was urged by the eloquent Dr John Erskine.

Meanwhile, the power of the evangelicals was growing. Wesley, who visited Scotland twenty-two times between 1751 and 1790, had less success than in England as he was neither a Calvinist nor a Presbyterian; yet influence he certainly had. Scotland felt repercussions from the 'Revival' in England which produced Robert Raikes' Sunday Schools, the London Missionary Society, and the British and Foreign Bible Society. In the nineties the Evangelical party was attracting to itself men of the first distinction, and was ready to confront the dangers and the opportunities which followed on the French Revolution.

Yet it must be remembered that Scotland had still a strong piety of her own. Behind all the Presbyterian dissensions remained a devotion to the Covenanting tradition, whose strength is revealed in an odd, but striking way. In the eighteenth century it was customary for an author to grace his book with an imposing list of noble and distinguished subscribers; when in 1791 there was published a second edition of Howie's *Scots Worthies** it was accompanied by a list of some 1,400 subscribers arranged according to their places of habitation, and most of these were plain working people whose status is recorded. There were a few ministers and students, a few small landholders and farmers, and a few merchants and manufacturers, but the great majority were manual workers: shoemakers, wrights, masons, sawyers, dyers, tanners, porters, and labourers are all recorded, but among the occupations mentioned that of weaver greatly predominated. The significance of the list is twofold. It shows how many plain people were able to read and willing to read of their spiritual ancestry; it was also, perhaps under the influence of the French Revolution, a deliberate assertion of the doctrine stated by Burns as 'A man's a man for a' that'. It was from the fusion of piety and independence that there was to emerge the political liberalism which played so great a part in the history of nineteenth-century Scotland.

Learning and Literature

The spirit of inquiry and achievement, manifest in the economic and ecclesiastical development of the age, informed the intellectual and literary development of Scotland to no less effect. In the Universities, Divinity still held formally pride of place, but there, as has been shown, new ideas were entering; new faculties of medicine and law made a modest appearance, and in philosophy (Arts) great changes were made.

The old system of regenting whereby the teacher took his students through the whole course was abandoned, first in Edinburgh, then in Glasgow, later in St Andrews and Aberdeen. Separate Chairs appeared and the occupants of these were often scholars of the first distinction. The

*In 1774 an Ayrshire farmer, John Howie of Lochgoin, who was a Cameronian, published a collection of the *Lives and Characters of the Heroes and Martyrs of the Reformation and of the Covenant*. The book became a classic.

Scottish mathematicians, like Simson of Glasgow and his pupils, Colin MacLaurin and Matthew Stewart of Edinburgh, were of great renown, at a time when in the English Universities mathematics was still untaught. In Edinburgh there developed a great school of medicine and science, to which contributions were made by the family of Gregory, originally from Aberdeen, and Cullen and Black from Glasgow.

At the beginning of the century, Scotsmen had been wont to study medicine in Leiden or in London, but before it was ended the Universities, especially Edinburgh, sent her doctors not only to London, but abroad, even to Russia. Peter the Great, Elizabeth, Catherine II, and Alexander I all had Scotsmen as their personal physicians. Several Scotsmen were employed as directors of Russian military hospitals, and one, Sir James Wylie, became virtually the head of the whole medical profession under Alexander I.

In Scotland itself, medical men (often trained in Leiden) took advantage of their rudimentary training in chemistry to enter the new world of manufacturing industry. Here James Roebuck is a good example: an Englishman who had been educated as a doctor in both Edinburgh and Leiden, he subsequently became a pioneer of sulphuric acid manufacture in Scotland and one of the founders of the Carron Ironworks in 1759. At one stage he helped to finance the experiments of James Watt, who was trying to design a more efficient steam engine. And if the Scottish universities not infrequently offered technical expertise to industry, Scottish industry in its turn often sustained intellectual endeavour. Thus James Hutton, the greatest geological thinker of the Scottish Enlightenment, owed his fruitful leisure to a fortunate partnership in a chemical works.

In almost every branch of learning, Scotland made her influence felt outside her boundaries. Voltaire had his tongue in his cheek when he said that 'at the present time it is from Scotland we receive rules of taste in all the Arts'; but there was truth as well as acidity in his remark. The works of David Hulme,)that bold speculator who did not admit to being an atheist and who was a good companion (it was said) drunk or sober, produced a great effect throughout Europe. His *Treatise of Human Nature*, written when Hume was only twenty-six, undermined the concept that it was possible to achieve certainty in most fields of human knowledge; and his political writings were only a shade less novel. Perhaps it was fortunate for the development of enlightened thought in Scotland that most people believed that Hume's iconoclastic views had been adequately refuted by the Aberdeen philosopher James Beattie, whose *Essay on the Immutability of Truth* was a reply to Hume.

In Edinburgh a brilliant group included Adam Ferguson and Dugald Stewart, philosophers both, who undertook investigations into political science and political economy. David Hume, John Home, Alexander Carlyle, and the learned lawyers Lord Kames and Lord Monboddo contributed much to the thought, and also to the cheerful life which distinguished the capital. John Millar, Professor of Law in Glasgow, who attracted students even from Rome, lectured on English as well as Scots Law; he it was who in his dedication to Fox of *An Historical View of English Government* (1787) first used the phrase 'Constitutional History'.

It was not in the Universities alone that learning flourished. It had been the custom for the sons of substantial gentlemen to make a tour abroad and, for this among other reasons, it was not unusual to employ scholars as tutors and to pay a person of distinction well. Adam Smith abandoned his Chair in Edinburgh to act as tutor to the young Duke of Buccleuch, and patronage gave a livelihood to men of learning who, like David Hume, could not obtain Chairs owing to their sceptical opinions. Yet when the count of *littérateurs* is taken it will be found that, in many cases, they were produced by the Church. It must not be supposed that, being Divines, they were remote from the world. This was the age of moderatism, and clerical members were found in the cheerful clubs – the Poker Club, for instance, in Edinburgh, or the Literary Society in Glasgow.

Such *camaraderie*, however, was not universal. The achievements of Sir James Steuart, author of *An Inquiry into the Principles of Political Economy* (1767), are not generally recognized because Adam Smith, who published his epoch-making *An Inquiry into the Nature and Causes of the Wealth of Nations* in 1776, disliked the Jacobite Steuart and made no reference to his writings. Smith's *Wealth of Nations* was immediately hailed as a seminal work for that tradition of economic thought which may be roughly described as 'laissez-faire' or 'liberal', yet the author was more than just an economist. Although he expounded his academic theories as a Professor in Glasgow, he began his academic career as a Professor of Belles Lettres in Edinburgh and he spent his last days in his native Kirkcaldy revising his *Theory of Moral Sentiments* which he had published in 1759. It did not occur to the philosophers of the time that economics could be separated from morality.

It was not only in philosophy that the work of Scotsmen attracted attention. The historical writings of William Robertson on Charles V and on America invited the interest of Europe, and his *History of Scotland* in the reigns of Mary and James VI was founded upon documents, some of which were not otherwise obtainable. David Hume wrote a history of the reigns of James I and Charles I which was somehow engulfed in the more facile work of Smollett, who covered eighteen hundred and three years in fourteen months. 'Hume and Smollett' became a classic. All these historical works were written in English, as were the 'Picaresque' novels by which Smollett, in private life very different from his heroes, is best remembered.

Poets, too, Scotland had. James Thomson of *The Seasons* and *Rule Britannia* lived and wrote in England; the English poetry written in Scotland was not of the first order, but James Macpherson's alleged translations of the works of an ancient Gaelic poet, Ossian son of Fingal, though they were in fact founded on little more than tradition, were universally acclaimed, save by a few sceptics like Johnson, and gave Scotland a place in the romantic movement in literature.

To that movement Scottish vernacular poetry was to make a more real contribution. A tradition had come down from the seventeenth century in which Robert Sempill (*d.* 1660?) had used with effect the six-line *rime couée* stanza (a a a b a b) which came to be known as 'Habbie Simson' from his poem *The Piper of Kilbarchan*. This had been known to Dunbar, and was later much used by Burns.

During the eighteenth century there was much interest in the works of earlier writers. In 1706 appeared Watson's 'Choice Collections' in which Hamilton of Gilbertfield's *Last Dying Words of Bonnie Heck* (a greyhound) was to be the model for Burns's poem on 'Poor Mailie' (a ewe). Original verse appeared too. Grisel Baillie, daughter and daughter-in-law of two distinguished Presbyterian victims of persecution under Charles II, yet wrote happy songs in good Scots; and Lady Wardlaw, born a Halkett of Pitfirrane, produced in *Hardyknute* a ballad which was published in 1719 and was long accepted as 'copied from "an old manuscript" '. It was in Allan Ramsay (1686–1758) that vernacular poetry found its great champion. A wig-maker in the Edinburgh Grassmarket, who enjoyed the patronage of men of letters and was made a member of the Easy Club (of a somewhat Jacobite complexion), he not only collected old songs and poems, but added verses of his own published in *The Tea Table Miscellany* (4 vols. 1724–32) and *The Evergreen* (1724). He also wrote an eclogue, *The Gentle Shepherd* (1725), which had a great vogue, and published *Thirty Fables* in verse.

Some of his contemporaries, like his patron the lawyer and antiquary Sir John Clerk of Penicuik, and William Hamilton of Bangour, wrote rather in English than in Scots, but among his followers the vernacular fared well in the hands of Jane Elliot who enshrined an old lament for Flodden in *The Flowers of the Forest*, of John Skinner, an Episcopal Aberdeenshire minister, who wrote *Tullochgorum*, and at a later day of Lady Anne Barnard of the house of Lindsay, the authoress of *Auld Robin Gray*. Conspicuous among his successors was the unhappy Robert

Fergusson (1730–54) who depicted the life of his times in the really good Scots, broad, but not coarse, then generally used in the Capital. Fergusson died insane at the age of twenty-four, and the tradition reached its climax in Robert Burns (1759–96) who lived to be only thirty-seven and a half.

The abundant praises lavished upon the poet in the countless Burns Suppers which celebrate the 25 January every year must not be allowed to obscure the fact that Burns was a genius who strove hard to perfect his spontaneous gifts and who united music, realism, comedy, and humanity in a manner seldom seen. To the same tradition, though with vast differences, belong two great prose writers of a somewhat later date. Sir Walter Scott (1771–1832) was a romantic conservative; John Galt (1779–1839) was a polished ironist; yet each of them was at his best when he portrayed with a vivid and humane pen the Scottish scene and the Scottish character.

A significant proof of the awakening of the public mind is given by the development of the newspaper. The *Edinburgh Evening Courant* (Whig) which appeared in 1718 was followed in 1720 by the *Caledonian Mercury* (Jacobite). *The Glasgow Courant* (1715) lasted only for a few months, but the *Glasgow Journal,* which appeared before the middle of the century, lasted, with several important interruptions it is true, for over a century, and the *Glasgow Herald,* as the *Glasgow Advertiser,* was founded in 1783. Papers appeared in Aberdeen, Dumfries, and other towns.

At first the news, mainly of politics at home and abroad, was provided from London, but soon economic and local news was supplied, and advertisements were published. Indeed, the papers of the smaller towns concerned themselves mainly with local and commercial affairs, but in the excitements which followed the French Revolution some of them entered into politics. By 1790 Scotland had twenty-seven newspapers and in the next ten years others appeared. Many of these inclined to 'reform', but after 1794 development was hindered by repressive legislation.

Meanwhile, the magazine had made its appearance. In 1739 was founded the *Scots Magazine* which dealt with both politics and literature and, in 1775, began the *Edinburgh Review*, the precursor of that review which after 1802 attained under the editorship of Francis Jeffrey great distinction as the mouthpiece of the Whigs.

Art

In art, as well as in all else, the eighteenth century witnessed a great development. Here too the seventeenth century had left a legacy, but this was mainly in the painting of portraits. In its early decades the last of the Scougalls was working; Sir John Medina (a Flemish Spaniard) lived until 1710, and among the pupils of both men were several competent artists. William Aikman, who had pursued his studies in Italy, was more than competent.

Landscape and decorative painting were at first represented mainly by the house-painting family of the Nories, who produced panels and murals. Before long, however, efforts were made to improve both the technique of the craft and the status of artists. In 1729 a group of *virtuosi* and artists, including William Adam the architect, the poet Allan Ramsay, and his son, founded the 'School of St Luke'. This had only a limited success, partly perhaps because one of its best products, Robert Strange,* a magnificent engraver, printed the Jacobite banknotes, and other members of the group joined the Prince's army.

In 1755 a 'Select Society for the Encouragement of Arts, Sciences, Manufacturers, etc.' came into being. It offered prizes for good work, only to discover that good work demanded good teaching, and in 1760 a 'School for Drawing' was established as part of the work of the Board for administering the 'Equivalents' (see pp. 261, 264). Meanwhile in Glasgow, Robert and Andrew Foulis, whose splended printing of the classics had won universal

*Returning from exile, Strange so impressed George III that he was knighted in 1787.

praise, boldly founded in 1753–4 an Academy of Arts on the Italian model. They established a salon in the lower half of the University Library, bought pictures abroad, hired teachers, and gave instruction in drawing, painting, modelling, and engraving. The school did not survive Andrew Foulis who died in 1775, deeply in debt as the result of his enterprise; but it produced some distinguished artists. Alexander Runciman (1736–85) who spent four years in Italy, produced classical paintings in the manner of Titian, as well as portraits; James Tassie (1735–99) made skilful medallion portraits which are still in great demand, and David Allan (1744–96) who, though he spent eleven years in Italy and produced classical pictures, yet was to earn his great renown as a painter of *genre* (e.g. *The Penny Wedding*) and as the illustrator of Allan Ramsay's *Gentle Shepherd* and Burns's *Songs*.

Great as were the services of these native academies they were less important for Scottish art than the visits to Italy by young painters, some of whom, from humble homes, were supported by enlightened aristocrats. For from Italy came the inspiration which transformed Scottish painting. Gavin Hamilton (1723–98), an archaeologist as well as an artist, painted classical scenes in the grand manner; Jacob More (1740–93) produced beautiful landscapes; but it is in the portraits of Allan Ramsay (1713–84) that the marriage of Scottish tradition with the craftsmanship and the taste of Italy produced its best results. The son of a literary wig-maker, who visited Italy four times between 1736 and 1782, he not only mastered a new technique in his craft but, discarding conventional 'poses', produced portraits which matched simplicity with elegance. He enjoyed the patronage of noble Scottish families and so commended himself to George III that in 1767 he was appointed 'Painter-in-Ordinary to the King'. At one time his reputation suffered because his school produced, at an alarming rate, royal portraits to which he himself made only a small contribution, but modern appraisal recognizes him as one of the really great portrait painters.

His successor, Henry Raeburn (1756–1823), was the son

of a yarn-boiler who had served an apprenticeship with a jeweller. The earliest portrait which survives is dated 1776. His marriage to a widow older than himself gave him both social status and the means to visit London, to meet Reynolds, and go on to Rome where he spent two years. Returning to Scotland at the age of thirty-one he began that great series of portraits in which a skilful technique enabled him to produce truth in beauty in a manner seldom equalled. Although he contemplated going to London and sent pictures to the Royal Academy, of which he became a full member in 1815, he did not leave Edinburgh, and when George IV visited Scotland in 1822, he received the honour of knighthood. Next year he died after an expedition to Fife with Sir Walter Scott, and Sir Walter's picture is one of his last.

Of almost equal distinction was David Wilkie (1785–1841) who brought to his *genre* painting a genius enriched by study abroad, and gained a reputation far beyond the bounds of Scotland. He was made Painter-in-Ordinary in 1830 and retained the office under William IV and Victoria. He was knighted in 1836.

Architecture. As with art, so with architecture; a native tradition was developed under the patronage of enlightened aristocrats who had made the Grand Tour. William Bruce (*d.* 1710), who had developed Holyroodhouse with a classicism which has been described as 'Frenchified' (see p. 246), had later introduced his new designs into his own mansion of Kinross House; he had also made plans for a new Hopetoun House. He employed, as what may be described as 'Clerk of Works', William Adam (1689–1748) of Kirkcaldy, who on his own account had undertaken much local building. Adam, benefiting from the patronage of Sir John Clerk of Penicuik (1684–1755), the Maecenas of his age, and of two successive Earls of Hopetoun, began to rebuild in a style modelled on the work of James Gibbs (a fellow Scot from Aberdeen) and Sir John Vanbrugh, who plied their work in England. His ideas were expanded by a visit to

English country houses which he made with Sir John Clerk in 1727 and after his return he rebuilt the seats of many Scots nobles and gentry. When he was not limited by his patron's instructions he built with a Vanbrughian exuberance, though he did not hesitate to introduce elements of his own into the Palladian style; and though he carefully watched the outlays, his employers sometimes found that the cost exceeded the estimates. Hopetoun House, begun by 1723, was not completed before 1742, and all over Scotland as far north as Duff House near Banff noble buildings with graceful and classic interiors bespeak the magnificence and also the costliness of his designs. Yet he did not confine himself to country houses. His hand is to be seen in some of the public buildings in Edinburgh (e.g. the Royal Infirmary). He became storekeeper of H.M. Works in Scotland and Master-Mason of the Ordnance Board. He also worked on many of the Royal Castles, and upon the forts built or strengthened after the Forty-Five, especially Fort George. His varied employments brought in much money; he acquired a considerable fortune and built Blairadam House where his son John succeeded him as laird when he died in 1748.

His sons, three of whom he had already employed as assistants, followed in his footsteps. Prudent John, the new laird, succeeded also to the office of Master-Mason, and acted in a general way as manager of the Adam firm, which continued with the lucrative contract at Fort George. He also collaborated with his brothers, though he seems to have been rather a designer than a builder. So too was James, whose ideas, as for the new Parliament Houses, were thought to be somewhat fantastic; yet he shared with his brother in the erection of the Adelphi in London (1759).

The fourth brother William pursued a business career in London. It was the second brother, Robert, who brought the name of Adam to its full glory. Having accumulated by his early efforts at Fort George and elsewhere the respectable capital of £5,000 he set off on the Grand Tour with Lord John Hope in October 1754; and though Lord John left Rome in September 1755, he himself remained there till May 1757, living *en prince*, cultivating British nobles who might be future patrons, meeting famous architects, assiduously making sketches and drawing plans. So famous did he become that he was invited to plan the new city of Lisbon destroyed by the disastrous earthquake of 1755.

Armed with a tremendous reputation he settled in London, and though much of his work was done in England, he also designed many buildings in Scotland. Among those in Edinburgh may be mentioned the Register House and Charlotte Square in the New Town, and in the Old Town, the University, of which the foundation stone was laid in 1789. The work was not completed until 1827 under the direction of another great architect, William Henry Playfair. Playfair was largely responsible for the building of the New Town whose stately lines command great admiration. Not only because its citizens were of an inquiring mind, but also because of its classic architecture did Edinburgh merit the name of 'Modern Athens'.

The culture of the eighteenth-century Scottish Enlightenment was indeed a classical one, in the sense that it rested on a balance between creative vitality and accepted rules of artistic decorum and discipline. Such a culture could not last indefinitely, least of all in a time of rapid economic and social change. The emphasis on order and discipline ultimately reflected the hierarchical structure of a society dominated by the landed aristocracy and although, of course, most of the concrete achievements of the Scottish Enlightenment were due to men of middle-class origins, none of them seriously challenged the values of a cosmopolitan aristocratic world. That mentality was, however, bound to be traumatically affected by the twin assaults of an industrial revolution – nowhere more spectacular than in Lowland Scotland – and a political revolution, which came to a head first in nearby France. From this clash of opposites a new synthesis was bound to emerge.

CHAPTER 17

UNREST AND REFORM

For almost four decades the political life of Scotland was dominated by the French Revolution and its consequences – by war with France from 1793 to 1815 and, thereafter, by efforts to remedy constitutional and economic grievances which had found no relief while the government met the crisis with a strong hand.

In Scotland, as in many other lands, the outbreak of the French Revolution seemed to liberal-minded men to presage the dawn of a new age, and the Scottish 'reformers' shared the enthusiasm expressed by Fox in England. As early as June 1789, the 'Reform Burgesses of Aberdeen' pledged 'the Estates General' at their annual dinner, and it was not only among politicians that hopes ran high. Amongst the intellectuals, Principal Robertson was at first 'dazzled'; Dugald Stewart, who visited Paris, came home convinced.

Of the Glasgow Professors, Millar gave warm support, Reid subscribed money, and Anderson presented to the Assembly some of his own military inventions, including a carriage designed to take the recoil of a gun. In February 1792, exciseman Robert Burns dispatched four carronades taken from a captured smuggler. Some ministers from the Established Church, as well as dissenters, publicly upheld the cause. The *Rights of Man* by Tom Paine was everywhere read, while Burke's *Reflections* served to produce Mackintosh's *Vindiciae Gallicae* as a counterblast.

Everywhere there was unrest; economic distress in some quarters was heightened by universal hopes that parliamentary reform would be achieved and slavery abolished everywhere; all over the country meetings were held and addresses were framed. In 1792 a 'Society of the Friends of the People' was formed from which many branches emanated; and, though its aims were constitutional, it was in touch with the 'London Corresponding Society' (founded by Thomas Hardy, a native of Falkirk), whose purpose was distinctly 'popular'. In that year there was a serious riot in Edinburgh on the King's birthday (4 June); a 'Tree of Liberty' was planted in Dundee and another in Perth; Dundas was burnt in effigy. In December there was held in Edinburgh a 'General Convention of the Friends of the People in Scotland' which indeed produced nothing more than a unanimous agreement that parliamentary franchise should be given to every man of twenty-one and over.

Dundas, who had been made Home Secretary in 1791, and his nephew, Robert, Lord Advocate (1789–1801), stood firm. They had the support of most of the landed classes; they were well-supplied with intelligence; they could call out the military in the last resort and, meanwhile, the ranks of the opposition were divided by the violence of the mobs. By 1793 the radicals' power was already waning and the events of that year weakened them still more. The French declaration of war upon Britain, the execution of the King, and the enthronement of a prostitute in Nôtre-Dame, seemed to show that the French Revolution with all its talk of 'liberty' and 'reason' was simply a murderous attack on established order, private property, and the Christian religion. Henceforth the government could brand its opponents as atheists and (at least potential) traitors, and could prosecute them for 'sedition', a crime unknown to Scottish law till 1795.

Full advantage was taken when the third General Convention of the Scottish Friends of the People, in October 1793, was joined by a few delegates from England, and declared itself 'the British Convention of Delegates Associated to Obtain Universal Suffrage and Annual Parliaments'. Its main purpose was to protest against a suspension of the Habeas Corpus Act in England and a similar Act in Scotland, though no doubt some vigorous language was used.

Already two conspicuous members of the Friends of the People, Thomas Muir, a young advocate, and Thomas

Palmer, an English Unitarian preacher, had been sentenced to transportation. Now the Convention was broken up by force and three of the delegates who were brought to trial were sentenced to fourteen years transportation. In 1795 the government muzzled the expression of political opinion by a new Treason Act and a Sedition Act and, in 1798, a Dundee weaver, George Mealmaker, also received a sentence of fourteen years. English juries had refused to convict even a firebrand like Hardy on similar charges. The Scottish political trials seldom allowed the accused to escape. The courts were dominated by ultra-conservative judges like Robert Macqueen, Lord Braxfield, who excelled in the violence of his vituperation, but was little worse than his fellows; the court was always biased against the accused. The best that can be said for the government is that it had some justification for the apprehension it displayed. The secret 'Society of United Scotsmen' was in touch with the 'United Irishmen'; a desperate plot to seize Edinburgh Castle, the banks, and the judges was uncovered in 1794; and in 1797 a proposal to meet the threat of invasion by the creation of a Scots militia was opposed by well-organized resistance in which eleven persons were killed in fighting at Tranent.

In the main, however, violent unrest died down as the rise of Napoleon made very clear the nature of French ambitions. Burns himself, that apostle of freedom and goodwill, wrote *Does Haughty Gaul Invasion Threat?* and joined the Dumfries Volunteers. Walter Scott, of course, was an early recruit to the Edinburgh Light Dragoons in which he was promoted quartermaster. The martial spirit of Scotland was aroused: new Highland Regiments were raised – the Camerons, the Gordons, and the Argyll and Sutherland Highlanders all took their origin between 1787 and 1799. In 1802, Scotland was given the militia which she had been refused in 1760.

The government recovered strength and passed some useful measures, finally emancipating the colliers in 1799, and providing schoolmasters with a very modest augmentation of their very modest stipends in 1803. But, meanwhile, there developed an opposition, all the more effective because it confined itself to 'constitutional' action. Prominent amongst its leaders was Henry Erskine who in January 1796 was deposed from his office as Dean of the Faculty of Advocates by a very great majority of his fellows, an action unprecedented and never repeated. The most admired member of the Bar, Erskine attracted to himself brilliant young advocates like Francis Jeffrey, the leaders of the popular party in the Kirk, professors like Dugald Stewart and John Playfair, and launched a campaign for a moderate, but definite, reform. The party found a most effective mouthpiece in the *Edinburgh Review*, founded in 1802, to which Sydney Smith, Brougham, and Francis Horner, besides Jeffrey himself, contributed powerful articles. Many various topics were covered, literary and philosophical as well as political, but mainly infused with the liberal spirit which they had imbibed as pupils of Dugald Stewart.

Whilst this opposition was mounting, the system of 'management' in Scotland received a blow from which it never recovered. Early in 1805, Henry Dundas, Lord Melville, was impeached for corruption as Treasurer of the Navy. He was acquitted, but his reputation was tarnished. Pitt, who died in February 1806, was succeeded by Grenville, under whose administration, mainly Whig, Henry Erskine was made Lord Advocate and Lauderdale, the only Scottish Whig peer, dispensed patronage as Keeper of the Great Seal. 'The Ministry of all the Talents', however, lasted for little more than a year. The business of carrying on the war and dealing with the difficulties which followed its conclusion was left to a succession of Tory administrations. Under these the office of 'Manager' was held after Melville's death in 1811 by his son, the second Lord Melville, but he, though he had ability and held high offices in the British government, never exercised complete control over the Scottish representation at Westminster.

The difficulties he faced at home were serious. Even in

1812 the Manchester Weavers' Committee had affiliations among malcontents in the south-west and, in the years of economic dislocation after Waterloo, the unrest attained proportions which led in 1817 to the suspension of the Habeas Corpus Act and a fresh law against sedition.

In Scotland four persons were prosecuted for taking a secret oath to obtain by physical force reforms which today seem far from shocking; but, thanks partly to advocacy of distinguished Whigs, the heaviest sentence imposed was one of six months' imprisonment. In 1820 there was a more serious affair when the unrest which had produced 'Peterloo' and the repressive 'Six Acts' flared up in Scotland into the 'Radical War'. A Committee of Organization for forming a Provisional Government called for a general strike and its summons was answered by 60,000 men. The riots which ensued were quelled in a few months by the yeomanry, but not without a small battle near Carron in which three of the insurgents were killed. Of forty-seven prisoners taken, twenty-six were brought to trial (by a special commission), two were acquitted, and though twenty-four were sentenced to death, three only were hanged. Thereafter, the urge for 'reform' expressed itself in less violent forms, though it was still vigorous.

The Economic Situation

There was both good and evil in the economic situation in Scotland during the early decades of the nineteenth century. The good, however, lay mainly in the promise for the future and the evil in present distress.

The Highlands. The distress was most obvious in the Highlands. There it produced emigration and 'Clearances'. For these it has been usual to blame the intruding sheep, the neglect by the chiefs of their ancestral duties, and the appearance of new landlords. All these things played their part; yet it must be noted that the population of the Highland counties increased remarkably until the census of

1831; that Argyll, largely given over to sheep, produced fewer emigrants than the Hebrides, little affected by sheep; that the rearing of black cattle which, in fact, gave little more employment than sheep-breeding, throve till 1800. It must be remembered too that, though some proprietors during the brief boom in kelp made large sums, others became very poor. When a bitter critic of the Clearances recounts with satisfaction that, while the exiles from Kintail flourished in Canada the House of Seaforth was ruined, and that the chiefs who cleared Glengarry were themselves ousted, he is really stating the case of the landlords, many of whom had fallen into the hands of trustees or creditors. Finally it must be noted that some of the old proprietors incurred heavy debts, and that some of the wealthy incomers spent great sums of their own money in endeavours, mainly vain, to increase employment on their estates.

The root causes of emigration and Clearances were overpopulation, land-hunger, near starvation (especially after a bad harvest), hopes founded on letters from relatives overseas, and dishonest promises by emigration agents. To these must be added the increased rents demanded by economically-minded landlords, and the reluctance of a conservative people to abandon the old methods – never productive of a great surplus of food – which became impossible as the population increased and the size of the croft dwindled. Yet, when all is said, this is a sorrowful tale.

The emigrations which marked the turn of the century differed from those which preceded the outbreak of the American War of Independence. Here was now no departure of fairly well-to-do tacksmen going often to places where the soldiers of Highland regiments had voluntarily settled down on land granted them on their discharge. This was the outflow of poor people going abroad as best they could from a land which could no longer maintain them, and that without sure prospects. True it is that the emigrants from each area of Scotland sought the same areas in distant Canada, but often they found that they had been misled by false promises. Sometimes indeed they were put ashore far from their destinations, because the St Lawrence was frozen, and left to find their new home as best they could. The ships bearing them were small: between 1800 and 1803 twenty-three ships, all save one from Highland or Island ports, carried 5,391 passengers.

It was hard to have a rational 'emigration policy'. Even when, between 1811 and 1817, the enlightened Earl of Selkirk tried to establish a well-organized settlement upon 1,600 square miles about the Red River, which he had purchased from the Hudson Bay Company, his effort was ruined by violent attacks from the rival North-Western Company, and by the latent hostility of the Hudson Bay Company itself. Both companies dreaded the approach of an agriculture which would threaten their lucrative fur trade.

The Clearances. It was bad enough when folk were driven to emigrate by grinding poverty, but worse still when they were forcibly evicted from homes where they wished to stay in spite of everything. The story of the Clearances is known to all; yet the Sutherland Clearances were part of a policy of improvement undertaken between 1811 and 1820 by the Marquis of Stafford, who had married the Countess of Sutherland in 1785. Aware of the 'improvements' which were being undertaken in Moray and of the hardship and famine which prevailed in his area, he called in experts from Moray, and began to move his tenants from the upland glens to the coast in the belief that there they could supplement the crofts, which he would supply, by fishing. At first he had some success when he moved people from Assynt to the west coast; but later he met with opposition which was repressed by violence, all the more resented when it was found that one of the factors employed, who was acquitted on a charge of homicide, himself entered into one of the sheep farms from which the evictions took place. The burning of wretched houses and the eviction of helpless people – some of them decrepit – aroused great condemnation, and the grievances reached the House of Commons. There and elsewhere it was shown that the Marquis, besides getting nothing from his Sutherland estate between 1811 and 1833, had spent £60,000 of his own money; but the stigma was not removed.

Meanwhile on the west coast a period of prosperity resulted from a boom in kelp, made from seaweed and valuable for the manufacture of glass, soap, and alum as a substitute for barilla (a similar substance imported from the Mediterranean). The import of chemicals was impossible during the war and, thereafter, it was for a time prohibited by the imposition of heavy duties. When these were removed in 1823 the resultant slump brought unemployment to those who had flocked to the sea-shore and had lost, to some extent, the taste for hard agricultural labour. Things were worse than ever. Between 1828 and 1851 some proprietors shipped surplus tenants overseas at their own expense, but in 1853 there occurred in Glengarry perhaps the most ferocious of the violent Clearances. This was not a matter of shifting people to the coast: whole families were put into ships and sent across the ocean, and sometimes men who sought refuge in the hills were hunted out like deer.

It is hard to ascertain the total number of the emigrants, but easy to understand the bitterness that they carried in their hearts. They were driven from the homes where their ancestors had lived for centuries. Life had never been easy in the old days; the tacksman was sometimes hard, but he was of their own kin, and when things were at their worst the chief would surely provide some meal. They did not realize that with the coming of better order, of better understanding of disease, and with the introduction of the potato, population was increasing to an extent which could not be supplied by the old economy. They did not realize – indeed, many of them may not have known – that money spent by landlords or by charitable societies on palliatives was spent in vain. All they saw was that land was being let to sheep-farmers who could pay three times the old rent and absorbed small crofts into bigger holdings. To them it seemed that nowadays chiefs preferred sheep to men – to men whose ancestors had served their ancestors for generations.

Lowlands. In the Lowlands there was distress as well as prosperity. Prosperity there certainly was, especially during the war years when Britain had to provide her own food and supply, not only herself, but her allies with the fruits of her industry. Scottish agriculture and stockbreeding reached a degree of efficiency which commanded the admiration of the visiting Cobbett (partly, it is true, because it enjoyed the protection of the Corn Laws until 1846). Yet the introduction of new techniques led to the employment of fewer labourers and it has been estimated that, even before 1786, 7,000 families had emigrated from the Lowlands, mainly from the Borders.

In the textile industry too the same sort of thing happened. There was immense expansion between 1780 and 1822; the annual output of cotton rose from 13,000,000 to 36,000,000 yards. Yet as the loom, as well as the spindle, came to be worked by machinery, the position of the craftsmen became steadily worse. The wages of a handloom cotton weaver fell to 4 shillings a week. As regards linen, the change came more slowly, because it was long before machines could rival the fine work of the craftsmen; but by 1834 the Forfarshire handloom weaver, who worked all day with the aid of his wife and children, could earn only 6 shillings a week and, by the middle of the century, even the skilled workers in towns were facing destitution. In the woollen industry of the Border, things were less difficult, for the mills were small and the transference to mechanical power was easier because one of their products found a ready market in the south. The English called it 'tweed' from a misreading of tweel (the Scots version of the French word for cloth: *toile*).

In the heavy industries too, great progress was made. Coal and iron ore were found in close proximity in the

Midland belt. David Mushet discovered extensive deposits of black-band iron-stone and, in 1828, James Neilson patented his hot-blast furnace which reduced by nearly three quarters the amount of coal required for smelting, and made the use of black-band iron-stone an economic proposition.

Ship-building developed greatly. Experimental steamships were made by William Symington in 1802 and Robert Fulton in 1807, and in 1812 the appearance on the Clyde of Henry Bell's 'Comet' marked the beginning of a large output of vessels in which steam was used as auxiliary to sail, and iron was used as well as wood, though for long the swift 'clippers' were to hold their own in the tea-trade.

Robert Napier enormously improved the marine engine and it was he and the Scottish ship-owner, George Burns, who were founders of the Cunard Line (1839–40). Before long, engineering was to become a great industry in itself. Meanwhile new coal-mines were being opened, new canals were used and there were vast improvements in the road system. The main roads of the Lowlands were built before 1814 mainly as the result of the adoption of the turnpike system whereby local subscribers to road improvement funds were allowed to recoup their expenditure by levying tolls on the improved roads. In 1803, after a report by Telford, a Highland Commission for Roads and Bridges came into being which, by 1820, had provided 930 miles of road and more than 1,100 bridges.

Yet amid all the expansion there was distress too. The plight of the textile workers has already been mentioned, and the dislocation resulting from economic change produced hardship in other quarters too.

Socially the age was one of great contrasts. The landed class still held its own in the main, though the merchants, according to Lord Cockburn a despised class about 1800, were winning their way into the upper ranks. Among these the old aristocratic outlook still prevailed. We read of balls so correct that the exact place of every dancer in each set was set forth on the ticket of invitation, and of dinner parties where it was *de rigueur* to drink the health of every diner. Sir Walter Scott was producing his romantic poems and (for long anonymously) his great series of historical novels which excited the admiration of the world and made Scotland appear from without as a land of romance. At the other end there was great poverty, which became more marked as the first impetus of the industrial revolution declined. It is true enough that the houses which the Highlanders had quitted were often miserable hovels, but life in the crowded slums in Edinburgh and Glasgow must also have been degrading.

Yet the picture must not be exaggerated. Food, though during the second half of the eighteenth century prices had doubled, was still very cheap. In Dundee beef was 6d. a lb., fish 1d. a lb., a hen 1s. 6d., and eggs 6d. a dozen. The old economic structure still prevailed to some extent; a draper, for example, was formally apprenticed to his master and though the boy was worked hard, he learned his trade thoroughly and might well become a successful master in the end if he kept a straight course. This he was encouraged to do by the Kirk which still kept a firm hold on its people. The 'Statistical Accounts' show that there was an abundance of churches of different denominations. Domestic piety was still strong.

It may be thought that this piety was an anodyne to make men accept unreasonable hardship in this world in the hope of a better hereafter, and sometimes this was so. Yet, among the weavers especially, piety went hand in hand with an independent mind, and the Paisley 'cork' or master-weaver was the type of a reading and thinking citizen. An educated middle class was coming into being.

It must be noticed too that it was not only to the working classes that the industrial revolution brought suffering. The *entrepreneurs* had their troubles too. For example, a wild joint-stock mania in 1825 and 1826 ruined thousands of speculators, and the attempt of the government to check inflation by forbidding the issue of the Scottish £1 note produced a violent agitation. To this Scott contributed by publishing three letters under the pseudonym of Malachi Malagrowther and, though his arguments were not equal to his vehemence, the government yielded to a display of Scottish patriotism which was well-nigh universal.

At this very juncture Scott himself was ruined with the fall of his publishers, Ballantyne and Constable, and by his own extravagances at Abbotsford. With undaunted courage, he wrote more busily than ever in order to discharge his liabilities, though his health was failing. He died in 1832. Throughout, he kept the admiration of most of his fellow countrymen and his death was not untimely, for 1832 witnessed the triumph of the 'Reform' which he had abhorred.

Victory of Reform

It would be quite wrong to regard the pre-1832 Scottish political system simply as corruption writ large. On the whole, the small electorate secured from its politicians what it most wanted: patronage which made jobs available, not only within Scotland but also far beyond its bounds. At an early stage, Scotsmen made their way into the diplomatic service of Great Britain – witness Sir Andrew Mitchell and Joseph Ewart at Berlin, Lord Cathcart in Russia, Sir Robert Murray Keith at Vienna, and Sir William Hamilton (whose wife became Nelson's mistress) at Naples. Henry Dundas, as President of the Board of Control for India, did much to facilitate the flow of Scotsmen to salaried positions in British India. Even after his fall from power, Lord Minto was appointed Governor-General (1807–13), and after his recall a galaxy of his henchmen (Sir John Malcolm, Mountstuart Elphinstone, Grant Duff, and Sir Thomas Munro among them) laid the foundations of a great administrative tradition. Naturally, the British army and navy also provided a field for the energies of the landed class which still dominated Scottish society. Sir John Moore, the hero of Corunna during the Peninsula War, and Admiral Adam Duncan, the victor of Camperdown during the French Revolutionary Wars, are but the two best-known examples.

But all this was not enough to satisfy the aspirations of the nation. While the sons of Scotland went abroad, Scotland enjoyed the successes and suffered the woes of economic expansion; yet, all along, the Reformers maintained their efforts on every front. Three successive statutes of 1808, 1815, and 1824 reorganized the judicial system of Scotland by establishing two divisions in the Court of Session and by introducing a jury court for civil cases. A beginning was made in the reform of local administration by the passing, between 1800 and 1825, of police statutes which allowed seven of the big towns to erect their own establishments to deal, not only with public order, but also with lighting, cleansing, and water supply; but though a Committee of Inquiry (1819–22) reported the grave abuses resulting from the self-election of burgh officials, nothing was gained save a law which gave the Court of Exchequer some power over burgh finances. An effort to curtail the growing powers of the Lord Advocate (1822–3) failed.

In 1827, however, the Whigs got what Dr Chalmers called 'a great deliverance'. Melville refused to serve under the moderate Canning who succeeded Liverpool as British Prime Minister, and 'management' came to an end. Canning's plan to administer Scotland through the Whig Home Secretary, Lansdowne, who was to have the advice of three stout reformers, was defeated by Canning's early death; and, though the Tories came into office, they did not regain their old power. Melville still declined to act as manager, and Wellington and Peel tried to conciliate the Whigs. In 1829 a great public meeting in Edinburgh, attended by leaders of both parties, supported the government's Bill for Roman Catholic Relief; in 1830 the office of Chief Baron of the Exchequer was given to a reformer, James Abercromby, over the head of Lord Advocate Rae, who had served the Tories well; and, also in 1830, the government passed the Scottish Judicature Bill which reduced the number of judges from fifteen to thirteen.

It seems likely that the complaisance of the Tories was due to their hope of creating a united front against a movement which they regarded as revolutionary – the movement for parliamentary reform. The abuses inherent in the parliamentary representation of Scotland arranged by the Act of Union had been multiplied by the economic developments of the eighteenth century. Some burghs, like the little Fife ports, had dwindled, while others, like Glasgow or Paisley, had increased with the influx of inhabitants from the countryside; election was still in the hands of unrepresentative burgh councils; some of the big new towns had no representation at all and, in the shires, election was dominated by family interests even when the pressure of management was relaxed.

The new urban population, particularly, showed a keen interest in the varying fortunes of the Reform Bill at Westminster and its passage on a second reading (March 1831) was hailed in Edinburgh by an illumination which the magistrates tried hard to forbid. The temper of the capital was made still more evident when, in the General Election of that year, Francis Jeffrey gained fourteen votes in the Dundas citadel against the seventeen cast for Mr Henry Dundas, and sailors from Leith had to be called in to quell the ensuing riots. Anger was turned to triumph when in July 1832 the Scottish Bill for Parliamentary Reform received the royal assent and, though a jubilant procession marched under an arch bearing the legend 'A United People makes Tyrants Tremble', the populace supported an address of loyalty and gratitude to the King.

With this extravagance of joy, the benefits conferred by the Act seem at first incommensurate. Scotland still kept only thirty representatives from the shires, though the six smaller counties were grouped in pairs which voted at every election and not alternately; and she received only eight additional burgh members. Yet, in the franchise and in the distribution of seats, great changes were made. In the counties the vote now was given to £10 owners and £50 occupiers. In the burghs the £10 householder was enfranchised. Edinburgh and Glasgow got two members apiece; Dundee, Aberdeen, and Perth each received one member; so did Paisley and Greenock, hitherto unrepresented; and eleven other burghs were given places in the fourteen 'districts' which were more sensibly arranged.

The Rubicon had been crossed and the returns for the General Election of 1833 bespeak the fall of privilege in burgh and shire alike: the Tories won only eight seats in the shires and one in the burghs. The triumphant Whigs went on to carry the reform into local administration. The Burgh Reform Acts of 1833 not only established the £10 householder as a municipal elector, provided for regular elections every November, and for the retirement annually of one third of the council; they also divided the burghs into wards, and enabled important burghs to adopt a new elective authority, the 'Commissioners of Police', which was authorized to regulate the order, the sanitation, and all the amenities of burgh life, with powers to impose assessments to meet their expenses.

At Westminster the tide of reform swept on. Colonial slavery was abolished, Ashley's Factory Act was passed, a grant was given to Education, the English Poor Law was amended (1834), and the Municipal Corporations reformed (1835). Penny postage was introduced in 1840. But the tide of reform in Scotland undoubtedly received a check when the spread of political agitation amongst the lower orders caused a conservative reaction in the possessing classes. The appearance of 'the People's Charter' (1838), and the rioting which followed its rejection, caused even Whig politicians to have some doubts. In Scotland the Chartist Riots were far less serious than they were in England, partly because some of the keen reformers were of evangelical piety, although there was some oratory and suspect newspapers like the *Black Dwarf* circulated. It is perhaps a sign of the times that no legislation followed the report (1831) of a Royal Commission to consider the state of the Scottish Universities, though that report made valuable suggestions and the evidence it collected has been of the first importance to historians. The Universities remained strongholds of the Kirk, and it was in the Kirk that 'reform', slowed up for the moment in the world of politics, pursued its advance.

The Disruption

In the great upsurge of liberal opinion the Kirk had a share which came to express itself in a very definite way. The discontents about the use of patronage to 'intrude' ministers still continued, and the ability of the authoritarians to repress them, with the aid of political management, declined. Professor Hill (p. 304) who had helped to fill so many parishes and, incidentally, to establish six of his own kinsmen in the senate of St Andrews University, died in 1819. Melville gave up 'management' in 1827 and, though the moderates found a resolute leader in another St Andrews Professor, George Cook, their citadel was shaken. The Samson who laid his hands upon their pillars was yet another St Andrews man, Thomas Chalmers, who entered the University at the age of eleven, and showed proficiency in mathematics. He began the divinity course when he was fifteen; observed that Hill did not really believe in the rigid Calvinistic orthodoxy which he preached; and, when he obtained a parish at Kilmany, took the view that a good minister could perform his duties to his people in two days of the week and devote the other five to his own intellectual development. He conducted in St Andrews classes, first of mathematics and then of chemistry, which attracted students away from the professors and justified his action with success. A severe illness, however, gave him a new outlook on life which revealed itself fully when, having been appointed to the good parish of the Tron in Glasgow, he deliberately abandoned it in 1819 for the new and much less distinguished Church of St John, because there he could carry out his self-appointed task of winning back the poor and the neglected.

In 1823 he became Professor of Moral Philosophy at St

Andrews and, from 1828 to 1843, he occupied the Chair of Divinity in Edinburgh. However, academic distinction had ceased to be his principal goal. Though generally conservative in politics, he was a staunch advocate of a liberal philosophy of self-help for the socially disadvantaged. His supreme aim was to make the Church of Scotland a powerful agent in the task of spreading the gospel, and reclaiming the lost.

The Evangelicals obtained control of the General Assembly for the first time in 1834. This enabled Chalmers to secure majority backing for his schemes to modernize the Kirk by law established. He succeeded remarkably well in raising large funds for the provision of new churches. Anxious to cooperate with the government, and never a believer in Disestablishment, Chalmers only very reluctantly became a leader in the 'Ten Years Conflict'. This protracted struggle between the General Assembly and the state, ultimately centering on the issue of lay patronage, culminated in the 'Disruption' of 1843 when some 451 ministers out of a total of about 1,200 left their manses and their livings and set out in faith to establish the Free Church. Most of the active ministers came out, and it has been calculated that the old Church lost about a third of its members.

The ministers who 'came out' found much support. They were able at once to establish in Edinburgh the New College which was to train their future ministers and, by 1847, they had over 700 churches of their own. When it seemed probable that school-teachers who adhered to them would be expelled from their posts, they created schools of their own and by 1869 they had nearly 600 of these.

Thus equipped, the Free Kirk became a force in politics; its attitude was in some ways conservative, for it believed that it was by spiritual right the Kirk of Scotland. Yet failure to achieve its great end and conflict with the Auld Kirk tended to drive it into alliance with other Dissenters who advocated Disestablishment.

CHAPTER 18

VICTORIAN SCOTLAND

THE Victorian Age was essentially one of 'Progress'. Modern critics who sneer at its smugness, its bad taste, and the morality which could combine Christian liberality with economic *laissez-faire* are inclined to forget its great achievement. In this achievement Scotland had a great share. In constitutional development, in economic expansion, in Empire-building and in a growing social conscience, Scotland went along with England, and her history is part of the history of the United Kingdom. Yet, with all this, Scotland retained her national identity. Much of the new legislation affected England and Scotland alike, yet Scotland still kept her old land laws and her own judicial organization. To some extent, too, her old electoral system survived in the groups of burghs. She kept much of her old educational system. She kept – and this was vital – her old Kirk or, by this time, Kirks. The wind of change which blew over the British Isles was the same on both sides of the Border, yet it did not blow upon identical countries.

Victorian Scotland was, on the whole, a contented and prosperous part of the United Kingdom. Its Protestant religion and increasingly dominant heavy industries ensured that it in no way shared the experience of Ireland, where lack of prosperity and cultural alienation bred political discontent.

In fostering the growing concord the Crown played a notable part. The visit of George IV in 1822, in arranging which Sir Walter Scott showed such energy and enthusiasm, was something of a spectacle in which clans and families paraded in the kilt. The monarch donned the kilt and judging from the speech he made at a banquet in the Parliament Hall may well have been under the impression that the government of the country was still largely a matter of chiefs and clans, but at least the Hanoverian Prince had been given a hearty reception. Queen Victoria, when first she came north in 1842, was impressed with the beauty of the country, and the hospitality of the nobles whom she visited, and by the people. She resolved to come back soon.

Holyroodhouse, though it had sheltered the exiled Royalty of France on two separate occasions, from 1795 to 1799 and, again, in 1831, was by this time hardly suitable for a royal residence; and, though the Queen and Prince Albert occasionally occupied the royal apartments there, they found a congenial home at Balmoral on Deeside, bought in 1848, and extended to the design of Prince Albert. It was as Countess of Balmoral that the Queen travelled abroad incognito and, after her husband's death, she came north with regularity. She came to have a real regard for the simplicities of the life of the Highlanders and for the services of the Kirk. She took communion according to the Presbyterian rite. She liked to regard herself as one of the Highland chiefs and, indeed, became something of a Jacobite. The Prince of Wales was entered in the High School of Edinburgh and, for some time, received instruction, privately however, in the University of Edinburgh. Queen Victoria was proud of her Scottish ancestry.

The Working of 'Reform'

The constitutional development of Scotland during the nineteenth century must needs be regarded as part of the history of the United Kingdom. Yet the approach of Scotland to the great questions of reform differed from that of England in several ways.

The social and political balance in Victorian Scotland was quite different from that of England. The Episcopal Church was strongly supported by the landed classes, but was still very small. If Presbyterians were divided, they were all at one in sustaining relatively radical social values. Their Elders were largely drawn from the business classes, and the vitality of the Lowland industrial economy bred a particularly aggressive and self-satisfied bourgeoisie. There was, of course, a powerful and rich landed aristocracy in Scotland, but in politics, especially after 1867, it had to play second fiddle to the natural middle-class leaders of a predominantly urban and industrial society.

It therefore comes as no surprise that the demand for reform in the State was closely allied with demand for reform of the Kirk. The 'Liberal Party' which developed had, in general, the support of the old Dissenters whose two main branches (see p. 302*n.*) joined in 1847 to form the United Presbyterian Church (U.P.) and of the great Free Church which arose from the Disruption. In Scotland the movement for political reform was closely bound up with the causes of Temperance, University Reform, and Disestablishment; and it is not unfair to say that, even towards the end of the century, the annual meetings of the two Assemblies and the U.P. Synod aroused as much interest in Scotland as did the proceedings at Westminster. One reason why Gladstone was so popular in Scotland was that he seemed to stand for moral principle.

As the electoral franchise was expanded, the representatives of Scotland were more able to make their presence felt. From 1853 on, Scottish members, led by Duncan McLaren, brother-in-law of John Bright, were demanding what was practically a manhood suffrage, a secret ballot, and a re-distribution of seats; and it was by their adhesion (on this matter alone) to Disraeli that he carried his Reform Bill of 1867. The resultant Act fell far short of Scottish aspirations. True, it was a great thing that, in Scottish Burghs and English Boroughs alike, the franchise was extended to all householders and £10 lodgers; but, for the county occupier, the lower limit was £14 in Scotland against £12 in England. Moreover, whereas Scotland, with between one ninth and one tenth of the population and contributing one eighth or one ninth to national taxation, might seem to be entitled to sixty-eight members out of 658, she was given only sixty in all. Of the seven additional seats, two went to the Universities, St Andrews being grouped with Edinburgh, and Glasgow with Aberdeen, and only five remained to be redistributed in response to change in the density of population. Nothing was then done about the secret ballot; which was introduced by Gladstone only in 1872.

The numerical inequality was remedied by Gladstone's Reform Act of 1884–5 which virtually established manhood suffrage. Scotland was now given twelve additional seats – in all seventy-two out of 670 – and the ratio of population to member was the same in both countries. The redistribution, too, proceeded on numerical lines. Glasgow gained four more seats, Edinburgh two, and Aberdeen one; of the counties, Lanark was given four extra members, Fife, Perth, and Renfrew one each. Yet some of the old inconvenience remained; two of the old districts of burghs, Haddington and Wigtown, were dissolved, but elsewhere the system of 'grouping' burghs was maintained.

The effect of these enlargements of the franchise was to strengthen the hands of the Reformers. Even the limited extension of 1832 resulted in the Liberals gaining forty-three out of fifty-three Scottish seats, and their preponderance (although threatened by a Tory revival in the 1840s and 50s) was confirmed by the Acts of 1867–8 and 1884–5. They usually controlled most of the burgh seats – on four occasions, all of them – and they had a good following in the northern counties too.

At Westminster, the Scottish representatives, along with the Irish, found that they could often sway the balance between the contending parties in England. It would, however, be absurd to argue that the whole of British policy was therefore dictated from the north. The leaders of the Liberal Party, and particularly Mr Gladstone, who for many years sat for a safe Scottish seat, contrived to make surprisingly few concessions to Scottish M.P.s, despite their immense strategic importance. Two reasons can be suggested for this. One is that the Scots were divided, especially over sectarian issues, and it proved possible to

play on those divisions to ensure that all Free Churchmen tended to support the Liberal Party in the hope of
securing Disestablishment, while most lay supporters of
the Church of Scotland also voted Liberal on purely
secular grounds. The second reason was simply that the
Scottish middle class wanted very little from the central
government. Prosperous and confident, they could afford
to treat politics as a source of psychological satisfaction,
rather than as a vital struggle for concrete interests. Mr
Gladstone left them with the feeling that they were on
God's side. It was enough.

There are many examples which illustrate the divergence
of interest between the English and the Scottish Liberals
during this period. English Liberals, for example, supported
the 'Maynooth Grant' to increase the financial support
given towards the education of Roman Catholic priests in
Ireland (1845), though this was vehemently opposed by all
Scottish parties; again, they were responsible for the
declaration of the war against Russia (1854), though this
was deplored by the advanced Scottish Radicals. Moreover,
some of the most important Acts, including the Poor Law
of 1845, the abolition of the Corn Laws of 1846, the
Reform Act of 1867 and the repeal of the Patronage Act
of 1874, though they represented Scottish Liberal aspirations,
were actually carried by Tory ministers, and in the passing
of others both parties had a share. None the less, it would
not be unfair to say that the general programme of reform
achieved at Westminster was in accord with the views of
Scotland whose representation was for long overwhelmingly
Liberal. To the movement for the abolition of the Corn
Laws they gave massive support. In Scotland it was a
popular cause. The idea of Free Trade had been familiar
since the days of Adam Smith; the new urban population
wanted cheap food; the Scottish farmers were more pro-
gressive than their neighbours in the south. The Dissenters
in a huge meeting organized by Duncan McLaren in 1842
denounced the Corn Laws as contrary to religion and the
principles of morality. Cobden and Bright, when they

visited Scotland, were astounded by the enthusiasm which was maintained by a campaign of speeches and pamphlets until the Potato Famine of 1845 brought things to a head. It was in his 'Edinburgh Letter' of 1845 that Lord John Russell made the declaration which rallied the Whigs to the cause, and a vast meeting addressed by Macauley resolved to petition Her Majesty for total abolition. This vigorous support from Scotland enabled Peel to defy the majority of his own party and abolish the Corn Laws altogether in 1846.

Meanwhile the Poor Law (Scotland) Act of 1845 had swept away the arrangement whereby each parish was responsible for its own poor, relying in most cases upon church-door collections rather than on a general levy. The system had worked fairly well and, in the main, humanely, though it did not assist the able-bodied poor and afforded only outdoor relief; but its day was done. Economic changes had made it ineffective, while the Secessions, and above all the Disruption, had weakened the claim and the ability of the Established Church to be responsible for the whole parish. Dr Chalmers still opposed a compulsory levy on the ground that relief of distress was the moral obligation of everyone, but a pamphlet by Dr Alison of Edinburgh (1840) had convinced public opinion that radical reform was necessary. A Royal Commission of inquiry was appointed and, on the basis of its report, a complete change was made by 1845. This provided for Parochial Boards and Inspectors of the Poor in every parish under the control of the Central Board of Supervision, and permission was given for the erection of poor-houses in parishes, or combinations of parishes mustering 5,000 inhabitants. It gave no relief to those able to work, but an applicant whose claim was refused might appeal to the sheriff. The Act expressed the spirit of the times: in the name of efficiency the State was taking over from the Kirk, and central authority was placing its hand on local institutions.

In the same way, the power of the central government

338

advanced on another front, namely that of education. In 1858 the Conservative Government passed the Universities (Scotland) Act, which had been drafted for the outgoing Liberal administrations by Lord Advocate Moncrieff. The Scottish Universities had not been inefficient. They had produced good scholars, good teachers, and good doctors. Yet their curricula, though still defended by critics who value a good foundation, had become too narrow for the times; and their government was largely in the hands of closed corporations of Professors. Dissatisfaction was felt by educationists, by students who were irked by an old-fashioned discipline, by graduates who had no part whatever in the corporation in which they had become masters, and by churchmen who felt that the old Kirk was a stronghold of outmoded authority. It is significant that among those who urged the Bill forward in Parliament were some who had been leaders in the Disruption.

In the government of the Universities the Act made a radical change. It established a General Council of Graduates and gave to it the right to elect the Chancellor; it gave the right of choosing the Rector to the students alone; and it entrusted the supreme authority to a synthetic University Court on which the Senate (the Professors) had but a slender representation. The Act had certain disadvantages, and these were not altogether removed by a second Act of 1889 which increased the size of the Court, removed finance from the control of the Senate, established a Students' Representative Council, provided for the admission of women, and extended the opportunities of study, envisaging extra-mural classes. It is under this Act, and Ordinances dependent thereon, that the Universities are administered today. Although the acceptance of government grants (very small in 1858) might seem to threaten the independence of the universities they remained, and still remain, to a large extent in control of their own affairs.

It has been argued that the Act dealt a serious blow to Scottish education by introducing new curricula which made the meticulous learning of Oxford and Cambridge its

339

supreme end, instead of a broad, and largely philosophical, basis for future experience. In fact, all the Act did was to pave the way to 'honours study' on a higher level in the existing Faculty of Arts and to open the door for new faculties of science and, ultimately, engineering. The course for the 'ordinary degree' was little changed. It still demanded the traditional seven subjects and these were normally Greek and Latin, Logic and Moral Philosophy, Mathematics and Natural Philosophy, and English (which was new). With the passage of time new subjects were introduced – Modern Languages, History, Political Economy, for example. But even when in 1907 the Universities agreed jointly to make it possible to get a degree on five subjects of which two must be taken again on a higher level, great care was taken in all cases to maintain a broad base. Well into the twentieth century the first year student, or 'bejant' (*bec jaune*), very often studied in his first year 'Latin, Greek, and Maths'.

This he was well prepared to do, for the Scottish schools, though their curricula moved with the times to some extent, still maintained the old tradition. Not only in the burgh schools and the parish schools, but even in the 'free schools', which multiplied after the Disruption, a boy was certainly taught Latin, often Greek if he required it, and some modern language. The tradition may have been maintained because among the masters there had always been not a few 'stickit ministers'. A 'stickit minister' was one who had not completed the studies which would enable him to 'wag his heid in the poo'pit'; but his failure to achieve the great hope of his parents was not always due to his inability to pass examinations. Sometimes the money ran out, for most students lived in any case on a very narrow margin; sometimes a young man realized that he had no vocation; and even if he had failed intellectually in the end, he had probably done at least the Classics and the Logic with which his course began; and of course he knew his Bible.

Mathematics, and such science as there was, unless the

master had a special aptitude, might be handed to an usher (not so called); but the 'Dominie' was a commanding figure to whom Scotland owes much. It is true that he gave most of his attention, sometimes in unpaid coaching, to the 'lad o' pairts' who went up to the University at a very early age, not only well-grounded in the essentials of character, and of learning, but also aware that success came from industry and application.

While the basis of the Scottish system was little shaken, the spirit of reform effected great changes, most of them salutary, in the whole fabric of the system. An act of 1861 had improved the status of the schoolmaster. It proved much more difficult to secure the passage of comprehensive legislation modernizing and rationalizing the Scottish school system on a national basis. Successive bills supported by the great majority of Scots M.P.s were rejected by the House of Commons. The delay lasted decades and pre-disposed many Scots to accept with relief the legislation of 1872, which by no means corresponded with their deepest desires, but did create, at last, a national Scottish school system. A new central authority, the Scotch (later Scottish) Education Department, was created. In the localities, ministers, heritors, magistrates, and town coun-cillors were replaced by popularly elected School-Boards, which gradually took control of all the schools provided by the Presbyterian Churches, though the Episcopal and Roman Catholic Churches might still continue as voluntary schools, and enjoy government grants. From teachers in the national schools (in Scotland, public schools) no religious profession was to be exacted. Education became universal, but it also became less individual so that there was some loss to be set off against the gain.

In the realm of administration, too, there was great development during the Victorian Age. The most notable innovation was in 1885 when the office of Secretary for Scotland was created in response to a major agitation led by Lord Rosebery, the rising hope of Scottish Liberalism. Rosebery clearly intended the Secretary to be a powerful minister, but his powers were curtailed and it was wholly typical that the first Secretary for Scotland was a man who had publicly expressed his conviction that the post was unnecessary. In practice the Secretary did little more than provide in a regular way the control hitherto exercised by the Lord Advocate. At a lower level, too, improvements were steadily made. In the burghs the police organization was extended, and charged with increased duties as regards public health; and in 1892 a consolidating Act, the Burgh Police (Scotland) Act, united the authority of magistrates and police commissioners and regulated the functions of all the officers. The Town Councils (Scotland) Act (1900) imposed on all a regular constitution of Provost, bailies, and councillors.

In the counties, progress was more spasmodic, for there the germ of the development was not a recognized institution like a Burgh Council, but the uncertain ill-organized 'Commissioners of Supply' upon whom the initial burdens were laid. It was to them that control was given when a county police force was made obligatory in 1856–7. In 1868 they were authorized to levy a county assessment; and gradually they were charged with various duties relative to public health, prisons, and highways. Only by the Local Government Act of 1889 were most of their duties transferred to the new County Councils. A similar development took place at a lower level. In 1845 Poor Relief had been transferred to a new Parochial Board, which took over Registration in 1854, and was soon charged with simple Public Health duties and authorized to levy a rate. The Poor Law, as administered by the Act of 1854, was not satisfactory and a great step forward was made when Acts of 1889 and 1894 brought into being the Local Government Board which took over the work of the arbitrary 'Board of Supervision', and gradually extended its powers over many matters of public health. This new Board was a Department of State.

In one way and another the old untidy machinery was thus superseded by uniform 'Authorities' derived directly from the central power, and the outline of a uniform system of administration came into being.

Yet, before the century was done 'reform' had lost much of its impetus. Its champions were no longer a united party. Gladstone was opposed to the Disestablishment demanded by some of his staunchest supporters; despite his triumphs in Midlothian, many of his followers disapproved of his proposals to give Ireland Home Rule, and a party of Liberal-Unionists came into being. He retired in 1894 and his successor Lord Rosebery, the third Scotsman to be Prime Minister, could not hold his place in the face of a mounting opposition. In the new General Election which became necessary Scotland returned 39 Gladstonians, 19 Conservatives, and 14 Liberal-Unionists; but in England the Conservatives had a huge majority. Their influence was increased by the enthusiasm of the Diamond Jubilee and before long the Liberal Party was greatly divided by varying opinions as to the justice of the Boer War. Rosebery and Asquith felt that their country must be supported till victory was won; Campbell-Bannerman and others were less sure about this.

Economic Expansion

The economic expansion which had begun before Victoria ascended the throne continued throughout her reign. Some new features, however, presented themselves. As Scotland's political life was more closely integrated with that of England, and, as the English economy was more and more involved with world markets, Scottish development came to depend on factors outside itself – for example, the Repeal of the Corn Laws, the Cotton Famine which followed the outbreak of the American Civil War, and the growth of the Colonies.

Agriculture. The high prices for farm produce which were obtained throughout the period of the Napoleonic Wars ensured that the adoption of improved methods of farming

343

became general in Lowland Scotland. There was a fall in agricultural prices after 1815, most marked in cattle prices. However, black cattle were primarily a product of the Highlands and the south-west, and Lowland farming as a whole was to some extent protected by the passing of the Corn Laws which secured a minimum price for home producers. In certain parts of Scotland the 1820s saw a major technological breakthrough in land improvement. Drainage had always been a problem to eighteenth-century improvers. The invention of tile drainage systems meant that, from the 1820s, very fertile but waterlogged clay soils (like those of the Carse of Stirling and the Carse of Gowrie, between Perth and Dundee) became rich agricultural areas.

This 'high farming' became characteristic of Lowland Scotland in the first half of the nineteenth century. In the Lothians, in particular, the adoption of steam power for many agricultural tasks made that fertile and highly-rationalized farming area the object of international admiration. The tide of prosperity lasted to the end of the Crimean War, but it was deeply affected by the agricultural depression which became general in the British Isles between 1873 and 1892. The so-called 'Great Depression' was due to the arrival on British markets of unprecedented quantities of low-price grain and livestock from overseas, especially from North and South America and from New Zealand. However it would be wrong to exaggerate the impact of these imports on Scottish farming. Wheat-farmers were the most seriously affected and, outside the Lothians, Scotland was not really a wheat-growing country: barley and oats remained the staple crops. Even in cattle markets, quality beef could still find a ready market, so improved breeds like the Aberdeen Angus and the Ayrshire continued to fetch good prices. Border sheep-farming also prospered, although it was only able to supply a part of the raw material requirements of the Border tweed industry, which was itself passing through a very prosperous phase. The price of efficient survival, however, was rationalization;

and, at the end of the century, little more than 200,000 people in Scotland were engaged upon the land as opposed to 500,000 in 1801.

The experience of the Highlands was, as usual, rather different. Ironically enough, large areas from which the inhabitants had been 'cleared' to make way for sheep-farming proved to be uneconomic producers of wool in the face of fierce competition from Australian imports. The result was that, over large parts of the Highlands, sheep were themselves 'cleared' to make way for that extra-ordinary, man-made, treeless desert: the 'deer forest'. These, in their heyday, offered high rents – not so much because of what they produced but because of the social status which an ambitious middle class derived from the systematic slaughter of deer and grouse. Millions of acres of the Highlands were devoted to this end and peat encroached more than ever on pasture ruined by reckless over-grazing.

Under these circumstances, and given the example of very grave agrarian unrest in Ireland after 1879, it is not surprising that a most serious crisis occurred in the relations between landlords and tenants in the Highlands. Highland people, it will be recalled, had been systematically moved out of the central glens and settled on comparatively small strips of land, often near the sea. These holdings were (and are still) known as 'crofts'. Even with their associated grazing rights they were never large enough to provide a family with a living: a 'crofter' is by definition a man of several employments – farming, fishing, weaving, or occasional work for a nearby hotel or estate all combined. The Clearances had always been accompanied by violent resistance, often led by women, and women were also prominent in fresh outbreaks of violence in the 1880s, culminating in the so-called 'Battle of the Braes' at Glendale in Skye. Though the British government landed parties of marines to control the situation, it lacked any effective apparatus permanently to enforce order in the Highlands and was fearful of the prospect of 'another

Ireland' on its doorstep. The result was the appointment of the Napier Commission on the crofting areas. By 1886 legilsation had revolutionized the position of the crofter, whose new-found political militancy had been expressed both in a great volume of evidence presented to the Napier Commission and in the emergence of a Highland Land League which successfully sponsored candidates for Parliament. Security of tenure and compensation for improvements were the foundations of the 'Crofters' Charter'. On the other hand, the legislation enacted in 1886 was guided by pure political expediency rather than by the precise recommendations of the Napier Commission. For example, the Commission had strongly opposed the granting of full crofters' rights to farming units that were so small as to be utterly uneconomic; but this distinction was disregarded by the Act. The result of the Crofting Act was undoubtedly a great triumph for human dignity and decency in the Highlands; but it was achieved only at the cost of artificially fossilizing a sometimes uneconomic situation.

Fishing. Attempts by such bodies as the British Fisheries Society to establish large-scale fishing in the Highlands proved abortive, though a few memorials remain (such as the planned 'fishing village' of Ullapool). Scottish fishing continued to be dominated by east-coast interests which could mobilize the increasingly large sums of capital needed as the century advanced and from Lerwick to Leith the herring fishing provided great if intermittent prosperity. In the late nineteenth century, steam trawling gradually spread northwards from England, and Aberdeen emerged as a great centre of mechanized fishing. This was partly because, given the range of the steam drifter, Aberdeen was the most northerly major port suitable for coaling vessels fishing the rich Faroese and Icelandic waters.

Communications. An expanding economy required an expanding network of communications. In the eighteenth century, coastal shipping had been essential to Scottish economic expansion, and it continued to play an important role in the early nineteenth century (which explains the bitter struggles for the control of harbour improvements before 1833 between the unreformed burgh authorities and the unenfranchised mercantile and manufacturing interests).* In the Western Isles, such coastal commerce remained important well into the twentieth century and the 'Clyde puffer' continued to provide a vital economic link between many scattered communities – as well as achieving immortality in Neil Monro's *Para Handy* tales.

Elsewhere, however, new communications systems came into use. Canals were the earliest innovation, but in Scotland they were something of a false start. The only profitable Scottish canal was the Forth–Clyde Canal, which was completed in the late eighteenth century after a very protracted period of construction. Elsewhere, geography was so hostile that such ventures as the Caledonian Canal along the Great Glen, and the Crinan Canal across the Mull of Kintyre, were financial disasters which had to be rescued by the British government.

The single most important innovation in the entire Victorian period was probably the railway. Its impact was, however, not entirely beneficial: it rendered most Scottish turnpikes (p. 295) hopelessly unprofitable, and thereby put an end to serious improvement in the Scottish road system until the motor car showed how inadequate that system was. Nevertheless, the increased facilities for the transport of goods and people offered by the railways had a great and stimulating effect on the whole Scottish economy. The wooden waggon-ways, common in coal-mining districts, had developed into locomotive-using railways by the 1820s, especially around Glasgow. The first 'inter-

*Many of the maritime burghs were heading for bankruptcy and some, like Aberdeen, Edinburgh, and Dundee, plunged right in. The merchants feared, quite rightly, that the unreformed corporations were anxious to secure control of the improved harbours in order to impose taxes on trade to service their mountainous debts.

city' line was opened between Edinburgh and Glasgow in 1842 and thereafter development was very rapid. Direct rail communication with England was soon established, on both the eastern and the western sides of the Border, and by the 1860s the Caledonian and the North British railways were engaged in a violent and frequently irrational rivalry which did at least produce very fast communication between Aberdeen and London, a tradition which culminated in the most famous British train of all: the 'Flying Scotsman'. This was a fact of considerable economic importance. Of course perishable goods had been sent from Scotland to London in the eighteenth century – even salmon had been sent, packed in ice, aboard the fast sailing smacks – but the railways made economic integration possible on an unprecedented scale. Thus the fruit-growers of Blairgowrie were by the late nineteenth century sending overnight 'Raspberry Specials', bearing their produce to the London market by rail. The opportunities offered by these new transport facilities served to enhance the dynamism of the Scottish economy and to increase the scale of business enterprise.

Industry. The growth of the railways and their location bespeaks the growth and the nature of the growth of Scottish industry. The salient feature was the increasing preponderance of the 'heavies' over the textiles.

The textiles by no means disappeared. Cotton continued to expand till about 1860, though rather slowly because, though some beautiful work was produced, the fine Glasgow muslin could not compete with Lancashire wares in the Indian market. After the American Civil War, however, the industry fell away, though Paisley, with her famous shawls, held a market till 1870 and, thereafter, profitably manufactured cotton thread. Today not much cotton is produced in Scotland, though some of the ancillary industries, chemicals, dyeing, and calico printing still remain.

Against the decline in cotton must be set important expansion in the jute and woollen industries. The manufacture of jute was rendered feasible, oddly enough, by the whaling industry, whose principal seat was in Peterhead but which also flourished briefly in Dundee. By 'batching' the stiff jute fibres (i.e. by softening them with a mixture of whale oil and water), it proved possible to use the existing machinery of the linen trade. Flax shortages during the Crimean War, and unprecedented demand for coarse textiles during that war and during the American Civil War, accelerated the transition from linen to jute production in east-central Scotland. By 1868, Dundee imported fifty times as much jute as she had done thirty years before.

In 1847 Kirkcaldy began the linoleum industry, which is still famous. Dunfermline continued to produce fine linen, but it was in the woollen industry that great progress was made, though the handloom was still used until 1850 in the relatively small mills. Expansion was the easier as abundant supplies of wool were obtained from the Colonies and, besides tweeds, hosiery and carpets were produced. Between 1858 and 1881 the number of persons employed trebled.

The Heavy Industries. One reason why the textiles declined was that the heavy industries were more profitable, and the reason for this prosperity was the close inter-relation of the railways, coal, iron, ship-building, and engineering. All these industries flourished together. The railways carried the coal to the furnaces, and helped to create a demand for the iron and steel produced.

As already shown, thanks to the discoveries of Mushet and Neilson, Scottish furnaces multiplied very rapidly in the first two decades of Victoria's reign, and not only pig-iron but malleable iron was being produced about Coatbridge. There was a threat of decline as the supply of native 'black-band' ore began to run out, but the discoveries of Bessemer and Siemens promoted the manufacture of steel; and after 1879, when the Middlesbrough Gilchrists discovered a process for handling phosphoric ores, foreign ores were very freely imported, and Scotland turned from malleable iron to steel. Great companies, nearly all of which owned coal-mines as well as furnaces, came into being and, in the 'industrial belt', mainly in the west, the steel industry throve.

Among reasons which created the great demand for steel was that the shipbuilders in the second half of the century turned from timber, first to iron and then to steel. In 1850 wood was still employed over most of Scotland, though on the Clyde iron had largely supplanted wood. With the advent of steel the use of timber for the hulls of vessels rapidly declined and, at the same time, steam-engines supplanted sails. First paddles and soon propellers came into use. The vessels built were not only capable of coastal trade, but of the longest voyages; and it was on the Clyde that some of the great shipping companies, as well as some of the greatest shipyards, came into being – the White Star, the Clan Line, the Anchor, and the Donaldson, besides the great Cunard which has already been mentioned.

Along with these developments in ship-building, came a great expansion in engineering which soon became a major industry in itself, producing locomotives, girders, bridges, and rails, besides textile machinery and machine tools. Big companies came into being to handle the great industries, and Scotland became one of the suppliers of the whole world.

To the abounding prosperity there is an ugly side. The evils of sweated labour had existed (more than is always recognized) even when manufacture was domestic; but, with the advent of factories, furnaces and shipyards, and the expansion of collieries these evils were accentuated. During the century the population had increased almost threefold to four and a half millions and, with the decline of the rural industries, crowding increased in the larger towns, where slums multiplied. Conditions were little better in the industrial villages which sprang up near pits and iron works. These were often rows of incommodious houses and offered little opportunities for entertainment except the public-house.

To a much greater extent than in England, the Scottish working class lived in large, crowded tenements in the great cities. Flats in these were relatively cheap to rent, but there was always a large homeless population because income levels in large sections of society were scarcely adequate to pay for even the most rudimentary housing. It is impossible to generalize about wages. On the one hand it is clear that, overall, Scotland was one of the most prosperous parts of Victorian Britain; on the other, the working population of entire cities like Dundee were effectively condemned to very low wages indeed. £1 a week was the average wage at the end of the nineteenth century; even given the much greater value of money at that time, this was barely a subsistence wage. Of course, skilled tradesmen in the shipyards and engineering works along the Clyde had much higher wages; but it must be remembered that the unskilled labour market was permanently and grossly oversupplied, partly due to the continuing mass immigration by very poor people from Ireland and from the Highlands. The inevitable result was very low wages and, even in Glasgow, a massive pool of chronically unemployed.

Scotland Overseas

As part of the free-trade economy of Great Britain, Victorian Scotland was very much integrated into a world-wide economic system. This fact can conveniently be illustrated by reference to the linen trade of east-central Scotland. In this area, centered on Dundee, the 'linen trade' was a term used both of jute and linen manufacture. The raw materials for both these industries came from abroad: jute almost exclusively from the Indian province of Bengal; flax largely from the Baltic provinces of Imperial Russia. The heavy textiles manufactured from these imported goods were subsequently exported all over the world. Sacking from Dundee was used in great quantities in the western hemisphere, from Argentina to Canada. In the same way, the heavy metallurgical industries of Scotland exported a high proportion of their products. American grain might well be taken in sacks made in Dundee, by locomotives manufactured in Springfield near Glasgow, to be loaded onto ships built on the Clyde.

At the same time, streams of capital and emigrants moved out of Scotland to take advantage of favourable economic opportunities abroad. It is no accident that Scotland pioneered the 'investment trust' whereby professional managers enabled large numbers of relatively modest investors to gain access to the rewards of large-scale investment. Cities like Edinburgh, Aberdeen, and Dundee came to hold enormous investments, particularly in North America where the expanding frontier of settlement offered very high rates of return on money invested. In a sense it was a circular process, because the dynamism behind the advancing frontier was the production of cheap meat and grain for the huge industrial market offered by free-trade Britain; while at the same time the spectacular growth of European settlement in both North and South America generated further demand for the heavy-engineering, and coarse-textile products which were the staples of the Scottish economy.

In such a cosmopolitan context, it is not at all surprising that emigration remained a conspicuous feature of Scottish life. It was true of Scotland, as of the United Kingdom as a whole, that throughout the nineteenth century the bulk of emigrants went, not to other parts of the British Empire, but to the United States. However, it is easier to trace those Scottish emigrants who remained under the British flag, and several of these groups made a distinctive contribution to the development of the overseas dominions of the Crown. Many Highlanders, driven out by the Clearances, made their way to Canada in the early nineteenth century. In the maritime provinces there they formed the last great wave of immigration and they contrived to establish extensive Gaelic-speaking enclaves in Newfoundland and Cape Breton which survived into the twentieth century. In New Zealand, the foundation of Dunedin in 1848 was largely the product of enthusiasm for emigration amongst members of the newly established Free Kirk. One of the leaders in this enterprise was the Reverend Thomas Burns, a nephew of the poet. Australia also attracted its fair share of Scottish immigrants (as well as its fair share of Scottish produce such as Dundee jute and, above all, Younger's Edinburgh Ale). In South Africa, finally, there were likewise many Scots among the English-speaking immigrants (mainly concentrated in the Cape and Natal) but the famous names among them were, significantly, nearly all missionaries.

The Victorian period was not only one of religious ferment within Scotland; it was also, to some extent, one of evangelical fervour in world-wide missionary activity. Scotsmen had taken a considerable part in the foundation of the 'interdenominational' London Missionary Society in 1795, and many went to Africa under its auspices. Amongst the greatest of these were Robert Moffatt (1795–1883) of Bechuanaland and his son-in-law David Livingstone (1813–73). Livingstone is all the more remarkable because he was outstanding in so many fields. As a doctor and as a missionary he would take a high place in the annals of European penetration of Africa; but it is perhaps as an explorer and a scientific geographer that he reached the peak of his achievement. Meanwhile, Scotland was founding her own missionary societies. In 1796 there was founded in Glasgow the Glasgow Missionary Society which until 1820 contributed rather money than men. But from 1821 onwards, ministers definitely Presbyterian established themselves in South Africa on the dangerous frontier between the colonists and the powerful tribe of the Khosas; and, in the face of great difficulties, including tribal wars, and the effects of the Disruption in Scotland, made Lovedale (1841) the headquarters of a great enterprise, not only to convert but to instruct and educate the Bantus. Further north, in Nyasaland, a unique combination of Scottish missionary and business enterprise can be traced to the impression made on a young Scottish probationer, James

Stewart, by an appeal made by Livingstone in an address given at Cambridge in December 1857 – 'I go back to try to make an open path for commerce and Christianity. Do you carry out the work which I have begun.' Stewart managed to persuade the Free Church Assembly in 1861 to consider a scheme for a mission to Nyasaland; and though his own visit to the Zambesi ended in sickness and disappointment he enlisted the help of some Glasgow businessmen who in 1874 inaugurated a mission to a country to be called Livingstonia in honour of the hero recently buried in Westminster Abbey.

There were also Scottish missionaries in British India, where the Church of Scotland has a small share in that remarkable phenomenon, the Indian ecclesiastical establishment. But the great majority of Scots in India were there in the service of the state, either as soldiers or as administrators. Since the eighteenth century, India had served as a major outlet for Scottish talent (p. 327). Indeed, the bad showing by Scottish candidates in the examinations for the Indian civil service immediately after 1857 (when these posts were thrown open to competition) was a major incentive towards changing the curricula in Scottish schools. However, the defect was soon remedied and in the latter part of the century many Scottish middle-class boys enjoyed impressive careers in both the Indian medical service and the Indian civil service. Scottish aristocrats on occasion were chosen to fill the high office of Governor-General (Lord Dalhousie, 1848–56; Lord Elgin, 1862–3, and his son 1894–8). Naturally the Indian army also contained a very substantial number of Scots: Sir Charles Napier conquered Sind, Sir Colin Campbell (Lord Clyde) saved Lucknow, and countless other Scots were among the 'martial races' on whose valour and discipline the British Raj ultimately rested.

In almost every way, Scotsmen were deriving benefit from the British Empire. It provided a field for emigration; it enabled some firms and individuals to make great commercial fortunes; above all it offered opportunities of employment to the sons of the ascendant Scottish middle class. But, in retrospect, it is clear that this great imperial structure carried within it the seeds of decay – possibly from as early as the 1870s, certainly from the 1890s, and irreversibly after the outbreak of the First World War in 1914.

CHAPTER 19

MODERN SCOTLAND

IN the great march of events which has transformed the
Britain of Queen Victoria into the Britain of today the
fortunes of Scotland were inextricably bound up. The
process of industrialization in Scotland, with all its unique
regional emphases, was nevertheless also a process of
integration with the industrial economy of Britain as a
whole. When modern types of political parties with elaborate organization reaching down into the constituencies
emerged in the second half of the nineteenth century, they
were organized on a British basis. By 1914 the Prime
Minister, the Liberal H. H. Asquith, sat for a Scottish seat
in Fife, while the leader of the Tory opposition, Andrew
Bonar Law, was a Glasgow iron-merchant turned politician. The British armies in France during the First World
War were led to victory by Field Marshal Sir Douglas
Haig (later Earl Haig) who, like Bonar Law, exemplified
the rise of the Scottish upper middle class, for he came from
a great whisky manufacturing dynasty. Perhaps examples
of this kind smack merely of the assimilation of individuals
within local ruling élites to the highest ruling class of
Britain. However, it is a fact that the history of twentieth-
century Scotland is part of the history of the United Kingdom, and that to treat only matters in which the Scottish
experience differed from that of England would be to
produce a distorted picture. Equally, it is impractical
simply to narrate the larger story, so what is here attempted
is a discussion of the particular experience of Scotland, as
a region within the United Kingdom.

Scotland shouldered her fair share of the burden of the
First World War. Indeed, before the introduction of conscription she probably bore more than her fair share, for
her industrial cities with their poverty and chronic unemployment were among the favourite recruiting grounds
of the regular British Army. Dundee, where it was difficult
for men to secure employment because of the predominantly
female labour force in the jute industry, had a far higher
proportion of serving soldiers and reservists than virtually
any other British city. Like all the other combatant countries, Scotland suffered heavy loss of life, and she had a
smaller population than some from which to make the
losses good. Such actions as the Battle of Loos, which
involved three full Scottish divisions, as well as other Scottish units, took an appalling toll of her young manhood.
As conscription was introduced from January 1916 the
effects of the great massacres in France affected every part
of Scotland. Just as the Isle of Skye had suffered disproportionate losses during the Napoleonic Wars, so the
Long Island of Lewis and Harris suffered some of the
highest casualties, in proportion to its population, of any
British region during the First World War.

Perhaps the scale of the losses helps to explain the unprecedented hysteria which swept through the traditional
leaders of Scottish society, lay and ecclesiastical. There had
been furious argument in Scotland over the Boer War at
the turn of the century. An Earl of Airlie died in it, like
so many of his forebears, at the head of his regiment of
horse, and Lord Lovat, chief of the Frasers, raised his own
regiment, the Lovat Scouts. On the other hand a very large
section of Scottish Liberalism, led by the future Prime
Minister Campbell-Bannerman, had opposed the war. Yet
the staggeringly greater loss of life between 1914 and 1919
merely brought out the latent belligerency, and emphasized
the capacity for self-righteousness which had always been
part of Liberal Scotland's collective personality. The clergy

of the Presbyterian churches in particular excelled themselves in depicting the war as a Homeric duel between Good and Evil. It is perhaps no accident that the Roman Catholic church in Scotland, many of whose Irish clergy had very mixed feelings about the war, suffered less from post-war disillusionment than most other churches. However, it must be said that the laymen who controlled the newspaper press of Scotland shared the apocalyptic vision of the war entertained by the bulk of their clerical contemporaries. There was certainly no serious pressure from Scotland for a coherent statement of British war aims, and, of course, Lloyd George only produced, grudgingly, a very vague statement of those aims as late as 1918. The only significant groups in the population which appear to have maintained some sense of detachment were those skilled workers on Clydeside who resisted attempts by the government to 'dilute' the ranks of skilled men with an influx of less skilled and cheaper labour. Lloyd George tried flattery and cajoling, and then went over to banning newspapers and jailing the men's leaders. The term 'Red Clydeside' which was coined to describe this outburst of labour militancy was a piece of nonsense. The leaders of resistance to government policy were nearly all to enjoy successful political careers in later years, and none of them displayed Lenin-like attributes. Their followers were predominantly traditionally minded trades unionists.

The war did have a profound, and on the whole unfortunate effect on the Scottish economy. It was one of the long-term weaknesses of that economy that it had evolved in such a way as to depend to a disproportionate extent on traditional heavy metallurgical industry (and associated coal-mining), and on coarse textiles. The First World War, a war of artillery fought over positions occupied by mass infantry armies dug into elaborate trench systems, tended to accentuate demand for heavy iron and steel products and coarse textiles. When Germany embarked on unrestricted submarine warfare in 1917, the loss of merchant shipping, already significant, became catastrophic, and the

British government needed every merchant ship which the Clyde yards could turn out. On the east coast, the Firth of Forth was by the end of the war a major base for repairs and servicing to the Grand Fleet. Much of this activity was conducted on an uneconomic basis. Peacetime demand under normal conditions was never likely to match wartime production levels, and very often the British government was so desperate to secure the product of an industry that price competition became irrelevant. An extreme case is the supply of sandbags, where the Scottish jute industry could not compete with the Indian industry in terms of price, but this did not matter for as long as the war raged. Many Scottish industrialists knew that peace must involve a drastic fall in demand for their products. The surprising event was not the post-war slump, but the fact that for most big Scottish industries it did not come until about 1921: as a result of post-war reconstruction and the demand it created, industrial activity remained at a high level until early in that year. Then the first of three major slumps hit the inter-war Scottish economy.

Inevitably, the later 1920s saw substantial overall recovery from this post-war slump, but certain sectors of the Scottish economy remained very depressed. Coal-mining is one example where there was no area in Scotland which registered an increase in its mining labour force between 1913 and 1931. Older western areas enjoying close linkages with iron and steel manufacture, like the Lanarkshire field, showed drops of up to 50 per cent in their work force. Only on the east coast did mining show relative vigour. In every part of industrial Scotland the slump which followed the collapse of the American stock exchange in 1929 bit deeply. By 1931–2 unemployment levels of up to 70 per cent were being registered in staple Scottish industries. The Clyde shipyards were so stricken that in 1933 the government gave financial aid to ensure the completion of the great trans-Atlantic liner, the 'Queen Mary'. In the late 1930s a certain measure of recovery set in, often at the price of the sort of consolidation which left Colvilles the only significant firm in what was left of the Scottish steel industry by 1936. Yet there was no parallel in Scotland to the boom in private housing construction which occurred in England, and by 1938 it was quite clear that the Scottish economy, with that of the rest of the United Kingdom, was re-entering a depressed phase.

From this downturn the Scottish economy was eventually rescued by the Second World War, though not immediately, for high unemployment persisted long after the outbreak of war in September 1939. Psychologically, the impact of the post-war depression from 1929, of the Great Depression from 1930, and of signs of renewed depression after 1938, was profound. The old Victorian self-confidence was gone for ever. It is significant that in 1937 George Malcolm Thomson published a book entitled *Scotland: That Distressed Area*. This was a reference to the largely nominal regional policies of the government of the day. At least the designation of Distressed Areas recognized the existence of a problem. The subsequent metamorphosis of Distressed Areas into Special Areas was pure verbal juggling.

Fundamentally, what was happening was that the conditions for Scotland's nineteenth-century prosperity were turning into the explanation of her twentieth-century failure. Unemployment in inter-war Scotland was persistently above the United Kingdom average. In 1932 the Scottish percentage of the workforce unemployed was 27.7 against a U.K. figure of 22.1; and in 1939 the U.K. figure was 10.8, the Scottish 15.9. Mainly, these high figures reflected the depression in Scotland's traditional staple industries. Tragically, the resulting poverty was a factor in discouraging the development of the new light-engineering consumer-oriented industries which, freed from the coalfields by the development of electrical power, tended to concentrate in relatively prosperous conurbations such as London. The gap between Scotland and south-east England widened with every decade.

Domestic Politics: The Struggle of Parties to 1939

The twentieth century began with the Liberal Party still the natural majority party in Scotland. Indeed, in 1906 it swept the Scottish constituencies in a fashion not seen since 1886, and it seemed that with their divisions over the Boer War behind them the Liberals were set for a long period of ascendancy in Scotland. They had suffered from disunity and feuds between the various Presbyterian churches, but by 1900 Scottish Presbyterianism was showing signs of a strong movement towards unity. In 1900 the Free Church with 1,100 parishes joined the United Presbyterian Church, with its 600 congregations, to form the United Free Church (see p. 302n.). The Church of Scotland or Auld Kirk had experienced a very considerable revival since the 1840s. It had been relieved of the incubus of lay patronage by a Tory government, and had survived campaigns for its disestablishment and disendowment to muster 1,457 parishes in 1900. It is true that changes in thought meant that it required parliamentary assistance in order to secure relaxation of its doctrinal standards, but this did not provoke the United Free Church to obstructive opposition, for the very simple reason that it was in desperate need of legislation itself. A minority in the former Free Kirk, claiming that the majority of that communion had violated the fundamental principles of their denomination by uniting with the United Presbyterians, claimed all the possessions of the Free Kirk. Improbably enough, the House of Lords accepted the claim of these 'Wee Frees', who had of course to be prised away from the Free Kirk endowments by legislation. The 'Wee Frees' were not ungenerously treated, and retained strong support in parts of the Highlands.

Another major advantage enjoyed by the Liberal governments of Sir Henry Campbell-Bannerman and Asquith before 1914 was the success and vigour of the Scottish economy. With such economic strength behind them, the traditional middle-class leaders of Scottish

Liberalism had every reason for the self-confidence which characterized them up to 1914. The Great War and the post-war slump of 1921 were appalling blows to Liberal vitality. During the war the Liberal Party itself split between a faction led by H. H. Asquith and a faction following the man who supplanted him as Prime Minister, David Lloyd George. The latter faction participated in a Coalition régime. This Coalition administration passed a major piece of Scottish legislation in November 1918 in the shape of the Education (Scotland) Act which finally abolished the parish as the basic unit of educational administration, replacing it with thirty-eight *ad hoc* electoral bodies based on the counties and larger burghs.

The Bolshevik Revolution in Russia in 1917 inevitably caused a stir in Scottish politics, especially in the Clydeside area where the remarkable Marxist and Scottish nationalist John Maclean tried to persuade the Trades Council of Glasgow to turn itself into a working revolutionary soviet. The idea was, to put it mildly, premature, and the 'coupon' election of 1918 came as a terrible shock to left-wingers and Asquithian Liberals alike. Only seven Labour members were elected and only six Liberals who did not possess the 'coupon' or letter of recognition sent to all Coalition candidates. Maclean was defeated and before he died in 1923 it was clear that he had failed in his gallant attempt to create an effective Scottish Workers Republican Party.

It was the 1922 election, following the break-up of the Coalition, which marked a major turning-point in Scottish politics. That election occurred against a background of massive slump and sustained socialist propaganda. No less than twenty-nine Labour M.P.s were returned as well as one Communist. At the same time, the Scottish Unionists (or Conservatives) followed a pattern which has become standard in twentieth-century Scotland: the country tends to be much more to the left in politics than England (the 1922 election saw a strong swing to the Conservatives in England), but at the same time Scottish Conservatives tend to be more passionately hostile to any proposed political change than English Conservatives. Thus the Scottish Unionists were opposed to the break-up of the Coalition and cooperated with Coalition Liberals to ensure that fourteen National Liberals were returned as well as fifteen Unionists. Significantly there were also fourteen 'Asquith' Liberals and three 'Lloyd George' ones. The Labour victory was especially impressive in and around Glasgow, whence the famous group of 'Clydesider' Labour M.P.s duly descended on Westminster. Their 'redness' can be wildly exaggerated for they were basically liberal-reformists with no serious Marxist content.

When in December 1923 the new Conservative leader, Stanley Baldwin, opted to hold a surprise election, perhaps more to bind his party together than to achieve his avowed programme, Scotland swung even more sharply to the left, returning thirty-five Labour M.P.s to sixteen Unionists and twenty-three Liberals. As Baldwin had threatened the great Liberal shibboleth of Free Trade, the Liberals showed signs of unwonted unity. However, the main result of the election was the formation in 1924 of a minority Labour government under Ramsay MacDonald, a strikingly handsome Scotsman from Lossiemouth whose mellifluous oratory tended to obscure the fact that he often had nothing to say, and who enjoyed an ill-deserved reputation as a left-winger due to his record of opposition to the First World War. Almost ideally cast as the man to show that Labour could be respectable in office, MacDonald leaned heavily on ex-Liberals such as his fellow Scotsman Lord Haldane, who served as Lord Chancellor, and even appointed a 'non-party' (i.e. Tory) Lord Advocate for Scotland, H. P. MacMillan. The only left-winger of any consequence in the government was John Wheatley, whose Housing Act was the only concrete legislative achievement of the régime. Based on close cooperation between government and the building industry it made a major attack on the task of redeveloping those urban slum areas which were so prominent in Scotland.

Labour 'moderates' argued that the conservative

policies of the government were both inevitable, due to its minority position, and desirable, as a way of courting middle-of-the-road voters. But in practice the Tories were able to compete very effectively for such votes, while the left of the Labour Party became increasingly crotchety and frustrated with a leadership which clearly liked the restrictions on its room for manoeuvre, because it did not want to do a great deal anyway. In Scotland the resulting friction was particularly damaging because the leftish Independent Labour Party, a body affiliated to the Labour Party, included the bulk of the Clydesiders led by Wheatley and his engaging, if rather emotional lieutenant, James Maxton. Ironically Ramsay MacDonald was precipitated into an election in 1924 by a cynical attack on his common-sense in trying to negotiate a trade agreement with Soviet Russia. The 'Red Scare' thus created helped to secure a great Conservative victory, though the swing to the right was less marked in Scotland than elsewhere: in the Scottish constituencies thirty-eight Unionists were returned against twenty-seven Labour M.P.s. The election did, however, mark the end of an era, for only nine Liberals survived. The old Liberal ascendancy in Scotland was now over, never likely to revive.

The General Strike of 1926, when the Independent Labour Party was far more militantly behind the strikers than the frankly embarrassed official Labour leadership, exacerbated the left–right tensions within the Labour Party. Nevertheless, when the Conservative leader Stanley Baldwin shambled rather casually into an election in 1929, Scotland made a substantial contribution to the strong Labour recovery, sending thirty-eight Labour men to Westminster, as against twenty-two Unionists and fourteen Liberals. A new pattern seemed to be emerging. The Representation of the People Act of 1918 had not only enfranchised women (in most cases over the age of thiry) but also left Scotland in a strong position with seventy-four M.P.s out of a total of 707, which by 1921 had fallen to 640 due to the secession of Southern Ireland. The Labour Party could usually only form a government when it secured a head-start by capturing a disproportionate share of Scottish (and, be it said, Welsh) seats. Certainly, this was one of the foundations of MacDonald's second minority Labour government of 1929. A new Labour ascendancy might have been in the making, but for the extraordinary events of 1931.

MacDonald included four Scotsmen in his Cabinet, but excluded, by his personal decision, Wheatley. Only two Independent Labour Party men were given (minor) office – Tom Johnston and Emanuel Shinwell – and both were known to be hostile to Wheatley and Maxton. It was an ill omen. The crisis which precipitated a split in the government involved pressure from foreign and domestic banking interests to introduce economies and especially cuts in unemployment benefit. Given the extremely conservative economic thought of the period, held strongly in its most rigorous form by Snowdon, MacDonald's Chancellor of the Exchequer, there was a strong case for MacDonald's refusal to continue in office in the face of resistance to cuts from his colleagues and the trade unions. What was infinitely less defensible was the fact that he then fought a notably bitter election against his own party, as the leader of a prospective National Government. In the Scottish constituencies the result of the 1931 election was spectacular. It cancelled the political developments of over a decade. In the 1929 election, the first fought in Britain under complete adult suffrage, the Labour Party held thirty-eight Scottish seats. In 1931 only seven Labour M.P.s survived, and they were largely concentrated in and around Glasgow. 'National' candidates won sixty-seven out of seventy-four Scottish seats, though it is significant that the Liberals, drawing on a maximum of Conservative support and goodwill in an almost complete electoral pact, could only win sixteen Scottish seats.

In Dundee even Neddy Scrymgeour, the Prohibitionist and socialist who had inflicted a well-deserved defeat on Winston Churchill at the polls in 1922, and who had survived the elections of 1924 and 1929, went tumbling to defeat as the burgh returned a Unionist and a National Liberal called D. Mackintosh Foot, subsequently better known as the English Labour M.P., Dingle Foot. One contemporary observer remarked that virtually all the Scottish press was hysterically in favour of the National Government and continually represented the choice before the voters as one between patriotism and treason.

Of course, the scale of the National Government's victory in Scotland in 1931 was exaggerated by the electoral system. A ten-to-one victory in representation was based on a two-to-one victory at the polls, and recovery by Labour was almost inevitable. To some extent it came in the form of Labour party gains in municipal elections. The National Government was overwhelmingly Conservative and the sheer size of its majority after 1931 rather discouraged any dynamism in its approach to such intractable regional problems as those of Scotland. In 1935 there was another general election at which Scotland returned forty-six pro-government M.P.s (thirty-seven of them Conservative), against twenty Labour members, four Independent Labour (that party having finally broken with Labour), three Liberals, and a Communist from West Fife. Such was the size of the National Government's majority at Westminster that the reappearance of Scotland's traditional 'bias to the left' hardly mattered.

The inter-war period was naturally not one dominated by any form of radical reconstruction in Scotland. One example of this was the way in which the Labour Party successfully slithered out of its originally very firm commitment to Scottish Home Rule. Ramsay MacDonald, like the father of the Labour Party, his fellow Scot Keir Hardie, had at one time been a militant believer in federal Home Rule for the United Kingdom, but the taste of office in 1924 produced unmistakable signs of a loss of enthusiasm on MacDonald's part for any form of devolution which might reduce the number of Labour M.P.s at Westminster, and which was in any case bitterly unpopular with the

Conservatives. A federal Home Rule bill, introduced by the Labour M.P. for the Gorbals, was not seriously supported by the government. This became MacDonald's standard technique, repeated in 1929: Home Rule bills were left to back-benchers and given only verbal support by government.

The Conservative response to Scottish pressures was purely administrative. In 1926 they upgraded the Secretaryship for Scotland to the status of a full Secretaryship of State, and in 1928 started a policy of administrative reorganization of the departments responsible to the Secretary of State for Scotland (at the time there were only three – health, agriculture, and prisons). This process culminated in 1939 in the removal of the Scottish departments from Whitehall to a new administrative building, St Andrew's House in Edinburgh. Whether this 'administrative devolution' was a bane or a blessing is debatable. Local government reform in 1929 had gone a long way towards destroying really local units which local people could hope to influence, and it would take a bold man to argue that St Andrew's House has shown itself more responsive to democratic pressures than Whitehall.

It is ironic that the 1920s – so barren of achievement in terms of legislation promoting effective political devolution – were a period of notable ferment of a nationalist kind in both politics and literature. The so-called 'Scottish Renaissance' in letters was first widely publicized as such by Lewis Spence, an able journalist who founded in 1926 a tiny group with the resounding title of the Scottish National Movement. In a broader perspective, the writers of the 'Scottish Renaissance' were a mixed bag, ranging from successful novelists using standard English, like Eric Linklater and Compton Mackenzie, to a literary phenomenon and poet deemed by some contemporaries to be of the stature of Burns, Hugh MacDiarmid (C. M. Grieve), who was deeply involved in an attempt to recreate a literary Scots language (Lallans). In between came a host of remarkable men like R. B. Cunninghame Graham, whose life was as romantic as his novels, James Bridie (Dr Osborne Mavor) who was a prolific playwright, and Neil Gunn, a serious novelist with a poet's gift for language whose greatness has slowly gained recognition. Every variety of language can be found in the work of this group, including even a contrived but effective Anglo-Scots in the novels of Lewis Grassic Gibbon (Leslie Mitchell).

In such an atmosphere, it is not surprising that the destruction of the Government of Scotland bill introduced by a Labour M.P., the Reverend James Barr, in 1927 should have precipitated the formation, mainly from earlier Home Rule groups, of the National Party of Scotland in 1928. Dominated by an extremely able young lawyer, John MacCormick, this party fought by-elections with conspicuous lack of success before it coalesced in 1934 with a small right-wing group called the Scottish Party. The result of the union was the Scottish National Party, but at first the new organization remained ineffectual and faction-ridden. The reason for its internal troubles was, of course, the multiplicity of strategies open to it, and the difficulty of deciding which, if any, was likely to be effective. Mac-Cormick had come to believe in a moderate Home Rule programme, within the framework of the United Kingdom, and like so many 'moderates' in politics had displayed great ruthlessness in purging the National Party in 1933 of anyone who seriously opposed this policy. MacCormick was determined to forge links with Labour and the Liberals but the brutal fact is that his policies produced no results and were therefore bound to be challenged within the new Scottish National Party. It was a divided self-doubting nationalist movement which entered the Second World War.

Scottish self-confidence was at a low ebb in 1939. Despite the political triumph of conservative elements in 1931, most old-established Scottish institutions felt threatened. The Church of Scotland, for example, had completed a major act of union with the United Free Church in 1929, and was full of ecumenical spirit, but it was also ravaged by the theological uncertainties and growing materialism and scepticism of the age. Even the Scottish working class, whose potential for political and social 'extremism' was the source of much middle-class paranoia, seems in the last analysis to have felt, however subconsciously, that with a collapsing regional economy around it, it needed all the help which Westminster could be persuaded to offer.

The Second World War and Post-War Reconstruction

The outbreak of war in September 1939 can be seen in retrospect as a major turning point in British history. That this is so is almost entirely due to the absurd misconceptions with which Neville Chamberlain, the Prime Minister and leader of a still nominally 'National' government, entered the war – misconceptions, be it said, shared by the great bulk of an expensive and conceited political establishment. Basically Chamberlain and his supporters expected to win, and to collect the credit for winning, a short war. The expected mechanism of victory was simple: the German economy was to collapse, conveniently and rapidly, under the strain of war. But, in fact, Hitler's early victories brought down not only Chamberlain but the liberal–capitalist consensus which his régime embodied.

Winston Churchill came into power in 1940 accompanied by a retinue of cronies of no real political standing like Lord Beaverbrook, Brendan Bracken, and Professor Lindemann, and as a result the Labour Party was able to enter a new coalition more or less on its own terms. Even in Scotland Churchill chose to buy acquiescence, and the price was the nomination of a Secretary of State for Scotland who for once had ability, initiative, and personal magnetism. This was Thomas Johnston, a Labour politician who was able to secure remarkable freedom of manoeuvre from Churchill and who set up a Council of State composed of ex-Secretaries to give a touch of bi-partisan approval to many of his measures. Johnston was able to establish the Scottish Council on Industry as well as the Scottish Tourist

369

Board and the North of Scotland Hydro-Electric Board. Using civil-defence hospital facilities, he created what amounted to a miniature national health service on Clydeside. Against the prevailing current of centralization, Johnston gave legitimacy to Scottish national sentiment while greatly accelerating administrative devolution. By the end of the war Johnston was shrewd enough to recognize that the time had come for him to retire.

The great Labour victory in the general election of 1945 was essentially a victory for centralization. The war years had seen a party truce which was designed quite simply to deprive the electorate of any influence over the government by ensuring that the major parties never opposed one another in by-elections. One of the odder results of this was to give Douglas Young, a poet and Greek scholar who had gained wide publicity by opposing industrial and military conscription on nationalist grounds, a chance to challenge the Labour grip on Kirkcaldy Burghs in 1944, where he gained 6,621 votes to the 8,268 for the Labour candidate. At Motherwell in 1945 a Scottish National Party candidate, Dr Robert McIntyre, actually won a by-election, though he was unseated in the general election when Labour secured thirty-seven Scottish seats, the Conservatives thirty-two, the Independent Labour Party three, and the Communists and Independents one each. The Liberals reached their nadir, and the Scottish National Party was reduced to its usual ineffectiveness.

Clement Attlee, the new Prime Minister, was an out-and-out centralizer with no more time for devolution than his Lord President of the Council, Herbert Morrison, who supervised an extensive programme of nationalization which was disproportionately significant in Scotland. Most of the new government's legislation was either bi-partisan, like the setting up of a National Health Service, or a series of rescue operations on ailing industries which had been either in trouble before the war, or so abused during it (like the railways) that their return to private control under normal conditions would have been very difficult indeed. Sir Hartley Shawcross, an upper-middle-class Labour lawyer, announced in 1945 that 'we are the masters now'. The sceptic may have been tempted to inquire if there had ever been a time when people like that had *not* been the masters in twentieth-century Britain; but the answer seems to be that the new establishment of ex-dons, trade-union bureaucrats, and 'moderate' politicians, all devoted to the interventionist pump-priming economics of Lord Keynes, was confirmed in the saddle it had occupied since 1940. Scotland's failure for once to swing as far or further left than England in 1945 may well have derived from a sense that the programme of the Labour leadership was not so much a revolution made as one prevented.

Despite pretensions to the contrary, the new government had no real long-term economic plans, and structural change in the Scottish economy between 1945 and 1951 was conspicuous mainly by its absence. There was a new willingness to maintain aggregate demand within the economy at levels which would ensure near full employment; and the scale of destruction during the war had been such that post-war demand for the sort of heavy capital goods which Scotland traditionally produced was enormous. The main problem was to produce the goods. Traditional rivals in world markets, such as Japan and Germany, were prostrate in defeat. The war had not been as technologically stultifying as the First World War, but surprisingly little of the new industries it bred became acclimatized in Scotland. In so far as new light industries did develop, they tended to be foreign, usually American-owned. In such fields as motor-car manufacture, the aircraft industry, and even electronics, Scotland in 1951 lagged far behind the south-east of England. The problems of Scottish agriculture were, it is true, to some extent brought under control by an elaborate structure of government supervision and subsidy, but the problems of depopulation and agricultural deterioration in the Highlands were scarcely scratched by the almost entirely powerless Highland

Advisory Panel, set up by the Attlee government as an exercise in public relations.

By 1951 the Labour government was clearly tired and losing the will to govern. It had exhausted the limited ideological capital of its leading members, a capital which was largely compounded of pre-war reformism and Keynesian economics. Ironically, the early 1950s also saw the end of the road for another political tradition hammered into shape in the 1930s – the nationalist one embodied in John MacCormick. That tireless man actually stood as a Liberal candidate in 1945. He had left the Scottish National Party in 1942 after failing to persuade it to convert itself purely into a propaganda organization dedicated to persuading other parties to accept an agreed measure of Home Rule for Scotland. Failing at the polls as a Liberal in 1945, MacCormick stood and lost as a 'National' candidate with Conservative support in a by-election in 1948. MacCormick's main organized support came from a Scottish Convention which was avowedly all-party in composition. With the failure of direct political action it turned to organizing a new Scottish National Covenant, a great petition for a measure of devolution within the United Kingdom which eventually secured two million signatures (including the usual multiple signatures by such individuals as Queen Victoria and Marshal Stalin). As a cheap and effective means of publicity and education, the Covenant proved valuable. It was also valuable in showing that mere opinion was of no interest to Westminster, where men dealt in power. By 1950 MacCormick was effectively retired from active politics, finishing on a fine note when he was elected Lord Rector of Glasgow University. His services to nationalism were great, not least in proving that it had no future if it relied on the effects of sweet reason applied to existing political structures.

Meantime the Scottish National Party had been totally re-organized by Dr Robert D. MacIntyre, who in retrospect is the father of modern political nationalism in Scotland. As Chairman of his party from 1947 to 1956 he set it on a clear path as a disciplined fighting group dedicated to winning elections against other parties. Gone were the days when political nationalism was compatible with membership of other parties, and this was too much for such an erratic genius as Douglas Young, who had at various times belonged to most known political parties. Nor did MacIntyre's hard line at first seem to yield much in the way of results. The main achievement of the Scottish National Party between 1942 and 1964 was simply to survive, whilst fighting off endless and importunate attempts to make it compromise on its central policy – independence for Scotland.

The two general elections of 1950–51 were crucial beyond the average. The first lamed the Labour administration; the second killed it, despite the fact that it had a majority of the popular vote in the United Kingdom. The electoral system gave Churchill a working majority under extremely favourable circumstances. Post-war difficulties were to some extent over; the world economy started to expand at an unprecedented pace; and the resulting prosperity more or less guaranteed those in power a long run in office. Conservative administrations in fact lasted from 1951 to 1964. Yet it was precisely in this era that Scottish self-government became a live political issue.

Scotland since 1960

After an initial period of *laissez-faire* (Churchill was, after all, an Edwardian Liberal), the Conservative administrations turned to planning for growth and to having a regional policy. It was probably politically counter-productive to do this in Scotland, for it drew attention to the yawning gulf between what the politicians promised and what actually happened. Indeed the greatest Conservative electoral triumph of the century in the Scottish constituencies came in 1955, shortly after Sir Winston Churchill had retired from a notably undynamic premiership. The Scottish Unionists (i.e. Conservatives) won an absolute majority

373

of Scottish votes cast in that election, and collected a useful thirty-six seats by so doing. Thereafter, the brief and disastrous premiership of Anthony Eden was followed by the long reign of Harold MacMillan, and by the early 1960s official and semi-official reports on the Scottish economy were appearing at regular intervals, all liberally laced with such words as 'growth' and 'development'. This reflected the post-Keynesian enthusiasm of professional economists for growth as the central issue of economics, as well as admiration in British government circles for the 'indicative planning' practised by the French government. Within a decade even professional economists were prepared to express doubts about whether such planning actually enhanced total growth in a mature industrial economy. Without the benefits of any comparable planning, for example, West Germany matched French growth rates in the 1960s. In Scotland there was sustained growth in the production of regional and national surveys and plans, but the economy was visibly running down at the same time, which may explain why the Conservative vote followed suit despite two more Scottish Prime Ministers (Harold MacMillan and Sir Alec Douglas-Home). It fell, in fact, from 1,349,298 in 1951 to 960,654 in 1966 and the Conservative haul of Scottish seats fell from thirty-six in 1955 to twenty in 1966. It was a very strategic loss of support, for Harold Wilson, the Labour leader, first scraped into office in 1964 by a tiny margin, wholly explicable in terms of Labour's head-start in Scotland.

Undoubtedly, the post-war Labour government had done much to alleviate the worst extremes of want in Scotland, and had even made a substantial dent in Scotland's appalling backlog of bad housing (albeit at the price of making municipal housing a cynically-abused counter in the political game). There had, however, been no significant change in the out-of-date bias of the Scottish economy towards heavy metallurgy and coarse textiles. By the 1950s old competitors were again active in world markets and the spread of primary industrialization in formerly under-

374

developed territories was continually creating new competitors, literally from Mexico to Korea. Unemployment in Scotland was usually about twice the United Kingdom average, and indeed in 1960 Scottish unemployment was about a third higher than it had been in 1948. Having lost out on most of the generation of new industries built up from the 1930s (motor-car manufacture, aircraft, heavy electrical engineering, etc.) Scotland was faring rather badly at attracting the new generation of science-based industries. Where she seemed successful, the success was often more apparent than real. Scottish electronics, for example, was very often simply a matter of assembly lines using cheap labour to put together the products of more sophisticated parts of the industry, situated anywhere but in Scotland.

On top of this, Scotland was unusually hard hit by such developments as the Beeching Report of 1963. Dr Richard Beeching was brought in from Imperial Chemical Industries to give expert blessing to decisions which the nationalized railways had obviously already taken in principle: mainly to cut, so far as was possible, peripheral railway lines running at a loss. Had the full report been implemented at once, large parts of northern and south-western Scotland would have been left very isolated. Road improvement and the spread of car ownership removed some of the sting from the inevitable contraction of rail services, but the increased cost of motoring and the run-down in bus services had, by the 1970s, made much of rural Scotland isolated as never before in the twentieth century, and particularly difficult for older people to live in. Urban Scotland had its own problems of environment, sometimes on a terrifying scale. Glasgow, for example, tried to cope with its dreadful heritage of central slums and overcrowding by forming peripheral housing estates, often of great size, and invariably devoid of social facilities or coherence. The result was, in human terms, a tragedy; but one which could be matched on a smaller scale by similar developments in other Scottish cities. All deprivation is relative;

so it is not unreasonable to say that the Scotland of 1965, for all its enhanced living standards, was relatively speaking a deprived society, and the natural result seemed to promise the emergence of a Labour ascendancy in its politics, comparable perhaps to the iron grip of the Labour Party in Wales, a grip which even the events of 1931 had failed to break.

That this did not happen can be explained largely by the policies followed by Harold Wilson and his Chancellor of the Exchequer, James Callaghan, after the election of 1966 had given the Labour government a clear majority, no longer strategically dependent on Scotland. First the régime embarked on a mulish but quite hopeless defence of a particular and unrealistic value for the pound sterling. Encouraged by the American government, the Wilson administration sacrificed most of its social and political priorities to this shibboleth. After the inevitable devaluation a new Chancellor, Roy Jenkins, pursued the most conservative of lines with a view to producing a favourable balance of payments. In Scotland this meant further deflation and unemployment and ensured that Scotland made its contribution to the unexpected electoral débâcle of 1970, which brought the Labour government down and installed a Conservative régime, at a time when few observers, and very few Conservatives, thought this likely.

At first it seemed possible that the Liberal party would be the principal beneficiary of Scotland's growing disenchantment with Labour. Peripheral rural areas, neglected in planning, hard-hit by transport cuts, and conservative in social structure, tended to vote for the party, which by 1966 held five Scottish seats, including Orkney and Shetland, and Highland and Border constituencies. Nevertheless, by 1968 there were unmistakable signs that the Scottish Liberals were past their peak, and losing their appeal. This was not really surprising. The party had long displayed a quite remarkable incapacity to make progress towards the Home-Rule-all-round policy which it had advocated with a view to turning the United Kingdom into a federal state. On almost all other issues it was not in fact hostile to the 'centrist' politicians who had come to dominate both the Labour and the Conservative Parties, and whose liberal, convergent ideas caused some commentators to coin the term Butskellism (compounded from the names of a leading Conservative and a leader of the Labour Party) to describe the phenomenon. A third party in a two-party system has to be a party of protest, but the Liberal leadership spent most of its time denouncing 'extremists' in the two large parties, on the ground that they threatened the existing political ascendancy in the United Kingdom. It was not a message calculated to set the heather on fire.

Under these circumstances it is really not surprising that the Scottish National Party eventually broke through electorally. It captured Hamilton from Labour at a by-election in November 1967. There was shock on all sides when Mrs Winifred Ewing won this once safe Labour seat, but the Scottish National Party went on to win striking victories in local elections in 1968. Hamilton reverted to its Labour allegiance at the general election of 1970, and academic commentators persuaded themselves that their initial shock over by-election results like Hamilton was misplaced, on the ground that such results were pure protest votes by disgruntled Labour supporters incapable of such independence when their votes really mattered. That Donald Stewart won the Western Isles from Labour for the Scottish National Party in 1970 seemed a quirk of fate and Highland politics, no more.

However, the 1970s saw the emergence of a substantial block of Scottish National Party M.P.s (eleven by 1977), and the adoption, at times clearly with very little real enthusiasm, of policies of political devolution by both big British parties. In Scotland this was particularly ironic, for the early 1970s saw a re-organization of local government which was specifically designed as an antidote to pressure for devolution and which was probably incompatible with the creation of a Scottish Assembly at Edinburgh. The original blueprint for the reconstruction of Scottish local government was a Scottish Office consultative document of astonishing durability, for its main recommendations were endorsed years later by the Wheatley Report (the result of the Royal Commission on Local Government in Scotland which sat from 1966 to 1969) and in turn enacted by subsequent legislation. One or two minor changes in the boundaries of the proposed new local government units were made, but the essence of the proposals as the same from start to finish. The historic counties and burghs of Scotland were all abolished,* to be replaced by a 'two-tier' structure of regional and district authorities. These new authorities were fully operative by 1975. They differed from the original proposals, including the Wheatley proposals, in one major respect only, but it was a highly significant respect: any suggestion that they should have an enhanced measure of financial autonomy from the central government was ignored. In the last analysis, the new units were meant to be as subservient to their central government paymaster as the old had become. On the other hand, the biggest of the new regions, Strathclyde, was so large in terms of population that it was difficult to see how it could coexist with any devolved body in Edinburgh.

The new local government arrangements undoubtedly fuelled a rising tide of discontent in Scotland. Apart from their remoteness, they proved roughly twice as expensive as their predecessors, after having been held up as virtuous examples of 'economies of scale'. However, the political ferment in Scotland in the mid 1970s was greater than anybody could have forecast. Partly this was because of unprecedented political events, such as the Conservative government's catastrophically unsuccessful gamble on an election early in 1974 at the height of a major confrontation with the National Union of Mineworkers. The recurring British economic crisis also played its part, on a graver scale than ever before, and to the accompaniment of un-

*Despite the fact that Article XXI of the Act of Union 1707 guaranteed their continuance 'in all time coming'.

precedented levels of inflation. Nor was the resurgence of Scottish national feeling unconnected with the discovery and exploitation of great stores of oil and gas in the seas off the Scottish coast. The Scottish National Party may have become obsessed with North Sea Oil, but then so was Her Majesty's Government at Westminster, to whom huge oil revenues looked rather like a lifebelt to a drowning man.

In a sense, the survival of Scotland as a distinct phenomenon balanced on a knife edge in the late 1970s. The Scottish economy had lost all real autonomy, being owned or controlled to an overwhelming extent from outside Scotland. The United Kingdom's governing class was clearly much more interested in participating in the construction of some sort of Western European super-state based on the European Economic Communities than in granting devolution to Scotland and Wales. As it was, many of the proposals for 'devolution' coming from the right wing in British politics were little more than an expensive cosmetic. The Scottish National Party, whose electoral success was the sole and necessary condition for the existence of a 'Scottish problem' at a significant political level was therefore a paradoxical phenomenon. It grew in strength and maturity just at the time when most of the traditional social and cultural peculiarities of Scotland were vanishing before a wave of social change and standardization. What the future of Scotland would be was something which no observer in the late 1970s, however well-informed and intelligent, could possibly predict with any confidence. The future of Scotland was intimately connected with the development of the balance of political power at Westminster, and that was problematical enough. What was clear was that Scotland was in fact over-represented at Westminster in terms of her population, and that the Labour Party had a massive vested interest in securing a disproportionate share of those Scottish M.P.s, especially when its electoral fortunes in England were running neck-and-neck with the Conservatives. Thus Labour had a much greater incentive to buy off Scottish discontent with concessions than the Conservatives; and for a long time this seemed to be the only mechanism capable of producing serious progress towards political devolution.

Yet the details of the political crisis of the 1970s were relatively unimportant compared with the central fact that Scottish identity)had emerged surprisingly strong after two and a half centuries of political union. There were deep divisions within Scotland as to exactly how that identity should find expression in the last quarter of the twentieth century. That was only natural, but it was clear that no significant group in Scotland could be accused of devotion to an anachronistic 'tartan' image of Scotland more suited to a misty, romantic past than to a challenging future. On the contrary, the essence of the debate about Scotland's future lay in the choice of the direction of change. That neo-Jacobite never-never land beloved of the American or Continental tourist was no longer the main source of a sense of Scottishness. The upshot was almost bound to be uncomfortable for Westminster and indeed the Western Alliance, for it was likely to mean that the political equation would contain a somewhat unpredictable Scottish factor. In that sense Scotland in the late 1970s was not what it had been, and this was the supreme and necessary evidence of Scotland's continuing significance and vitality as a human community.

SUGGESTIONS FOR FURTHER READING

The standard modern history of Scotland is *The Edinburgh History of Scotland* in four volumes: A. A. M. Duncan, *Scotland: The Making of the Kingdom* (1975); R. Nicholson, *Scotland: The Later Middle Ages* (1974); G. Donaldson, *Scotland: James V – James VII* (1971); W. Ferguson, *Scotland: 1689 to the Present* (1968). These volumes render all previous multi-volume histories of Scotland obsolete, and each contains a very adequate bibliography of its subject up to the date of publication. A lively introduction to Scottish history will be found in R. Mitchison, *A History of Scotland* (London, 1970) and there is a very good one-volume introduction to Scottish history before 1603 in the shape of the third edition of W. C. Dickinson's, *Scotland from the Earliest Times to 1603* (Oxford, 1977), a book which has been very extensively rewritten by W. C. Dickinson's own pupil A. A. M. Duncan, in such a way as both to bring it up to date, and to preserve the original flavour of this very distinguished work. There exists a good introduction to the social history of early modern Scotland in T. C. Smout, *A History Of The Scottish People 1560–1830* (London, 1969). The economic history of Scotland is covered by S. G. E. Lythe and J. Butt, *An Economic History of Scotland 1100–1939* (Glasgow, 1975), and by B. Lenman, *An Economic History of Modern Scotland 1660–1976* (London, 1977). All these works have extensive bibliographies. There is no satisfactory ecclesiastical history of Scotland available but G. Donaldson, *Scotland: Church and Nation through Sixteen Centuries* (2nd edn, Edinburgh, 1972) provides a very sensible brief survey. Highland history is not well supplied with up-to-date surveys, but W. R. Kermack's, *The Scottish Highlands*:

A Short History (Edinburgh, 1957), if brief, is very good up to the eighteenth century, and J. Hunter, *The Making of the Crofting Community* (Edinburgh, 1976) is a study of the main theme in modern Highland history.

INDEX

384

393

395

Langholm, 99, 295
Langside, battle of (1568), 165
Largs, battle of (1263), 45
La Rochelle, 94
Last Dying Words of Bonnie Heck (Hamilton of Gilbertfield), 309
Laud, William, archbishop of Canterbury, 157, 195, 201, 202, 203, 217
'Laud's Liturgy' (1637), 203, 205, 206, 241
Lauder, 92, 101
Lauderdale, James Maitland, 8th earl of, 319
Lauderdale, John Maitland, 2nd earl and 1st duke of, 232, 234, 236–9
Law, Andrew Bonar, 356
Law, early development of, 51
Law, Scots, 245, 261, 263
Learning and literature: in the 15th century, 95; at the Renaissance and under the New Monarchy, 112, 117–21; under James VI and I, 197; in the 18th century, 305–11; in the 20th century, 367–8
Leicester House Party, 285
Leicester, Robert, Lord Dudley, earl of, 162
Leighton, Robert, archbishop of Glasgow, 234, 237
Leith: burgh or port of, 121, 152, 160, 208, 223, 255, 297, 329, 346; industry in, 229; treaty of (1560), *see* Edinburgh, treaty of (1560)
Lennox, Charles Stewart, 6th Stewart, earl of, 175
Lennox, Esmé Stuart, lord d'Aubigny, and duke of, 168 169
Lennox, John Stewart, 3rd Stewart, earl of, 128
Lennox, Ludovick Stewart, 2nd duke of, 188
Lennox, Malcolm, 5th earl of, 74
Lennox, Margaret, countess of, 127
Lennox, Matthew Stewart, 4th Stewart, earl of, 128, 162, 166

Lennox earldom of, 49, 168; earls of, 94
Lerwick, 227 and n., 346
Leslie, Alexander, 1st earl of Leven, 208, 209, 213, 216, 223
Leslie, David, 217, 223, 224
Lethington, Maitland of. *See* Maitland
Leuchars, church of, 203
'Levellers' of Galloway (1724), 290
Lewis, Isle of, 190, 273, 357
Leyden, university of, 306
Liberal Party, 335, 336, 343, 361, 362, 363, 364, 368
Liberal-Unionists, 343
Lichfield, 278
Lindemann, Professor, 369
Lindsay, family or house of, 41, 98n., 99, 109, 300
See also Crawford
Lindsay, Sir David, 119, 129, 131, 143
Lindsay, Sir James, 179, 185
Lindsay, Robert, of Pittscottie, 197
Lindsay, Lady Sophia, 240
Linen industry, 293, 324, 349
Linklater, Eric, 367
Linlithgow, burgh of, 60, 74, 75, 128, 143, 166, 182, 193, 205; castle of, 84; palace of, 131–2, 134
Linton, Bernard de. *See* Bernard
Lisbon, 315
Liverpool, Robert Jenkinson, 2nd earl of, 328
Lives and Characters of the Heroes and Martyrs of the Reformation and of the Covenant (Howie), 305n.
Livingstone, Sir Alexander, 97, 98
Livingstone, David, 353–4
Livingstonia, 354
Lloyd George, David, 1st earl, 358, 362
Loarn, 18
Local Government, 192, 328, 330
Local Government Board, 342
Loch Awe, 43
Lochbay (Skye), 295
Loch Duich, 273

402

130, 202, 208, 241, 246, 254, 255, 292; judicial enactments of, 104, 105, 116, 130, 189, 232, 233; judicial functions of, 52, 83–4, 104, 116, 130; military enactments of, 98n., 103, 121, 130, 235, 241, 259; record of sittings of, 106; representation in, 78, 83, 103, 107, 180, 183, 192, 194, 208, 246, 254, 282; royal relations with, 192, 199, 202, 203, 232, 234, 250, 253–4, 256; speaker to be elected, 103; and taxation, 78, 83, 107; and covenanters, 205–11; and Union (1707), 257–65. See also General Council; and under names of sovereigns

Parliamentary Hall, 333

Parliamentary reform. See Reform Acts

Parliamentary representation of Scotland, 225–6, 261, 262, 267, 282ff., 329ff., 334ff.

Parochial Boards, 342

Paterson, William, 255

Patrick's Places (Hamilton), 146

'Patriots' the (party), 284, 285. See also 'Squadrone'

Patronage Act, repeal of (1874), 337

Patronage in the Church, 252, 268, 300, 301

Paulet, Sir Amyas, 173

Pavia, battle of (1525), 128, 132

'Peat' Einar, 29

Pedersen, Christian, 146

Peel, Sir Robert, 328, 338

Pembroke, Aymer, earl of, 72, 73

Penda, king of Mercia, 21

Penicuik, 293, 313

Penny Wedding, The (Allan), 312

Penrith, 91

Pentland Hills, 12, 235, 236

Pentland Rising (1666), 236. See also Rullion Green

Perth: agitation for reform in during 1790s, 317; burgh of, 72, 74, 91, 97, 115, 145, 151, 182, 184, 195, 216, 224, 272, 276; North Inch of, 96; parliamen-

tary representation of, 330, 336; treaty of (1266), 45

Perth, James Drummond, 4th earl of, 243

Perth, James Drummond, 3rd duke of, 289

Perthshire, 289, 302

Peterhead, 272, 349

Peterloo, 320

Philip II, king of Spain, 162, 169, 170, 173, 179

Philip IV, king of France, 68

Philip VI, king of France, 80

Philiphaugh, battle of, (1645), 217

Pictland, 24, 25, 27–8

Picts, 16, 18, 23, 25, 26, 27, 46

Pinkie, battle of (1547), 138

Piper of Kilbarchan, The (Sempill), 309

Pitcairne, Archibald, 246

Pitreavie, battle of (1651), 224

Pitscottie. See Lindsay, Robert, of

Pitt, William, earl of Chatham, 280

Pitt, William, 'the Younger', 287, 288, 319

Pius II, pope, 111

Playfair, John, 319

Playfair, William Henry, 315

Pluscarden, priory of, 55

Poitiers, battle of (1356), 81

'Poker Club', the (Edinburgh), 286, 307

Police, 328, 342

Pontefract, 125

Poor Law (Scotland) Act (1845), 337–8

Poor Relief, 154, 338, 342

Population: increase of in 18th century, 296–7. See also under separate burghs

Port Royal, 196

Porteous, Captain John, and Porteous Affair, 285

Prague, 145

Prayer Book (English), 236

Prayer Book, Second, of Edward VI, 148

'Praying Societies', 302

Predestination, 301

Prelacy. See Episcopacy

Premonstratensians, 54

Signet, 105, 106, 250
Sigurd the Mighty, 29
Sigurd the Stout, 29
Simson, Professor John, 301
Simson, Robert, 306
Sinclair, Oliver, 134
Siward, earl of Northumbria, 33–4
Skinner, John, 309
Skye, Isle of, 273, 279, 357
Slains, 177
Smith, Adam, 307, 308, 337
Smith, Sydney, 319
Smollett, Tobias, 308
Snell Exhibition, 246
Society and social life, 23–4, 32, 57–8, 84–7, 108–10, 326, 350
'Society Folk' or 'Society People', 239–40, 241, 242, 299, 300n. *See also* Cameronians
'Society of Improvers in the Knowledge of Agriculture in Scotland' (1723), 289
'Society of the Friends of the People', 316–17
'Society of United Scotsmen', 318
Solway Moss, battle of (1542), 134, 137, 147
Somerled, ancestor of Clan Donald, 43, 74. *See also* Scandinavian problem
Somerset Herald. *See* Young, John
Somerset, Edward Seymour, duke of. *See* Hertford
Sophia, Electress of Hanover, 256
Sorbonne, 95
South Africa, 353
South Australia, 353
South Carolina, 255
Spain, 123, 127, 159, 160, 162, 169, 178, 179, 255
'Spanish Blanks', 177
Spottiswoode, John, Archbishop of Glasgow, later of St Andrews, 189, 194, 195, 197, 198, 201–2, 203, 205
Spuilzie, 51, 106
Squadrone Volante, party, 259, 284, 285, 302–3n.
Stafford, George Granville Leveson Gower, 2nd marquis of, 322–3

Stair, James Dalrymple, 1st viscount, 240, 245
Stair, John Dalrymple, 3rd viscount and 2nd earl, 289
Stalin, Marshal Josef, 372
Standard, battle of the (1138), 36
Steenkirk, battle of, 254, 266
Steuart, Sir James, 308
Steward, office of, 51
Stewart. *See also* Stuart
Stewart, Alexander, archbishop of St Andrews, 118
Stewart, Alexander, wolf of Badenoch, 89, 109
Stewart, Alexander, son of Alexander, wolf of Badenoch, 89
Stewart, David, earl of Strathearn. *See* Strathearn
Stewart, Donald, 377
Stewart, Dugald, 307, 316, 319
Stewart, James, 353–4
Stewart, John, earl of Ross, 97
Stewart, Matthew, 306
Stewart, Mary, daughter of James II, 99–100 and 100n.
Stewart, Robert, son of earl Patrick, 191
Stewarts, family of, 49, 51
Stewarts of Appin, 276
Stirling, burgh of, 60, 98, 99, 151, 152, 163, 165, 166, 205, 217, 224, 244, 272; castle, 71, 74, 75, 76, 278; earl of, *see* Alexander, Sir William; field of, *see* Sauchieburn, battle of; minister of, *see* Erskine, Ebenezer; royal residence at, 48, 131
Stirling Bridge, battle of (1297), 70
Stone of Destiny. *See* Scone, stone of
Stornoway Castle, 115
Story, John, 119
Stracathro, 68
Strachan, Colonel, 221
Stralsund, 208
Strange, Robert, 311
Strathbogie, 34, 177
Strathcarron, 19

411

412

READ MORE IN PENGUIN

In every corner of the world, on every subject under the sun, Penguin represents quality and variety – the very best in publishing today.

For complete information about books available from Penguin – including Puffins, Penguin Classics and Arkana – and how to order them, write to us at the appropriate address below. Please note that for copyright reasons the selection of books varies from country to country.

In the United Kingdom: Please write to *Dept. EP, Penguin Books Ltd, Bath Road, Harmondsworth, West Drayton, Middlesex UB7 0DA*

In the United States: Please write to *Consumer Sales, Penguin USA, P.O. Box 999, Dept. 17109, Bergenfield, New Jersey 07621-0120.* VISA and MasterCard holders call 1-800-253-6476 to order Penguin titles

In Canada: Please write to *Penguin Books Canada Ltd, 10 Alcorn Avenue, Suite 300, Toronto, Ontario M4V 3B2*

In Australia: Please write to *Penguin Books Australia Ltd, P.O. Box 257, Ringwood, Victoria 3134*

In New Zealand: Please write to *Penguin Books (NZ) Ltd, Private Bag 102902, North Shore Mail Centre, Auckland 10*

In India: Please write to *Penguin Books India Pvt Ltd, 706 Eros Apartments, 56 Nehru Place, New Delhi 110 019*

In the Netherlands: Please write to *Penguin Books Netherlands bv, Postbus 3507, NL-1001 AH Amsterdam*

In Germany: Please write to *Penguin Books Deutschland GmbH, Metzlerstrasse 26, 60594 Frankfurt am Main*

In Spain: Please write to *Penguin Books S. A., Bravo Murillo 19, 1° B, 28015 Madrid*

In Italy: Please write to *Penguin Italia s.r.l., Via Felice Casati 20, I–20124 Milano*

In France: Please write to *Penguin France S. A., 17 rue Lejeune, F–31000 Toulouse*

In Japan: Please write to *Penguin Books Japan, Ishikiribashi Building, 2–5–4, Suido, Bunkyo-ku, Tokyo 112*

In South Africa: Please write to *Longman Penguin Southern Africa (Pty) Ltd, Private Bag X08, Bertsham 2013*

READ MORE IN PENGUIN

HISTORY

London: A Social History Roy Porter

'The best and bravest thing he has written. It is important because it makes the whole sweep of London's unique history comprehensible and accessible in a way that no previous writer has ever managed to accomplish. And it is angry because it begins and concludes with a slashing, unanswerable indictment of Thatcherite misrule' – *Independent on Sunday*

Somme Lyn Macdonald

'What the reader will longest remember are the words – heartbroken, blunt, angry – of the men who lived through the bloodbath ... a worthy addition to the literature of the Great War' – *Daily Mail*

Aspects of Aristocracy David Cannadine

'A hugely enjoyable portrait of the upper classes ... It is the perfect history book for the non-historian. Ample in scope but full of human detail, accessible and graceful in its scholarship, witty and opinionated in style' – *Financial Times*

The Penguin History of Greece A. R. Burn

Readable, erudite, enthusiastic and balanced, this one-volume history of Hellas sweeps the reader along from the days of Mycenae and the splendours of Athens to the conquests of Alexander and the final dark decades.

The Laurel and the Ivy Robert Kee

'Parnell continues to haunt the Irish historical imagination a century after his death ... Robert Kee's patient and delicate probing enables him to reconstruct the workings of that elusive mind as persuasively, or at least as plausibly, as seems possible ... This splendid biography, which is as readable as it is rigorous, greatly enhances our understanding of both Parnell, and of the Ireland of his time' – *The Times Literary Supplement*